Communications
in Computer and Information S

T0238720

Manoj Singh Gaur   Mark Zwolinski
Vijay Laxmi   Dharmendra Boolchandani
Virendra Singh   Adit D. Singh (Eds.)

VLSI Design and Test

17th International Symposium, VDAT 2013
Jaipur, India, July 27-30, 2013
Revised Selected Papers

 Springer

Volume Editors

Manoj Singh Gaur
MNIT, Jaipur, India
E-mail: gaurms@mnit.ac.in

Mark Zwolinski
University of Southampton, UK
E-mail: mz@ecs.soton.ac.uk

Vijay Laxmi
MNIT, Jaipur, India
E-mail: vlaxmi@mnit.ac.in

Dharmendra Boolchandani
MNIT, Jaipur, India
E-mail: dbool@ieee.org

Virendra Singh
IIT Bombay, Mumbai, India
E-mail: virendra@computer.org

Adit D. Singh
Auburn University, AL, USA
E-mail: adsingh@eng.auburn.edu

ISSN 1865-0929   e-ISSN 1865-0937
ISBN 978-3-642-42023-8   e-ISBN 978-3-642-42024-5
DOI 10.1007/978-3-642-42024-5
Springer Heidelberg New York Dordrecht London

Library of Congress Control Number: Applied for

CR Subject Classification (1998): B.6, B.7, B.8, C.0, C.1, C.2, F.3, D.2, D.4

Typesetting: Camera-ready by author, data conversion by Scientific Publishing Services, Chennai, India

Printed on acid-free paper

Springer is part of Springer Science+Business Media (www.springer.com)

Publicity Co-chairs

Sushanta Chakraborty   BESU, India
M. Jimson   University of Bristol, UK

Industrial Liaison Co-chairs

S. Gulawadi   ARM, India
Pradeep Thakkar   Maxim, India
S. Uma Mahesh   Indrion Technologies, Bangalore, India
Arvind Dixit   Advance, CDG, India

Local Arrangements Co-chairs

Ghanshyam Singh   MNIT Jaipur, India
Smita Naval   MNIT Jaipur, India

Registration Co-chairs

Kuldeep Pareek   MNIT Jaipur, India
Sonal Yadav   MNIT Jaipur, India
Amaar Bharmal   MNIT Jaipur, India
Rimpy Bishnoi   MNIT Jaipur, India

Program Committee

Abhijit Asati   BITS Pilani, India
Abhijit Chatterjee   Georgia Tech., USA
Abhijit Karmakar   CEERI Pilani, India
Alok Jain   Cadence Noida, India
Amit Patra   IIT Kharagpur, India
A.N. Chandorkar   IIT Bombay, India
Anshul Kumar   IIT Delhi, India
Anu Gupta   BITS Pilani, India
Anzhela Matrosova   TSU, Russia
A.S. Mandal   CEERI Pilani, India
B. Sikdar   BESU, India
Bharadwaj Amrutur   IISc. Bangalore, India
Bhargab B. Bhattacharya   ISI, India
Bhaskar Murlidharan   IIT Bombay, India
Debdeep Mukhopadhyay   IIT Kharagpur, India
Debesh K. Das   Jadavpur University, India
Dharmendra Boolchandani   MNIT Jaipur, India
Dhiraj Pradhan   University of Bristol, UK
Dinesh Sharma   IIT Bombay, India
Dipanwita Roy Chowdhury   IIT Kharagpur, India
Dong Xiang   Tsinghua University, Beijing, China
Erik Larsson   University of Lund, Sweden

Organization

VDAT 2013 was organized by the Department of Computer Engineering and the Department of Electronics and Communication Engineering, Malaviya National Institute of Technology, Jaipur.

Organizing Committee

General Co-chairs
M.S. Gaur   MNIT Jaipur, India
Mark Zwolinski   University of Southampton, UK

General Vice Co-chairs
Vijay Laxmi   MNIT Jaipur, India
D. Boolchandani   MNIT Jaipur, India

Program Co-chairs
Adit Singh   Auburn University, USA
Virendra Singh   IIT Bombay, India

Finance Co-chairs
Girdhari Singh   MNIT Jaipur, India
Lava Bhargava   MNIT Jaipur, India

Tutorial Co-chairs
V. Kamakoti   IIT Madras, India
Usha Mehta   Nirma University, India

Workshop Co-chairs
Abhijit Karmakar   CEERI Pilani, India
Niranjan Devashrey   Nirma University, India

Fellowship Co-chairs
Kolin Paul   IIT Delhi, India
D. Boolchandani   MNIT Jaipur, India
Naveen Chaudhary   MPUAT Udaipur, India

Publication Co-chairs
Sushmita Sur Kolay   ISI, India
Erik Larsson   University of Lünd, Sweden
Sonal Yadav   MNIT Jaipur, India

5. A. Srivastava and E. Dakshinamoorthy: "Electromigration: Design and Reliability Challenges in Advanced Logic Libraries"
6. Jose Flich: "gMemNoCsim: A Simulation and Emulation-Based Platform for Network-on-Chip Architectural Exploration and Analysis"

Subsequently, educational talks by eminent researchers working in VLSI were delivered on the second day of the symposium dedicated to VLSI educational awareness. These talks were delivered by M. Balakrishnan (IIT Delhi, India), Abhijit Chatterjee (Georgia Tech, USA), Mark Zwolinski (Southampton, UK), Vishwani Agrawal (Auburn University, USA), and Narendra Ahuja (UIUC, USA). Panel discussions were held to decide the future course of VLSI R&D in academia as well as industry. The panel included eminent researchers such as Dinesh Sharma (IIT Bombay, India), Abhijit Chatterjee (Georgia Tech, USA), Mark Zwolinski (University of Southampton, UK), Vishwani Agrawal (Auburn University, USA), M. Balakrishnan (IIT Delhi, India), M.S. Gaur and Vineet Sahula (MNIT Jaipur, India), Adit Singh (Auburn University, USA), Chandrashekhar and Raj Singh (CEERI Pilani, India), and Narendra Ahuja (UIUC, USA). A PhD forum, held on the same day provided a platform for research scholars wherein they received critical review of their work.

The VDAT 2013 symposium was an event geared to bringing academia and VLSI industry into close interaction for their mutual benefit. Several invited talks and keynote speeches were delivered by experts from India and abroad. K.S. Dasgupta (Director IIST, India), Masahiro Fujita (Tokyo University, Japan), Jose Flich (UPV, Spain), Dinesh Sharma (IITB, India), Chandrashekhar (CEERI, Pilani), and Scott Roy (University of Glasgow, UK) enlightened participants about various aspects of emerging issues in VLSI research. The conference comprised six sessions and each session had two parallel tracks. We hope that this conference provided an opportunity to all delegates to carry with them new ideas and shall result in better academic and research output. The research articles presented in the conference are published in these proceedings and we hope that this is to the technical satisfaction of the readers.

On behalf of VDAT 2013, we would like to thank all conference delegates especially the authors and reviewers, as their contribution was a must for the success of this event. We take this opportunity to acknowledge the support of the EasyChair conference system. We would also like to thank Springer for consenting to publish the proceedings even at short notice. Our special thanks go to all invited speakers. We would like to thank Ms. Sonal Yadav, who single-handedly compiled the VDAT 2013 and VSI digest proceedings. Last but not least, we would like to thank the MNIT administration for providing support and the student volunteers who worked round the clock.

July 2013   M.S. Gaur
                                                                          Mark Zwolinski

Preface

The VLSI Design and Test Symposium (VDAT 2013) was the 17th in the series of symposia that started in 1997. This annual event is devoted to research discussions at the frontiers of the design and testing of VLSI components, circuits, and systems. In view of the fact that silicon design is approaching its physical limits, fault tolerant computing is becoming a major research area. The idea behind the VDAT Symposium is to promote R&D in all aspects of VLSI and to act as a forum for academicians and professionals from India and abroad to discuss emerging topics of VLSI and related fields. In VDAT 2013, research contributions in the following areas were invited:

1. **VLSI Design:** analog and RF mixed signal design; design and modeling of digital circuits and systems; FPGA prototyping of algorithms; synthesis; optoelectronic devices and circuits; MEMS, deep submicron and nanometer devices and circuits; power analysis and low-power design; thermal analysis and temperature-aware design; physical design, packaging and board design; technology CAD; high-performance computing; networks-on-chip; system-on-chip designs
2. **Testing and Verification:** design for testability; test generation and fault simulation; built-in self-test; verification (simulation and formal); design for manufacturability and yield analysis; testing memories and regular logic arrays
3. **Embedded Systems:** hardware/software codesign and verification; audio, image and video processing; reconfigurable systems; applications in communications, encryption, security, compression, etc.; embedded software tools; FPGA prototyping of complete systems; CAD for embedded systems
4. **Emerging Technology:** nanoscale computing and nanotechnology; reversible computation

Overall, 162 research papers were submitted to VDAT 2013. After a process of rigorous review, 44 contributions were selected as regular papers as part of the proceedings (the acceptance ratio was 27.16%) and 12 were selected as poster papers to be published separately as a VSI digest. The symposium hosted one full-day and five half-day tutorials as follows:

1. Adit Singh and Virendra Singh: "Concept to Silicon"
2. Chetan Parikh and Subhajit Sen: "Design of Simple Electronic Hearing Aid"
3. Suraj Sindia, Vishwani Agrawal, and Abhijit Chatterjee: "Analog Design and Test"
4. Neerav Nanavati and Mahesh Rawal: "DFT Techniques for Low Power Methodology for 40nm and Below"

Gaurab Banerjee	IISc. Bangalore, India
Hafizur Rahman	BESU, India
Huawei Li	Chinese Academy of Sciences, China
Indranil Sengupta	IIT Kharagpur, India
Jaan Raik	TUT, Estonia
Jacob Abraham	University of Texas, USA
Jimson Mathew	University of Bristol, UK
Jose Flich	University of Valencia, Spain
Kewal K. Saluja	University of Wisconsin, USA
Kolin Paul	IIT Delhi, India
Koushik Maharatna	University of Southampton, UK
Krishnendu Chakrabarty	Duke University, USA
Kurvilla Varghese	IISc. Bangalore, India
Lava Bhargava	MNIT Jaipur, India
M. Balakrishnan	IIT Delhi, India
M. Fujita	University of Tokyo, Japan
Madhu Mtyam	IIT Madras, India
Mark Zwolinski	University of Southampton, UK
Michiko Inoue	NAIST, Japan
Nagesh Tamrapalli	AMD, India
Navakat Bhatt	IISc. Bangalore, India
Nilanjan Mukherjee	Mentor Graphics, USA
Nitin Chandrachoodan	IIT Madras, India
Preeti Ranjan Panda	IIT Delhi, India
Raimund Ubar	TUT, Estonia
Raj Singh	CEERI, Pilani, India
Rajat Moona	CDAC Pune, India
Rohit Sharma	IIT Ropar, India
Rubin Parekhji	Texas Instruments, India
S. Batterywala	Synopsys, India
Sachin Patkar	IIT Bombay, India
Sandip Kundu	University of Massachusetts, USA
Satoshi Ohtake	University of Oita, Japan
S.C. Bose	CEERI Pilani, India
Sergey Ostanin	TSU, Russia
Shalabh Gupta	IIT Bombay, India
Shankar Balachandran	IIT Madras, India
Siddharth Duttagupta	IIT Bombay, India
S.K. Nandi	IISc. Bangalore, India
Somyendu Raha	IISc. Bangalore, India
Srivaths Ravi	Texas Instruments, Bangalore, India
Sudhakar Reddy	University of Iowa, USA
Sukumar Nandi	IIT Guwahati, India
Supratik Chakravarty	IIT Bombay, India
Susanta Chakravarty	BESU, India
Tomokazu Yoneda	NAIST, Japan

V. Kamakoti   IIT Madras, India
Vijay Laxmi   MNIT Jaipur, India
Vineet Sahula   MNIT Jaipur, India
Vishwani Agrawal   University of Auburn, USA

Advisory Committee

I.K. Bhat   MNIT Jaipur, India
M.M. Salunkhe   CURAJ, India
P.K. Kalra   IIT Jodhpur, India
Dinesh Sharma   IIT Bombay, India
Vishwani Agrawal   Auburn University, USA
Chandrashekhar   CEERI, Pilani, India
Kewal Saluja   Wisconsin University, USA

Additional Reviewers

Abhijit Asati	Kota Solomon Raju	Satoshi Ohtake
Abhijit Karmakar	Kusum Lata	Saurabh Lodha
Amit Prakash Singh	Lakshminarayanan G.	Sergey Ostanin
Ankush Srivastava	Lars Wanhammar	Shabbir Batterywala
Ansuman Banerjee	Lava Bhargava	Shalabh Gupta
Anu Gupta	Lokesh Garg	Sharat Chandra Varma
Anzhela Matrosova	Madhu Mutyam	Shashikant Sharma
Aritra Hazra	Manodipan Sahoo	Siddharth Duttagupta
Arnab Sarkar	Manoj Singh Gaur	Srihari P. Rao
Arun Chandorkar	Mark Zwolinski	Subash Chandra Bose
Arun Parakh	Martin Burbidge	Subrat Panda
Bhaskar Pal	Maryam Shojaei	Sudeb Dasgupta
Bogaraju	Masahiro Fujita	Supratik Chakraborty
Chandan Giri	Michiko Inoue	Suraj Sindia
Debaprasad Das	Mousumi Saha	Suryakant Toraskar
Debesh Das	Naveen Choudhary	Swaroop Ganguly
Dinesh Sharma	Parthasarathi Dasgupta	Takeshi Matsumoto
Dipankar Saha	Prasenjit Basu	Tomokazu Yoneda
Dong Xiang	Prasun Ghosal	Usha Mehta
Eric Kerherve	Preeti Ranjan Panda	Vaibhav Jain
Hemangee Kapoor	Renu Kumawat	Venkateshwara Reddy
Janak Porwal	Rohit Sharma	Vijay Laxmi
Jaynarayan Tudu	S. Qureshi	Vinay B.Y. Kumar
Jimson Mathew	Sachin Patkar	Vineet Sahula
Jose Flich	Santanu Mahapatra	Virendra Singh
Kaligana S. Gowtham	Santosh Biswas	
Kolin Paul	Sapna Khandelwal	

Sponsoring Institutions

Malaviya National Institute of Technology Jaipur
Indian Institute of Technology Bombay
Central University, Rajasthan
CEERI Pilani

Table of Contents

Process Aware Ultra-High-Speed Hybrid Sensing Technique for Low
Power Near-Threshold SRAM 1
   Bhupendra Singh Reniwal and Santosh Kumar Vishvakarma

A Novel Design Methodology for High Tuning Linearity and Wide
Tuning Range Ring Voltage Controlled Oscillator 10
   *Gudlavalleti Rajahari, Yashu Anand Varshney, and
   Subash Chandra Bose*

A Low-Power Wideband High Dynamic Range Single-Stage Variable
Gain Amplifier 19
   Vivek Verma and Chetan D. Parikh

An Ultra-Wideband Baseband Transmitter Design for Wireless Body
Area Network 26
   *R.K. Naga Mahesh, Akash Ganesan, Manchi Pavan Kumar, and
   Roy P. Paily*

Computational Functions' VLSI Implementation for Compressed
Sensing 35
   *Shrirang Korde, Amol Khandare, Raghavendra Deshmukh, and
   Rajendra Patrikar*

A Novel Input Capacitance Modeling Methodology for Nano-Scale
VLSI Standard Cell Library Characterization 44
   *Akhtar W. Alam, Esakkimuthu Dhakshinamoorthy,
   Prince Mathew, and Narender Ponna*

An Area Efficient Wide Range On-Chip Delay Measurement
Architecture 49
   Rahul Krishnamurthy and G.K. Sharma

10 Gbps Current Mode Logic I/O Buffer 59
   Akhil Rathore and Chetan D. Parikh

Kapees: A New Tool for Standard Cell Placement 66
   Sameer Pawanekar, Kalpesh Kapoor, and Gaurav Trivedi

Preemptive Test Scheduling for Network-on-Chip Using Particle Swarm
Optimization 74
   *Kanchan Manna, Shailesh Singh, Santanu Chattopadhyay, and
   Indranil Sengupta*

Energy Efficient Array Initialization Using Loop Unrolling with Partial
Gray Code Sequence 83
   Sumanta Pyne and Ajit Pal

Design and Simulation of Bulk Micromachined Accelerometer
for Avionics Application 94
   Amit Sharma, Ravindra Mukhiya, S. Santosh Kumar, and B.D. Pant

Performance Analysis of Subthreshold 32-Bit Kogge-Stone Adder
for Worst-Case-Delay and Power in Sub-micron Technology 100
   *Himadri Singh Raghav, Sachin Maheshwari, and
   Brahmadeo Prasad Singh*

Characterization of Logical Effort for Improved Delay 108
   Sachin Maheshwari, Himadri Singh Raghav, and Anu Gupta

A Dual Material Double-Layer Gate Stack Junctionless Transistor
for Enhanced Analog Performance 118
   Ratul Kumar Baruah and Roy P. Paily

An Improved g_m/I_D Methodology for Ultra-Low-Power Nano-Scale
CMOS OTA Design 128
   Somnath Paul, Abhijit Dana, and Soumya Pandit

An Efficient RF Energy Harvester with Tuned Matching Circuit 138
   Sachin Agrawal, Sunil Pandey, Jawar Singh, and P.N. Kondekar

A Modified Gate Replacement Algorithm for Leakage Reduction Using
Dual-T_{ox} in CMOS VLSI Circuits 146
   Surabhi Singh, Brajesh Kumar Kaushik, and Sudeb Dasgupta

Impact of Fin Width and Graded Channel Doping on the Performance
of 22nm SOI FinFET 153
   Jose Joseph and Rajendra Patrikar

Power Reduction by Integrated Within_Clock_Power Gating and Power
Gating (WCPG_in_PG) 160
   Debanjali Nath, Priyanka Choudhury, and Sambhu Nath Pradhan

Design and Analysis of a Novel Noise Cancelling Topology for Common
Gate UWB LNAs 169
   Mohd Anwar, Syed Azeemuddin, and Mohammed Zafar Ali Khan

A Combined CMOS Reference Circuit with Supply and Temperature
Compensation 177
   Madhusoodan Agrawal and Alpana Agarwal

Convex Optimization of Energy and Delay Using Logical Effort Method
in Deep Sub-micron Technology.................................. 185
   Sachin Maheshwari, Rameez Raza, Pramod Kumar, and Anu Gupta

A Cache-Aware Strategy for H.264 Decoding on Multi-processor
Architectures   194
   Arani Bhattacharya, Ansuman Banerjee, Susmita Sur-Kolay,
   Prasenjit Basu, and Bhaskar J. Karmakar

Random-LRU: A Replacement Policy for Chip Multiprocessors   204
   Shirshendu Das, Nagaraju Polavarapu, Prateek D. Halwe, and
   Hemangee K. Kapoor

Analysis of Crosstalk Deviation for Bundled MWCNT with Process
Induced Height and Width Variations   214
   Jainender Kumar, Manoj Kumar Majumder,
   Brajesh Kumar Kaushik, and Sudeb Dasgupta

Congestion Balancing Global Router   223
   Shyamapada Mukherjee, Jibesh Patra, and Suchismita Roy

CMOS ASIC Design of a High Performance Digital Fuzzy Processor
That Can Compute on Arbitrary Membership Functions   233
   Anirban Guha and Shubhajit Roy Chowdhury

Variation Robust Subthreshold SRAM Design with Ultra Low Power
Consumption   242
   Saima Cherukat and Vineet Sahula

Modeling of High Frequency Out-of-Plane Single Axis MEMS
Capacitive Accelerometer   249
   Prashant Singh, Pooja Srivastava, Ram Mohan Verma, and
   Saurabh Jaiswal

CPK Based IO AC Timing Closure to Reduce Yield Loss and Test
Time   257
   Sandip Ghosh and Rohit Srivastava

Optimization of Underlap FinFETs and Its SRAM Performance
Projections Using High-k Spacers   267
   Pankaj Kr. Pal, Brajesh Kumar Kaushik, and Sudeb Dasgupta

On-Chip Dilution from Multiple Concentrations of a Sample Fluid
Using Digital Microfluidics   274
   Sudip Roy, Bhargab B. Bhattacharya, Sarmishtha Ghoshal, and
   Krishnendu Chakrabarty

Automatic Test Bench Generation and Connection in Modern
Verification Environments: Methodology and Tool   284
   Rohit Srivastava, Gaurav Gupta, Sarvesh Patankar, and
   Nandini Mudgil

A Methodology for Early and Accurate Analysis of Inrush and Latency
Tradeoffs during Power-Domain Wakeup 294
   Vipul Singhal, Ayon Dey, Suresh Mallala, and Somshubhra Paul

Fault Aware Dynamic Adaptive Routing Using LBDR 304
   Rimpy Bishnoi, Vijay Laxmi, Manoj Singh Gaur, and Mohit Baskota

Architectural Level Sub-threshold Leakage Power Estimation of SRAM
Arrays with Its Peripherals 312
   Nupur Navlakha, Lokesh Garg, Dharmendar Boolchandani, and
   Vineet Sahula

On Designing Testable Reversible Circuits Using Gate Duplication 322
   Joyati Mondal, Debesh Kumar Das, Dipak Kumar Kole,
   Hafizur Rahaman, and Bhargab B. Bhattacharya

Circuit Transient Analysis Using State Space Equations 330
   Kai Chi Alex Lam and Mark Zwolinski

3D CORDIC Algorithm Based Cartesian to Spherical Coordinate
Converter 337
   Anita Jain and Kavita Khare

Level-Accurate Peak Activity Estimation in Combinational Circuit
Using BILP 345
   Jaynarayan T. Tudu, Deepak Malani, and Virendra Singh

Design and Optimization of a 2x2 Directional Microstrip Patch
Antenna 353
   Cerin Ninan, Chandra Shekhar, and M. Radhakrishna

A New Method for Route Based Synthesis and Placement in Digital
Microfluidic Biochips 361
   Pranab Roy, Samadrita Bhattacharya, Hafizur Rahaman, and
   Parthasarathi Dasgupta

Defect Diagnosis of Digital Circuits Using Surrogate Faults 376
   Chidambaram Alagappan and Vishwani D. Agrawal

Author Index 387

Process Aware Ultra-High-Speed Hybrid Sensing Technique for Low Power Near-Threshold SRAM

Bhupendra Singh Reniwal and Santosh Kumar Vishvakarma

Nanoscale Devices, VLSI/ULSI Circuit & System Design Lab Indian Institute of Technology Indore, India
{phd11120202,skvishvakarma}@iiti.ac.in

Abstract. Significant speed degradation is one of the severest issues encountered in low-voltage Static Random Access Memory (SRAM) operation. In addition, Sense Amplifier (SA) stability deterioration is another problem in low-voltage operation. These phenomena occur because the random transistor variation becomes larger as the process scaling progresses. In this work a highly robust and novel Ultra-High-Speed (UHS) hybrid current/voltage sensing technique is developed for low power and high speed SRAM. The Precisely sized Current Mode Circuit (CMC) is designed for local differential current mode sensing at bit-lines to achieve low power and high-speed. Local cross coupled inverters latch configuration is designed which convert differential voltage developed at data-lines to full logic swing at output. High speed SRAM sensing technique is designed using a 45nm CMOS standard process. With focus on the current sensing, we have shown that latch makes an excellent second-stage comparator after a local differential current sensing. Extensive post-layout simulation has been verified that our design operates down to 0.7V and achieves 95ps sensing delay at 1V supply voltage. Operating frequency is 1 GHz and power consumption is 2.18μW and 0.10μW at 1V and 0.7V respectively. The primary advantage of the proposed amplifier over previously reported sense amplifiers is the excellent immunity to inter-die and intra-die variations, making it more reliable against device mismatch and process variations.

Keywords: SRAM, CMC, UHS, Yield, SA.

1   Introduction

In nanometer technologies, embedded SRAM occupy significant portion of system on chips (SoCs) and has large impact on chip yield. As the motivation to increase the capacity of on-chip cache, SRAM is predicted to occupy about 94% of die-area by 2014 [1]. Increasing inter-die statistical variations in the process parameters (channel length (L), width (W), and transistor threshold voltage (V_{th})) has emerged as a serious problem in the nano-scaled circuit design [2]. With the increase in random variation with scaling due to Random Dopant Fluctuation (RDF), Line Edge Roughness (LER) and other sources, SRAMs become extremely sensitive to process variations especially as the supply voltage is reduced. Similarly, SA suffer from random variations,

M.S. Gaur et al. (Eds.): VDAT 2013, CCIS 382, pp. 1–9, 2013.
© Springer-Verlag Berlin Heidelberg 2013

which increase the SA input offset (due to its differential nature, and small signal operation) and deteriorates SRAM read access yield (Y_{read}) [3], [4], [5]. Hence, the failure probability of a SA is directly related to the yield of a memory chip. The sensing margin required by SRAM is dominated by the sense amplifier offset and bit-line (BL) level offset. SA offset is caused by device mismatch resulting from process variations. Hence SA input referred offset directly slows the access times of SRAMs and limits the amount of integration of cells on a column.

Substantial amount of research have so far been reported regarding sensing speed improvement, offset reduction and yield improvement of SA [6-14], like latch based SA [6], Voltage Mode SA(VMSA) [7], Decoupled latch [8] [9], Hybrid Mode SA (HMSA) [10], Automatic power down (APD) SA [11], etc. Among the above mentioned techniques, voltage & current mode implementations are popular to the researchers, which also serve the limitations. [6], [8] shows the conventional voltage mode SA The self shut-off mechanism of VSA has made it a pervasive choice in today's SRAM design. The input offset of sense amplifier in voltage mode sets the higher levels for the required bit-line discharge [8], [12], thereby increasing the energy consumption. This offset affects the sensing delay or even the functionality of the circuit, depending on the extent of process variation, therefore determining the worst case possibility of process variation highly significant in sense amplifier. The minimal target value of the required bit-line discharge depends on the technology, sense amplifier design, sizing and the target yield level [5] [12]. Current sense amplifiers (CSA) have long been proposed as a promising approach for high speed applications since they do not require large bit-line voltage swing for detection. The new read scheme to maximize the utilization of I_{cell}, hence offering a better performance in terms of sensing speed proposed in [10], nevertheless, such hybrid mode sense amplifier consumes more power than a typical latch type sense amplifier due to its dc bias current. On the other hand, the automatic power down scheme was implemented in parallel [11] fashion, resulted better speed and power with the penalty of hardware than earlier reported SAs implementation. In this work, a highly robust and novel Ultra High-Speed (UHS), hybrid current/voltage mode Sense Amplifier (SA) technique is developed for low power SRAM using 45nm CMOS standard process. This paper is organized as follows: Section 2 describes the proposed sensing technique and its operation and Section 3 discusses the impact of process variation, sensing failure and design yield. Simulation results are discussed and compared in Section 4. Finally, Section 5 concludes the paper.

2   Proposed Sensing Technique

The Proposed Design Sense Amplifier (PDSA) with simplified read-cycle only memory system is shown in Fig. 1. The circuit is evaluated in terms of the propagation del-delay and power dissipation vs supply voltages, process variations and temperature. It consists of nine PMOS (MP2-MP10) and seven NMOS transistors (MN1-MN7). MP2-MP5 configures the Current Mode Circuit (CMC) [12]. It has zero input (ideally) resistance during sensing. This property makes it insensitive to the bit-line capacitance. CMC eliminates the bit-line equalization circuit due to virtual short circuit at

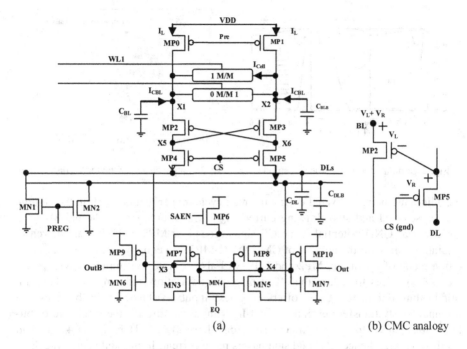

Fig. 1. Schematic of proposed SA

node X1 and X2 because the gate to source voltage of MP2 and MP4 will be same, since their currents are equal, their sizes are equal and both devices are in saturation. Same is the case for MP3 and MP5. Hence the voltage at node X1 is $V_L + V_R$ [Fig. 2]. Similarly voltage at X2 will be the same. Transistors MP0 and MP1 are used to pull the bit-lines close to the supply voltage to attain memory cell stability and soft error immunity. CMC transfers the differential current to data-lines. Second sensing stage consists of three PMOS (MP6-MP8) and seven NMOS (MN1-MN5) transistors. Here MN1, MN2 are used to precharge the data-lines (DLs) to GND. The cross coupled inverter amplifies the small voltage difference on the DLs to the full CMOS logic level. MP9-MP10 and MN6-N7, forms two output inverters, serving as buffers to drive the potentially large output loads to full CMOS logic output levels. Before any read cycle MP0 and MP1 precharge the bit-line capacitances to V_{DD}. Precharge transistors are upsized to charge large bit-line capacitances up to 3pF in order to account for the effect of parasitic capacitances associated with large cells in the array. Simultaneously, MN1 and MN2 precharge the data-line capacitances to GND. Meanwhile, Equal (EQ) signal turns on MN4 to equalize nodes X3 and X4 to the same potential. MP6 is kept in cut-off mode by asserting SAEN logic "HIGH", thereby saving static power. Nodes X3 and X4 will also be at low potential (near V_{th}) during standby as a result, implying both the NMOS devices (MN6, MN7) operates in cutoff mode consuming no DC current by these buffers except subthreshold current. The second sensing stage ensures that the standby current of the circuit and thus the power dissipation is minimized because of sleeping MP6. Once Word Line (WL1) and Column Select

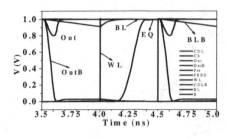
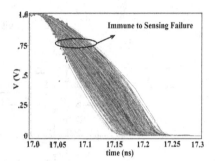

Fig. 2. Simulated voltage at various nodes   **Fig. 3.** Output characteristic for V_{th} distribution

(CS) lines are being activated during the read cycle, upper memory cell in the column will be selected and start drawing current 'I_{cell}'. Since drains of MP4 and MP5 are already near GND potential, once CS signal goes low MP4 and MP5 are driven to saturation. Since all the devices of CMC (MP2-MP5) are equally sized to ensure saturation mode of operation, MP2 and MP3 will also operate in saturation. We up size the CMC devices to reduce the effect of process variation, reducing the delay until self loading dominates. CMC offers very less input resistance to the bit-lines and instantaneously transfer currents I_L' and I_R without waiting for the discharge of bit-line capacitances to current transporting data-lines (DLs). Here $I_L'=(I_L+I_{CBL})$ and $(I_R=I_L+I_{CBL}-I_{cell})$, hence left hand side passes more current, $I_L'>I_R$ and charge the data-line capacitances producing differential voltage at the source terminal of the NMOS devices (MN3 & MN5) of the cross coupled inverters. Thereafter, Sense Enable Signal (SAEN) goes low and EQ signal is deasserted, turning device MP6 on and MN4 off respectively, and cross coupled inverter quickly finishes the latching process pulling node X3 to V_{DD} while node X4 is discharged to near ground. Two inverters are designed here to drive large loads and provide full logic swing at the output. Since no differential discharging of capacitance is required to sense the cell data, these signals propagate almost instantaneously from CMC to the data-lines. Precharge (GND) time of data-line capacitances through NMOS devices MN1-MN2 is crucial here at near threshold. The increase in the number of column increases data-line capacitance, in which case the sizing of MN1-MN2 play a major role to discharge the data-line capacitances. Data-line capacitance value also depends on the sizing of PMOS devices in CMC. Through carefull sizing of the CMC devices we achieved optimum delay. Fig. 2 shows waveform at various nodes of design.

3   Process Mismatch Analysis and Yield Optimization of SA

Random within-die variation in process parameters (principally, V_{th} variation due to random dopant fluctuations) results in different types of parametric failures in an SA. The parametric failures in SA are principally due to offset (reduction in the bit-differential produced while accessing the cell), incorrect flipping of latch in SA while reading, A column of an SRAM array is defined to be faulty if any of the SA in that column is faulty. An entire SRAM array is said to be faulty (memory failure) if number of faulty column is more. A typical memory chip may contain a large number of sense amplifiers. If some sense amplifiers malfunction then it causes loss of functional yield. Hence it is necessary to design robust sense amplifiers that have lower failure probability against process variations. Sense amplifiers and SRAM cells in particular, are vulnerable to within-die WID [14].

$$P(failure) = \frac{Frequency\ of\ incorrect\ samples}{Total\ number\ of\ inter\text{-}die\ Monte\ Carlo\ samples} \times 100 \qquad (1)$$

To estimate the yield of an SA design, Monte Carlo simulations for inter-die distributions of V_{th} (assumed to be Gaussian) need to be performed.

Proper sizing of the SA transistors can reduce the failure (due to within-die variation) probability of a cell at nominal inter-die corner. To understand this, we applied a certain amount of V_{th} shift to all the transistors in an SA (represents an inter-die V_{th} shift). To reduce the probability of sensing failure, NMOS transistors (MN3, MN5) are slightly upsized in the proposed design. The upsizing of NMOS transistors lower the trip point voltage that flips the cross-coupled inverters at a lower output voltage. Symmetric layout is a critical piece of our design strategy to reduce mismatch in bit-line and data-line capacitances, which reduces the probability of sensing failure and increases yield. Post layout circuit characteristic with inter-die variation, obtained by Monte Carlo simulation of 1000 iterations with 3σ parameter variation are shown in

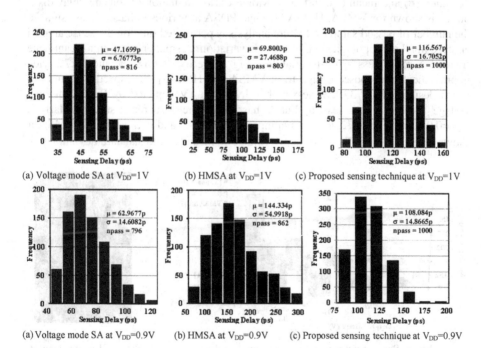

Fig. 4. Sensing Delay histogram of the designs in comparison , results are from 1000 sample Monte Carlo simulation that vary local parameters (3σ) at room temperature and $C_{BL}=C_{DL}=100fF$

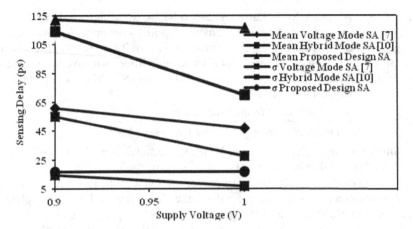

Fig. 5. Mean and standard deviation of sensing delay variation with supply voltage. Obtained by Monte Carlo Simulation for 1000 iterations.

Fig. 3. Fig. 3 shows for PDSA that all the samples yield correct result. A typical value equal to 100fF for bit-line and data-line capacitances is used to account the effect of large cells of array in bit-line and data-lines at 1V, standard 6T cell with same cell current (I_{cell}) is used for all simulations. The problem of variability defined as standard deviation (σ) and mean (μ). In Fig. 4, Monte Carlo simulation of sensing delay distribution is shown for VMSA, HMSA [10] and PDSA at various voltages. npass signifies the number of passed samples. Failure analysis is performed only on the sense amplifier stage in all the topologies for 3σ process variation. A smaller σ is a significant benefit for SA robustness against variability. Fig. 4, verify that 18.4% and 19.7% yield improvement in proposed design from VMSA and HMSA [10] respectively, and proposed design exhibit 39.18% less σ than hybrid at 1V depicted by Fig. 4, although voltage mode SA has less σ, but it has lower yield characteristic. Similarly at V_{DD}=0.9V, σ value is 72.96% less compared to HMSA and comparable to VMSA as shown in Fig. 4. Fig.5 Plots the supply voltage vs mean (μ) and standard deviation (σ).

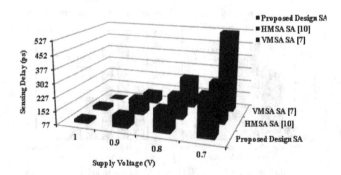

Fig. 6. Sensing delay variation with supply voltage

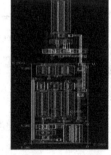

Fig. 7. Layout view of proposed design SA

4 Analysis Methodology and Simulation Environment

Sensing delay is a critical design metric for the nanoscaled memories. All the designs in comparison with proposed design SA have been optimized extensively and simulated using Cadence Spectre circuit simulator at 45nm technology node, balancing the trade-off between area, speed and power consumption. Simulation setup is shown in Fig. 1, with one standard column. The size of the equilibrating device MN4 (Fig. 1) is kept minimum to ensure retention operation is faster. A standard 6T SRAM memory cell is used for the simulation. Sensing delay is defined as the difference between the time when Sense Enable (SAE) is turned on (i.e. SAE=0.5 V_{DD}) to the time outB (i.e. the node that is finally discharged) is reduced to $0.5V_{DD}$ [7], for VMSA. In HMSA and PDSA delay is equal to the time when CS signal reaches half V_{DD} ($V_{DD} = 0.5$) to the time when the node that is fully discharging reaches half V_{DD}. Design is simulated at various supply voltages and can operate lower down till $V_{DD} = 0.7V$. Fig. 6 plots sensing delay vs supply voltage at C_{BL}=100fF for all topologies and C_{BL}=C_{DL}=100fF for HMSA [10] and PDSA. Fig. 7 shows layout of PDSA for area consideration. Fig.8, shows power consumption vs supply voltage plot, which verifies an 32.86%, 86.32% improvement of the proposed design compared to VMSA and HMSA respectively.

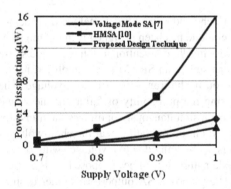 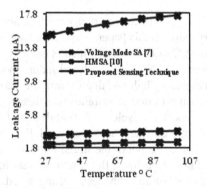

Fig. 8. Power dissipation vs. supply voltage   **Fig. 9.** Leakage current at various temperature

Table 1. Comparison with other published work

	Sensing Delay (ps)	Power (μW)	Power Delay Product (fJ)	Silicon Area (μm²)	Yield (%)
VMSA[7] (45nm)	77	3.257	0.2507	3.009	81.6
HMSA[10] (45 nm)	99.71	16.004	1.5957	12.923	80.3
Proposed (45nm)	95.32	2.188	0.2085	10.310	100

This results because of the reduced voltage swing at bit-lines, as with the cross coupled inverter finishing the latching process no direct current flows from V_{DD} to GND thus reducing the power dissipation. Table 1 shows post-layout comparisons with other proposals. Since VLSI circuits often operate at elevated temperatures, we have simulated for varying temperature in the range from 27°C to 100°C for the estimation of leakage power because leakage power becomes incremental at higher temperature. The leakage current for the three designs are shown in Fig. 9 for C_{BL}=100fF and C_{DL}=100fF at 1V supply voltage. In standby mode, terminal voltage at X3 and X4 are at a potential of 534.7mV and body to source voltage (V_{bs}) of MP4 and MP5 become slightly positive, resulting in an increase in threshold voltage (larger body effect) of MP4 and MP5 respectively, and thereby reducing their subthreshold leakage (I_{sub}) to some extent. From Fig. 1, it may appear that proposed SA may consume higher standby power as it has more leakage components. However, interestingly, it consumes less hold power and overall leakage component is reduced at array level because cross coupled inverter stage with output buffers are shared among the number of column. The pair of output buffers in proposed design contributes a large portion of leakage current.

5   Conclusion

Sense amplifier is a crucial block of SoC Cache and affects functional yield of memory chip. In this paper, a hybrid sensing technique has been designed using 45nm standard CMOS process, which is competitive with the conventional voltage mode sense amplifier. We have analyzed failure mechanisms in an SRAM sense amplifier, namely sensing failures, due to intra-die variation in the transistor threshold voltage. The sensing-failure probability is estimated using the probability of failure of individual events. The developed hybrid design approach simultaneously optimizes the transistor sizes to enhance the design yield. For SRAM circuit operating near threshold voltages reliable readout of the stored information is challenging due to a voltage swing of tens of mV at bit-lines. Because of current mode nature at bit-lines proposed design offers less offset and enhances sensing speed. The proposed SA outperforms other designs and sense lower voltage differences and operates at a high frequency of 1GHz which is highest among the recent SA designs.

References

[1] International Technological Road Map Survey ITRS (2009)
[2] Bhavnaganuala, A.J., et al.: IEEE Journal of Solid-State Circuits, 658-665 (2001)
[3] Heald, R., Wang, P.: Variability in sub-100nm SRAM designs. In: ICCAD, pp. 347–352 (2004)
[4] Houle, R.: Simple statistical analysis techniques to determine minimum sense amp set times. In: CICC, pp. 37–40 (2007)
[5] Abu-Rahma, M.H., et al.: A methodology for statistical estimation of read access yield in SRAMs. In: DAC, pp. 205–210 (2008)

[6] Wicht, B.: Current Sense Amplifiers for Embedded SRAM in High-Performance System-on-a-Chip Designs. Springer, Heidelberg (2003)

[7] Wicht, B., Nirschl, T., Landsiedel, D.S.: Yield and speed optimization of latch-type voltage sense amplifier. IEEE Journal of Solid-State Circuits 39, 118–158 (2004)

[8] Singh, R., Baht, N.: An offset compensation technique for latch type sense amplifiers in high-speed low-power SRAMs. IEEE Transactions on Very Large Scale Integration (VLSI) Systems. Trans. Briefs 12, 652–657 (2004)

[9] Lovett, S.J., Cibbs, G.A., Pancholy, A.: Yield and matching implications for static RAM memory array sense-amplifier design. IEEE Journal of Solid-State Circuit 35, 1200–1204 (2000)

[10] Tuan Do, A., Zhi-Hui, K., Yeo, K.-S.: Hybrid Mode SRAM Sense Amplifiers: New Approach on Transistor Sizing. IEEE Trans. Circuit and Systems-II 55, 986–999 (2008)

[11] Lia, Y.C., Huang, S.Y.: A Resilient and Power-Efficient Automatic-Power Down Sense Amplifier for SRAM Design. IEEE Transaction on Circuits and Systems II: Express Brief 55, 1031–1035 (2008)

[12] Seevinck, E., Beers, P.J.V., Ontrop, H.: Current-mode techniques for high-speed VLSI circuits with application to current SA for CMOS SRAM's. IEEE Journal of Solid-State Circuits 26(5), 525–536 (1991)

A Novel Design Methodology for High Tuning Linearity and Wide Tuning Range Ring Voltage Controlled Oscillator

Gudlavalleti Rajahari[1,2], Yashu Anand Varshney[1,2], and Subash Chandra Bose[1,2]

[1] CSIR-Central Electronics Engineering Research Institute (CSIR-CEERI),
Pilani, Rajasthan, India
{rajahari,subash}@ceeri.ernet.in
[2] Academy of Scientific and Innovative Research
yvarshney@gmail.com

Abstract. This paper presents a novel design methodology of a CMOS current starved ring Voltage Controlled Oscillator (VCO) for wide tuning range and high linearity. The f-V tuning characteristic of the ring VCO depends on the current-voltage (I_{bias}-$V_{control}$) characteristic of the replica bias and region of operation of current sources/sinks transistors (CSTs). The proposed design methodology linearizes the I_{bias}-$V_{control}$ characteristic and ensures the CSTs to operate in saturation region during switching and consequently enhances the tuning range without additional circuitry. The design is implemented in UMC 0.18 µm CMOS technology at 1.8 V supply voltage. The overall circuit consumes 260 µW power at 404.5 MHz, has a wide tuning range of 66 MHz to 875 MHz having 94.5% tuning linearity.

Keywords: Ring VCO, Wide Tuning Range, Tuning Linearity, Current Starved, Design Methodology.

1 Introduction

Phase-Locked Loop (PLL) is one of the important analog/mixed signal circuits for clock generation, frequency synthesis *etc*., in a System-on-Chip. VCO is the critical building block that affects the tuning range, jitter, power and area of the overall PLL. A linear and wide tuning range of the VCO is an important performance parameter in various applications [1][2]. A linear frequency-voltage (f-V) tuning characteristic of the VCO leads to a constant loop gain K_{VCO} (Hz/Volt) providing the widest possible tuning range to the PLL. A nonlinear and high K_{VCO} can result in increasing noise and spurious power of the PLL owing to frequency modulation of the control voltage noise [3]. Such non-linearity also degrades the closed loop performance parameters such as loop bandwidth and settling behavior of PLLs [4]. In Frequency based Delta Sigma Modulator (FDSM) where VCO acts as an alternative to op-amp based integrator has performance degradation due to VCO non-linearity. If the VCO is nonlinear, it will introduce a harmonic distortion to the output signal. Also, the Signal

M.S. Gaur et al. (Eds.): VDAT 2013, CCIS 382, pp. 10–18, 2013.
© Springer-Verlag Berlin Heidelberg 2013

to Noise and Distortion Ratio (SNDR) along with the resolution of the ADC employing FDSM architecture will be limited by the VCO non-linearity [5][6][7]. Thus, a linear frequency-voltage (f-V) tuning characteristics and wide tuning range of the VCO are essential for high performance PLL and FDSM based ADCs.

A VCO can be implemented using LC oscillator, ring oscillator and relaxation oscillator. However, ring oscillator has been a popular choice for VCO as it occupies less area, has wide-tuning range and can be easily integrated on-chip as compared to other oscillator architectures. In literature [8][9][10], design methodology of ring VCO has been addressed considering center frequency, power dissipation, jitter, tuning range as the specification parameters. The optimization is done for area and center frequency resulting in optimal transistor sizes. Tuning linearity in VCOs has been addressed using techniques such as an on chip servo loop [11], post-correction techniques [12], source degeneration [13], and a Frequency Locked Loop (FLL) as VCO [14]. This paper proposes a design methodology for a CMOS current starved ring voltage controlled oscillator considering tuning bandwidth and linearity as the design parameters without additional circuitry and thus reducing the power consumption. The proposed designed methodology enhances tuning linearity and consequently tuning range for the current starved ring VCO. The design has been implemented in UMC 0.18 µm CMOS technology at 1.8 V supply voltage. The overall circuit consumes 260 µW at 404.5 MHz, has a wide tuning range of 66 MHz to 875 MHz having 94.5% tuning linearity. However, supply rejection and noise are the major issues of ring VCO and research has been done to mitigate this problem [15], [16]. The present work assumes a constant supply voltage from a stable supply regulator. In the next section, the analysis and design of the current-starved VCO design is discussed along with the comparison of conventional [13] and proposed design procedure. In section 3, the outline of the proposed design procedure is presented. Section 4 presents the simulation results and finally conclusion is given in section 5.

2   Current-Starved VCO Design

A Current Starved Voltage Controlled Oscillator (CSVCO) as shown in Fig. 1 consists of a ring oscillator formed by an odd chain of inverters (M_p, M_n) biased by current source and sink (M_{ps}, M_{ns}). The transistors (M_{pb}, M_{nb}) act as the bias stage and bias current (I_{bias}) is mirrored from bias stage to each stage of the ring oscillator.

The time taken by each inverter stage of the ring VCO to charge/discharge the total capacitance (C_{tot}) from 0 to V_{SP} with I_{bias} when CSTs are in saturation region is given by

$$t_{ch} \propto C_{tot} \frac{V_{SP}}{I_{bias}} \tag{1}$$

The total capacitance is the sum of the input and output capacitances at each output of the inverter stage and is given by

$$C_{tot} = \frac{5}{2}C_{ox}(W_nL_n + W_pL_p) \qquad (2)$$

where, C_{ox} is the gate oxide capacitance per unit area, (W_p, W_n) are the widths and (L_p, L_n) are the lengths of the M_p and M_n respectively. The VCO's oscillation frequency is inversely proportional to sum of the charging and discharging time (t_{dis}) and is given by [13]

$$f_{osc} = \frac{1}{N(t_{ch} + t_{dis})} = \frac{I_{bias}}{NC_{tot}V_{DD}} \qquad (3)$$

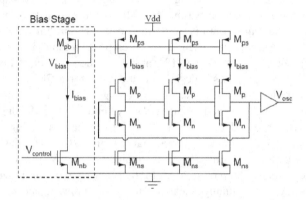

Fig. 1. Conventional Current-Starved Ring Voltage Controlled Oscillator

In eq. (3), the number of stages N, V_{DD} are initially specified for the ring VCO. C_{tot} and I_{bias} can be varied to obtain the desired frequency tuning. In the present work, I_{bias} in the replica bias stage is varied to tune the frequency of oscillations. By varying I_{bias}, the time t_{ch} (=t_{dis}) in each stage of the oscillator varies and therefore, frequency tuning is obtained. I_{bias} is a function of control voltage ($V_{control}$). Thus, the frequency range and linearity of the VCO depends upon the variation of I_{bias} with $V_{control}$. Also, the loop gain K_{VCO} of the VCO depends on the slope of I_{bias}-$V_{control}$ characteristic. Therefore, a constant K_{VCO} across the tuning range of the VCO requires a constant I_{bias}-$V_{control}$ slope. The variation of I_{bias} with $V_{control}$ can be obtained using large signal analysis of the bias stage (shown in fig. 1). Assuming current sources M_{pb}, M_{ps} and current sinks M_{nb}, M_{ns} are matched respectively, for $V_{control} \geq V_{tn}$ the current I_{bias} varies linearly with $V_{control}$ till control voltage reaches $V_{bias}+V_{tn}$ as M_{nb} and M_{pb} operate in the saturation region. For $V_{control} \geq V_{bias}+V_{tn}$, M_{nb} enters linear region and M_{pb} still remains in saturation region, under this condition I_{bias} in the bias stage is governed by

$$\left[(V_{control} - V_{tn})V_{bias} - \frac{V^2_{bias}}{2}\right] = \frac{\beta_{pb}}{2}\left(V_{DD} - V_{bias} - |V_{tp}|\right)^2 \qquad (4)$$

Since M_{pb} remains in the saturation region for the entire range of $V_{control}$, the non-linearity in I_{bias} variation is attributed to M_{nb} operating in the linear region. V_{tn} and V_{tp} are the threshold voltages of NMOS and PMOS transistors respectively.

In conventional design procedure, this non-linear variation of I_{bias} with $V_{control}$ leads to a non-linear K_{VCO} of the VCO. The nonlinearity of I_{bias} can be reduced if M_{nb} can be kept in saturation region till $V_{control}$ reaches V_{DD}. This eventually increases the linearity of the oscillation frequency in the tuning range as f_{osc} is proportional to I_{bias}. Assuming $V_{tn} = | V_{tp} | = V_t$ and solving eq. (4) for V_{bias} gives

$$
\begin{aligned}
V_{bias} \\
= -\frac{2\left[\beta_{nb}(V_t - V_{control}) + \beta_{pb}(V_t - V_{DD})\right]}{2\left(\beta_{nb} + \beta_{pb}\right)} \\
\pm \frac{2\beta_{nb}\left[(V_t - V_{control})^2 + \dfrac{\beta_{pb}}{\beta_{nb}}(V_t^2 - V_{DD}^2 - 2V_{control}V_t + 2V_{control}V_{DD})\right]^{0.5}}{2\left(\beta_{nb} + \beta_{pb}\right)}
\end{aligned}
\tag{5}
$$

Substituting $V_{control} = V_{DD}$ and finding out minimum V_{bias} gives

$$
V_{bias(min)} = V_{DD} - V_t - \frac{V_{DD} - V_t}{\sqrt{1 + \left(\beta_{pb}/\beta_{nb}\right)}}
\tag{6}
$$

$$
\frac{W_{pb}}{W_{nb}} = \frac{K_{nb}}{K_{pb}}\left[\left(\frac{V_{DD} - V_t}{V_{bias(min)} - V_{DD} + V_t}\right)^2 - 1\right]
\tag{7}
$$

Thus, eq. (7) yields the minimum ratio of the widths of M_{pb} and M_{nb} such that M_{nb} can be kept in saturation region till $V_{control} = V_{DD}$. This ratio can be used to size the current source/sink transistors such that current mirrored from the bias stage to each stage of the oscillator varies linearly, consequently improving the overall f-V characteristic. Fig. 2 and Fig. 3 show the variation of I_{bias} and V_{bias} with $V_{control}$ using conventional and proposed design method.

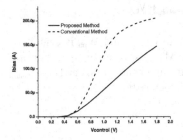

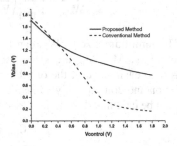

Fig. 2. Variation of I_{bias} with $V_{control}$ for proposed and conventional design procedure

Fig. 3. Variation of V_{bias} with $V_{control}$ for proposed and conventional design procedure

In addition to I_{bias}-$V_{control}$ characteristic, the operating region of current source/sink transistors (CSTs) also determines the linearity of the VCO. When $V_{control}$ is low, the CSTs operate in saturation region and a wide range of frequencies are possible resulting in high K_{VCO}. When $V_{control}$ is high, CSTs operate in triode region and their gate voltages have less effect on I_{bias} [17]. The delay in each stage of the oscillator when CSTs operating in saturation region is given by eq.(1). In triode region, the delay in each stage is determined by the resistance of the CST (R_{ps},R_{ns}) and the inverter stage (R_p,R_n) and is given by

$$t_d \propto \left(R_{ps,ns} + R_{p,n} \right) C_L \tag{8}$$

Where $R_{ps,ns}$ is given as

$$R_{ps,ns} = \cfrac{1}{\mu_{eff} C_{ox} \cfrac{W}{L} \left(V_{gs} - V_{th} \right)} \tag{9}$$

This is further exacerbated by the switching inverter currents giving rise to switching voltages at the source/drain terminals of $M_{p,n}$/$M_{ps,ns}$. The result is a reduction in tuning range and K_{VCO}. Thus, the causes of tuning nonlinearity determined by CSTs operating in triode region and non-linear starving currents (I_{bias}) from replica bias stage when $V_{control}$ is high can be solved with the proposed design method.

3   Design Procedure

The summary of the design methodology for current starved ring VCO can be outlined as follows:

1) The starving current I_{bias} is calculated from power dissipation specification given by

$$I_{bias} = \frac{P_{avg,dc}}{V_{DD}}$$

2) For M_{nb} to operate in saturation for entire range of $V_{control}$, V_{bias} should be set atleast to V_{DD}-V_t. From eq. (7), we obtain the ratio of W_{pb} and W_{nb}.

$$\frac{W_{pb}}{W_{nb}} = \frac{K_{nb}}{K_{pb}} \left[\left(\frac{V_{DD} - V_t}{V_{bias(min)} - V_{DD} + V_t} \right)^2 - 1 \right]$$

   The minimum size of W_{nb} can be chosen for low area and W_{pb} is calculated accordingly. M_{ps}, M_{ns} are sized same as M_{pb}, M_{nb} respectively to mirror I_{bias} current to each stage of the oscillator. This condition ensures a linear I_{bias}-$V_{control}$ variation and consequently a linear f_{osc}-$V_{control}$ characteristic.

3) C_{tot} can be calculated from the formula given by eq. (3)

$$C_{tot} = \frac{I_{bias}}{N f_{osc} V_{DD}}$$

4) From C_{tot}, the sizes of the current starved inverters in the ring oscillator can be obtained. $W_p = (K_n/K_p)W_n$ for the symmetric switching of the inverters and $L_n = L_p = L$ for all transistors. W_p, W_n can be calculated using eq. (2) given by

$$C_{tot} = \frac{5}{2}C_{ox}(W_n L_n + W_p L_p)$$

From the above procedure, we obtain the sizes for the current source/sink transistors and inverters in the ring oscillator.

4 Simulation Results

The design method given in section 3 is implemented to calculate the aspect ratios of transistors for three stage current starved ring VCO (shown in Fig. 1) with a center frequency of 404.5 MHz. Spectre simulation results for the design implemented in UMC 0.18 μm process parameters at 1.8 V supply voltage are shown in Fig. 4. and Fig. 5. It is observed from Fig. 4. that the proposed design method shows a linear f-V characteristic as compared to conventional design method. Fig. 5. shows the percentage non-linearity of f_{osc}-$V_{control}$ characteristic obtained from the proposed design method. The linear f-V characteristic for N=5 and N=7 stages shown in Fig. 6. indicates that the method is independent of number of stages.

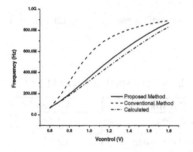

Fig. 4. Linearity comparison of conventional vs. proposed design method

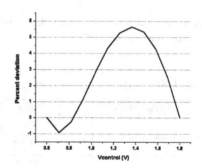

Fig. 5. % non-linearity of f_{osc} -$V_{control}$ for the proposed design method

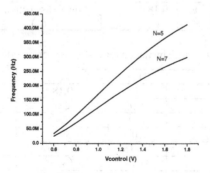

Fig. 6. Linearity of f_{osc}-$V_{control}$ for N=5 and N=7

The summary of the transistor sizes and simulation performance parameters are shown in Table 1 and Table 2 respectively. Fig. 7(a). shows the comparison of post-layout and schematic simulation of three stage CSVCO. Fig. 7(b). shows the corresponding layout of the three stage CSVCO.

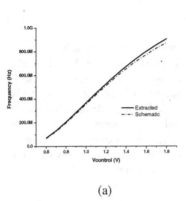
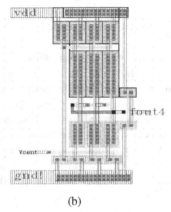

(a)   (b)

Fig. 7. (a) Comparison of post-Layout simulation and schematic simulation (b) Layout of 3 stage current starved ring VCO

Table 1. Summary of design parameters

Parameters		Value
Bias stage transistors	W_{pb}	2.40 µm
	W_{nb}	0.24 µm
Current Source / Sink Transistors (CSTs)	W_{ps}	2.40 µm
	W_{ns}	0.24 µm
Current starved inverters	W_p	5.87 µm
	W_n	2.94 µm
Channel length	L	0.18 µm

Table 2. Simulated performance of CSVCO

Parameters	Value
Technology	0.18 µm
Supply Voltage	1.8 V
Current (I_{bias}) @ (f_0)	88 µA
Oscillation centre frequency (f_0)	404.5 MHz
Tuning Range	66 – 875 MHz
% Full Scale Non-Linearity	5.567%
Power dissipation @ (f_0)	260 µW

Table 3. Comparison of the simulation results with work reported in literature

Parameters	[11]	[1]	This Work
Technology (µm)	3	0.18	0.18
Supply Voltage (V)	5.0	2.0	1.8
Power (mW)	150	22	0.26
Center frequency (MHz)	10	390	404.5
Tuning range (MHz)	1 – 15	20 – 807	66 – 875
Linearity	99.8%	-	94.5%
Phase Noise (@1 MHz offset)	-	-108 dBc/Hz	-82.28 dBc/Hz
Figure of Merit (FOM)	-	-	-140.27 dBc/Hz

5   Conclusion

In this paper a novel design methodology of a CMOS current starved ring Voltage Controlled Oscillator (VCO) for wide tuning range and high linearity has been achieved. The f-V tuning characteristic of the ring VCO depends on the current-voltage (I_{bias}-$V_{control}$) characteristic of the replica bias and region of operation of current source/sink transistors (CSTs). The proposed design methodology linearizes the I_{bias}-$V_{control}$ characteristic and ensures the CSTs to operate in saturation region. Consequently, tuning range is enhanced without additional circuitry and thus, reducing the power consumption and area of the CSVCO. The design is implemented in UMC 0.18 µm CMOS technology at 1.8 V supply voltage. The overall circuit consumes 260 µW power at 404.5 MHz, has a wide tuning range of 66 MHz to 875 MHz and having 94.5% tuning linearity. The post-layout extraction simulation results closely match with the schematic simulation results.

Acknowledgement. The authors would like to thank Dr. Chandra Shekhar, Director, CSIR-CEERI, Pilani for his constant guidance and support. The authors also thank DeitY/MCIT, New Delhi for project sponsorship and support.

References

1. Choi, J., Lim, K., Laskar, J.: A Ring VCO with Wide and Linear Tuning Characteristics for a Cognitive Radio System. In: IEEE Radio Frequency Integrated Circuits Symposium, pp. 395–398 (2008)
2. Brownlee, M., Hanumolu, P.K., Mayaram, K., Moon, U.-K.: A 0.5-GHz to 2.5-GHz PLL with Fully Differential Supply Regulated Tuning. IEEE J. Solid-State Circuits 41(12), 2720–2728 (2006)
3. Kim, C.-W., Koo, K.-H., Yoon, S.-W.: Fully-integrated wideband CMOS VCO with improved f–V linearity and low tuning sensitivity. IEEE Electronics Letters 46(1) (2010)
4. Razavi, B.: Design of Analog CMOS Integrated Circuits. McGraw Hill (2001)
5. Hamilton, J., Yan, S., Viswanathan, T.R.: A Discrete-Time Input Δ ∑ADC Architecture Using a Dual-VCO-Based Integrator. IEEE Trans. Circuits Syst. II, Express Briefs 57(11), 848–852 (2010)
6. Cao, T.V., Wisland, D.T., Lande, T.S., Moradi, F.: Low Phase-Noise VCO utilizing NMOS Symmetric Load for Frequency-based Delta-Sigma Modulators. In: IEEE International Conference on Electronics Circuits and Systems (ICECS), pp. 767–770 (2009)
7. Wismar, U., Wisland, D.T., Andreani, P.: Linearity of Bulk-Controlled Inverter Ring VCO in Weak and Strong Inversion. In: NORCHIP Conference, pp. 145–148 (2005)
8. Panda, B.P., Rout, P.K., Acharya, D.P., Panda, G.: Design of a Novel Current Starved VCO via Constrained Geometric Programming. In: International Symposium on Devices MEMS Intelligent Systems and Communication (ISDMISC 2011), Sikkim, India, pp. 224–227.
9. Ghai, D., Mohanty, S.P., Kougianos, E.: Parasitic Aware Process Variation Tolerant Voltage Controlled Oscillator (VCO) Design. IEEE Trans. VLSI Syst. 17(9), 1339–1342 (2009)

10. Lee, T.-H., Abshire, P.A.: Design Methodology for a Low-Frequency Current-Starved Voltage-Controlled Oscillator with a Frequency Divider. In: International Midwest Symposium on Circuits and Systems, MWSCAS (2012), pp. 646–649 (2012)

11. Wakayama, M.H., Abidi, A.A.: A 30 MHz Low-Jitter High-Linearity CMOS Voltage-Controlled Oscillator. IEEE J. Solid-State Circuits 22(6), 1074–1081 (1987)

12. McNeill, J.A.: Interpolating ring VCO with V-to-f linearity compensation. IEEE Electronics Letters 30(24), 2003–2004 (1994)

13. Baker, R.J.: CMOS: Circuit Design, Layout and Simulation, 3rd edn. Wiley-IEEE (2010)

14. Ayranci, E., Christensen, K., Andreani, P.: Enhancement of VCO Linearity and Phase Noise by Implementing Frequency Locked Loop. In: EUROCON: The International Conference on Computer as a Tool, pp. 2593–2599 (2007)

15. Park, Y.S., Choi, W.-Y.: Supply Noise Insensitive Ring VCO with On-Chip Adaptive Bias-Current and Voltage-Swing Control. In: IEEE International Symposium on Circuits and Systems (ISCAS), pp. 229–232 (2011)

16. Herzel, F., Razavi, B.: A Study of Oscillator Jitter Due to Supply and Substrate Noise. IEEE Trans. Circuits Syst. II: Analog and Digital Signal Processing 46, 56–62 (1999)

17. McNeill, J.A., Ricketts, D.S.: The Designer's Guide to Jitter in Ring Oscillators. Springer (2009)

A Low-Power Wideband High Dynamic Range Single-Stage Variable Gain Amplifier

Vivek Verma[1] and Chetan D. Parikh[2]

[1] vivekverma23@gmail.com
[2] Institute of ICT, Ahmedabad University, Ahmedabad, India
chetan.parikh@ahduni.edu.in

Abstract. This paper presents a low-voltage, low-power, wideband, single-stage variable gain amplifier (VGA) that provides a 57-dB gain variation. It consumes 1.35 mW, which is one of the lowest power consumptions reported for similar VGAs in the literature. The 3-dB bandwidth varies from 110 MHz at 25 dB gain to 3.8 GHz at -32 dB gain.

Keywords: Amplifier, analog circuits, CMOS, variable gain amplifier (VGA).

1   Introduction

Variable gain amplifiers (VGAs) are used to maximize the dynamic range of electronic systems in medical equipment, telecommunication, disc drives and many other systems where the signal amplitude may experience large variations and hence requires an inverse change in gain. In communication systems, VGAs play a role in automatic gain control by sensing the power level of incoming signals and normalizing the average amplitude of the signal to a reference value.

There are two broad approaches for designing VGAs. One is by analog gain control [1–6], and the other is discrete gain steps with digital control [7,8]. Digitally controlled VGAs use binary weighted arrays of resistors or capacitors for varying the gain, and analog VGAs use a variable transconductance or a variable resistance. An example application of analog VGAs is in code division multiple access (CDMA) systems, which require a power control range larger than 80 dB, and a continuously variable gain is preferred because it avoids signal phase discontinuity [9,10].

In this paper, we propose a single-stage CMOS VGA which uses capacitance cancellation technique to achieve wideband operation, and a pseudo-exponential MOSFET circuit with parallel driver and load paths for the dc currents of the differential amplifier, to achieve a wide dynamic range, and minimized chip area and power consumption.

M.S. Gaur et al. (Eds.): VDAT 2013, CCIS 382, pp. 19–25, 2013.
© Springer-Verlag Berlin Heidelberg 2013

2 Approximated Exponential Functions

To achieve a wide dynamic range, it is necessary that the gain variation be an exponential function of the control voltage. As MOSFET characteristics are not exponential, different pseudo-exponential functions have been proposed [2,11,12] that enable implementation in MOSFET circuits. The following are three such functions:

$$f(x) = e^{2ax} \cong \frac{(a+ax)}{(a-ax)} \qquad (1) \qquad f(x) = \frac{1}{2}[1+(1+2ax)^2] \qquad (2)$$

$$f(x) = \frac{[k+(1+ax)^2]}{[k+(1-ax)^2]} \qquad (3)$$

Of these, the first two functions provide a linear range of about 15dB; the third, obtains a range of more than 90 dB, for $k = 0.12$ [2]. We use the third function.

3 VGA Circuit Design

3.1 Control Circuit Design

Figure 1 shows a control circuit [2] which generates (3). The numerator and denominator of (3) are proportional to the currents I_{C2} and I_{C1} in Fig. 1, respectively. To minimize channel length modulation, the lengths of M1 and M2 must be kept large. The current ratio (I_{C2} / I_{C1}) as a function of the control voltage V_C is given in (4)

$$\frac{I_{c2}}{I_{c1}} = \frac{\dfrac{I_o}{K(V_{dd} - |V_{TH}|)^2} + \left(1 + \dfrac{V_c}{(V_{dd} - |V_{TH}|)}\right)^2}{\dfrac{I_o}{K(V_{dd} - |V_{TH}|)^2} + \left(1 - \dfrac{V_c}{(V_{dd} - |V_{TH}|)}\right)^2} \qquad (4)$$

which is equivalent to (3) with

$$k = \frac{I_o}{K(V_{dd} - |V_{TH}|)^2} \qquad \text{and} \qquad a = \frac{1}{(V_{dd} - |V_{TH}|)}$$

Equation (4) is derived by assuming $V_{DD} = V_{SS}$, with V_C in the range ($V_{SS} + V_{thn}$) to ($V_{DD} - |V_{thp}|$). If V_{DD} and V_{SS} are V_{supply} and 0 V, respectively, then V_C stays in the range V_{thn} to ($V_{DD} - |V_{thp}|$). Circuit simulation results of the circuit of Fig. 1 are shown in Fig. 2, which shows that a 90dB range of $\sqrt{(I_{C2}/I_{C1})}$ is achieved.

3.2 Proposed VGA Design

Figure 3 shows the circuit of the proposed variable gain amplifier (VGA). The circuit includes a common-mode feedback (CMFB) circuit [2]. In the figure, the core amplifier consists of the differential pair (M9 and M12) and diode connected loads (M10 and M11). The sizes of M9 and M12 are equal, and the sizes of M10 and M11 are equal. The differential gain of this amplifier cell is (g_{m-M9}/g_{m-M10}), with the assumption that the R_{out} of the current sources is high. Note that this configuration is different from the conventional differential amplifier, in that in a conventional circuit, the same current flows in the input and load transistors, while in the proposed circuit, the currents in the input and load transistors are $I_{C1}/2$ and $I_{C2}/2$, respectively, which are not equal; and it is by controlling these two currents by the control voltage, by the circuit of Fig. 1, that a wide dynamic range VGA is obtained.

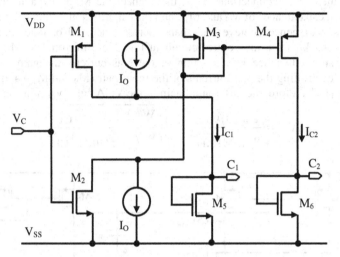

Fig. 1. Circuit diagram of control stage [2]

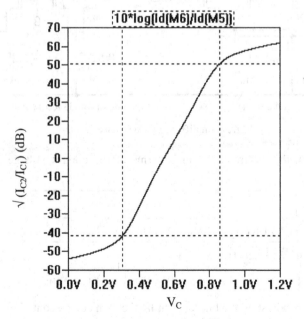

Fig. 2. Decibel scale plot of current ratio $\sqrt{(I_{C2}/I_{C1})}$ of control circuit

To reduce the Miller effect experienced by the gate-drain capacitances of the input transistors M_9 and M_{12}, a capacitive cancellation technique [13] is used. This is implemented using transistor M_{23} and M_{24} acting as capacitances. This technique has been used to increase the bandwidth of multistage amplifiers in wideband circuits [14]. The principle here is that the Miller capacitances due M_{23} and M_{24} are negative because of their cross-connections. Thus they cancel the Miller capacitances due to the gate-drain capacitances of M_9 and M_{12}, and thus significantly reduce the net Miller capacitances, and hence achieve wide-band performance. Also, note that the two currents I_{C2} and I_{C1} from the control circuit in Fig. 1 are mirrored to M_{13} and M_{14}. Since the transconductance is a function of the bias current, the gain variation is obtained by controlling the bias currents of the input-pair (M_9 and M_{12}) and the loads (M_{10} and M_{11}). Therefore, the differential gain of the VGA cell shown in Fig. 3 is:

$$A_v = \frac{g_{m-M9,12}}{g_{m-M10,11}} = \sqrt{\frac{(W/L)_{M9,12}\, I_{C2}}{(W/L)_{M10,11}\, I_{C1}}} \tag{5}$$

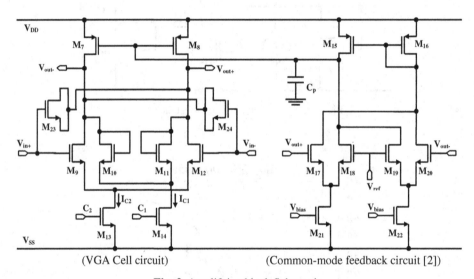

(VGA Cell circuit)   (Common-mode feedback circuit [2])

Fig. 3. Amplifying block Schematic

From (4) and (5), the differential gain in terms of the control voltage V_C can be expressed as

$$A_v = \sqrt{\frac{(W/L)_{M9,12}}{(W/L)_{M10,11}} * \frac{\dfrac{I_0}{K(V_{dd}-|V_{TH}|)^2} + \left(1+\dfrac{V_c}{(V_{dd}-|V_{TH}|)}\right)^2}{\dfrac{I_0}{K(V_{dd}-|V_{TH}|)^2} + \left(1-\dfrac{V_c}{(V_{dd}-|V_{TH}|)}\right)^2}} \tag{6}$$

In this equation, by adjusting the bias current I_0, the gain can be controlled. For the I_0 value corresponding to k = 0.12, the circuit yields more than 60 dB gain variation.

In Fig. 3, as noted above, the amplifier gain is varied by controlling the currents through M_{13} and M_{14}. Hence the currents through M_7 and M_8 must also vary as a function of the control voltage. A common-mode feedback (CMFB) circuit [2] is used to prevent any transistor from entering the triode region and to maintain a constant common-mode output voltage, as the control voltage varies.

4   Simulation Results

The proposed VGA circuit was designed in a standard 0.18 μm CMOS technology. Simulations were carried out in LT-Spice. V_{DD} was 1.2 V, and V_{SS} was 0 V.

The frequency response of the VGA for different gains is shown in Fig. 4. For a maximum gain of 25 dB, the bandwidth is 110 MHz. The bandwidth increases with reduction in gain. At the minimum gain of -32 dB, the bandwidth is 3828 MHz.

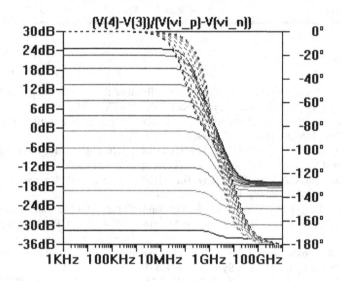

Fig. 4. Frequency Response of the Proposed VGA at different Gain Settings

The simulated performance of the VGA is shown in Table I. The Table also compares the proposed VGA with similar VGA's reported in the literature. The Table shows that the proposed VGA achieves the best performance in terms of the dynamic range of the gain variation, power consumption, and bandwidth, for a single-stage circuit.

5   Conclusion

A CMOS VGA with a high bandwidth and low-power consumption is proposed. The proposed circuit uses a capacitive neutralization technique to achieve wideband operation, and parallel driver and load paths for the dc currents of the differential amplifier. With an exponential approximation function a wide decibel linear range is achieved, so that only a single VGA stage is needed.

Table 1. Comparison of the proposed circuit with previously reported VGAs

Ref.	Technol. (μm)	Supply Voltage (V)	Power (mW)	Bandwidth (MHz)	Gain Variation / No. of Stages	Gain Variation in 1-Stage (dB)	Year
[1]	0.6	(*)	10	20	25dB / 2	15	1995
[11]	0.6	3.3	21	20	34dB / 2	17	2000
[12]	0.5	3.3	13	150	15dB / 1	15	1998
[6]	0.35	1.5	25	21	26dB / 1	26	2000
[15]	0.25	3	14	2100	15dB / 1	15	2002
[2]	0.18	1.8	7	32 - 1050	95dB / 2	47	2006
[16]	0.18	1.8	20	380-2200	27dB / 1	27	2012
This Work	0.18	1.2	1.4	110 – 3828	57dB / 1	57	2013

References

1. Harjani, R.: A low-power CMOS VGA for 50-Mb/s disk drive read channels. IEEE Trans. Circuits Syst. II, Analog Digit. Signal Process. 42, 370–376 (1995)
2. Duong, Q.-H., et al.: A 95-dB linear low-power variable gain amplifier. IEEE Trans. Circuits Syst. I. 53(8), 1648–1657 (2006)
3. Duong, Q.-H., et al.: An all CMOS 743 MHz variable gain amplifier for UWB systems. In: International Symposium on Circuit and System, pp. 678–681 (2006)
4. Song, W.C., Oh, C.J., Cho, G.H., Jung, H.B.: High frequency/high dynamic range CMOS VGA. Electron. Lett. 36(13), 1096–1098 (2000)
5. Lee, H.D., Lee, K.A., Hoang, S.: A wideband CMOS variable gain amplifier with exponential gain control. IEEE Trans. on Microwave Theory and Technique 55(6) (June 2007)
6. Green, M.M., Joshi, S.: A 1.5-V CMOS VGA based on pseudodifferential structures. In: Proc. IEEE Int. Symp. Circuits Syst., pp. IV-461–IV-464 (May 2000)
7. Orsatti, P., Piazza, F., Huang, Q.: A 71-MHz CMOS IF-baseband strip for GSM. IEEE J. Solid-State Circuits 35(1), 104–108 (2000)
8. Elwan, H.O., Ismail, M.: Digitally programmable decibel-linear CMOS VGA for low-power mixed-signal applications. IEEE Trans. Circuits Syst. II, Analog Digit. Signal Process. 47(5), 388–398 (2000)
9. Yamaji, T., Kanou, N., Itakura, T.: A temperature-stable CMOS variable-gain amplifier with 80-dB linearly controlled gain range. IEEE J. Solid-State Circuits 37(5), 553–558 (2002)
10. Carrara, F., Palmisano, G.: High-dynamic-range VGA with temperature compensation and linear-in-dB gain control. IEEE J. Solid-State Circuits 40(10), 2019–2024 (2005)
11. Christopher, W.M.: A variable gain CMOS amplifier with exponential gain control. In: Dig. Tech. Papers IEEE Symp. VLSI Circuits, pp. 146–149 (2000)
12. Huang, P., Chiou, L.Y., Wang, C.K.: A 3.3-V CMOS wideband exponential control variable-gain-amplifier. In: Proc. IEEE Int. Symp. Circuits Syst., pp. I-285–I-288 (May 1998)

13. Meyer, R., Gray, P.: Analysis and Design of Analog Integrated Circuits. Wiley, New York (2001)
14. Galal, S., Razavi, B.: 10-Gb/s limiting amplifier and laser/modulator driver in 0.18-/spl mu/m CMOS technology. IEEE J. Solid-State Circuits 38(12), 2138–2146 (2003)
15. Koh, K.-J., Youn, Y.-S., Yu, H.-K.: A gain boosting method at RF frequency using active feedback and its application to RF variable gain amplifier (VGA). In: Proc. IEEE Int. Symp. Circuits Syst., pp. III.89–III.92 (May 2002)
16. Huang., Y.-Y., et al.: Compact Wideband Linear CMOS Variable Gain Amplifier for Analog-Predistortion Power Amplifiers. IEEE Transactions on Microwave Theory and Techniques 60(1) (January 2012)

An Ultra-Wideband Baseband Transmitter Design for Wireless Body Area Network

R.K. Naga Mahesh, Akash Ganesan, Manchi Pavan Kumar, and Roy P. Paily

Dept of Electrical and Electronics Engineering
Indian Institute of Technology,
Guwahati, Assam - 781039, India
{r.mahesh,akash.ag,m.pavan,roypaily}@iitg.ernet.in

Abstract. This paper presents a low-power ultra-wideband baseband transmitter designs for wireless body area networks (WBAN). This is the first time a baseband architecture for UWB PHY is implemented according to the standard IEEE 802.15.6. Since WBAN is the network around the humanbody there are stringent requirements associated with it such as high security, low power consumption and reliable communication. To incorporate these features in baseband transmitter, an efficient, simple BCH encoder is used for random error protection and to combat burst errors an optimum size interleaver is used. A low complexity transmitter controller and an efficient algorithm for determining the interleaver size has been implemented. Two different architectures have been implemented in 0.13 μm CMOS technology which are operated at 487.5 kHz system clock with 1.08 V supply.

1 Introduction

Wireless body area network (WBAN) is an emerging technology that combines continuous health care monitoring and consumer electronic applications around the human body [1],[2]. WBAN consists of small, intelligent devices attached on or implanted in the body and are capable of establishing a wireless communication link [3],[4]. Current wireless personal area networks do not support the combination of reliability, quality of service (QOS), low power, data rate, and non-interference required to broadly address the breadth of body area network (BAN) applications[5]. So a separate wireless standard IEEE 802.15 Task Group 6 (IEEE 802.15.6) was exclusively developed for WBAN applications. The standard defines a Medium Access Control (MAC) layer and several supporting physical layers (PHYs) to enable body area networks used in, on, or around a body. The IEEE 802.15.6 specifies a total of three PHYs namely narrowband (NB) PHY, ultra wideband (UWB) PHY, and human body communication (HBC) PHY.

The UWB PHY specification is designed to offer robust performance for BANs and to provide a large scope for implementation opportunities for high performance, robustness, low complexity, and ultra low power operation [5]. This physical layer is targeted at both medical and non-medical applications. For high data

M.S. Gaur et al. (Eds.): VDAT 2013, CCIS 382, pp. 26–34, 2013.
© Springer-Verlag Berlin Heidelberg 2013

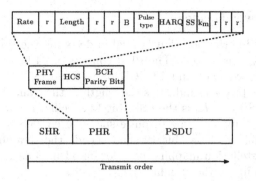

Fig. 1. Ultra wideband Physical layer Frame Format

rate applications, UWB physical layer is best suitable compared to other physical layers because of larger bandwidth (500 MHz) availability [6]. In this paper, two architectures are considered for UWB PHY baseband transmitter designs for WBAN applications. The details of implementations of the architectures and their differentiating features are explained in section III of this paper. We also discussed the hardware implementation of each block in the baseband processor. To the best of our knowledge, it is the first time an architecture for the standard is implemented.

2   Ultra Wideband PHY Specification

The operating frequency bands of UWB PHY layer divided into two band groups: low band (3.244 to 4.742 GHz) and high band (6.240 to 10.23 GHz). The low band is divided into 3 channels, high band into 8 channels and each channel's bandwidth is 499.2 MHz. The standard [5] defines two modes of operations: default mode and high QOS mode. The default mode shall be used in medical and non-medical applications and the high QOS mode in high priority medical applications. In this paper, default mode implementation is considered.

The PLCP layer constructs the UWB PHY frame format or physical layer protocol data unit (PPDU) by concatenating the synchronization header (SHR), physical layer header (PHR) and physical layer service data unit (PSDU) respectively, as shown in Fig. 1. Detailed descriptions of SHR, PHR and PSDU are given below.

2.1   Synchronization Header

The synchronization header (SHR) shall be divided into two parts: Preamble, intended for timing synchronization, packet detection, and carrier frequency offset recovery; The frame delimiter, which is used for frame synchronization[5].

2.2 Physical Layer Header

The PHR contains information that is vital in decoding the PSDU. The length of the PHR (N_{header}) is 40 bits. The PHR consists of 24 bits of PHR frame, 4 bits of Head check sequence and 12 BCH parity bits. In PHR, frame bits 0-2 indicates data rate; bits 4-11 indicates the length of the frame body (L_0 to L_7), where L_7 is the MSB and L_0 is the LSB; bit 14 specifies if burst mode is being used; bits 15-16 specify the type of pulse shaper used; bits 17 & 18 are used in HARQ retransmission flow; bit 19 shall encode the scrambler seed; bit 20 represents the constellation mapping used for on-off modulation. All other bits are reserved according to the standard.

2.3 Physical Layer Service Data Unit

The PSDU contains the MPDU and the BCH parity bits. The MPDU is formed is by prepending the 7-octet MAC header to the MAC frame body and appending a 2-octet FCS to the result. The maximum size of the MAC frame body is 255 octets, and this information is carried in the PHY header in octets.

3 Ultra Wideband Baseband Transmitter Design

The overall block diagram of a compliant digital baseband transmitter for UWB PHY specification is shown in Fig. 2. The baseband module can be divided into two parallel processing blocks. One of the blocks is used for the creation of the physical layer header (PHR). The other block is for the generation of PSDU from MPDU. To increase the robustness of the PHR frame, it is protected by a CRC4 as well as a BCH channel code. The CRC4 will append 4-bits for error detection. The HCS (CRC4) is implemented by using ones complement of the remainder generated by modulo-2 division of the PHR information by the polynomial, as shown in equation 1. After the HCS phase, the PHR frame consisting of 24 bits data and the 4-bits checksum will be processed by a shortened BCH(40,28) encoder. The BCH(40,28) channel code is derived from a BCH(63,51,t=2) code by appending 23 zero bits (called shortening bits) to the 28 information bits. After BCH encoding, the shortening bits are removed and the PHR frame is stored in a shift register, from which it is later read while it is being sequenced with the PSDU.

$$g(x) = 1 + x + x^4 \tag{1}$$

The construction of the PSDU from the MPDU is as follows: The MAC enqueues the MPDU packet in the TXFIFO. From TXFIFO, the data is processed by an additive scrambler with the generator polynomial $x[n]$ given in equation 2. The scrambler has two seed values which is set by the MAC.

$$x(n) = 1 + x^2 + x^{12} + x^{13} + x^{14} \tag{2}$$

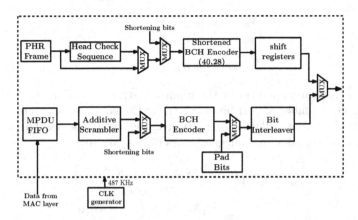

Fig. 2. Block diagram of UWB baseband transmitter

After scrambling, the data goes to the channel coding block. The channel coding employed in the baseband processor is BCH(n=63, k=51, t=2), a systematic cyclic code which has very simple encoding and decoding structures. The generator polynomial employed for BCH(63,51) is given by equation 3. The parity bits are determined by computing the remainder polynomial $r(x)$ as shown in equation 4, where $m(x)$ is the message polynomial $m(x) = \sum_{i=0}^{50} m_i x^i$.

$$g(x) = 1 + x^3 + x^4 + x^5 + x^8 + x^{10} + x^{12} \tag{3}$$

$$r(x) = \sum_{i=0}^{11} r_i x^i = x^{12} m(x) \bmod g(x) \tag{4}$$

The total number of bits in the MPDU is shown in the equation 5 where $N_{MACheader}$ is the number of octets in the MAC header, $N_{MACframebody}$ is the number of octets in the MAC frame body, and N_{FCS} is the number of octets of the FCS. The number of codewords (N_{CW}) in a PSDU frame is given by the equation 6. Bit stuffing is performed such that modulo ((MPDU+ stuffing), 51) is zero. This is done so that the BCH encoder always has full blocks to process. Mathematically, if the rem(N_{MPDU},k)≠0, the last codeword requires N_{bs} bits stuffing which is shown in equation 7. The total number of bits before encoding is given by equation 8. After sending 51 information bits to BCH encoder, it will add 12 parity bits to the output stream. So, the pipeline should be stalled for 12 clock cycles.

$$N_{MPDU} = 8(N_{MACheader} + N_{MACframebody} + N_{FCS}) \tag{5}$$

$$N_{CW} = \left\lceil \frac{N_{MPDU}}{k} \right\rceil \tag{6}$$

$$N_{bs} = N_{CW}k - N_{MPDU} \tag{7}$$

$$N_{PSDU} = N_{MPDU} + N_{bs} \tag{8}$$

Pad bits shall be appended to the input bit stream to align on the symbol boundary. The number of pad bits is given by the equation 9, where M is the cardinality of the constellation of a given modulation scheme. The standard defines two constellation mappings schemes (M=2 ,M=16).

$$N_{pad} = \log_2(M) \left\lceil \frac{N_{PSDU} + (n - k)N_{CW}}{\log_2(M)} \right\rceil - [N_{PSDU} + (n - k)N_{CW}] \tag{9}$$

If M=2, then the number of pad bits is zero which is evident from equation 9 and if M=16, the number of bits in the PSDU frame should be divisible by 4. By using mathematical deduction, the pad bits depends only on the number of stuff bits which are inserted at the last code word of BCH encoder.

After adding the pad bits, interleaving is carried out in order to protect the data from burst errors. Interleaving turns burst errors into random errors. The algebraic interleaver is is given in equation 10:

$$\prod(n) = nb_s ModN_I \tag{10}$$

where N_I is interleaver's length. The interleaver's length is set to 192 and seeding parameter b_s , to 37. If N_{rem}=rem(N_T,N_I)$\neq$ 0, the last interleaver block, N_I is set to N_{rem}. Two design methodologies are considered in this paper and their details are given below.

3.1   Architecture 1 (A1)

In this architecture, a synchronous pipeline is used and the design is described in Verilog. A low complexity transmitter controller controls all the activities of the PHY layer. It controls the dataflow in the pipeline. The dataflow control is achieved by running enable lines to the various blocks from the controller. It stalls the scrambler while the BCH coder generates the parity bits. The functions of the controller are stated below.

- Getting information about the MPDU to be transmitted, from the MAC.
- Generating stall signals for the pipeline.
- Calculation of interleaver's block size.
- Calculation of number of pad bits to be inserted and pad bit enable signal generation.
- PHR and PSDU sequencing is controlled by this block.

The working of the front-end controller is shown in the flowchart Fig 3. The *length* in the flowchart has to be initialized with the total length of MPDU.

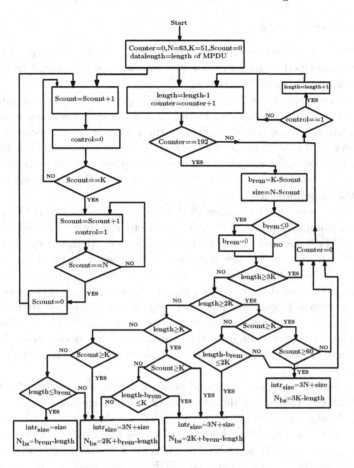

Fig. 3. Flowchart of transmitter controller of A1

The *Scount* is a mod-63 counter that sets *contol* to '1' when *Scount* is greater than 51. When *contol=1*, the output of the scrambler is stalled, while the BCH encoder outputs the parity bits. The $intr_{size}$ represents the size of the last interleaving block and n_{bs} represents number of bits to be stuffed in the last BCH block.

The interleaver consists of two banks, each a 192 bit register. At any given instance, one of the banks will act as the input bank and the other will act as the output bank. The input bank will take the input from the BCH coder, while the output is taken from the other bank. The input bank will be fully filled and the output bank will be fully drained at the same instance, and the roles will be reversed. The address is generated internally with information about the block size from the controller. The PHR frame is initially processed and then stored in a 40-bit register. The controller generates a PHR enable signal, which when active, pipes the output from the PHR register to the output. Once finished, the PSDU is provided to the next stage.

3.2   Architecture 2 (A2)

This architecture is described in Bluespec SystemVerilog[7]. Bluespec allows designs to be described in terms of rules or internal behaviors and transactions
with other modules through interfaces.

This architecture, unlike A1, uses an elastic pipeline. An elastic pipeline is
based on the Producer-Consumer model. In this model, whenever a consumer
block is ready to accept new data, it asks the producer it is associated with to
feed it, provided it can. This is in contrast to A1, where the control is centralized.
This producer-consumer model allows for easy replacement and modification of
modules without changing the other blocks, as long as the replacement module
provides the same interface.

The pipeline structure is implemented using First in First out (FIFO). FIFOs
allow for communication between blocks using enqueue (enq) and dequeue (deq)
operations. These methods are guarded; i.e., an enq operation can occur only
if the FIFO can accept the new data and a deq operation can happen only if
the FIFO is not empty. Hence, for each stage to have a one clock latency, a
2-element FIFO is needed or a 1-element FIFO which can simultaneously enq
and deq on empty is needed. The latter has a combinational path from the
input to the output and also consumes less area and power. The combinational
path translates to a reduction in the maximum frequency of operation. But, this
reduction in the clock frequency was a non-issue as the timing requirements were
easily met.

As previously hinted, the front-end controller does not perform heavy duty
tasks such as controlling the dataflow in A2. It does specifies/tags the end of
frame bit. It also specifies the scrambler seed. It also specifies whether BCH
encoding is done or not. This scheme is employed by HARQ mechanism.

The design of the PHR block is also different. To make sure that no bubbles
were present at the overall output, the PHR stream must be immediately followed by the payload without bubbles in between. Bubbles are essentially caused
by the use of shortened BCH code, which drops bits from the BCH coder it is
derived from. To prevent bubbles, the entire word was computed and stored in
a register the size of the PHR, in architecture A1. To achieve a reduction in
the register count, partial computation of the PHR was employed in A2. A 25-
element FIFO was used. This allowed for computations to happen partially. As
soon as the PHR FIFO starts draining, new values are computed. Initially, these
are the values to be dropped, which are not enqueued. During the last value
that is dequeued, the data to be present is calculated and added to the FIFO.
Thus, the bubbles in the pipeline are avoided at a reduced cost in power and
area when compared to A1.

4   Results and Discussion

The performance characteristics of both the architectures are tabulated below.
These characteristics are for the 0.13 μm CMOS technology, operating at a
supply voltage of 1.08 V with clock frequency of 487.5 kHz. The Bluespec code

Table 1. Performance characteristics of the architectures

Parameters	Architecture 1	Architecture 2
Core Size (μm^2)	35244.8	34490
Critical Path (ns)	8.2	10.2
Total Power (μW)	26.04	25.46

of architecture A2 was converted into Verilog code by the Bluespec compiler and the flow is same for both the designs. One of the major advantages of A2 is that any block can be replaced without modifications to the control logic of the other blocks.

The interleaver consumes the most power (around 16 μ W for both architectures) due to the two 192-bit banks and its associated address generation logic. It accounts for about 70 % of the total power consumption in both the architectures. In architecture A1, the interleaver block has a latency of 192 clock cycles and 40 bit PHR is inserted before the interleaver output such that the overall latency of the design reduces to 152 clock cycles. In architecture A2, the maximum latency is 192 bits, while for any thing less than this, it becomes a multiple of 63.

5   Conclusion

In this paper a low power and high energy efficiency baseband transmitter has been implemented for WBAN. The design includes a low complexity physical layer which is compliant to the standard IEEE 802.15.6. As WBAN mostly deals with medical data, highly reliable communication is essential which is provided by the low power forward error correction block. Two different architectures for UWB-PHY transmitter baseband were designed, synthesized, and compared. The two architectures have been implemented in 0.13 μm CMOS technology targetting a data rate of 487.5 kbps and consuming only 26 μW power.

References

1. Patel, M., Wang, J.: Applications, challenges, and prospective in emerging body area networking technologies. IEEE Wireless Communications 17, 80–88 (2010)
2. Cao, H., Leung, V., Chow, C., Chan, H.: Enabling technologies for wireless body area networks: A survey and outlook. IEEE Communications Magazine 47, 84–93 (2009)
3. Chen, M., Gonzalez, S., Vasilakos, A., Cao, H., Leung, V.: Body Area Networks-A Survey. Springer publication (2010)
4. Pantelopoulos, A., Bourbakis, N.: A survey on wearable sensor-based systems for health monitoring and prognosis. IEEE Transactions on Systems, Man, and Cybernetics, Part C: Applications and Reviews 40, 1–12 (2010)
5. IEEE Computer Society: IEEE standard for local and metropolitan area networks - part 15.6: Wireless body area networks. IEEE Std 802.15.6-2012, 1–271 (2012)

6. Lee, C., Kim, J., Lee, H.S., Kim, J.: Physical layer designs for wban systems in ieee 802.15.6 proposals. In: ISCIT 2009. 9th International Symposium on Communications and Information Technology, pp. 841–844 (2009)
7. Bluespec Inc.: Bluespec System Verilog Version3.8 Reference Guide (2005)

Computational Functions' VLSI Implementation for Compressed Sensing

Shrirang Korde, Amol Khandare, Raghavendra Deshmukh, and Rajendra Patrikar

Electronics Engineering Department, VNIT, SA Road, Nagpur-440010
{shrirang.korde,amolkhandare2}@gmail.com,
mona1810@yahoo.com, rajendra@computer.org

Abstract. Compressed Sensing (CS) is found to be promising method for sparse signal recovery and sampling. The paper proposes the architecture for computing various computational functions useful in realizing CS recovery consisting of Singular Value Decomposition (SVD) using Bi-diagonalization method; L_1 norm of vector, L_2 norm of vector calculations. This is one of the early VLSI implementation attempt for CS recovery. We have verified the design for speed and accuracy of results on FPGA.

Keywords: Compressed Sensing, Compressive Sensing, Architecture.

1   Introduction

Compressed Sensing (CS) has been receiving a lot of interest as a promising method for sparse signal recovery and sampling. As a general principle, a sparse solution x to an under-determined linear system of equations "Ax = y" may be obtained by minimizing the L1 norm of x. Minimizing ||x||1 is recognized as a practical avenue for obtaining sparse solutions x. If the "observation" y is contaminated with noise, then an appropriate norm of the residual (Ax − y) should be minimized. If there is noise in y, the L1-regularized least square problem (LSP) [1-4]

$$\text{minimize} \|Ax - y\|_2^2 + \lambda \|x\|_1 \tag{1}$$

$$\lambda > 0, \|x\|_1 \to L_1 \text{ norm}, \|Ax - y\|_2 \to L_2 \text{ norm}$$

Numerous schemes have been proposed for obtaining sparse solutions of underdetermined systems of linear equations; popular methods have been developed from many viewpoints: L1-minimization, convex regularization and nonconvex optimization [2-5], matching pursuit [2-5], iterative thresholding methods and subspace methods [6-7], Singular Value Decomposition (SVD) methods [8-10]. These specific proposals are often tailored to different viewpoints, ranging from formal analysis of algorithmic properties to particular application requirements.

As per our review, Patrick et al [7] work is an early paper proposing VLSI Implementation for CS recovery using message passing/iterative methods. Yeyang et al [10] proposes to use SVD as data-adaptive sparsity basis for compressed sensing Magnetic Resonance (MR) images and is able to give sparser representation for

M.S. Gaur et al. (Eds.): VDAT 2013, CCIS 382, pp. 35–43, 2013.
© Springer-Verlag Berlin Heidelberg 2013

broader range of MR images as it is better than the conventional transforms like Discrete Cosine Transform and Discrete Wavelet transform.

We reviewed various CS recovery algorithms. Matrix and vector processing is most suited to implement various computational functions. The paper contributes in identifying and implementing various computational functions required for VLSI implementation. The functional verification of the VLSI implementation was done by using LAPACK/LINPACK/TNT (Template Numerical Toolkit) software wherever required.

The paper is organized as follows. The section 2 give Computational Functions, Section 3 give Design and Implementation and Section 4 give results. The conclusion and future scope is presented in section 5.

2   Computational Functions

The review of various CS recovery algorithms [1-10], highlight use of L_1 norm of vector, L_2 norm of vector, matrix SVD function as basis for implementing various CS algorithms. The current work focuses on following CS recovery algorithms: L_1-minimization, convex regularization [2-4], iterative thresholding methods [6-7] and Singular Value Decomposition (SVD) [8-10].

The computational functions are defined as follows: L_1 norm of vector = $\Sigma_i |x_i|$, L_2 norm of vector = Squareroot ($\Sigma_i |x_i|^2$) and Matrix SVD includes solving least square problem (eq. 1), i.e. computing the following equation:

$$x = \arg \min \|Ax - y\|^2 \qquad (2)$$

To compute equation (2), SVD is computed as factorization of matrix $\mathbf{A}$ (= USV^T). U, S, V denote matrix factorization of $\mathbf{A}$

There are two methods for computing the SVD: Bi-diagonal form with QR algorithm and Jacobi rotation method. The QR algorithm is computationally much more efficient than the Jacobi method. On the other hand, Jacobi methods exhibit much more inherent parallelism than the QR. The review indicates SVD FPGA implementation [11-15] using Jacobi rotation. Jacobi SVD [15] analyzes small and mid sizes matrices around 8X8 size. The Jacobi method works well for real symmetric matrices. However the algorithm is slower for matrices of order greater than about 10, by a significant constant factor, than the Bi-diagonal form with QR method [16].

Compressed sensing recovery normally deals with larger matrix sizes. We require SVD method dealing for dense, real non-symmetric matrices which is not the case with Jacobi method. The accuracy requirement is also important and requires floating point operations. We propose SVD calculation as Householder's reduction to Bi-diagonal form (Bi-diagonalization) followed with QR algorithm. The Householder's reduction [17, 18] reduces a matrix to bi-diagonal form by repeated transformation. Transformation annihilates the required part of whole column and whole corresponding row by using a Householder matrix of the form $P = 1 - 2w.w^T$.

3   Design and Implementation

3.1   Design

We designed various architectural entities and have presented the architecture. These entities are used multiple times in the CS recovery schemes. The details are as follows:

- L_1 norm of vector
- L_2 norm of vector
- SVD calculation using Bi-diagonalization of matrix with QR algorithm (Bi-diagonalization entity , Sum1, Sum2 and Squareroot entities)

The design and RTL implementation of L_1 norm of vector, L_2 norm of vector and Bi-diagonalization are given below. The QR algorithm's functional implementation has been used for testing SVD.

L_1 Norm and L_2 Norm:
The **Fig. 1** gives iterative design and RTL implementation of L_1 norm and L_2 norm for a vector. To our knowledge L_1 norm and L_2 norm architecture is not available in literature comes as our contribution.

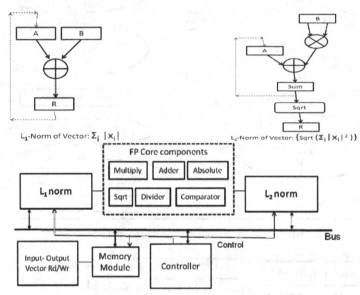

Fig. 1. (a) L_1 norm of vector (b) L_2 norm of vector (c) RTL view

Bi-diagonalization:
The Householder's reduction [17-18] to Bi-diagonal form is designed and implemented in VHDL. The Bi-diagonalization steps are given below:

1. Compute the transformation on matrix A for the ith column and place the ith diagonal in vector1, Apply transformation
2. Place the ith row of Matrix A into vector2 for the row transformation and it's calculation
3. Store the transformation in U

4. Find the ith row transformation and place the ith super-diagonal in vector2, Apply transformation
5. Store the transformation in V
6. Order the Matrix to bi-diagonal form, storing the diagonal elements in vector1 and the super-diagonal element in another vector2
7. Generate U
8. Generate V

The **Fig. 2** gives the overview of Bi-diagonalization design and **Fig. 3** gives Bi-diagonalization entity RTL view and SVD implementation. To our knowledge Bi-diagonalization architecture is not available in literature and comes as our contribution.

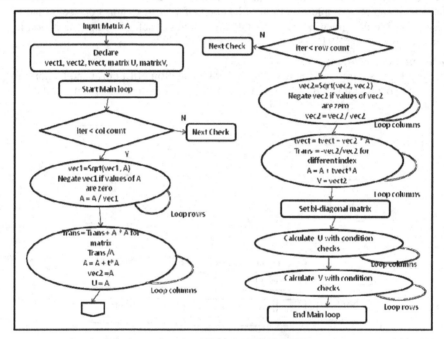

Fig. 2. Overview of Bi-diagonalization design and implementation

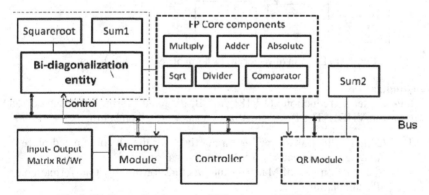

Fig. 3. Bi-diagonalization entity RTL view and SVD Implementation

The **Fig. 4** gives Sum1, Sum2 and Square root entities. The Bi-diagonalization entity (and SVD) is based on these entities. For Sum2 and Square root entities we use two multipliers (floating point) and there by introducing parallelism in operations.

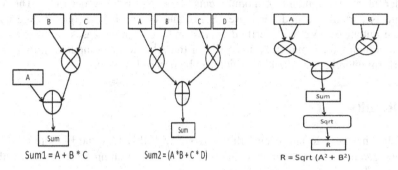

$$Sum1 = A + B * C$$ $$Sum2 = (A*B + C*D)$$ $$R = Sqrt (A^2 + B^2)$$

Fig. 4. (a) Sum1 (a) Sum2 (c) Square Root

3.2   Implementation

We have implemented and synthesized L_1 norm of vector, L_2 norm of vector, Bi-diagonalization of matrix, Sum1, Sum2, Square root. The Bi-diagonalization entity uses Sum1 and Squareroot entities and other FP core entities. The architectural entities are implemented and synthesized on Xilinx Artix-7 with ISE-14.x and the implementation is done in VHDL. The Floating Point core (FP) 6.0 is used.

The Xilinx FP Core (blocking mode) gives the results of calculation after certain duration. The duration is multiple (N) of clock cycles for operations like Multiply, ADD/SUB, DIV etc.

We have implemented following techniques:

- For repetitive operations, 'for loop' i.e. for functional we have provided a control flag (gated if with clock) which controls the execution to next stage. The flag is updated when all the required operations are done in each of the iteration.
- Wait for the floating point operations is implemented by using a variable to count the desired number of cycles on clock along with a flag whether to proceed to next stage or not.
- We have used above techniques for creating L1 norm of vector, L2 norm of vector, Bi-diagonalization of matrix synthesizable entities.

The **Fig. 1** gives RTL view of L_1 norm of vector and L_2 norm of vector. The memory module uses LogiCore to define memory. The controller interacts with L_1 norm entity and L_2 norm entity. The controller along with memory module gets data in/out for processing.

The **Fig. 2** gives the brief overview of Bi-diagonalization. It indicates that there are multiple loops and nested loops along with conditional checks. The design decision to create the entities like Sum1, Sum2 and Squareroot and techniques enabled us to create synthesizable entity for Bi-diagonalization.

We also have done VHDL implementation of SVD using Bi-diagonalization entity and other entities as shown in **Fig. 3**. The memory module uses LogiCore to define memory. The controller interacts with Bi-diagonalization entity and QR module. The controller along with memory module gets data in/out for processing. The QR algorithm is part of test code and uses Sum2 and other FP components. We have tested the output of SVD and verified against matlab. For the cases when rows are less than columns for a matrix A, the SVD of the A^T is to be computed initially and then perform interchanges U and V which can be part of testcode.

4   Results

The scheme has been tested using Xilinx Artix-7 with ISE-14.x and FP core 6.0. The test input given to the system was random. The device summary details are also given below for various synthesized entities.

L_1 Norm:
We have implemented L_1 norm for various vector sizes. This can be configured as per user need. We verified the output of L_1 norm using matlab as reference output and no error was observed. The time to compute L_1 norm for few vector lengths is given below and the time scales in proportion of the length.

Vector Lengths	Time
10, 100	1.305 us, 13.005 us

L_2 norm:
We have implemented L_2 norm for various vector sizes. This can be configured as per user need. We verified the output of L_2 norm using matlab as reference output and no error was observed. The time to compute L_2 norm for few vector lengths is given below and the time scales in proportion of the length.

Vector Lengths	Time
100, 49	23.695 us, 11.969 us

Bi-diagonalization:
We have implemented Bi-diagonalization and verified its output with the reference software implementation and the results were matching. The timing for a matrix size is given below and found to be acceptable for SVD implementation.

Matrix	Time
4X4	24.915 us

Device Summary for L_1 Norm of Vector and L_2 Norm of Vector and Bi-diagonalization:
Selected Device: xa7a100tcsg324-2i.

Parameters	L_1 norm	L_2 norm	Bi-diag
Number of Slice Registers*	32	97	137
Number of Slice LUTs **	32	66	76
Number used as Logic **	NA	2	12
Number of LUT FF pairs used	64	98	213
Number of bonded IOBs ***	97	97	65

(* out of 1268000, ** out of 63400, *** out of 210)
Note[1]

Design Summary of Sum1, Sum2, Squareroot:
Selected Device: xa7a100tcsg324-2i.

Parameters	Sum1	Sum2	Squareroot
Number of Slice Registers*	65	240	282
Number of Slice LUTs **	1	117	67
Number used as Logic **	1	53	67
Number of LUT FF pairs used	66	253	304
Number of bonded IOBs ***	64	161	97

(* out of 1268000, ** out of 63400, *** out of 210)

SVD:
The SVD implementation is done using various synthesized Architectural entities given above. The **Table 1** gives comparison of first diagonal element of 'S' Matrix (equation (2)) of VHDL implementation and Matlab implementation, though we have the complete Matrix (U, S, V) available, the first diagonal element being the dominant value of SVD is used for comparison in the table. We compared the timing for our SVD calculation to the implementation in [15] for size 16 X 32 and have found to be faster by a factor of 2.7. Our implementation for 32X16 takes 1.969 ms while implementation given in [15] takes 5.344 ms. The clock period used is 10 ns for getting the results but it can be reduced to 3 ns as lower limit, so the above values in the table can reduce to 1/3rd.

The Xilinx ISE value and the Matlab value indicated in the table are output of SVD for various sample input vectors. The ISE values and Matlab values are observed to be almost same and the error is negligible compared to implementation done by [15] which has error of around 1.4% for first diagonal element for 16X32 size.

---

[1]   The device summary does not add the hardware resources used by FP core. The resource utilization for Artix7 is available in the document, LogiCORE IP Floating-Point Operator v6.2 Product Guide PG060 December 18, 2012.

Table 1. SVD results

Matrix Size	Xilinx ISE value	Matlab value	Time
4x4	4	4	41.330 us^2
4x4	2	2	18.130 us
4X4	1.999999	2	49.750 us
32x16	16	16	1.969 ms
32x32	22.62739	22.6274	4.578 ms
96x96	67.88227	67.8823	50.904 ms
128x128	90.50966	90.5097	90.869 ms

(The timing values given above can be 1/3rd if minimum clock period of 3ns is used)

5   Conclusion

In this paper we have implemented and synthesized the computational functions required for doing compressive sensing recovery. We believe ours is one the early attempts to carry out VLSI implementation and synthesis of computational functions for compressive sensing recovery. We could not get any reference for L_1 norm of vector and L_2 norm of vector implementations and could not do comparison. Similarly, Bi-diagonalization architecture is also our contribution. Our SVD implementation has been found to be faster and more accurate compared to implementations done in [15].

We also studied algorithms (second order methods) like interior point method which can be solved in the polynomial time ($O(N^3)$) and it uses preconditioned conjugate gradient (PCG) method to approximately solve linear systems in a truncated Newton framework. Iteration methods (first order) are studied for L_1-minimization and literature has compared iterative algorithms (Hard /Soft, IST/IHT) along with its tuning. For certain very large matrices it can rapidly apply and without representing as a full matrix and in such settings, the work required scales very favorably with N. In future we plan to consider implementation of SVD based method/ first order method, along with calculation of power and present compressive sensing recovery architecture.

References

[1] Maleki, A.: Approximate Message Passing Algorithms for compressed sensing, PhD Thesis, Stanford University (September 2011)
[2] Kim, S.-J., Koh, K., Lustig, M., Boyd, S.: An Interior-Point Method for Large Scale l1-Regularized Least Squares. IEEE Journal of Selected Topics in Signal Processing 1(4), 606–617 (2007)
[3] Kim, S.-J., Koh, K., Lustig, M., Boyd, S.: An Efficient Method for Compressed Sensing. In: IEEE International Conference on Image Processing, vol. 3, pp. III-117–III-120, http://www.stanford.edu/~boyd/l1_ls/

---

^{2} The timing corresponds to the same input that was also used for bi-diagonalization testing.

[4] Hale, E.T., Yin, W., Zhang, Y.: A Fixed Point Continuation method for l1-Regularized Minimization with Applications to Compressed Sensing, CAAM Technical Report TR07-07, Dept of Computational and Applied Mathematics, Rice University, Houstan, Texas (July 7, 2007)

[5] Baraniuk, R., Davenport, M.A., Duarte, M.F., Hegde, C.: An Introduction to Compressive Sensing. In: Connexions. Rice University, Houston (2011)

[6] Maleki, A., Donoho, D.L.: Optimally Tuned Iterative Reconstruction Algorithms for Compressed Sensing. IEEE Journal of Selected Topics in Signal Processing 4(2) (April 2010)

[7] Maechler, P., Studer, C., Bellasi, D.E., Maleki, A., Burg, A., Felber, N., Kaeslin, H., Baraniuk, R.G.: VLSI Implementation of Approximate Message Passing for Signal Restoration and Compressive Sensing. Submitted to IEEE Journal on Emerging and Selected Topics in Circuits and Systems

[8] Xu, L., Liang, Q.: Compressive Sensing Using Singular Value Decomposition. In: Pandurangan, G., Anil Kumar, V.S., Ming, G., Liu, Y., Li, Y. (eds.) WASA 2010. LNCS, vol. 6221, pp. 338–342. Springer, Heidelberg (2010)

[9] Peng, Y., He, Y.: A Reconstruction Algorithm for Compressed Sensing Noise Signal. Journal of Computational Information Systems 8(14), 6025–6031 (2012)

[10] Yu, Y., Hong, M., Liu, F., Wang, H., Crozier, S.: Compressed Sensing MRI Using Singular Value Decomposition based Sparsity Basis. In: 33rd Annual International Conference of the IEEE EMBS, Boston, Massachusetts USA, August 30-September 3 (2011)

[11] Ahmedsaid, A., et al.: Improved SVD systolic array and implementation on FPGA. In: Proceedings of the 2003 IEEE International Conference on Field-Programmable Technology, FPT (2003)

[12] Ma, W., et al.: An FPGA based Singular Value Decomposition processor. In: IEEE Canadian Conference on Electrical and Computer Engineering, CCECE 2006 (2006)

[13] Rahmati, M., et al.: FPGA Based Singular Value Decomposition for Image Processing Applications. In: IEEE International Conference on Application-Specific Systems, Architectures and Processors, ASAP 2008 (2008)

[14] Szecówka, P.M., et al.: CORDIC and SVD Implementation in Digital Hardware. In: IEEE 17th International Conference on Mixed Design of Integrated Circuits and Systems, MIXDES 2010, Wrocław, Poland, June 24-26 (2010)

[15] Ledesma-Carrillo, L.M.: Reconfigurable FPGA-Based Unit for Singular Value Decomposition of Large m × n Matrices. In: IEEE 2011 International Conference on Reconfigurable Computing and FPGAs (2011)

[16] Numerical Recipes- The Art of Scientific Computing, 3rd edn. Cambridge University Press

[17] Golub, Reinsch: Singular Value Decomposition and Least Squares Solutions. Handbook Series Linear Algebra, Numer. Math. 14, 403–420 (1970)

[18] Strang, G.: Linear Algebra and its Applications, 4th edn. Cengage Learning

A Novel Input Capacitance Modeling Methodology for Nano-Scale VLSI Standard Cell Library Characterization

Akhtar W. Alam, Esakkimuthu Dhakshinamoorthy,
Prince Mathew, and Narender Ponna

ARM Embedded Technologies, Bangalore, India
{Akhtar.alam,Esakkimuthu.Dhakshina,Narender.Ponna,
Prince.Mathew}@arm.com

Abstract. As the technology scales to 55nm and below, the traditional modeling methodology of input capacitance results in high deviation between the back-annotated delay values and the measured delay in Silicon. To reduce such a high deviation, novel modeling methodologies of input capacitance have been proposed in this paper. The proposed model have been used across different process and technology nodes using different test cases and back-annotated delay values were shown to have good agreement with the measured delay in Silicon. The proposal can be used to understand the device behavior; and based on device behavior; the methodology can be used to model the input cap accurately.

Keywords: pin capacitance, input cap, hspice, silicon, correlation.

1 Introduction

In this paper we talked about the basic method of improving the Silicon Vs STA (Static Timing Analysis) correlation [6]. As technology advances, the integration scale is shooting up. The timing constraint of a design has become very critical hence the redundant design margin need to be reduced to get better performance. To close any design, STA is the only viable method for chip-level timing analysis and therefore its accuracy should be of up most important.

There are many factors that affect the accuracy of STA. Among them, the input capacitance modeling of logic gates is an important factor because a significant amount of load capacitance is still occupied by the input capacitances of gates except for interconnects dominated sections such as clock trees and busses. In STA, the input capacitance of a gate is modeled as a lumped capacitance. There are a few papers that explain the importance of the capacitance modeling [1]–[4]. However, no paper has justified about choosing Max cap or average cap. Also, no paper has studied the input capacitance variation across different bias condition of PMOS and NMOS device. Also, although Synopsys Siliconsmart for library characterization measure input capacitance different input slew and output load condition [5], it is common to measure capacitance from 20% to 80% rise of input-signal. And among all measured

M.S. Gaur et al. (Eds.): VDAT 2013, CCIS 382, pp. 44–48, 2013.
© Springer-Verlag Berlin Heidelberg 2013

value of cap, the Siliconsmart picks the max or min or average capacitance in a timing library. In case of max-cap, the STA can predict the longest delay without optimism so that we can safely check set-up constraints. On the other hand, if we want to analyze the shortest-path delay, the resulting timing is overestimated and there is a possibility of existing shorter delays, which will lead to hold violations.

In case of average-cap, the STA can predict the longest delay with some optimism in critical path; which can cause silicon failure. This paper talked about how to reduced pessimism and optimism in input pin capacitance measurement.

1.1   Input Pin Capacitance: HSPICE vs STA

STA reads input pin capacitance from the Liberty to calculate corresponding output delay and slew. As the liberty has only one static value of input pin capacitance, STA takes total FO cap and uses it to map the delay. In general Liberty takes average value of input pin capacitance calculated across different condition (from 20% to 80% input slew). As FO increase, the inaccuracy gets multiplied. To evaluate the discrepancy between actual gate cap and the gate cap seen by STA, an experiment is done on RO shown in Figure 1, it is found that the input-cap at nodes net1, net2, net3, ... is always more than the input pin capacitance calculated by STA at these nets. This gives basic reason of miscorrelation of HSPICE vs STA.

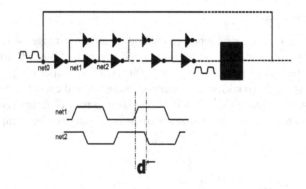

Fig. 1.

Figure 5 show input pin capacitance measured at each nets of the circuit shown in Figure 1. The capacitance in Liberty [5], which is based on average capacitance across different input slew and output load, is always less than the capacitance estimated by HSPICE simulation. SiliconSmart, the characterization tool, have option to choose range of integration for input pin cap. Default range is 20-80. However, for given range, the tool calculates the input pin capacitance for combination of slew/load.

1.2   Variation in Input Pin Capacitance

To study the input pin capacitance very closely, we have devised a method to estimate the instantaneous capacitance at each instance of input rise/fall. Figure 2 shows the instantaneous capacitance at each voltage level of input slew, the plot is done across different input slew. The graph shows input pin capacitance variation more than 2X. It is a challenge to estimate one unique capacitance for Liberty file for a given cell.

To understand the behavior of input capacitance, we came up with new terms called Capacitance range which is described in next section.

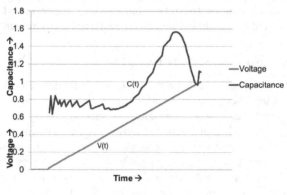

Fig. 2.

1.3   Capacitance Range

Capacitance range is the Capacitance calculated at different range of input slew. It starts from mid-point of input slew for very small range Δ, $(50-\Delta/2)\%$ to $(50+\Delta/2)\%$ and ends at the full range 0 to 100%. The Figure 4, shows input ramp(Aqua color), Instantaneous Cap (light Black), and capacitance range(dotted curve).

Ideally, input pin capacitance should be constant across different range of input slew, however, in reality, the cap changes with different range of input cap.

$$C = \frac{\int_{t_1}^{t_2} C(t)\, dt}{t_2 - t_1}$$

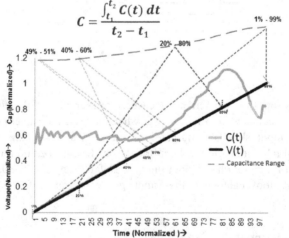

Fig. 3.

2   Limiting Capacitance (LC)

Figure 4 shows different range cap curve at different output load.

LC cap is coming out to be the best estimation of input cap. Correlation data shows LC cap correlates much better than traditional input cap.

Table 1 is the correlation result (Tradition Cap vs LC). Negative correlation number shows that STA is faster than HSPICE simulation. The Liberty with LC capacitance gives out very accurate correlation than the Liberty with traditional capacitance.

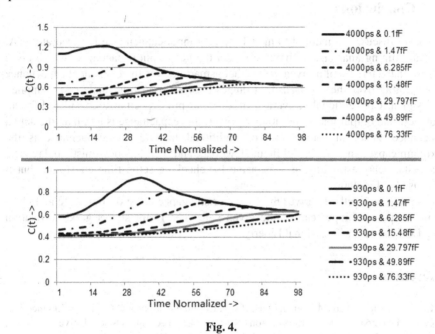

Fig. 4.

	net0	net1	net2	net3	net4	net5	net6	net7	net8
Slew Rise (ps)	75.58	96.62	96.83	96.79	96.83	96.79	96.79	96.79	96.75
Slew Fall (ps)	79.48	93.68	94.40	94.13	94.41	94.41	94.41	94.41	94.38
Average Cap(fF) 20% to 80%	6.04	6.05	6.04	6.04	6.04	6.04	6.04	6.05	6.04
Average Cap(fF) 0% to 100%	6.93	7.06	7.01	7.01	6.99	6.99	6.96	7.04	6.98
CAP from dotLib	5.5	5.5	5.5	5.5	5.5	5.5	5.5	5.5	5.5

Fig. 5.

TEST CASE	Regular Liberty (NLDM/CCS)		LC Liberty (NLDM/CCSN)	
	STA nldm to spice	STA ccsn to spice	STA nldm to spice	STA ccsn to spice
INV CHAIN	-15%	-22%	2%	2%
BUF CHAIN	1%	-8%	3%	3%
DLY CHAIN	-2%	-2%	1%	1%

Fig. 6.

3   Conclusions

This paper discusses a method to model the gate input capacitance for accurate STA. For static timing analysis, we have to model the gate input capacitance, which gives the best characteristic of a given gate. Siliconsmart derives the equivalent capacitance by integrating over the full transition range or 20-80 transition range of the applied input signal. Conventionally, average of all input pin capacitance considered for all input slew and output load condition. However, this capacitance is less than the actual capacitance. Also, in some cases of traditional method, the capacitance is the maximum capacitance across all input slew/load; and it results pessimistic delay. The pessimistic delay estimation is reasonable for checking setup time constrains, but it can cause hold violation.

The proposed method derives the characteristic capacitance of logic gate and gives the most optimum input cap of the given gate. The result shows good correlation using LC Liberty Vs Traditional Liberty.

References

1. Kouno, T., Hashimoto, M., Onodera, H.: Dept. Communications and Computer Engineering. Kyoto University, Dept. Information Systems Engineering, Osaka University Input Capacitance Modeling of Logic Gates for Accurate Static Timing Analysis
2. Bailey, D.W., Benshneider, B.J.: Clocking design and analysis for a 600-MHz alpha microprocessor. Journal of Solid-State Circuits 33, 1627–1633 (1998)
3. Singhal, V., Bittlestone, C., Hill, A., Arvind, N.V.: Architecting asic libraries and flows in nanometer era. In: Proceedings of Design Automation Conference, pp. 776–781 (June 2003)
4. Subramaniam, P.: Modeling MOS VLSI circuits for transient analysis. Journal of Solid-State Circuits 21, 276–285 (1986)
5. Synopsys. SiliconSmart™ ACE Version (June 2012)
6. Synopsys. PT Static Time Analysis
7. Synopsys "CCS Timing White paper" (1996)

An Area Efficient Wide Range On-Chip Delay Measurement Architecture

Rahul Krishnamurthy and G.K. Sharma

ABV-Indian Institute of Information Technology and Management
National Highway #92, Gwalior - 474 015(M.P.), India
krishnamurthy.rahul@gmail.com, gksharma@iiitm.ac.in

Abstract. Aggressive design practices in nanoscale era has led to an increase in the performance of circuit at the cost of reduced slack margins. Reduced margin increases the risk of path failures due to small additional delays. In this paper, an on-chip path delay measurement architecture is designed to identify paths which violates timing constraints. A new method of measuring delay based on crossovers is proposed. Simulation results show precise measurement of path delays. Maximum path delay measured by the proposed architecture is 4.3 times the maximum delay measured by Modified Vernier Delay Line (MVDL) architecture and the area is 74% less than the area of MVDL.

Keywords: Time to Digital converter, Vernier Delay Line, Path Delay Characterization.

1 Introduction

In advanced CMOS technology, detection of timing related failures has become primary testing challenge. Increasing gap between the operating frequency of circuits and external Automatic Test Equipments(ATEs) has compelled researchers to design on-chip circuits which will assist detection of delay defects. An on-chip delay sensor proposed in [7], converts time-to-voltage to measure path delays. Drawback of this technique is its dependence on the voltage across a capacitor which may vary due to leakage.

Another on-chip technique to detect delay defects is to use a Time to Digital converter(TDC). In [3], a single delay line TDC is embedded in one core of System-on-Chip(SOC). That core is dedicated for the purpose of detecting delay defects in neighbouring cores and interconnects. However, precision of delay measurement in a single delay line TDC is limited by the minimum gate delay.

In [4], a Modified Vernier Delay Line (MVDL) architecture using scan flip-flops is designed to facilitate detection of small delay and gross delay faults. The major drawback of MVDL is the trade-off that exist between the number of stages and the minimum delay that can be measured. Smaller delay range of a stage gives a high precision measurement. However, to detect delays over a wide range, a large number of stages will be required. This increases the area overhead and reduces the accuracy of measurement, as the long delay lines are susceptible

M.S. Gaur et al. (Eds.): VDAT 2013, CCIS 382, pp. 49–58, 2013.

to process variation. In [5], a Fine and Coarse Block architecture is proposed to reduce number of delay stages required in a Vernier Delay Line (VDL) based architectures. However, since the delay range in each block is constant, a large number of stages are still required to measure path delays over a wide range.

In [6] and [2], delay range of each stage in a VDL based design increases by a factor of two. Such a delay range allows measurement of delay over a wide dynamic range with reduced area overhead as compared to previous designs. However, for a wide range of delay measurement, size of buffer increases exponentially, which increases the area overhead.

Motivated by the results of a variable delay range in VDL architecture, a VDL based design is proposed in which the delay range in each stage depends on a crossover. After a crossover, delay range of subsequent stages is reduced and the signal transition which occurs earlier is delayed more than the other signal transition. This reduces the number of buffers used in each stage and also enables a wide range delay measurement.

2   Proposed Architecture

Proposed architecture consists of delay stages and every delay stage has D flip flop (DFF), multiplexers, Buffers (BUFs) and Programmable Delay Elements (PDEs), as shown in Figure 1 . Input and output of the Path Under Test (PUT) are connected to START1 and STOP1, respectively.

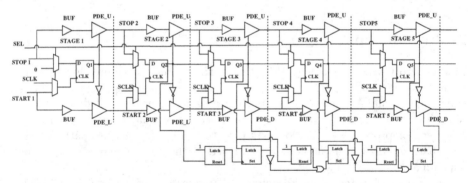

Fig. 1. Proposed architecture with variable delay range to measure path delay

Input signals to an ith delay stage are represented by STARTi and STOPi, which are delayed form of START1 and STOP1, respectively. STARTi passes through lower delay chain comprising of either a PDE_L or PDE_D and a BUF. STOPi passes through upper delay chain, which comprises of PDE_U and a BUF. In i^{th} delay stage, STARTi signal and STOPi signal are connected to the clock port and data port of DFF, respectively. The output of DFF is denoted by Qi, where i denotes the stage index. DFF of all the stages are initially reset to zero. Output of DFF indicates the signal transition which occurs earlier in a delay stage, as shown in the Figure 2 .

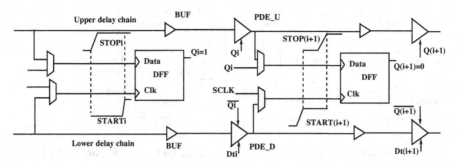

Fig. 2. Qi=1 shows that STOPi signal transition occurs earlier than STARTi signal transition. Q(i+1)=0 indicates that STARTi signal transition occurs earlier than STOPi signal transition.

The delay range is defined as modulus of the difference between the delay produced by upper delay chain PDE(PDE_U) and lower delay chain PDE(PDE_L or PDE_D).

$$\text{delay range} = |\text{upper PDE delay} - \text{lower PDE delay}| \tag{1}$$

When a slow moving signal in a delay chain crosses a fast moving signal due to different delays applied to these signals, a crossover is said to have taken place. Crossover is identified by different output of DFFs in adjacent delay stages.

In [6], the signal passing through delay chain connected to the input of PUT is either delayed more or given an equal delay compared to the delay given to signal passing through the delay chain connected to output of PUT. Such a delay mechanism require buffers of two different sizes in delay chain of each stage. In the proposed approach, the signal transition which occurs earlier is delayed more than a slow signal transition, irrespective of whether the signal transition passes through upper delay chain or lower delay chain. This reduces the number of required buffers in a delay stage as compared to [6].

Number of delay stages in the proposed architecture is reduced by employing high delay range stages, till a first crossover takes place. After first crossover, when two signals crosses each other in a delay stage, the delay range of the subsequent stages is reduced and again the signal transition which occurs earlier is given more delay as compared to the delay given to signal with slow transition. Path delay measurement with high precision is completed after three crossovers.

We now perform analysis of time difference between the signals at delay stages during crossovers. In Figure 3 , t1, t2 represents time at which signal transition takes place. The transition that occurs earlier is given a delay which is D1 more than the delay given to other signal transition. D1 is the delay range prior to first crossover. Till the first crossover the STARTi of an ith stage is given D1 more delay than the delay given to STOPi signal.

Suppose first crossover occurs after N1 stages, then the time relationship between the input signals in stage (N1+1) is as shown in Figure 3 . In an ith

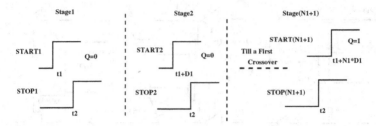

Fig. 3. Time relationship between the input signals at each stage in the design till a first crossover

delay stage after a first crossover the STOPi signal transition occurs earlier than the STARTi signal transition till the second crossover. Hence the delay given to STOPi is D2 more than the delay given to STARTi till a second crossover takes place. D2 is the delay range after first crossover. This is shown in Figure 4 where a second crossover is assumed to have taken place in stage(N1+N2+1). After second crossover START(N1+N2+1) is given a delay D3 more than the delay given to the STOP(N1+N2+1). D3 is the delay range after second crossover. Small value of D3 gives a higher delay measurement resolution.

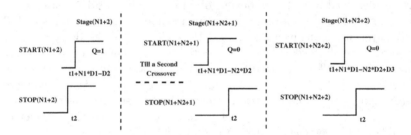

Fig. 4. Time relationship that exists between the input signals in a delay stage after a first crossover

In Figure 5 , relation between time difference of input signals in two adjacent delay stages during third crossover is shown. After the analysis till the third crossover a mathematical equation (2) can now be derived from Figure 5 which gives the time difference between START1 and STOP1 signal with D3 measurement resolution. Eq. (4) considers a case for maximum path delay between t1 and t2 when no crossover occurs between two input signals. In (4), N denotes total number of delay stages in measurement architecture.

$$t1 + (N1 \times D1) - (N2 \times D2) + (N3 - 1) \times D3 \le t2 \le$$
$$t1 + N1 \times D1 - N2 \times D2 + N3 \times D3$$

$$(2)$$

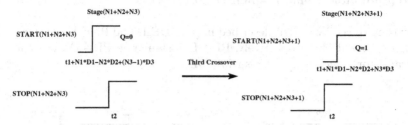

Fig. 5. Time relationship between the input signals in the third crossover stage and its preceding stage

$$N1 \times D1 - (N2 \times D2) + ((N3 - 1) \times D3) \leq$$
$$(t2 - t1) \leq N1 \times D1 - (N2 \times D2) + (N3 \times D3) \tag{3}$$

$$\text{Max.Path Delay} \leq (N - 1) \times D1 \tag{4}$$

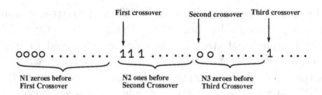

Fig. 6. General form of output containing sequence of ones and zeroes

Data stored in all the DFF, forms a sequence of zeroes and ones as shown in the Figure 6 . N1, N2 and N3 in Figure 6 , represents the count of these zeroes and ones. Delay is measured by observing this sequence which is shifted to output by connecting DFF of all the stages in the form of shift register.

3   Implementation Details

The proper working of the architecture lies in its ability to change the delay range when a crossover takes place. It must differentiate between the initial output of DFF and output of DFF after second crossover. This section gives implementation details of the proposed delay measurement architecture.

3.1   Programmable Delay Element(PDE)

The delay is produced by a PDE described in [1]. PDE_D and PDE_U are shown in the Figure 7a and 7b , respectively. PDE_L is similar to PDE_D except for the M9 transistor, which is not present in PDE_L.

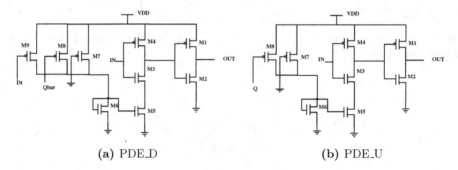

(a) PDE_D   (b) PDE_U

Fig. 7. Programmable delay elements designed to generate a high and low delay ranges depending on the output of DFF and Detect block

In a ith delay stage where $i \in [3, N]$, STARTi and inverted output of DFF is connected to IN port and Qbar port of the PDE_D, respectively. The output signal Detect(Dt) from the Detect block(which is explained in next section) is connected to the Dt port of PDE_D. In a ith delay stage where $i \in [1, N]$ STOPi and output of DFF is connected to IN port and Q port of the PDE_U, respectively. PDEs enable the generation of delay ranges as shown in Table 1 . In Table 1 , Qi is the output of DFF in i^{th} stage and Dti is the output of Detect block controlling i^{th} stage PDE_D.

Buffer BUF is also a PDE with a constant delay value designed to delay input signals of a delay stage until the output of DFF attains a stable value.

Table 1. Delay ranges based on all possible combinations of Q(i-1), Qi and Dti

Q(i-1)	Qi	Dti	Delay range(ps)	Remarks
0	0	-	300	For i={1,2}, Dt is not required.
0	R	-	90	When a first crossover occurs in stage 2
0	0	1	300	For $i \in [3, N]$, till a first crossover. D1=300ps
0	R	1	90	A first crossover condition. D2=90ps
R	R	1	90	Delay range is maintained till a 2nd crossover
R	0	0	12	A second crossover condition. D3 is 12ps

3.2   Detect Block

Detect block is designed to detect a condition in which the output of DFF in a preceding stage is a rising one and the next stage DFF output remains zero. To implement this, two positive level sensitive latch are used to form one Detect block. Figure 8 , shows two such adjacent Detect blocks. Qi represents DFF output of ith stage, where $i \in [3, N]$ in a N stage measurement architecture. The first latch in a Detect block is initially reset to '0' with a '1' at its data input and Qi connected to its clock input. The second latch is initially set to '1' with Q(i+1) connected to its data input. The output of first latch triggers second latch. The output of the second latch is called Detect(Dt) and the inverted form of Dt is called Detectbar(Dtbar). Once a Dt in any preceding Detect block becomes '0', the second latch of the subsequent Detect Block's should be triggered irrespective of the output of first latch. This is implemented by using Dtbar(i) signal and an 'OR' gate.

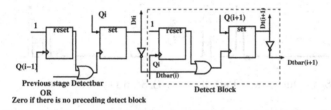

Fig. 8. Two adjacent Detect Blocks each containing two positive level sensitive latch

All type of possible sequences of a DFF output at the input of Detect block is shown in the Table 1 . The output of DFF rises to a one from initial value of zero, which is represented by R in Table 1 . When Dt becomes zero, a second crossover is said to have taken place.

4   Experimental Results

The proposed architecture is integrated with the C880 benchmark circuit [9], using a delay measurement scheme employed in [6]. This integrated architecture was simulated in SPICE using TSMC 180nm CMOS process to validate the working of proposed approach. The transition pattern is generated using KF-ATPG tool. The details of this tool is described in [8]. Transitions are generated on four different paths of C880 benchmark circuit. The output stored in the DFF is shifted out serially using a clock SCLK with a period of 1ns. Figure 9 shows the serially shifted data after the completion of measurement. Values of N1,N2 and N3 can be found from Figure 9 and then path delay can be calculated using (3). The path delay measured across these paths is shown in Table 2 . Path delay column is subdivided into Using Arch. column which shows the path delay measured using proposed architecture and simulation column which shows the path delay measured using SPICE simulation.

Table 2. Delay Measurement of 4 different paths of a C880 benchmark circuit

C880 bench. paths	First crossover		Second crossover		Third crossover		Path Delay	
	D1	N1	D2	N2	D3	N3	Using Arch.	Simulation
Fig. 9a	304ps	3	90ps	2	12ps	3	756-768ps	761ps
Fig. 9b	304ps	1	90ps	1	12ps	3	238-250ps	246ps
Fig. 9c	304ps	1	90ps	2	12ps	7	196-208ps	207ps
Fig. 9d	304ps	3	90ps	1	12ps	3	846-858ps	854ps

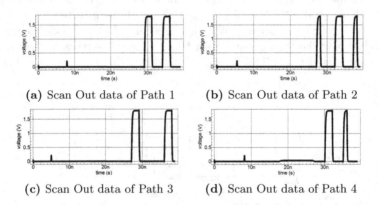

(**a**) Scan Out data of Path 1   (**b**) Scan Out data of Path 2

(**c**) Scan Out data of Path 3   (**d**) Scan Out data of Path 4

Fig. 9. Waveform shows the data obtained at the end of measurement. Measurement is done by counting number of zeroes and ones starting from the last bit and moving towards first bit till a third crossover bit is found.

In Table 3 , MVDL and OCDM refers to designs implemented by using the techniques proposed in [4] and [6], respectively. These designs are implemented and simulated in SPICE for the purpose of accurate comparison with the proposed work in 180nm and 90nm CMOS technology. We estimated the area of all designs in Table 3 by measuring the layout area of all the transistors using SPICE netlist.

Area of OCDM increases due to the use of six buffers in each stage and size of these buffers increases exponentially with increase in stages. In 90nm CMOS process, delay of buffer decreases and more number of transistors are required to make a buffer as compared to buffers in 180nm technology. This is another reason of increase in area of OCDM as compared to proposed design in 90nm. Estimated area of the proposed design containing 14 stages, with values of D1,D2 and D3 equals to 300ps, 100ps and 13ps, respectively is reported in Table 3 . Maximum path delay that can be measured by the proposed architecture is 3900ps, which is 4.3 times the maximum delay measured by MVDL. In worst case, path delays upto 900ps can be measured with a precision of 13ps.

Delay difference below DFF setup time was lost in the delay measurement. To compensate for this loss, a DC compensation unit given in [6], is used in this design. The design can only measure delay between two rising signals.

Table 3. Comparison with previous designs in 180nm and 90nm CMOS

Design	Area in 180nm (μm^2)	Area in 90nm (μm^2)	Min.delay(ps)	Max.delay(ps)
Proposed	3,728.5	2,041.87	13	3900
MVDL[4]	14,441	5,979.6	14	900
OCDM[6]	4,849	2,918.44	7	805

To measure delay difference between all type of signals, whether falling or rising, a DG gate used in [5], is incorporated in the proposed design.

5   Conclusion

In this paper a delay measurement architecture for path delay characterization has been proposed. A new delay mechanism is employed in which the signal transition that occurs earlier is delayed more in each delay stage irrespective of whether the signal travels through upper or lower delay chain. Stages with high delay range are used to reduce the number of stages and increase the measurement range, without affecting the resolution of measurement which depends on the delay range after second crossover. This makes it possible to detect a small path delay as well as very large path delay using same architecture. Simulation results on C880 benchmark circuit validates effectiveness of the proposed on-chip path delay measurement architecture.

References

1. Maymandi-Nejad, M., Sachdev, M.: A digitally programmable delay element: design and analysis. IEEE Transactions on Very Large Scale Integration (VLSI) Systems 11(5), 871–878 (2003)
2. Zhang, Y., Yu, H., Xu, Q.: Coda: A concurrent online delay measurement architecture for critical paths. In: 2012 17th Asia and South Pacific Design Automation Conference (ASP-DAC), January 30-Feburary 2, pp. 169–174 (2012)
3. Yotsuyanagi, H., Makimoto, H., Hashizume, M.: A boundary scan circuit with time-to-digital converter for delay testing. In: 2011 20th Asian Test Symposium (ATS), pp. 539–544 (November 2011)
4. Datta, R., Sebastine, A., Raghunathan, A., Carpenter, G., Nowka, K., Abraham, J.A.: On-chip delay measurement based response analysis for timing characterization. J. Electron. Test. 26(6), 599–619 (2010), http://dx.doi.org/10.1007/s10836-010-5188-1
5. Tsai, M.-C., Cheng, C.-H., Yang, C.-M.: An all-digital high-precision built-in delay time measurement circuit. In: 26th IEEE VLSI Test Symposium, VTS 2008, April 27-May 1, pp. 249–254 (2008)
6. Pei, S., Li, H., Li, X.: A high-precision on-chip path delay measurement architecture. IEEE Transactions on Very Large Scale Integration (VLSI) Systems 20(9), 1565–1577 (2012)

7. Ghosh, S., Bhunia, S., Raychowdhury, A., Roy, K.: A novel delay fault test-ing methodology using low-overhead built-in delay sensor. IEEE Transactions on Computer-Aided Design of Integrated Circuits and Systems 25(12), 2934–2943 (2006)
8. Yang, K., Cheng, K.-T., Wang, L.-C.: Trangen: a sat-based atpg for path-oriented transition faults. In: Proceedings of the ASP-DAC 2004 Asia and South Pacific, Design Automation Conference, pp. 92–97 (January 2004)
9. Perform the SPICE Simulation of ISCAS85 Benchmark Circuits for Research, http://www.ece.uic.edu/~masud/iscas2spice.htm

10 Gbps Current Mode Logic I/O Buffer

Akhil Rathore[1] and Chetan D. Parikh[2]

[1] Dhirubhai Ambani Institue of Information and Communication Technology,
Gandhinagar, India
[2] Institute of ICT, Ahmedabad University, Ahmedabad, India
chetan.parikh@ahduni.edu.in

Abstract. A new architecture for a high speed CML buffer is presented. The
buffer is designed for OC-192/STM-64 applications to be used in the limiting
amplifier which is a critical block in optical communication systems. OC-
192/STM-64 works around 10Gbps. The proposed architecture is also more
efficient in terms of area.

1   Introduction

In high speed serial links and optical communication, buffers create a bottleneck. In
such systems, Current- mode logic (CML) buffers [1] are commonly used. Using
current as the signaling variable rather than voltage, allows for low voltage
swings between the high and low digital levels. Systematic design procedures for
CML buffers have been reported by Heydari and Mohanvelu [1] and by Green and
Singh [3]. In conventional CML buffers inductive peaking [1] is used to enhance
bandwidth but it requires monolithic inductors, which needs a large silicon area.
Current architectures of output buffers use f_T doublers and inductive peaking together
and can obtain data rates of up to 10 Gbps, but these also require a large silicon area
[3]. The conventional CML buffer suffers from the Miller effect which degrades high
frequency operation.

This paper presents a new architecture which avoids miller effect and works around
10 Gbps in a $0.18\,\mu$ m CMOS technology. It requires less chip area and power than
existing architectures. The contents of the paper are as follows: Section 2 describes the
conventional CML buffer, its operation and its limitations at high frequencies.
Sections 3 and 4 describe the proposed architecture, its working and the various design
issues. In section 5 simulation results are shown and section 6 concludes this paper.

2   CML Buffer

This section describes the basics of a conventional CML buffer, its advantages,
and its limitations at high frequencies. The various design issues related to a CML
buffer are discussed in [1, 3, 4].

M.S. Gaur et al. (Eds.): VDAT 2013, CCIS 382, pp. 59–65, 2013.
© Springer-Verlag Berlin Heidelberg 2013

2.1   Overview

Figure 1 shows the basic CML buffer. It consists of a differential pair with two NMOS transistors, which act as switches. When the differential input ($V_{IN+} - V_{IN-}$) varies from 0 to V_{DD}, the output in each branch varies from V_{DD} to ($V_{DD} - I_{SS}R_D/2$), or vice versa. Thus, the differential output voltage swing achieved is $I_{ss}R_D$. Low switching noise, higher common mode rejection due to differential architecture & low swing signaling make CML an attractive choice for high frequency applications.

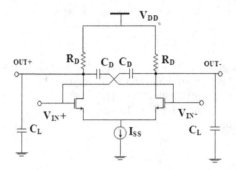

Fig. 1. Conventional CML Buffer

2.2   Limitations of a CML Buffer at High Frequencies

Figure 2 shows the half circuit diagram of the CML buffer which is a standard common-source amplifier.

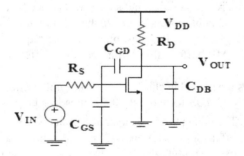

Fig. 2. Half circuit of CML buffer buffer

The dominant pole (ω_{p1}), and the first non-dominant pole (ω_{p2}) of this circuit are given approximately by

$$\omega_{p1} = 1 / [R_S(1 + g_m R_D)C_{GD} + R_S C_{GS} + R_D(C_{GD} + C_{DB})] . \qquad (1)$$

$$\omega_{p2} = \frac{R_S (1 + g_m R_D)C_{GD} + R_S C_{GS} + R_D (C_{GD} + C_{DB})}{R_S R_{D(} C_{GD} C_{DB} + C_{GD} C_{DB} + C_{GD} C_{DB})} . \quad (2)$$

Due to the Miller effect, the gate-drain capacitance (C_{GD}) contributes significantly to the frequency response (through the term $R_s g_m R_D C_{GD}$ in the denominator of Eqn. (1). Also, the transfer function exhibits a zero given by $\omega_Z = g_m/C_{GD}$, located in right half plane. C_{GD} creates a feed forward path from the input to the output at high frequencies, causing distortion in the output.

3   Proposed Architecture

The above mentioned issues because of miller capacitance can be resolved if source coupled pair is used instead of common source amplifier in half circuit. This architecture not only avoids input-output coupling, but also reduces the input capacitance, thereby increasing the maximum frequency of operation. Figure 4 shows the proposed architecture, which is two source coupled (or differential) amplifiers connected to provide a differential input and a differential output. One of the inputs of each differential amplifier (gates of M_2 and M_3) are connected to a 'dc' voltage, while to the other (Gates of M1 and M4), the differential input signals are applied. The outputs are taken at the drains of M2 and M3. When used as a buffer, for the case when the input voltage of M_1 goes high, M_2 is turned off, the entire tail current switches to M_1, and the output voltage at the drain of M_2 becomes V_{DD}. Simultaneously, the input at the gate of M_4 will go low, thus turning off M4, and the entire tail current of that differential pair flows through M_3, causing the drain of M_3 to be at $(V_{DD} - I_{SS}R_D)$. Thus the differential output voltage of the circuit will be $I_{SS}R_D$.

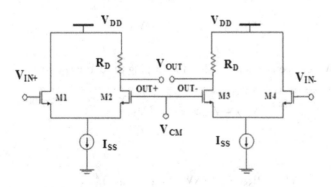

Fig. 3. Proposed Architecture

For this architecture approximate expressions for the dominant pole (ω_{p1}), and the first non-dominant pole (ω_{p2}), for a differential input voltage, are found to be:

$$\omega_{p1} = 1/[(R_{s+}R_D)C_{GD} + (R_s + 1/g_m)0.5 C_{GS} + R_D C_{DB})] \ . \tag{3}$$

$$\omega_{p2} = 1/K[R_s R_D (C_{GD} C_{DB+} C_{GD} C_{DB} + C_{GD} C_{DB})] \ . \tag{4}$$

Where, $K = (C_{GD} C_{DB+} C_{GD} C_{GS} + C_{GS} C_{DB}) (R_s + 1/g_m) R_{D+}(R_D/g_m)$

$(C_{DB+} C_{GD} + C_{GS}) (C_{DB+} C_{GD} + C_{GS3} + C_{DB3}) +$
$R_D [R_s C_{GD} (C_{GD} + C_{DB}) + C_{DS} C_{DS/} g_m)] \ .$

where R_S is the resistance of the voltage sources (not shown in the figure) connected at the inputs, the transconductance, and the capacitances are for the transistors M_1 and M_2 (which are assumed to be identical), unless there is a subscript "3" in the name, in which case they refer to the transistor M_3. Comparison of Eqns. (1) and (3) shows that the proposed architecture has a much higher dominant pole frequency, compared to the conventional CML buffer,   Moreover, due to the source-coupled configuration of the former, two gate-source capacitances (C_{GS}) are seen in series by the input terminal, thus reducing this capacitance by a factor of 2 in the dominant pole expression.

4   Design Issues

The load resistor R is determined by impedance matching requirements (being typically between $50\,\Omega$ and $100\,\Omega$) and was taken to be $75\,\Omega$. For a given voltage swing (V_{SWING}), the current I_{SS} is given by $I_{SS} = V_{SWING}/R_D$.
For the entire tail current to flow only in one branch [1],

$$0.5V_{in} > [2I_{SS}L / \mu CoxW]^{1/2} \ . \tag{5}$$

from which W_1 can be calculated. Also, for keeping the current source in saturation,

$$V_{CM} - V_{GS} > V_{BIAS} - V_T . \tag{6}$$

which yields,

$$W_1 > 2I_{SS}L / \mu CoxW(V_{CM} - V_{BIAS})^2 \ . \tag{7}$$

W_1 then must be chosen to satisfy both Eqns. (5) and (7).

5   Simulation Results

The proposed circuit was designed in MOSIS 180nm CMOS technology [5] and simulated with Cadence Spectre. The supply voltage used was 1.8 V, with a common-mode dc voltage (V_{CM} in Fig. 3) of 1.2 V. At high speed the effect of package and transmission line parasitics must also be considered for off-chip loads. The package model was taken from Maxim's 3840 10-Gbps equalizer [6], and the transmission line model of Spectre was used .

Figure 4 shows the differential output of the buffer before package, for differential input of 10 GHz. The output shows a differential peak to peak of about 800 mV. Fig 5(b) shows the output of the buffer at offchip load(R_0C_0) as shown in Fig5(a)

Table 1 shows the different parameter values obtained from Fig. 4 and Figure 5 shows the output waveform for the same inputs at the off-chip load (includes effect of package and transmission line) which is 600 mV differential peak to peak.

Table 2 shows the rise and fall times obtained at the driver output, after the package and at the off-chip load.

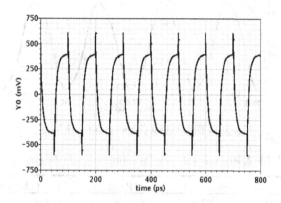

Fig. 4. Differential output at the output of buffer line

Table 1. Summary of buffer performance at the driver output

Parameter	Value
Rise time (T_r)	13.82s
Fall Time (T_f)	18ps
V_{OH}	1.78V
V_{OL}	1.39V
Vswing(single ended)	0.39V
Power dissipiation	22.32mW

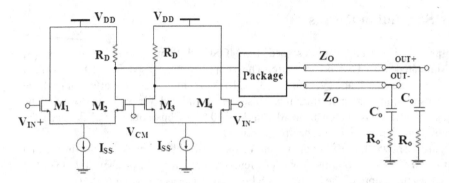

Fig. 5(a). Complete Schematic of output buffer with package and transmission line output at offchip load

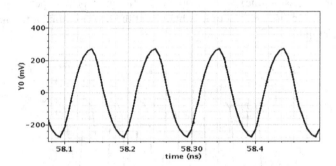

Fig. 5(b). Differential Output at off chip load

Table 2. Rise and Fall times at various point in the system

	At Driver	After Package	At off chip load
Rise time (T_r)	13.82ps	26.45ps	29.4ps
Fall Time (T_f)	18ps	28.32ps	28.4ps

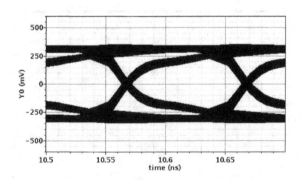

Fig. 6. Eye diagram of output for a 10 Gbps pseudo-random bit sequence input

At the off-chip load, an eye diagram is simulated using a pseudo-random bit sequence (2^5 -1) as input. Figure 6 shows the eye diagram obtained. Peak to peak jitter is calculated to be 4.95 ps, and an eye opening of ±125 mV which is quite acceptable for the OC-192 application.

6   Conclusion

A new high-speed CMOS buffer is proposed that can work at up to 10 Gbps, without the need of an inductive peaking architecture, thus saving on valuable chip area. The power consumption is comparable to previously reported work [7].

References

1. Heydari, P., Mohanavelu, R.: Design of Ultrahigh -Speed Low Voltage CMOS CML Buffers and Latches. IEEE Trans. VLSI Syst. 12, 1081–1093 (2004)
2. Razavi, B.: Design of Analog CMOS Integrated Circuits. McGraw-Hill, New York (2001)
3. Green, M.M., Singh, U.: Design of CMOS CML circuits for high speed broadband communications. In: Proc. Int. Symp. Circuits and Systems, pp. II-204–II-207 (2003)
4. Tsuchiya, A., Kuboki, T., Onodera, H.: Low -Power Design of CML Drivers for On Chip Transmission Lines. IEICE Trans. Electron. E90-C, 1274–1281 (2007)
5. MOSIS Integrated Circuit Fabrication Service, http://www.mosis.org
6. Maxim Corporation, 'MAX3804 I/O model 10Gbps equalizer' (2008), http://www.maximic.com/tools/spice/fiber/app_3804ete.pdf
7. Galal, S., Razavi, B.: 10 Gb/s Limiting amplifier and laser/modulator driver in 0.18 μm CMOS technology. IEEE J. Solid-State Circuits 38, 2138–2146 (2003)

Kapees: A New Tool for Standard Cell Placement

Sameer Pawanekar[1,*], Kalpesh Kapoor[2], and Gaurav Trivedi[1]

[1] Department of Electronics and Electrical Engineering
Indian Institute of Technology Guwahati, India
{p.sameer,trivedi,kalpesh}@iitg.ernet.in
[2] Department of Mathematics
Indian Institute of Technology Guwahati, India

Abstract. We consider the well-known problem of efficient cell placement on a fixed die. We investigate minimization of half perimeter that is required for a design that in turn results into minimal routed wire length and thus wire delay. We describe a new method, *Kapees*, for large scale standard cell placement. Our technique is based on recursive partitioning of placement circuit which is modeled as a hypergraph. It uses partitioning during the global placement phase and a greedy approach is followed to reduce the wire length during detailed placement phase. Our results show a significant improvement in comparison to Cadence Encounter's Amoeba and Capo tools by 9% and 5%, respectively.

1 Introduction

Standard Cell Placement is a well studied problem over several years. The objective of standard cell placement is to find coordinates of all the standard cells in a netlist in such a way that the wire length connecting them is minimum. The wire length is modeled as Half Perimeter wire length (HPWL) which can be defined as sum of all the perimeters of the smallest bounding box enclosing each net of the design. There are four broad approaches to solve this problem: 1. Min-cut [1–3], 2. Simulated annealing [4], 3. Analytic [5], and 4. Force directed [6]. Although both academic and commercial tools for placement are available, there is a scope for improvement because of inherent complexity of the problem [7]. This is also apparent from the ISPD placement contests held in the recent past in which none of the placers dominated across the entire benchmark set. A comparative study has also shown that the current state of the art is far from optimal [8].

Our approach to solve this problem is based on partition driven placement. Net cut objective follows wire length objective at initial hierarchical levels. At later hierarchical levels, net cut objective no longer follows wire length objective. This is when the number of cells are less than say 10. After this step detail placement (DP) follows. The existing placers such as Capo [1], Dragon [2] and feng shui [3] use different approaches during detailed placement.

---

* Sameer Pawanekar is currently a senior engineer with SiConTech, Bangalore. He is enrolled as a part-time Ph.D. student at IIT Guwahati.

M.S. Gaur et al. (Eds.): VDAT 2013, CCIS 382, pp. 66–73, 2013.

The tool feng shui does k-way partitioning and legalization and carries out the detailed placement by a branch and bound method [3]. In addition to traditional partitioning with hMetis, feng shui also uses large-scale k-way partitioning by iterative deletion to obtain initial terminal propagation information. Both Capo and Dragon uses a top-down hierarchical partitioning approach. Capo uses the hypergraph partitioner tool MLPart [9]. Dragon performs bin swapping for net cut optimization and low temperature annealing in its global and detailed placement phases, respectively [2].

Partition driven placement tools rely on terminal propagation to a large extent. This technique is capable of obtaining better cuts with regard to placement. Work in [10] relies heavily on the terminal propagation technique. It helps the partitioner to gather the characteristics of cut nets and derive hence good wire length results. The tool NTUPlace [11] proposes a terminal propagation method which was a generalized version of a method presented in Theto [10].

We present a new method, *Kapees*, for the cell placement which has two steps (a) partitioning in global placement phase, and (b) low temperature annealing in detailed placement phase, followed by greedy cell swapping. We compare our HPWL results with two existing tools: Cadence Encounter's Amoeba and Capo [12].

The rest of the paper is organized as follows. In Section 2, we present the flow of our algorithm and our global placement strategy. Section 3 presents low temperature annealing algorithm. Finally, experimental results and comparison with three other tools and the conclusion are given in Section 4.

2   Global Placement Phase

Our placement tool works in two phases – Global Placement Phase and Detailed Placement Phase. We describe these phases in detail below. The former phase involves partitioning of hypergraph using hMetis package [13]. We recursively bipartition the circuit and perform the arrangement. An arrangement is a step in which coordinates are assigned to the bins in all possible ways. We continue to partition until an optimum level is reached. We aim to use bisection because of the fact that we got better partitioning and wirelength results in case of bisection compared to using k-way partitioning and our partitioning approach is not aimed at obtaining the slicing of floorplan In the next phase, we use a simulated annealing algorithm with multiple objectives which is then followed by a greedy algorithm for Half Perimeter Wire Length (HPWL) reduction. In global placement phase we recursively bipartition the given circuit. We first partition the circuit horizontally followed by vertically partitioning the two sub-circuits that are obtained in the previous step. In the second step, these four partitioned circuits are bisected. This continues until an optimum level is reached which is defined as $\log(number\ of\ rows)$. If the number of rows is four, we can recursively bipartition the circuit up to two levels. At the end of partitioning phase we are left with $4^{\log(number\ of\ rows)}$ sub-circuits that we refer to as bins. Each bin typically has between five to ten cells. During global phase all the cells in a

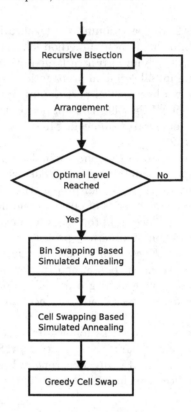

Fig. 1. Flow of Kapees

bin have the same coordinates. At every level an arrangement of the bins in all possible locations is performed. For the first level, entire circuit forms a bin and is placed at the center. In the second level, there are four bins and 24 possible ways of arranging the four bins in four locations. In the third level we have $4 \times 4 = 16$ bins. Here each bin in the third level is arranged in 24 ways within the region of its parent bin.

The existing placers such as [2] and [10] typically carry out terminal propagation. In terminal propagation, when the cells of circuit is partitioned into two bins, dummy cells are introduced into each bins. These dummy cells are included in external (cut) nets. When the two bins are possible candidate for further partitioning, external nets carry information that they are connected to a bin externally, and hence they do not get cut. As a result better wire length is obtained. However, in our experiment with terminal propagation we did not find noticeable improvement in the wire length resulting from terminal propagation scheme. So we do not perform terminal propagation but instead swap and move cells within bins. This is equivalent to improve upon the cuts obtained at Global placement phase. We discuss Cell Swapping in section 3.2.

3   Detailed Placement Phase

In Detailed placement phase we perform bin swapping based simulated annealing and cell swapping based simulated annealing followed by greedy cell swapping.

3.1   Bin Swapping Based Simulated Annealing

In bin swapping phase, we use a simulated annealing algorithm (see Algorithm 1) with two objectives. These are (A) reduction of wire length, and (B) balancing row width, respectively.

To implement Multi-Objective Simulated Annealing, the objective function, C, has to be equal to a sum of two objective functions $C = \alpha A + \beta B$. It is difficult to determine the ratio α and β as these values may not be the same for different designs. We overcome this problem by selecting the moves in such a way that any move that causes an imbalance is not accepted. We swap coordinates of the bins to achieve HPWL reduction along with the condition that row imbalance should not occur. The minimization function, $F(x)$, is the x-direction HPWL estimate and is given by Equation (1) from [14], where n_H and e_H are the node and edge sets of the hypergraph H, respectively.

$$F(x) = \sum_{e_k \in e_H} \max_{\forall i,j \in n_H} |x_i - x_j| \tag{1}$$

Algorithm 1. Multi Objective Simulated Annealing

---

  while init_temp $\geq$ final_temp **do**

    P $= e^{\delta \text{WL}/\text{init\_temp}}$

    Perturb   ▷ *Will cause swapping of bin coordinates*

    if δ WL ≤ 0 and row_imbalance ≤ 0 **then**

      Accept the perturbation

    else

      if random_number $\leq$ P and row_imbalance ≤ 0 **then**

        Accept the perturbation

      else

        Revert the perturbation

      end if

      if sufficient_number_of_perturbations **then**

        Decrease init_temp

      end if

    end if

  end while

3.2   Cell Swapping Based Simulated Annealing

We do not perform terminal propagation therefore it is important for us to improve the cuts obtained during global placement phase. This is achieved by performing cell swapping between the bins. In this step all cells within a bin are placed on top of each other, that is, there exists overlap between the cells. All the cells of a bin have the same coordinates. After completion of cell swapping between the bins, all the cells are spread out to remove overlap. Spreading is placing of the cells of the bins adjacent to each other in such a way that there is no overlap between them. It is important that the wire length obtained after spreading out all the cells must correlate with the changes that are done during cell swapping phase. Cell swapping and cell movement between the bins is studied by [15] and implemented in Dragon version 2.1. They attempt to achieve a bin width balance by swapping of cells. By doing this they achieve a correlation between the wire length of spread out cells and wire length during cell swapping. We tried two approaches for doing annealing based on cell swapping.

Algorithm 2. Perturbation Method 1

Randomly Select Two Bins in sufficiently close vicinity
Select one Cell from Each Bin
Calculate Incremental Cost = Cost1
Swap the Cell coordinates
Calculate Incremental Cost = Cost2
Return $\delta WL = Cost1 - Cost2$

Algorithm 3. Perturbation Method 2

Randomly Select Two Bins in sufficiently close vicinity
Select one Cell from Each Bin
Calculate Incremental Cost = Cost1
Swap the Cell coordinates and arrange all Bins to the right of the selected Bins separated by a distance equal to their widths
Calculate Incremental Cost = Cost2
Return $\delta WL = Cost1 - Cost2$

In the first approach we did not move the bin location ie, all the bins have fixed coordinates. Here the bin coordinates are not changed and there exists even spacing between the bins. Here we randonly select the bins which are within a distance of *numberofrows*/3 bins. For us this method does not correlate well with the spread out wire length.

In the second approach Figure 2, bins are placed at a distance equal the their widths and we shift the bins towards right by the difference in cell widths. Let Cell A belongs to Bin A and Cell B belongs to Bin B, then after swapping the cells, all the bins to the right of Bin A will be moved by a difference amount (Width(cellB)-width(cellA)) where as all the bins to the right of Bin B Bin B will be moved to right with a difference amount (Width(cellA)-width(cellB)). If we spread out the cells after the first method, we get worse wire length. This is

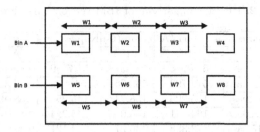

Fig. 2. Method 2 for Perturbation

because the estimates for bin width separation are not correct. We do not aim to obtain a balance for bin widths but only for row widths. In the second method the wire length during cell swapping stage correlates well with spread out cost.

3.3   Greedy Cell Swapping

In this stage, initially, all the cells for the bins are spread out. Then we randomly pick two cells in sufficiently close vicinity and see if swapping their coordinates with each other can reduce the wire length. The swapping is done in such a way that there does not exist any overlap between the adjacent cells. All the cells to the right of the selected cells are spread out.

Table 1. Characteristics of IBM version 2 benchmarks

Circuits	Cell Count	Net Count	Rows	core utilization
IBM01_easy	12028	11753	132	85.12%
IBM01_hard	12028	11753	130	88.00%
IBM02_easy	19062	18688	153	90.42%
IBM02_hard	19062	18688	149	95.28%
IBM07_easy	44811	44681	233	89.95%
IBM07_hard	44811	44681	226	95.30%
IBM08_easy	50672	48230	243	90.03%
IBM08_hard	50672	48230	236	95.16%
IBM09_easy	51382	50678	246	90.24%
IBM09_hard	51382	50678	240	95.12%
IBM10_easy	66762	64971	321	90.22%
IBM10_hard	66762	64971	313	95.08%
IBM11_easy	68046	67422	281	90.11%
IBM11_hard	68046	67422	273	95.33%

4   Experimental Results and Conclusion

We selected the IBM version 2.0 benchmarks to test our tool. These benchmarks have cell counts ranging from 12028 to 68046. Most of the current state of art

Table 2. HPWL comparison for IBM version 2 benchmarks

Circuits	Amoeba (A)	Capo (C)	Kapees (K)		
	$\times 10^6$	$\times 10^6$	$\times 10^6$	K/A	K/C
IBM01_easy	58.0278	55.8873	51.7759	0.89	0.92
IBM01_hard	57.6793	55.1354	51.456	0.89	0.93
IBM02_easy	165.906	158.743	146.253	0.88	0.92
IBM02_hard	164.541	156.048	145.224	0.88	0.93
IBM07_easy	373.388	368.7	354.121	0.94	0.96
IBM07_hard	359.586	355.686	353.964	0.98	0.99
IBM08_easy	406.834	387.502	352.928	0.86	0.91
IBM08_hard	395.116	379.512	363.081	0.91	0.95
IBM09_easy	341.532	317.126	311.554	0.91	0.98
IBM09_hard	338.188	321.029	321.057	0.94	1.00
IBM10_easy	605.746	636.689	601.824	0.99	0.94
IBM10_hard	642.065	629.543	624.721	0.97	0.99
IBM11_easy	521.413	481.637	478.191	0.91	0.99
IBM11_hard	514.758	476.332	472.878	0.91	0.99
			Average	0.91	0.95

placers have reported their work on these benchmarks. For our experiments and HPWL comparison we obtained the tool Cadence Encounter's Ameoba (version 9.1) and Capo (version 8.8) [12] from its respective websites.

The implementation of our tool, Kapees, for large scale standard cell placement, is done in C language. The experiments are performed on 1.5 GHz, 32-bit, 2GB RAM, Intel dual core machine running Ubuntu, a variant of GNU-Linux, as operating system. We compared our tool with Capo as they are run on the same machine, whereas Amoeba run results are extracted on a different machine.

The run time of our tool is 10 times more when compared to that of Capo for designs with cells less than 2000. For the design IBM01_easy, run time of Capo is 21 seconds, whereas, runtime of Kapees is 428 seconds, which means kapees is 22 times slower than Capo for this design. For the design IBM12_hard, run time of Capo is 205 seconds, whereas, runtime of Kapees is 9084 seconds, which means kapees is 44 times slower than Capo for this design. We observed that the runtime of Kapees increases with the growth of number of cells. This is primarily due to the use of simulated annealing technique wherein we perform HPWL calculation for each iteratve move. We plan to improve run-time in future.

As reported in Table 2, the experiments show that the half perimeter wire lengths obtained for these designs by Kapees are on an average 9% and 5% less than that obtained from Amoeba and Capo, respectively. We get superior results over other simulated annealing techniques because of our contribution as the method2. Instead of using terminal propagation, we use method2 to improve the already obtained cuts during global placement.

References

1. Caldwell, A.E., Kahng, A.B., Markov, I.L.: Can recursive bisection alone produce routable, placements? In: Proceedings of Design Automation Conference, pp. 477–482 (2000)
2. Wang, M., Yang, X., Sarrafzadeh, M.: Dragon2000: standard-cell placement tool for large industry circuits. In: Proceedings of IEEE/ACM International Conference on Computer Aided Design (ICCAD), pp. 260–263 (2000)
3. Agnihotri, A., Yildiz, M.C., Khatkhate, A., Mathur, A., Ono, S., Madden, P.H.: Fractional cut: improved recursive bisection placement. In: Proceedings of International Conference on Computer Aided Design (ICCAD), pp. 307–310 (November 2003)
4. Sechen, C., Sangiovanni-Vincentelli, A.: The timberwolf placement and routing package. IEEE Journal of Solid-State Circuits 20(2), 510–522 (1985)
5. Kahng, A.B., Wang, Q.: Implementation and extensibility of an analytic placer. IEEE Transactions on Computer-Aided Design of Integrated Circuits and Systems 24(5), 734–747 (2005)
6. Cong, J., Xie, M.: A robust detailed placement for mixed-size ic designs. In: Proceedings of Asia and South Pacific Conference on Design Automation, pp. 188–194 (January 2006)
7. Shahookar, K., Mazumder, P.: VLSI cell placement techniques. ACM Computing Surveys 23(2), 143–220 (1991)
8. Chang, C.C., Cong, J., Romesis, M., Xie, M.: Optimality and scalability study of existing placement algorithms. IEEE Transactions on Computer-Aided Design of Integrated Circuits and Systems 23(4), 537–549 (2004)
9. Alpert, C.J., Caldwell, A.E., Kahng, A.B., Markov, I.L.: Hypergraph partitioning with fixed vertices (VLSI CAD). IEEE Transactions on Computer-Aided Design of Integrated Circuits and Systems 19(2), 267–272 (2000)
10. Selvakkumaran, N., Karypis, G.: Theto - a fast and high-quality partitioning driven global placer. Technical report, in university of minnesota - computer science and engineering technical reports (2003)
11. Chen, T.C., Hsu, T.C., Jiang, Z.W., Chang, Y.W.: Ntuplace: a ratio partitioning based placement algorithm for large-scale mixed-size designs. In: Proceedings of the 2005 International Symposium on Physical Design, ISPD 2005, pp. 236–238. ACM, New York (2005)
12. Capo: Tool, http://vlsicad.eecs.umich.edu/BK/PDtools/tar.gz/Placement-bin/ (accessed 17 January 2013)
13. Karypis, G., Kumar, V.: Multilevel k-way hypergraph partitioning. In: Proceedings of 36th Design Automation Conference, pp. 343–348 (1999)
14. Kennings, A., Markov, I.: Analytical minimization of half-perimeter wirelength. In: Proceedings of Design Automation Conference (ASP-DAC), pp. 179–184 (June 2000)
15. Yang, X., Choi, B.K., Sarrafzadeh, M.: A standard-cell placement tool for designs with high row utilization. In: Proceedings of the 2002 IEEE International Conference on Computer Design: VLSI in Computers and Processors, pp. 45–47 (2002)

Preemptive Test Scheduling for Network-on-Chip Using Particle Swarm Optimization*

Kanchan Manna[1], Shailesh Singh[2],
Santanu Chattopadhyay[3], and Indranil Sengupta[4]

[1] School of Information Technology
[2,3] Dept. of Electronics and Elec. Comm. Engg.
[4] Dept. of Computer Science
Indian Institute of Technology Kharagpur, India - 721 302
{kanchanm@sit,santanu@ece,isg@cse}.iitkgp.ernet.in,
shailesh17.singh@gmail.com

Abstract. Network-on-Chip (NoC) has evolved as a promising technique for the present-day's communication in the VLSI design paradigm. It ensures reusability, parallelism and scalability. To reduce the testing cost of such a system, the existing communication structure ca be reused. In this paper, we have proposed a Particle Swarm Optimization (PSO) based mixed test scheduling approach to test the cores in the NoC environment. It incorporates both non-preemptive and preemptive tests. Experimental results for ITC'02 System-on-Chip (SoC) benchmarks show that the PSO based mixed test scheduling approach efficiently reduces the overall test application time compared to other existing works.

Keywords: NoC testing, PSO, Non-preemptive testing and preemptive testing.

1 Introduction

Network-on-Chip (NoC) has evolved as a very promising methodology to implement core based systems, in which, a number of simple routers are interconnected following some topology (most commonly, mesh). The cores are attached to the routers. Electrical signal exchanges between the cores are replaced by message passing via the router network. Such an environment, though well suited for the VLSI design paradigm based on reuse of IP-cores, testing becomes a major challenge. Since the input-output lines of all IP-cores are not available at system input-output pins, a major task is to transport the test patterns from system input to the inputs of individual IP cores, collect their responses and transfer to the system output. Moreover, to reduce system-level pin count and area overhead, it is advisable to use the on-chip network itself for test data transportation.

---

* This work is partially supported by Department of Information and Technology, Govt. of India (9(5)/2010-MDD), Dated 23/11/2011.

M.S. Gaur et al. (Eds.): VDAT 2013, CCIS 382, pp. 74–82, 2013.

To reduce test application time, a proper scheduling is necessary for the cores. Even if we assume the availability of multiple I/O channels from the *Automated Test Equipment* (ATE), system pins may be associated with only a few cores, primarily dedicated for input-output operations. Test patterns are to be routed from such an input core to an output core. Thus, even if multiple I/O cores are available, test parallelism may be restricted by the availability of routing resources through the NoC.

As a result, NoC test scheduling has become a major research area. The non-preemptive version of the problem is *NP-hard* [1]. The fully preemptive version is solvable optimally in $O(n^3)$ time [1], n being the number of cores. The problem can be solved as an instance of job-shop problem. The test session for the sequential and BIST based core, in practice, may be nonpreemptive [2]. Therefore, all cores in a NoC need not be preemptive. Purely combinational cores may be taken as preemptive, sequential or BIST based core testing is not preemptive. Preemption also depends on type of fault-model assumed. In particular, the assumption does not hold for transition and linked faults. Ideally, a NoC will contain cores such that, only a subset of them support preemptive testing. Thus, the overall scheduling problem remains NP-hard. A judicious mix of sequences testing preemptive and non-preemptive cores can have better flexibility in utilizing test times which may otherwise remain idle, due to resource conflicts. This has motivated us to formulate a *Particle Swarm Optimization* (PSO) problem to identify test schedule for NoCs having both types of core.

The rest of the paper is organized as follows. Section 2 presents the problem definition along with the test time computation for individual cors. Section 3 presents a survey of related works on test scheduling. Section 4 and 5 enumerates the PSO formulation. Result has been discussed in Section 6. Section 7 draws conclusion.

2   Problem Definition

The input to the test scheduling problem consists of the following.

- A set $C = \{C_i, 1 \le i \le N_c\}$ of N_c cores in the NoC.
- Each core C_i has a test set T_i associated with it. The test may be preemptive or non-preemptive in nature. A non-preemptive test set has to be applied to the core as a single group. On the otherhand, a preemptive test can be divided into multiple test sessions for a single core.
- A set of pairs P of cores marked as input-output pairs. The overall test scheduling problem is to identify the schedule to test all cores in the system.

To test a core, a test wrapper interfaces between the core and NoC environment. Test wrappers convert core scan-chains into wrapper scan-chains (each of almost equal length). In this work, we have used test wrapper design algorithm proposed in [4]. A mesh based NoC implementation of ITC benchmark *d695* [5] has been shown in Fig. 1. It has two number of I/O pairs indicated by the incoming and outgoing arrows. A channel of an *Automatic Test Equipment* (ATE)

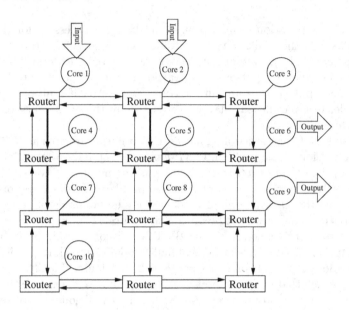

Fig. 1. d695 SoC implemented in NoC environment

is used to connect to each I/O pairs. Cores 1 and 9 form an I/O pair. The other
I/O pair consists of core 2 and 6. If core 7 has to be tested by the I/O pair (1,9),
core 1 (source) will feed the test pattern to core 7. The test and response packets
will move through the NoC following a deadlock free deterministic xy-routing
technique. Test responses will be collected at core 9 (sink). The solid arrows
indicate the entire routing path. Test and response packets move in pipelined
fashion through this path.

A core supporting preemption, can be scheduled in either preemptive or
non-preemptive manner. As the path to test a core via each I/O pair is fixed,
the path will remain same throughout the test session. Test packets are moved
in a pipelined fashion which can be interrupted, if the core allows preemption.
The preemptive scheduling approaches often result in lower test time than non-
preemptive one, because tests are preempted to avoid resource conflicts that
can create idle time durations in test resources. In preemptive policy, this idle
time can be used to test other cores. The preemptive test strategy does not
significantly increase the ATE's control complexity. It stores the test patterns
in the same way as in non-preemptive strategy, except that the sub-sequences
of test patterns are reordered in ATE memory. The scheduler has to do little
switching between core test and isolation modes.

Test time corresponding to a block of patterns for a core can be calculated
as follows. Let p denote the number of test patterns, l the maximum scan-chain
length (flit length) and the distances (interms of hops) from source to core and
core to sink be denoted by $h_{s \rightarrow c}$ and $h_{c \rightarrow k}$ respectively. As each flit is unpacked
in one clock cycle and flits move in pipelined fashion, the time to send test packet
from source to the core plus the time to collect response packet in the sink is

given by $h_{s \to c} + (l + 1) + 1 + h_{c \to k} + (l - 1)$. The minimum inter-arrival time between consecutive flits is given by $Max\{$ *time required to shift-in a flit into core, time required to shift-out a response from core + unit cycle to unpack the flit + time taken to generate the response*. Therefore, entire test time for for a particular core is obtain by

$$h_{s \to c} + (l-1) + 1 + [1 + Max\{h_{s \to c} + (l-1), h_{c \to k} + (l-1)\}] \times (p-1) + h_{c \to k} + (l-1)$$

$$\Rightarrow [1 + Max\{h_{s \to c}, h_{c \to k}\} + (l - 1)] \times p + [Min\{h_{s \to c}, h_{c \to k}\} + (l - 1)]$$

Now, the test schedule problem can be formulated as

Given an NoC with the test information such as core type (preemptive/non-preemptive), number of wrapper scan-chain, number of test patterns etc. and m number of test port (I/O pair), find an assignment of cores to test ports and its duration in such a way that the overall test application time is minimized.

3   Related Works

An *Integer Liner Programming* (ILP) based non-preemptive test strategy has been developed in [6]. It is computationally expensive when system has more number of cores. A *Genetic Algorithm* (GA) based meta-search technique has been developed for non-preemptive test schedule [7]. In that work, cores and I/O pairs are embedded separately into chromosome structure. A non-preemptive scheduling strategy has been developed based on another meta-search technique named *Simulated Annealing* (SA) [8]. Different types of wrappers have been assigned to each core for reducing the test application time. Another SA based technique have been presented in [9]. In this approach, dynamic routing path has been selected to reduce the test application time. Flit size has been computed using Pareto-optimal strategy. The core location has been decided using a mapping algorithm. An ant colony based meta-search technique has been used to minimize the test application time in NoC based SoC environment [10]. A non-preemptive test scheduling based on *Particle Swarm Optimization* (PSO) based meta-search have repotted in [3]. In this work, each core tested by a clock rate, all cores are assumed to be nonpreemptive and each particle consists of two parts—core part and IO pair part. Many other strategies have been proposed in the literature for multi-frequency testing [11], power and thermal-aware strategies [12–16] and so on. However, these works mostly consider non-preemptive policy. This paper presents a basic mixed test scheduling policy having both preemptive and non-preemptive cores. The policy can be extended easily to-words power and thermal-aware tests.

4   Continuous and Discrete Particle Swarm Optimization

Particle Swarm Optimization (PSO) based evolutionary strategy has been developed in 1995 [17]. It is a population based stochastic search and optimization technique, each particle represents a potential solution. Evolution of particles over generation is guided by both the self and the swarm intelligence.

Let the kth particle in the ith generation is denoted by P_k^i and its position in the n-dimensional search space is represented as $< P_{k,1}^i, P_{k,2}^i, ..., P_{k,n}^i >$. The local best of kth particle be represented by $pbest_k$. It corresponds to the best position that this particle has come across in the evolution so far. The quantity $gbest^i$ denotes the global best particle position of ith generation. Based on the evolution policy, PSO can be classified into two group – discrete PSO (DPSO) and continuous PSO. The continuous PSO evolves particle positions by updating their velocities in each dimension. The evolution is guided by the following equations.

$$V_k^{i+1} = wV_k^i + C_1 R_1 (pbest_k - P_k^i) + C_2 R_2 (gbest^i - P_k^i); \; P_k^{i+1} = P_k^i + V_k^{i+1}$$

where, C_1 and C_2 are the self confidence (cognitive) and swarm confidence (social) respectively. R_1 and R_2 are two random numbers in the range between 0 to 1. Inertia is represented by w. The velocity of the kth particle in the ith generation is denoted by V_k^i. The updated velocity of the particle is captured by V_k^{i+1} for the $(i+1)^{th}$ generation. The new position of the particle is denoted by P_k^{i+1} for the $(i+1)^{th}$ generation.

For discrete PSO, the new position is obtained as, $P_k^{i+1} = (\gamma \times I \oplus \alpha \times (P_k^i \vdash pbest_k) \oplus \beta \times (P_k^i \vdash gbest^i))P_k^i$.

Here, $\vdash$ is a transform operator on two sequences. Given two sequences m and n, $m \vdash n$ identifies the minimum set of swappings to be applied on m to transform it to n. For example, if $m = < 6, 8, 9, 7 >$ and $n = < 7, 6, 8, 9 >$, $m \vdash n = < swap(1,4), swap(2,4), swap(3,4) >$. The numbers inside the $swap()$ are index of the sequence. The inertia, self confidence and swarm confidence are incorporated via the parameter γ, α, and β respectively. The fusion operator has been denoted by $\oplus$. The fusion of two sequences, m and n, $m \oplus n$ signifies that the sequence of swaps in m will be followed by those in n. The operation $\alpha \times (m \vdash n)$ implies the swap in the sequence $(m \vdash n)$ will be performed with probability α. Identity swap is represented by I that is, $swap(1,1), swap(2,2), ..., swap(n,n)$. The overall operation $(\gamma \times I \oplus \alpha \times (P_i \vdash lbest^k) \oplus \beta \times (P_i \vdash gbest_i))$ is applied to particle P_k^i to get P_k^{i+1}.

5   Core Test Scheduling as a Combined PSO Problem

To minimize the test application time, we have mapped test scheduling problem into combined PSO. It is a combination of continuous and discrete PSO. In the following, we present a formulation of the same.

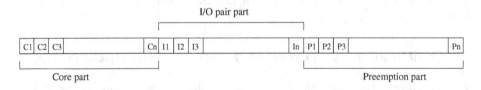

Fig. 2. Particle structure for test scheduling

5.1 Particle Structure and Fitness Calculation

The individual particles of the formulated PSO consists of three parts (shown in Fig. 2) – the *core part*, the *I/O pair part* and the *preemption part*. For an NoC with n cores, each part has got n entries in it. The *core part* is a permutation of numbers *1* through n, identifying the order in which the scheduler will attempt to schedule the testing of cores. If the NoC has k number of I/O pairs, the ith entry in *I/O pair part* identifies the I/O pair through which core i will be tested. Each preemption part entry is a number between *0* and *1*. For non-preemptive cores, the entry is always *1*. For a preemptive core, if the corresponding entry is x and the core has a total of m test patterns, $x * m$ number of patterns will be tested as a single block. Thus, testing of entire core is distributed over a number of blocks, each block being scheduled independent of others. However, since the same I/O pair is attached to the core in each test session, the same routing resources will be utilized for them. The overall test time resulting from the scheduling of all cores is the fitness of the particle.

5.2 Evolution Process

The initial population of particles is generated randomly, their fitness values are computed and the *gbest* particle is identified. Local best for each particle is taken to be the same as the particle itself. To evolve particles of generation i to generate $i + 1$, evolution using both continuous and discrete PSO policy are utilized. The *core part* and the *I/O pair part* evolve via discrete PSO, while the *preemption part* evolves via continuous PSO. The evolution process continues till either a maximum number of generations has been evolved, or, the best solution does not improve over a pre-decided number of generations.

Table 1. Test scheduling result for 10% preemptive cores

SoC	Number of I/O ports					
	(2,2)		(3,3)		(4,4)	
	PSO	Heu. [2]	PSO	Heu. [2]	PSO	Heu. [2]
d695(10)	19618	20815	13238	14633	10104	12368
g1023(14)	29117	29608	18880	20543	14794	18248
p22810(28)	290125	313582	187800	223021	141630	175275
p34392(19)	263172	321815	176322	260332	162626	188035
p93791(32)	318199	346219	204424	235398	150200	193033
t512505(31)	500222	613211	330579	402660	249130	412922
Avg.% improvement	9.9		16.1		22	

6   Result for ITC'02 Benchmarks

The experimental results have been shown in this section for some ITC'02 benchmarks [5]. Mesh based topology has been used for this experiment. We have run

Table 2. Test scheduling result for 30% preemptive cores

SoC	Number of I/O ports					
	(2,2)		(3,3)		(4,4)	
	PSO	Heu. [2]	PSO	Heu. [2]	PSO	Heu. [2]
d695(10)	19618	20881	13304	14881	10104	12368
g1023(14)	29148	30611	18938	21500	14794	18248
p22810(28)	290125	399524	187899	290149	142669	243412
p34392(19)	263172	321815	176326	260332	162626	269270
p93791(32)	318199	385386	204055	312737	149606	248914
t512505(31)	500222	642196	330318	469036	249393	367846
Avg.% improvement	16		25.7		31.7	

Table 3. Test scheduling result for 70% preemptive cores

SoC	Number of I/O ports					
	(2,2)		(3,3)		(4,4)	
	PSO	Heu. [2]	PSO	Heu. [2]	PSO	Heu. [2]
d695(10)	19618	22276	13238	14939	10104	13448
g1023(14)	29148	31794	18969	22098	14794	19204
p22810(28)	290125	463407	187772	316998	144901	267732
p34392(19)	263172	413903	177109	369769	162626	236771
p93791(32)	318199	398182	204568	334965	150168	304154
t512505(31)	500222	642419	330545	512972	250079	487773
Avg.% improvement	22.6		32.2		37.3	

the experiment in Dell PowerEdge T410 system having 8 number of cores (Intel Xeon processor, E5606@2.12 GHz), 64 GB RAM. For our experiment, we have considered 300 particles and the evolution stops when there is no improvement in test time (in the global best) over last 50 number of generations. Tables 1, 2 and 3 show the results preemptive scheduling policy. In each table, the first column identifies the SoC benchmark. The number within the parenthesis is the number of cores present in the corresponding benchmark. The column marked (2,2) is the case in which two number of I/O pairs are assumed to be present. Similarly, (3,3) and (4,4) correspond to three and four I/O pairs respectively. The test time results have been noted for our PSO based approach and the heuristic approach proposed in [2] (marked as "Heu" in tables). Table 1 noted the results in which 10% cores are assumed to be preemptive. For the two I/O pairs case, the PSO based strategy requires on an average 9.9% less test time than [2]. These savings increase to 16.1% and 22% respectively for three and four number of I/O pairs. Table 2 notes the results with 30% cores assumed to support preemption. Table 3 note the result with 70% preemptive cores.

Table 4 shows a comparison between non-preemptive and preemptive approaches. The non-preemptive approach applies all test patterns of a core in a single block while the mixed one performs preemptive scheduling. In the table, preemptive results are for 10% cores being preemptive. It can be observed that

Table 4. Non-preemptive Vs. Mixed scheduling result (10% cores are being preemptive)

SoC	Number of I/O ports					
	(2,2)		(3,3)		(4,4)	
	Non preemptive [3]	Mixed	Non preemptive [3]	Mixed	Non preemptive [3]	Mixed
d695(10)	19618	19618	13868	**13238**	10545	**10104**
g1023(14)	29148	**29117**	19277	**18880**	14794	14794
p22810(28)	290125	290125	188695	**187800**	162951	**141630**
p34392(19)	263172	263172	184387	**176322**	162626	162626
p93791(32)	318199	318199	207003	**204424**	155148	**150200**
t512505(31)	500222	500222	330685	**330579**	250631	**249130**

in most of the cases, preemptive scheduling could utilize the idle time slots left otherwise by a non-preemptive schedule, thus reducing the overall test time. Out of 18 test cases, in 11 cases (shown in bold in Table 4) preemptive schedule could obtain better test times.

7   Conclusion

This approach shows a new way to test the core-based SoC system in NoC environment. It is a combination of both non-preemptive and preemptive scheduling approach. In preemptive scheduling approach test session for each core is divided into multiple number of test sessions whereas in non-preemptive scheduling a single test session is devoted for each core. Experimental results for ITC'02 benchmarks show that our approach outperforms other works presented in [2] and [3]. This work can extended towards power-aware and thermal-aware scheduling.

References

[1] Iyenger, V., Chakrabatry, K.: System-on-a-Chip Test Scheduling With Precedence Relationships, Preemption and Power Constraints. IEEE Trans. on Computer-aided Design of Integrated Circuit and Systems 21(9), 1088–1094 (2002)

[2] Cota, E., Liu, C.: Constrain-Driven Test scheduling for NoC-Based Systems. IEEE Trans. on Computer-Aided Design of Integrated Circuit and Systems 25(11), 2465–2478 (2006)

[3] Manna, K., Khaitan, P., Chattopadhyay, S., Sengupta, I.: Particle Swarm Optimization based Technique for Network-on-Chip Testing. In: Proceedings of IEEE Intl. Conf. EAIT, pp. 66–69 (2012)

[4] Iyengar, V., Chakrabarty, K.: Test wrapper and test access mechanism co-optimization for system-on-chip. Journal of Electronic Testing: Theory and Appl. 18, 213–230 (2002)

[5] Marinissen, E.J., Iyengar, V., Chakrabarty, K.: A Set of Benchmarks for Modular Testing of SOCs. In: Proceedings of International Test Conference, pp. 519–528 (2002)

[6] Liu, C., Cota, E., Sharif, H., Pradhan, D.K.: Test scheduling for Network-on-Chip with BIST and precedence constraints. In: Proceedings of International Test Conference, pp. 1369–1378.

[7] Kundu, S., Sathi, M., Chattopadhyay, S.: Genetic Algorithm based Test Scheduling for Network-on-Chip. In: Procedings of IEEE VLSI Design and Test Symposium (2007)

[8] Zou, W., Reddy, S.M., Pomeranz, I., Huang, Y.: SoC Test Scheduling Using Simulated Annealing. In: Procedings of IEEE VLSI Test Symposium (VTS 2003), pp. 325–330 (2003)

[9] Farah, R., Harmanani, H.: A method for efficient NoC test scheduling using deterministic routing. In: Proceedings of IEEE International SOC Conference (SOCC), pp. 363–366 (2010)

[10] Ahn, J., Kang, S.: Noc-based soc test scheduling using ant colony optimization. ETRI Journal 30, 129–140 (2008)

[11] Salamy, H., Harmanani, H.M.: An optimal formulation for test scheduling network-on-chip using multiple clock rates. In: Proceedings of the 24th Canadian Conference on Electrical and Computer Engineering (CCECE), pp. 215–218 (2011)

[12] Cota, E., Carro, L., Wagner, F., Lubaszewski, M.: Power-aware noc reuse on the testing of core-based systems. In: Proceedings of International Test Conference, pp. 612–621 (2003)

[13] Rosinger, P., Al-Hasmi, B.M., Chakrabarty, K.: Thermal-safe Test Scheduling for Core-Based System-on-Chip Integrated Circuit. IEEE Trans. on Computer-aided Design of Integrated Circuit and Systems 25(11), 2502–2512 (2006)

[14] Liu, C., Iyengar, V., Pradhan, D.K.: Thermal-aware Testing of Network-on-Chip Using Multiple-Frequency Clocking. In: Proceedings of VLSI Test Symposium, pp. 46–51 (2006)

[15] He, Z.,, Z.: A heuristic for thermal-safe SoC test scheduling. In: Proceedings of International Test Conference, pp. 1–10 (2007)

[16] Yao, C., Saluja, K.K., Ramanathan, P.: Power and Thermal Constrained Test Scheduling Under Deep Submicron Technologies. IEEE Trans. on Computer-aided Design of Integrated Circuit and Systems 30(2), 317–322 (2011)

[17] Kennedy, I., Eberhart, R.C.: Particle Swarm Optimization. In: Proceedings of IEEE International Conference on Neural Networks, NJ, pp. 1942–1948 (1995)

Energy Efficient Array Initialization Using Loop Unrolling with Partial Gray Code Sequence

Sumanta Pyne and Ajit Pal

Department of Computer Science and Engineering
Indian Institute of Technology Kharagpur, West Bengal, 721 302, India
{spyne,apal}@cse.iitkgp.ernet.in

Abstract. The present work introduces a software technique to reduce energy consumed by the address bus of the on-chip data memory. This is done by reducing switching activity on the address bus of the on-chip data memory, with the help of loop unrolling with partial Gray code sequence. The present work introduces the translation of a loop with array initialization to its loop unrolled version with partial Gray code sequence. The expressions for switching activity consumed on the address bus of data memory are derived for both unrolled loop with and without partial Gray code sequence. The proposed translation method finds a relocatable base address of the array so that the partial Gray code sequence is maintained, without any energy-performance overhead and achieves a considerable amount of energy reduction without any performance loss. The proposed method achieves 25-50% reduction in switching activity on the address bus of on-chip data memory. The present work is evaluated on five benchmark programs and is suitable for programs where array initialization time is more than computation time.

Keywords: Energy reduction, array initialization, address bus of on-chip L1-data cache, switching activity, loop unrolling, unrolling factor, loop unrolling with partial Gray code sequence, translation.

1 Introduction

Energy/power consumed by VLSI circuits is directly proportional to the switching activity. The address and data bus connecting memory and processor are highly capacitive which leads to the switching power dissipation when $0-to-1$ and $1-to-0$ bit transitions occur on the buses at high frequency. As the technology scales down to the deep-submicron region, the inter-wire capacitance (C_I) becomes significant compared to the wire-to-substrate capacitance (C_L). As C_I is the dominant capacitance in deep sub-micron era, it has two significant effects, large propagation delay due to opposite transitions on adjacent wires [1,2,3] and power dissipation associated with driving the on-chip buses [2]. The expression for average bus wire power consumption can be written as $P_{avg} = \frac{1}{2} \times C_{bus} \times V_{dd}^2 \times n_{trans} \times f$ where, C_{bus} is the bus capacitance, V_{dd} is the supply voltage, f is the frequency of operation. $n_{trans} = \frac{\sum_{t=0}^{N-1} HD(d^t, d^{t+1})}{N}$, which

M.S. Gaur et al. (Eds.): VDAT 2013, CCIS 382, pp. 83–93, 2013.

is the average number of bit transitions (switching activity) on the bus caused by transfer of N bit patterns. $HD(d^t, d^{t+1})$ is the Hamming Distance between two consecutive bit patterns d^t and d^{t+1}. The present work reduces n_{trans} on the address bus of data memory. This work focuses on systems that use Harvard architecture employing independent data and instruction address buses. This work considers the address bus between L1-data cache and the processor, where the L1-data cache is on-chip. The present work exploits the sequential access of adjacent memory locations, when a set of sequential locations (like an array) is initialized within a small loop, and introduces loop unrolling with partial Gray code sequence. This technique reduces on-chip bus switching activity on the address bus of data memory, thereby saving energy. The proposed work does not require any extra hardware for encoding and decoding address on the address bus. Programmers and/or compilers can exploit this idea to reduce switching activity on address bus of data memory, when they encounter loops which initialize array of considerable size. Loop unrolling reduces the number of loop manipulation instructions by loop unrolling factor (uf) saving both time and energy. Array initialization using loop unrolling with partial Gray code sequence can save more energy by reducing switching activity on the address bus of on-chip L1-data cache.

1.1   Related Work

Several hardware based approaches to reduce bus switching activity has been proposed earlier which require extra hardware in the form of encoders and decoders which consume more silicon space (increasing the design cost), power and degrades performance. Since, the present work is a software based technique, the hardware approaches are not discussed. In [4] the authors proposed the idea for instruction scheduling to reduce switching activity. The authors of [5] studied Gray code addressing to reduce switching activity on the instruction address bits and introduced an instruction scheduling technique called cold scheduling to reorder instruction sequence to reduce the switching activities. In [6,7] Lee et al proposed a greedy bipartite-matching instruction scheduling scheme to reduce switching activity in the instruction bus. In [8] Parikh et al proposed instruction scheduling algorithms considering the activity of switching from one instruction to another instruction as circuit-state effect (circuit-state cost or inter-instruction cost). In [9] the authors proposed an algorithm to reduce both schedule length by 11.5% and bus-switching activities by an average of 19.4% for applications with loops. In [11] the authors proposed an algorithm to reduce bus-switching activities by 52.2% and schedule length by an average of 20.1% while performing scheduling and allocation simultaneously. The method proposed in [10] modifies operation placement orders within VLIW instructions to reduce the switching activity between successive instruction fetches by 34% on an average.

2   Present Work

2.1   Basic Approach

```
                              ♯define n 1000000              ♯define n 1000000
                              int main()                      int main()
                              {                               {
                                register int i;                 register int i;
                                int a[n];                       int a[n];
                                for(i = 0; i < n; i = i + 16)   for(i = 0; i < n; i = i + 16)
                                {                               {
♯define n 1000000                   a[i] = 0;                       a[i] = 0;
int main()                          a[i + 1] = 0;                   a[i + 1] = 0;
{                                   a[i + 2] = 0;                   a[i + 3] = 0;
  register int i;                   a[i + 3] = 0;                   a[i + 2] = 0;
  int a[n];                         a[i + 4] = 0;                   a[i + 6] = 0;
  for(i = 0; i < n; i + +)          a[i + 5] = 0;                   a[i + 7] = 0;
  {                                 a[i + 6] = 0;                   a[i + 5] = 0;
      a[i] = 0;                     a[i + 7] = 0;                   a[i + 4] = 0;
  }                                 a[i + 8] = 0;                   a[i + 12] = 0;
  return 0;                         a[i + 9] = 0;                   a[i + 13] = 0;
}                                   a[i + 10] = 0;                  a[i + 15] = 0;
                                    a[i + 11] = 0;                  a[i + 14] = 0;
(a) Original Program                a[i + 12] = 0;                  a[i + 10] = 0;
                                    a[i + 13] = 0;                  a[i + 11] = 0;
                                    a[i + 14] = 0;                  a[i + 9] = 0;
                                    a[i + 15] = 0;                  a[i + 8] = 0;
                                  }                               }
                                  return 0;                       return 0;
                                }                               }
```

(b) Original Program with loop   (c) Original Program with unrolled loop
unrolling   having partial Gray code sequence

Fig. 1. Programs for array initialization

Figure 1(a) shows a program where all the $'n'$ elements of an array $'a'$ are initialized to an integer value $'0'$. This array initialization involves sequential access of $'n'$ memory locations, where the index variable $'i'$ is stored in a CPU register. The program in Fig. 1(b) is the loop unrolled version of the program in Fig. 1(a), where the loop unrolling factor (uf) is $'16'$. Loop unrolling reduces the number of loop manipulation instructions by a factor $'uf'$, saving time and energy. The program in Fig. 1(c) is a loop unrolled version of the program in Fig. 1(a), where the array $a's$ memory address references within the body of the unrolled loop follows a Gray code sequence. So, the number of $'0 - to - 1'$ and $'1-to-0'$ bit transitions for array $a's$ memory address references within the body of the unrolled loop, referred as intra-iteration switching, is restricted to $'uf-1'$. The present work refers a simple unrolled loop as LU, and an unrolled loop with partial Gray code sequence as LUG. The number of $'0 - to - 1'$ and $'1 - to - 0'$ bit transitions (switchings) on the address bus of the data memory for LU and LUG are referred as S_{LU} and S_{LUG}, respectively. Figure 2 shows the generalized form of the original loop, LU and LUG, where an array $'a'$ is initialized with $'value'$. Where, $value$ is either a constant or a variable stored in CPU register. Let, $data\_type$ be the type of data stored in the array $'a'$, $data\_type$ may be $char$,

register int i;
data_type a[n];
for(i = 0; i < n; i++)
{
    a[i] = value;
}
(a) Original Loop

register int i;
data_type a[n];
for(i = 0; i < n; i = i + uf)
{
    a[i] = value;
    a[i + 1] = value;
    a[i + 2] = value;
    a[i + 3] = value;
    ...
    a[i + uf − 2] = value;
    a[i + uf − 1] = value;
}
(b) LU

register int i;
data_type a[n];
for(i = 0; i < n; i = i + uf)
{
    a[i] = value;
    a[i + 1] = value;
    a[i + 3] = value;
    a[i + 2] = value;
    ...
    a[i + $\frac{uf}{2}$ + 1] = value;
    a[i + $\frac{uf}{2}$] = value;
}
(c) LUG

Fig. 2. Generalized form of the original loop, LU and LUG

int, long int, float, double, etc. Each element belonging to a data_type consumes $sizeof(data\_type)$ bytes of memory space, where $sizeof(data\_type)$ is a power of 2. Let, $base\_address(a)$ be the base address or the starting address of the array 'a'. Let, b be obtained by shifting $base\_address(a)$ $log_2 sizeof(data\_type)$ bits right. The value of b signifies the portion (bits) of the address of array elements involved in switching activity. The $log_2 sizeof(data\_type)$ least significant bits (lsbs) of the address of the array elements are not involved in switching activity, and remain same for all elements of the array. Let, 'a' be an array of $n = 2^\alpha$ elements and $uf = 2^\beta$ be the loop unrolling factor, where $\alpha \geq \beta$ and α, β are natural numbers. The unrolled loop iterates, $\frac{n}{uf} = 2^{\alpha-\beta} = 2^\gamma$ times. The expressions for S_{LU} and S_{LUG} are derived in sections 2.2 and 2.3, respectively, considering $base\_address(a) = 0$ and n is divisible by uf.

2.2   Derivation of S_{LU}

S_{LU} is dependent on intra-iteration switching (S_{LU_intra}) and inter-iteration switching (S_{LU_inter}). So, S_{LU} can be written as shown in equation (1)

$$S_{LU} = S_{LU\_intra} + S_{LU\_inter} \tag{1}$$

S_{LU_intra} is the total number of $'0 - to - 1'$ and $'1 - to - 0'$ bit transitions on the address bus of the data memory, which takes place due to the memory address references of the elements of array 'a', i.e. $a[i], a[i+1], ..., a[i+uf-2], a[i+uf-1]$ (in $(\frac{i}{uf} + 1)^{th}$ iteration, where, $0 \leq i < n$ and i is a multiple of uf), within the body of the unrolled loop. For each iteration β lsbs of b follows the sequence $0, 1, 2, 3, \cdots, uf-2, uf-1$. So, S_{LU_intra} can be written as shown in equation (2)

$$S_{LU\_intra} = \frac{n}{uf} \times t_\beta \tag{2}$$

where t_β is the number of intra-iteration switchings per iteration. t_β can be expressed by the recurrence relation as shown in equation (3)

$$t_\beta = 2 \times t_{\beta-1} + \beta, \ for \ \beta > 1 \ , and \ t_1 = 1 \tag{3}$$

The solution of the recurrence relation in equation (3) is shown in equation (4)

$$t_\beta = 2^{\beta+1} - \beta - 2 \tag{4}$$

Substituting equation (4) in equation (2) S_{LU_intra} is obtained in equation (5)

$$S_{LU\_intra} = \frac{n}{uf} \times (2^{\beta+1} - \beta - 2) = \frac{n}{uf} \times (2 \times uf - log_2 uf - 2) \tag{5}$$

Let, i_{curr} and i_{next} be the values of i in the current and next iterations,

			Inter-iteration bit transition for LU			Inter-iteration bit transition for LUG		
Iteration	i_{curr}	i_{next}	$b_{a[i_{curr}+uf-1]}$	$b_{a[i_{next}]}$	$\sharp Switching$	$b_{a[i_{curr}+\frac{uf}{2}]}$	$b_{a[i_{next}]}$	$\sharp Switching$
1	0	16	0000 1111	0001 0000	5	0000 1000	0001 0000	2
2	16	32	0001 1111	0010 0000	6	0001 1000	0010 0000	3
3	32	48	0010 1111	0011 0000	5	0010 1000	0011 0000	2
4	48	64	0011 1111	0100 0000	7	0011 1000	0100 0000	4
5	64	80	0100 1111	0101 0000	5	0100 1000	0101 0000	2
6	80	96	0101 1111	0110 0000	6	0101 1000	0110 0000	3
7	96	112	0110 1111	0111 0000	5	0110 1000	0111 0000	2
8	112	128	0111 1111	1000 0000	8	0111 1000	1000 0000	5

Fig. 3. Inter-iteration switching on the address bus of data memory for first eight iterations of LU and LUG in Fig. 2 (b) and (c), respectively, where, $uf{=}16$ and $base\_address(a) = 0$

$(Iteration(\eta), \sharp Switching)$
$(1, \beta+1)$
$(2, \beta+2), (3, \beta+1)$
$(4, \beta+3), (5, \beta+1), (6, \beta+2), (7, \beta+1)$
$(8, \beta+4), (9, \beta+1), (10, \beta+2), (11, \beta+1), (12, \beta+3), (13, \beta+1), (14, \beta+2), (15, \beta+1)$
$\cdots$

$(2^{\gamma-2}, \beta+\gamma-2+1), (2^{\gamma-2}+1, \beta+1), \cdots, (2^{\gamma-1}-2, \beta+2), (2^{\gamma-1}-1, \beta+1)$
$(2^{\gamma-1}, \beta+\gamma-1+1), (2^{\gamma-1}+1, \beta+1), \cdots, (2^\gamma-2, \beta+2), (2^\gamma-1, \beta+1)$

(a) Inter-iteration switching after each iteration from iteration 1 to iteration $2^\gamma - 1$

Iteration Range	Total $\sharp Switching$	
1	$\sigma_1 = \beta+1$	$= 2^0 \times \beta + 2^1 - 1$
2 to 3	$\sigma_2 = \beta+2+\beta+1 = 2 \times \sigma_1 + 1$	$= 2^1 \times \beta + 2^2 - 1$
4 to 7	$\sigma_3 = \beta+3+\beta+1+\beta+2+\beta+1 = 2 \times \sigma_2 + 1$	$= 2^2 \times \beta + 2^3 - 1$
8 to 15	$\sigma_4 = 2 \times \sigma_3 + 1$	$= 2^3 \times \beta + 2^4 - 1$
$\cdots$	$\cdots$	
$2^{\gamma-2}$ to $2^{\gamma-1} - 1$	$\sigma_{\gamma-1} = 2 \times \sigma_{\gamma-2} + 1$	$= 2^{\gamma-2} \times \beta + 2^{\gamma-1} - 1$
$2^{\gamma-1}$ to $2^\gamma - 1$	$\sigma_\gamma = 2 \times \sigma_{\gamma-1} + 1$	$= 2^{\gamma-1} \times \beta + 2^\gamma - 1$

(b) Total inter-iteration switching in mentioned iteration ranges

Fig. 4. Inter-iteration switching on the address bus of data memory for LU in Fig. 2(b), where, $base\_address(a) = 0$

respectively. Where, $i_{next} = i_{curr} + uf$. S_{LU_inter} is the total number of $'0 - to - 1'$ and $'1 - to - 0'$ bit transitions on the address bus of the data memory, which takes place due to the last memory address reference (of $a[i_{curr} + uf - 1]$) in the $(\frac{i}{uf} + 1)^{th}$ iteration (current iteration), and the first memory address reference (of $a[i_{next}]$) in the $(\frac{i}{uf} + 2)^{th}$ iteration (next iteration). Let, $b_{a[i_{curr} + uf - 1]}, b_{a[i_{next}]}, b_{a[i_{curr} + \frac{uf}{2}]}$ be the portion (bits) of the address of array elements $a[i_{curr} + uf - 1]$, $a[i_{next}], a[i_{curr} + \frac{uf}{2}]$, rescpectively, which are involved in inter-iteration switching activity. Figure 3 shows the inter-iteration switching on the address bus of data memory for first eight iterations of LU and LUG in Fig. 2 (b) and (c), respectively, where, $uf = 16$ and $base\_address(a) = 0$. S_{LU_inter} can be obtained from Fig. 4. Figure 4(a) shows the inter-iteration switchings for each iteration (from iteration 1 to iteration $2^\gamma - 1$). In Fig. 4(b) the total inter-iteration switching in mentioned iteration ranges forms a series whose summation forms the S_{LU_inter}. This can be written as, $S_{LU\_inter} = \beta \times (2^0 + 2^1 + 2^2 + \cdots + 2^{\gamma-2} + 2^{\gamma-1}) + (2^1 + 2^2 + 2^3 + \cdots + 2^{\gamma-1} + 2^\gamma) - \gamma = \beta \times (2^\gamma - 1) + (2^{\gamma+1} - 2) - \gamma$. The final expression for S_{LU_inter} can be written as shown in equation (6).

$$S_{LU\_inter} = (log_2 uf + 2) \times \left(\frac{n}{uf} - 1 \right) - log_2 \frac{n}{uf} \qquad (6)$$

Substituting equations (2) and (6) in equation (1), the expression of S_{LU} is obtained as $S_{LU} = \frac{n}{uf} \times (2 \times uf - log_2 uf - 2) + (log_2 uf + 2) \times \left(\frac{n}{uf} - 1 \right) - log_2 \frac{n}{uf}$.

2.3   Derivation of S_{LUG}

S_{LUG} is dependent on intra-iteration switching (S_{LUG_intra}) and inter-iteration switching (S_{LUG_inter}). So, S_{LUG} can be written as shown in equation (7).

$$S_{LUG} = S_{LUG\_intra} + S_{LUG\_inter} \qquad (7)$$

S_{LUG_intra} is the total number of $'0 - to - 1'$ and $'1 - to - 0'$ bit transitions on the address bus of the data memory, which takes place due to the memory address references of the elements of array $'a'$, i.e. $a[i], a[i + 1], a[i + 3], a[i + 2], ..., a[i + \frac{uf}{2} + 1], a[i + \frac{uf}{2}]$ (in $(\frac{i}{uf} + 1)^{th}$ iteration, where, $0 \le i < n$ and i is a multiple of uf), within the body of the unrolled loop. For each iteration β $lsbs$ of b follows the Gray code sequence $0, 1, 3, 2, \cdots, \frac{uf}{2} + 1, \frac{uf}{2}$. So, S_{LUG_intra} can be written as shown in equation (8)

$$S_{LUG\_intra} = \frac{n}{uf} \times (uf - 1) \qquad (8)$$

where, $(uf - 1)$ is the intra-iteration switching per iteration due to a Gray code sequence of address references within the body of the unrolled loop. S_{LUG_inter} is the total number of $'0 - to - 1'$ and $'1 - to - 0'$ bit transitions on the address bus of the data memory, which takes place due to the last memory address reference (of $a[i_{curr} + \frac{uf}{2}]$) in the $(\frac{i}{uf} + 1)^{th}$ iteration (current iteration), and

$(Iteration(\eta), \sharp Switching)$

$(1, 2)$

$(2, 3), (3, 2)$

$(4, 4), (5, 2), (6, 3), (7, 2)$

$(8, 5), (9, 2), (10, 3), (11, 2), (12, 4), (13, 2), (14, 3), (15, 2)$

$\cdots$

$(2^{\gamma-2}, \gamma - 2 + 2), (2^{\gamma-2} + 1, 2), \cdots, (2^{\gamma-1} - 2, 3), (2^{\gamma-1} - 1, 2)$

$(2^{\gamma-1}, \gamma - 1 + 2), (2^{\gamma-1} + 1, 2), \cdots, (2^{\gamma} - 2, 3), (2^{\gamma} - 1, 2)$

(a) Inter-iteration switching after each iteration from iteration 1 to iteration $2^{\gamma} - 1$

Iteration Range	Total $\sharp Switching$	
1	$s_1 = 2$	$= 2$
2 to 3	$s_2 = s_1 + 3 \times 2^0 = 2 + 3$	$= 5$
4 to 7	$s_3 = s_2 + 3 \times 2^1 = 5 + 6$	$= 11$
8 to 15	$s_4 = s_3 + 3 \times 2^2 = 11 + 12$	$= 23$
...	...	...
$2^{\gamma-2}$ to $2^{\gamma-1} - 1$	$s_{\gamma-1} = s_{\gamma-2} + 3 \times 2^{\gamma-3}$	$= 3 \times 2^{\gamma-2} - 1$
$2^{\gamma-1}$ to $2^{\gamma} - 1$	$s_{\gamma} = s_{\gamma-1} + 3 \times 2^{\gamma-2}$	$= 3 \times 2^{\gamma-1} - 1$

(b) Total inter-iteration switching in mentioned iteration ranges

Fig. 5. Inter-iteration switching on the address bus of data memory for *LUG* in Fig. 2(c), where, $base\_address(a) = 0$

the first memory address reference (of $a[i_{next}]$) in the $(\frac{i}{uf} + 2)^{th}$ iteration (next iteration). S_{LUG_inter} can be obtained from Fig. 5. Figure 5(a) shows the inter-iteration switchings for each iteration (from iteration 1 to iteration $2^{\gamma} - 1$). In Fig. 5(b) the total inter-iteration switching in the mentioned iteration ranges forms a series whose γ^{th} term is obtained from the recurrence relation as shown in equation (9)

$$s_{\gamma} = s_{\gamma-1} + 3 \times 2^{\gamma-2}, \ for \ \gamma > 1 \ , and \ s_1 = 2 \tag{9}$$

The solution of the recurrence relation in equation (9) is shown in equation (10)

$$s_{\gamma} = 3 \times 2^{\gamma-1} - 1. \tag{10}$$

The S_{LUG_inter} can be obtained from the summation of the series obtained in Fig. 5(b). This can be written as $S_{LUG\_inter} = 3 \times (2^0 + 2^1 + 2^2 + \cdots + 2^{\gamma-1}) - \gamma = 3 \times (2^{\gamma} - 1) - \gamma$. The final expression for S_{LUG_inter} can be written as shown in equation (11).

$$S_{LUG\_inter} = 3 \times \left(\frac{n}{uf} - 1 \right) - log_2 \frac{n}{uf} \tag{11}$$

Substituting equations (8) and (11) in equation (7), the expression of S_{LUG} is obtained as $S_{LUG} = \frac{n}{uf} \times (uf - 1) + 3 \times \left(\frac{n}{uf} - 1 \right) - log_2 \frac{n}{uf}$. Table 1 compares S_{LU} and S_{LUG} considering $n = 2^{10}$. For any n, $n \geq uf$ reduction in S_{LUG} is minimum (25%) when $uf = 2^2$ and maximum (50%) when a loop is totally unrolled ($n = uf$). But, total loop unrolling is impractical due to hardware limitations of the system.

Table 1. Comparision between S_{LU} and S_{LUG}

uf	$\frac{n}{uf}$	S_{LU}	S_{LUG}	Gain(%)
2^2	2^8	2036	1525	25.09
2^3	2^7	2036	1270	37.62
2^4	2^6	2036	1143	43.86
2^5	2^5	2036	1080	46.95
2^6	2^4	2036	1049	48.47
2^{10}	1	2036	1023	49.75

2.4   Translation to LUG

In section 2.2 and 2.3 the expressions for S_{LU} and S_{LUG} have been derived, respectively, assuming $'0'$ as the $base\_address(a)$. But, in reality when the program in Fig. 2 will execute, the $base\_address(a)$ may not be $'0'$. The $base\_address(a)$ may vary for different executions because it depends on system's memory manager that allocates space for array a at runtime. So, it is not possible for a compiler to predict the actual base address $base\_address(a)$. The present work considers both b and n are divisible by uf. When the array a is allocated at compile time the compiler does not know the actual base address $base\_address(a)$, but knows the relocatable base address of the array, which is an offset address. The compiler finds a relocatable base address such that the logic values corresponding to the intra-iteration switching bits are 0, which implies that b is divisible by uf. If the array a is allocated in runtime then the dynamic memory allocation subroutine can be directed to find a base address such that b divisible by uf.

3   Experimental Results

The present work is evaluated on five benchmark programs on XEEMU simulator [12]. XEEMU is a power-performance simulator which simulates Intel's XScale processor. Each benchmark program (as described in Table 3) have array initialization loops (as in Fig. 2(a)) which are translated to LUG (as in Fig. 2(c)). Table 2 shows the reduction in switching activity, execution time, energy consumption by the translated loop (E_{TL}) and energy drawn by the address bus of dl1-cache ($E_{dl1-addr\_bus}$) for the programs in Fig. 1. Since $E_{dl1-addr\_bus}$ is directly propotional to S_{LUG} they experience equal amount of reduction. Table 4 shows the time taken and energy consumed by the benchmark programs having the original loop (Org), LU, and LUG. $SCount$ and $CSort$ with LUG achieves more gain in total energy (E_{Tot}) because their array initialization time (T_{init}) is much longer than computation time (T_{comp}). KS, TI and DFS with LUG have less gain in E_{Tot} because their T_{init} is much lesser than T_{comp}. Thus, LUG is more applicable for the programs having $T_{init} \geq T_{comp}$.

Table 2. Comparision of Switching activity, Time and Energy consumption of the programs in Fig. 1

Program	Metric	Value	Metric	LU's Gain wrt Org (%)	LUG's Gain wrt Org (%)	LUG's Gain wrt LU (%)
Original	♯Switching	1999986	♯Switching	-	-	-
(Org)	Time(ms)	36.90	Time	-	-	-
	E_{TL}(mJ)	28.10	E_{TL}	-	-	-
	$E_{dl1-addr\_bus}$(mJ)	5.69	$E_{dl1-addr\_bus}$	-	-	-
Loop Unrolling	♯Switching	1999986	♯Switching	0.0	-	-
(LU)	Time(ms)	27.60	Time	25.20	-	-
	E_{TL}(mJ)	19.90	E_{TL}	29.18	-	-
	$E_{dl1-addr\_bus}$(mJ)	5.69	$E_{dl1-addr\_bus}$	0.0	-	-
Loop Unrolling	♯Switching	1124989	♯Switching	-	43.75	43.75
with partial	Time(ms)	27.60	Time	-	25.20	0.0
Gray code	E_{TL}(mJ)	16.70	E_{TL}	-	40.56	16.08
sequence (LUG)	$E_{dl1-addr\_bus}$(mJ)	3.2	$E_{dl1-addr\_bus}$	-	43.75	43.75

Table 3. Benchmark Programs

Benchmark	Description	T_{init} T_{comp}
Symbol Count ($SCount$)	Finds frequency of symbols in a string of size $\omega = 10^3$, each symbol belongs to a set of $n = 2^{20}$ symbols. $uf = 2^4$	$O(n)$ $O(\omega)$
Counting Sort ($CSort$)	A linear time sort on an array of $m = 10^3$ integers, each integer lies between 0 and $n = 2^{20}$. $uf = 2^4$	$O(n)$ $O(m)$
0-1 Knapsack (KS)	Given costs and weights of $r = 3$ types of items, fill a knapsack of capacity $n = 10^6$ such that the sum of cost of the elements to fill it is maximum. $uf = 2^4$	$O(n)$ $O(r \times n)$
Treasure Island (TI)	Given an $n \times n$ grid, each coordinate of the grid has a cost, staring from the lower-left corner $(1, 1)$ one has to reach upper-right corner (n, n), either by moving upward or rightward in each step, such that the cost of the path traversed is maximum. $n = 2^9$, $uf = 2^4$	$O(n)$ $O(n^2)$
Depth First Search (DFS)	Depth First Traversal of a randomly generated graph with $n = 2^{10}$ vertices and $e = O(n^2)$ edges. $uf = 2^4$	$O(n)$ $O(max\{n, e\})$

4   Conclusion

The present work introduces a software based approach to reduce energy consumed on the address bus of the data memory. This is done by reducing switching activity on the address bus of the data memory, with the help of LUG. Translation of a loop with array initialization to LUG is introduced. The expressions for switching activity on the bus for LU and LUG are derived. The proposed translation technique finds a relocatable base address of the array so that the partial Gray code sequence is maintained, without any energy-performance overhead and achieves a considerable amount of energy reduction without any performance loss. The proposed method achieves 25-50% reduction in switching activity on the address bus of on-chip data memory. The proposed work is evaluated on five benchmark programs. LUG is more applicable for the programs having

Table 4. Comparision of Time and Energy consumption of the benchmark programs

Benchmark	Metric	Org	LU	LUG	Metric	LU's Gain wrt Org (%)	LUG's Gain wrt Org (%)	LUG's Gain wrt LU (%)
$SCount$	$Time$ (ms)	40.6	29.3	29.3	$Time$	27.83	27.83	0.0
	E_{Tot} (mJ)	30.7	21.1	17.7	E_{Tot}	31.27	42.34	16.11
	E_{TL} (mJ)	30.5	20.9	17.5	E_{TL}	31.47	42.62	16.26
$CSort$	$Time$ (ms)	160.7	142.2	142.2	$Time$	11.51	11.51	0.0
	E_{Tot} (mJ)	116.7	102.2	99.7	E_{Tot}	12.42	14.46	2.44
	E_{TL} (mJ)	36.6	22.1	19.5	E_{TL}	39.61	46.72	11.76
KS	$Time$ (ms)	766.1	751.1	751.1	$Time$	1.95	1.95	0.0
	E_{Tot} (mJ)	576.9	564.1	559.7	E_{Tot}	2.21	2.98	0.78
	E_{TL} (mJ)	52.0	39.3	35.0	E_{TL}	24.42	32.69	10.94
TI	$Time$ (ms)	124.5	120.1	120.1	$Time$	3.53	3.53	0.0
	E_{Tot} (mJ)	91.2	88.0	87.4	E_{Tot}	3.5	4.16	0.68
	E_{TL} (mJ)	15.4	12.3	12.1	E_{TL}	20.12	21.42	1.62
DFS	$Time$ (ms)	246.5	246.4	246.4	$Time$	0.04	0.04	0.0
	E_{Tot} (mJ)	180.23	180.212	180.211	E_{Tot}	0.01	0.01	0.0
	E_{TL} (mJ)	0.0583	0.0499	0.0466	E_{TL}	14.40	20.06	6.61

$T_{init} \geq T_{comp}$. The future work will investigate on other software techniques to reduce switching activity on address, data and control bus of instruction and data memory.

References

1. Caignet, F., Delmas-Bendhia, S., Sicard, E.: The Challenge of Signal Integrity in Deep-submicrometer CMOS Technology. Proceedings of the IEEE 89(4), 556–573
2. Sylvester, D., Hu, C.: Analytical Modeling and Characterization of Deepsubmicrometer Interconnect. Proceedings of the IEEE 89(5), 634–664
3. Victor, B., Keutzer, K.: Bus Encoding to Prevent Crosstalk Delay. In: Proceedings of ICCAD, pp. 57–63 (2001)
4. Tiwari, V., Malik, S., Wolfe, A.: Compilation Techniques for Low Energy: An Overview. In: Proceedings of Symposium on Low-Power Electronics, San Diego, CA (October 1994)
5. Su, C.-L., Tsui, C.-Y., Despain, A.M.: Reducing Power Consumption at Control Path of High Performance Microprocessors. IEEE Design and Test of Computers (December 1994)
6. Lee, C., Lee, J.K., Hwang, T.T.: Compiler Optimization on Instruction Scheduling for Low Power. In: Proceedings of 13th International Symposium on System Synthesis, pp. 55–60 (2000)
7. Lee, C., Lee, J.K., Hwang, T.T., Tsai, S.: Compiler Optimization on VLIW Instruction Scheduling for Low Power. ACM Transactions on Design Automation of Electronic Systems (TODAES) 8(2), 252–268
8. Parikh, A., Kim, S., Kandemir, M., Vijaykrishnan, N., Irwin, M.J.: Instruction Scheduling for Low Power. Journal of VLSI Signal Processing 37(1), 129–149

9. Shao, Z., Xiao, B., Xue, C., Zhuge, Q., Sha, E.H.M.: Loop scheduling with timing and switching-activity minimization for VLIW DSP. ACM Transactions on Design Automation of Electronic Systems (TODAES) 11(1), 165–185
10. Shin, D., Kim, J., Chang, N.: An Operation Rearrangement Technique for Low-Power VLIW Instruction Fetch. In: Proceedings of DATE, p. 809 (2001)
11. Shao, Z., Xiao, B., Xue, C., Sha, E.H.M.: Algorithms and analysis of scheduling for loops with minimum switching. Int. J. Computational Science and Engineering 2(1/2)
12. Herczeg, Z., Kiss, Á., Schmidt, D., Wehn, N., Gyimóthy, T.: XEEMU: An Improved XScale Power Simulator. In: Azémard, N., Svensson, L. (eds.) PATMOS 2007. LNCS, vol. 4644, pp. 300–309. Springer, Heidelberg (2007)

Design and Simulation of Bulk Micromachined Accelerometer for Avionics Application

Amit Sharma[1], Ravindra Mukhiya[2], S. Santosh Kumar[2], and B.D. Pant[2]

[1] Arya College of Engineering & IT, Jaipur, India
amitsharma.ceeri@gmail.com
[2] CSIR-Central Electronics Engineering Research Institute (CEERI),
Pilani-333 031, India
{rmukhiya,santoshkumar,bdpant}@ceeri.ernet.in

Abstract. In the present paper, the design and simulation of a MEMS polysilicon piezoresistive based bulk micromachined accelerometer for avionics application i.e. ± 10g has been presented. The maximum acceleration this design can bear is ± 50g. The accelerometer design presented in this paper consists of a trapezoidal shaped proof-mass suspended by four flexures. The piezoresistors are placed at the maximum stress locations on the beams, worked out through simulation tool COMSOL^{TM} Multiphysics. The optimum size of the sensor structure, stress, displacement of proof-mass and output voltage are analytically calculated. For 10g acceleration the relative resistance change is 3.66×10^{-3} and output voltage is 18.29 mV. Sensitivity of this accelerometer is 0.366 mV/V/g. A comparison of the analytical and simulation results is also presented.

Keywords: MEMS, Bulk micromachining, Accelerometer.

1   Introduction

Accelerometer is a mechanical device which measures the linear acceleration of a moving object. A large number of different types of accelerometers have been developed until now. The conventional accelerometers are found to be bulky and large, and consume high power. They also need careful maintenance and large operational cost. With the evolution of Micro-Electro-Mechanical Systems (MEMS) technology a new class of micro mechanical sensors has been developed, including accelerometers.

MEMS accelerometer is one of the most desired miniature sensors for a wide variety of mechanical measurement applications. Although, several types of MEMS accelerometers are now available in commercial market, yet there is always a demand of devices for customised applications with superior characteristics and lower cost.

In MEMS technology it is possible to batch fabricate and to scale down the size of accelerometers leading to low power consumption and economy. These remarkable properties of new generation accelerometers open up new application segments in industrial as well as in consumer electronics. In micro scale regime, most commonly available accelerometers are based on piezoresistive and capacitive transduction mechanism [1]. Each type of accelerometer has its own advantages and limitations.

M.S. Gaur et al. (Eds.): VDAT 2013, CCIS 382, pp. 94–99, 2013.
© Springer-Verlag Berlin Heidelberg 2013

In the present work, piezoresistive type transduction has been explored in a specific type of mass-spring system. In piezoresistive type accelerometers; there is elongation or shortening of suspension beam when the proofmass moves relative to the reference/support frame under external acceleration. The piezoresistors are placed at the fixed ends of the suspension beams at the maximum stress regions. As the proof-mass moves under applied acceleration the induced stress changes the resistance of the piezoresistors. The main advantage of piezoresistive accelerometers is that they are simple in structure, easy to fabricate and less susceptible to parasitic capacitance or electromagnetic interference (EMI) [2, 3]. The major drawback is that they have large temperature drift.

The type of design discussed in this paper is aimed for an acceleration of ± 10g. In the current design, four piezoresistors are placed in a Wheatstone bridge configuration as shown in Fig. 1. In case of zero acceleration the bridge is balanced and output voltage is zero, as all the four resistors have the same resistance value. Under acceleration, the proofmass moves in opposite direction of the acceleration and there is elongation or shortening of suspension beam which causes maximum stress at the fixed ends of the beams. This stress is sensed by the piezoresistors and this causes change in the value of its resistance. Due to this change in resistance, the bridge is no longer balanced and there is an output voltage corresponding to the acceleration. Fig. 1 shows the arrangement of piezoresistors and corresponding increase and decrease in resistances. The resistances of R_1 and R_3 increase, whereas R_2 and R_4 decrease, as a result of applied stress under the acceleration.

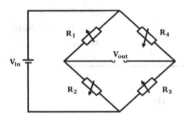

Fig. 1. Wheatstone bridge configuration of piezoresistors

2   Device Configuration

Top and bottom view of the proofmass and suspension system (supporting beam) is shown in Fig. 2. The structure is to be realized using bulk micromachining of a silicon (100) substrate. Polysilicon piezoresistors are placed along [110] direction on the substrate. The die size is 6 mm × 6 mm. The central proof-mass is trapezoidal with height of 310 μm and size of 2.8 mm × 2.8 mm (top) and 2.362 mm × 2.362 mm (bottom). The flexures or beams dimensions are $(800{\times}150{\times}20)$ μm^3 and piezoresistors have dimensions of $(70{\times}10{\times}0.5)$ μm^3. Detail design parameters of the accelerometer are given in Table 1.

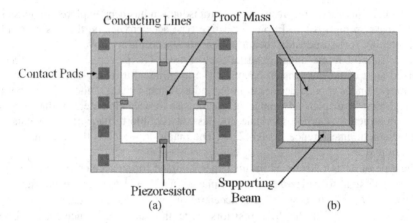

Fig. 2. (a) Top-view of the accelerometer with piezoresistors and metal lines interconnections (b) Bottom-view of the accelerometer

Table 1. Accelerometer design parameters

Design parameter	Dimensions
Die size	6 mm × 6 mm
Beam length(l)	800 μm
Beam width(w)	150 μm
Beam thickness(t)	20 μm
Proofmass size (top) B	2.8 mm × 2.8 mm
Proofmass size (bottom) b	2.362 mm × 2.362 mm
Proofmass height	310 μm
Piezoresistor size	70 μm × 10 μm × 0.5 μm

3   Design Calculations

Prior to implementation of the design in COMSOL, analytical design optimization is performed using the first order equations (1) to (8) given in Table 2, as follows:

Table 2. Accelerometer design parameter equations

Parameter	Formula	Equation no.
Volume of a single spring	$V_b = l \times w \times t$ μm³	(1)
Volume of proofmass	$V_{pm} = 1/3 \ (B^2 \times H - b^2 \times h) + V_s$ μm³	(2)
Proofmass	$M = 2.329 \times 10^{-9} \times V_{pm}$ mg	(3)
Spring constant (single spring)[4]	$K = (E \times w \times t^3)/(l^3)$ N/m	(4)
Displacement	$X = (M \times a)/(4 \times K)$ μm	(5)
Maximum stress [5]	$T = (3 \times M \times a \times l)/(4 \times w \times t^2)$ Pa	(6)
Relative resistance change [6]	$\Delta R/R = (\pi_l \times T_l) + (\pi_t \times T_t)$	(7)
Voltage output	$V_{out} = \Delta R/R \times V_{in}$ Volt	(8)

where,

H = pyramidal height

h = H − height of trapezoidal proof-mass (310 μm)

V_s = Volume of upper block

E = Young's modulus of single crystal silicon (SCS) = 170 GPa

a = Acceleration

π_l, π_t = effective piezoresistive coefficient of polysilicon in lateral and transverse directions, respectively

T_l, T_t = stress in lateral and transverse directions respectively.

4   Finite Element Analysis

A finite element method based simulations are carried out using MEMSCAD tool COMSOL. For same configurations the von-Mises stress and total deflection variations along the beam length, obtained by simulations are shown in Figs. 3-4, respectively.

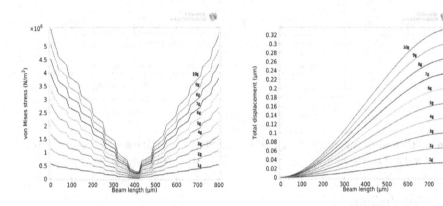

Fig. 3. Beam length vs. von-Mises stress   **Fig. 4.** Beam length vs. displacement

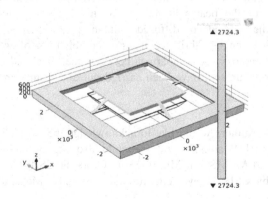

Fig. 5. First mode natural frequency

From modal analysis of this design we found the shapes and natural frquencies for first three modes, Fig. 5 shows the first mode natural frequency.

The natural frequencies for first three modes are 2.7243, 4.5759 and 4.5766 kHz, respectively. Fig. 6 (a) shows variation of displacement and that of maximum stress against the acceleration (1g to 10g) for analytical as well as simulated results. Wheatstone bridge output voltage for applied acceleration is shown in Fig. 6 (b). From Fig. 6 (a), we observe that analytical results are in close agreement with the simulated results. For a fixed bias of 5 V the output is 18.29 mV for 10g applied acceleration. Sensitivity of this accelerometer is 0.366 mV/V/g.

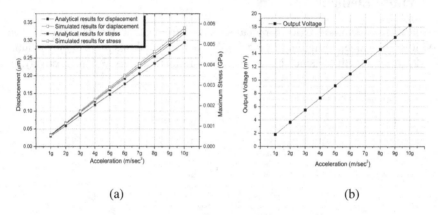

(a)   (b)

Fig. 6. (a) Comparison of analytically calculated and FEM simulated results for acceleration vs. displacement and acceleration vs. von-Misses stress (b) Acceleration vs. Output voltage.

5   Conclusions

Design and simulation of an out-of-plane Z-axis bulk micromachined accelerometer has been presented and discussed. In the present design polysilicon piezoresistors are placed on the top of the beams at maximum stress regions which have higher sensitivity than the embedded diffused silicon piezoresistors. The proposed accelerometer design can be fabricated using a combination of wet and dry bulk micromachining technology. A comparison between analytical and simulated results using COMSOL software tool have been carried out and results are found to be in close agreement.

Acknowledgments. Authors would like to acknowledge the generous support of the Director, CSIR-CEERI, Pilani. The authors would also like to thank all the scientific and technical staff of MEMS and Microsensors Group at CSIR-CEERI, Pilani. The financial support by CSIR, New Delhi through PSC-201: MicroSensys project is gratefully acknowledged.

References

1. Kal, S., Das, S., Maurya, D.K., Biswas, K., Ravi Sankar, A., Lahiri, S.K.: CMOS compatible bulk micromachined silicon piezoresistive accelerometer with low off axis sensitivity. Microelectronics Journal 37, 22–30 (2006)
2. Suminto, J.T.: A Simple High Performance Piezoresistive Accelerometer. In: Proceedings of the International Conference on Tranducers, Sunnyvale CA, p. 104 (1991)
3. Haris, M., Qu, H.: A CMOS-MEMS Piezoresistive Accelerometer with Large Proof Mass. In: Proceedings of the 2010 5th IEEE Conference on Nano/Micro Engineered and Molecular Systems, Xiamen-China, p. 309 (2010)
4. Liu, C.: Foundations of MEMS. Pearson Education, Inc. (2006) ISBN 0-13-147286-0
5. Labontiu, N.: Dynamics of Microelectromechanical System. Springer Science+Business Media, LLC (2007) ISBN 978-0-387-28731-7
6. Hsu, T.-R.: MEMS & Microsystems Design and Manufacture. Tata McGrawHill Edition (2002) ISBN 0-07-048709-X
7. Reck, K.: Piezoresistanc in Silicon Nanowires for Sensor Applications, M.Sc. Thesis (February 2008)

Performance Analysis of Subthreshold 32-Bit Kogge-Stone Adder for Worst-Case-Delay and Power in Sub-micron Technology

Himadri Singh Raghav[1,*], Sachin Maheshwari[2], and Brahmadeo Prasad Singh[1]

[1] Faculty of Engineering and Technology, MITS Lakshmangarh, India
{himadri.singh.raghav,sachin.mahe}@gmail.com
[2] Department of Electrical and Electronics Engineering, BITS, Pilani, India
bpsingh@ieee.org

Abstract. Subthreshold logic operation can drastically reduce power, if the decreased frequency operation is of secondary importance. In this paper, a 32-bit Kogge-Stone (KS) adder, which is a basic functional unit of most computational platforms, in sub-threshold logic using UMC 180nm and UMC90nm CMOS technology is presented. The performance parameters of the adder such as average power, worst-case-delay and power-delay-product at all five corners with temperature ranging from 0^0C to 100^0C are investigated. The 32-bit adder is simulated using Spectre Simulator in Cadence environment. Finally, Monte-Carlo Simulation was done to calculate the worst case delay for 180nm CMOS Technology.

Keywords: average power, kogge-stone, low power, sub-threshold, worst-case-delay.

1   Introduction

A large number of sensors and medical applications like hearing-aids, pacemakers, and other implantable devices demand ultralow power consumption, so that the user does not have to recharge or replace the batteries often. Therefore, the robustness of the device is very challenging in this situation. The main factor in subthreshold design is maintaining a good trade-off between power consumption, performance and robustness.

A paper by Kwong and Chandrakasan reported that upsizing is necessary to achieve robustness at reduced voltages and proposed a design methodology to meet yield constraints but at the expense of increased energy consumption in the subthreshold region [1]. EKV models the short channel effects accurately for deep submicron devices even at subthreshold operation (Vgs < Vt).EKV model has been used to reduce power consumption when compared to BSIM4 model for 8-bit RCA's in 32nm predictive technology [2]. In [3] multi-operand adder architecture and in [4] low power energy-efficient 32-bit carry skip adder in 45nm predictive technology in

---

* Corresponding author.

M.S. Gaur et al. (Eds.): VDAT 2013, CCIS 382, pp. 100–107, 2013.
© Springer-Verlag Berlin Heidelberg 2013

subthreshold region is proposed but it is not robust as the process variations greatly affect the minimum energy point whereas, in [5] a 32-bit bridge style adder in 32nm technology is proposed which has considerable improvement in power consumption. Twelve different subthreshold 1-bit full adders are used for designing 4-bit adders using Carry-Ripple and Carry Look-Ahead adders in 65nm and 90nm CMOS technology node [6] and the best adder is determined by comparing different performance metrics.

In subthreshold circuit design the functionality can be compromised without proper design for PVT variations. Before exploring the performance metrics for an inverter we first demonstrate the challenges of designing a circuit in subthreshold region. Then, the Monte-Carlo Simulation for 100 points was done for inverter for different channel length and frequency in UMC180nm at 350mV supply voltage. Based on this, we have designed a 32-bit KS adder in subthreshold region using UMC180nm and UMC90nm technology. The design was simulated for all five corners with temperature ranging from 0^0C to 100^0C. The robustness of the adder is shown through Monte-Carlo analysis done for 100 point in UMC180nm technology. The same adder circuit was simulated in UMC90nm technology at 200mV power supply, to show a comparison in terms of average power, worst-case-delay and power-delay-product.

2   Delay Challenges of Subthreshold Design

2.1   Delay

The first and foremost challenge of circuit operation in the subthreshold region is the relatively weak current flow resulting in longer delays and lower frequencies. Using a combination of above-threshold and subthreshold circuits for different components of the same system provides one means of bypassing this limitation. Another possibility is lowering the supply voltage while a system is in "standby" or low performance mode.

2.2   Low Voltage Operation

Operation in the subthreshold region for an inverter in UMC 90nm technology is limited by a minimum operating voltage. This voltage has been calculated to be 3 to 4 V_{TH} (V_{TH}, the thermal voltage is equal to kT/q) . This degradation of circuit operation at lower Vdd values is shown in Fig. 1. The gain of the VTC lowers for lower values of Vdd, until it approaches loss of functionality at Vdd=70mV.

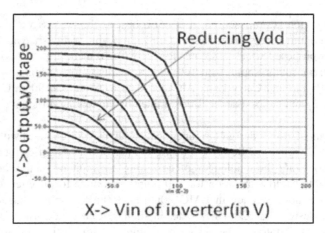

Fig. 1. VTC as a function of supply voltage for a minimum sized inverter at 27⁰C in UMC 90nm process

2.3   Process Variations

As mentioned above, the subthreshold current is exponentially dependent on the transistor's threshold voltage. Accordingly, process variations that substantially affect the threshold voltages can cause a large variance in the behavior of subthreshold circuits. In extreme cases, this can even cause certain circuits to malfunction, and so, special means need to be taken to deal with this issue. Fig. 2 shows the VTC of a minimum sized inverter in UMC90nm process for VDD at 200mV. A substantial shift of the VTC in SF and FS corner.

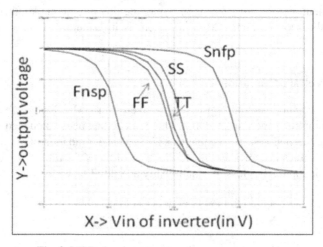

Fig. 2. VTC of an inverter at various process corners

2.4   Temperature

Another challenge for digital design in the subthreshold region is the effect of temperature variations on circuit behavior. During strong inversion operation, a rise in temperature generally slows down circuits due to mobility degradation. However, a rise in temperature causes a fall in threshold voltage, V_T which exponentially increases subthreshold current. At a certain temperature, this increase overtakes the mobility degradation and subthreshold circuits get faster. On the other side of the temperature scale, cooling down a circuit not only increases mobility, but also minimizes subthreshold leakage. At very low temperatures, the drain leakage becomes so minimal that the temperature insensitive gate leakage becomes the primary leakage. Further drops in temperature don't change the leakage. The effect of temperature change from 0^0C to 100^0C on the VTC of a minimum sized inverter in UMC 90nm process at a typical corner is shown in Fig. 3.

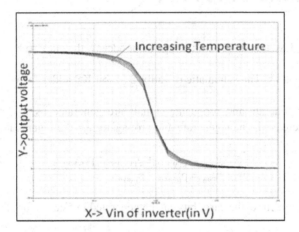

Fig. 3. VTC of an inverter at various operating temperatures

2.5   Impact of Scaling

It might appear that since the target frequencies for the subthreshold circuits are of the order of MHz or lower, scaling is unnecessary. However, scaled subthreshold circuits have the following advantages for conventional planar MOSFETs: (1) Smaller devices have lower capacitance and hence, lower switching power. (2) Gate oxide thickness (tox) is smaller, which increases the gate control.

3   32-Bit Kogge-Stone Adder Architecture

The concept of KS adder is used in order to reduce the delay of the digital circuits. This adder has the complexity of O(log2n) [7]. It combines two carry words at a time at each level of hierarchy. The total adder requires 129 complex logic gates each to implement the dot operator. In addition, 32 logic modules are needed for the generation of the propagate and generate signals at the first level (pi and gi) as well as 16

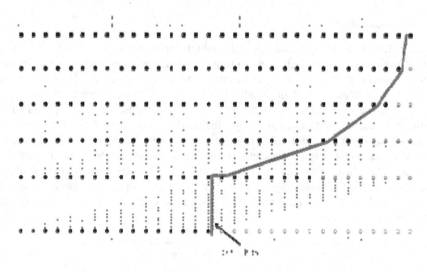

Fig. 4. Radix-2 32-bit Kogge-Stone adder with critical path

sum-generation gates. The schematic of radix-2 32-bit KS adder for with critical path is shown in Fig. 4.

In KS adder generate and propagate signals are generated using AND logic and XOR logic. Whereas, the new generate and propagate signal are generated as;

$$g_{new} = g_{present} + g_{previous} * p_{present} \tag{1}$$
$$p_{new} = p_{present} * p_{previous} \tag{2}$$

Using this architecture, the carry bits can be generated in 5stages for 32-bit KS adder.

3.1   Worst Case Condition

Since, the carry is available for sum 16th to sum 31st at the same time, so the worst case is when the carry delay is maximum for sum 16th bit.

$$C_{out16} = g_{new16} + p_{new16} * C_{in} \tag{3}$$

Since, g_{new} and p_{new} are available at the same instant of time hence the worst case is dependent on the product term that is $p_{new16} * C_{in}$. Also, C_{in} is available with inputs, it is totally dependent on p_{new16}.

Let us assume that initially, C_{in} is logic 1, so as soon as the value of p_{new16} is logic 1 the C_{out16} is produced. p_{new16} depends on p0, p1, p2 upto p16. So, the inputs should such that p_{new0}, p_{new1}, p_{new2} and so on upto p_{new15} should be logic 1. So the worst case input combination is:

$$A = xxxxxxxxxxxxxxx1111111111111111$$
$$B = xxxxxxxxxxxxxxx1111111111111110$$
$$C_{in} = 1$$

The analysis of the KS adder is done at different process corners in UMC 90nm and UMC180nm CMOS technology at particular temperature.

4   Simulation Results

The KS adder design was simulated using spectre in UMC 180nm and UMC90nm technology with minimum sized two input gates that are carefully laid out to function below the threshold voltage. The simulation was done for the worst case delay condition for all five corners are tabulated in table 1. The supply voltage used are 0.35V for 180nm and 0.2V for 90nm. Monte-Carlo simulations was also done for 100 points in UMC180nm Technology. The transistor sizes taken are L=180nm and W=240nm.

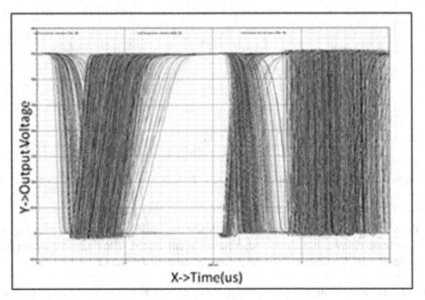

Fig. 5. KS adder output bits v/s time using Monte Carlo Simulation for 100 points in UMC180nm

Table 1. The worst case delay and power dissipation of kogge-stone adder at different process corners in UMC 180nm

S.No.	Process corners	Temperature (^{0}C)	Power Dissipation ($*10^{-6}$W)	Worst-case delay(us)	Power-Delay-Product ($*10^{-15}$)
1	TT	27	0.09	0.709	63.81
2	SS	100	0.14	0.505	70.70
3	FF	0	0.20	0.359	71.80
4	SNFP	27	0.26	0.513	133.38
5	FNSP	27	0.20	1.159	231.80

Simulation shows that there is slight variation in the delay from the sum 16th bit to sum 31st bit but suddenly the delay increased from level 1 (sum1) to level 5 (from sum 16 to sum 31). Since, there was huge load on g0, p0 bit as it is used by other g_{new} and p_{new}, the delay for the sum0 bit was maximum (approximately 900ns).The worst case delay was coming out be 1.35us through Monte-Carlo simulation in UMC180nm is also shown in fig.6.

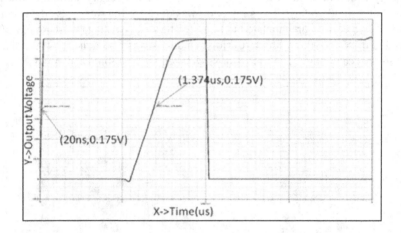

Fig. 6. Worst case delay of Kogge stone adder through Monte Carlo Simulation in UMC 180nm

Similarly, the analysis was done for the UMC90nm at different process corners, and the worst case delay and the power dissipation is calculated. The transistor sizes taken are L=85nm and W=120nm. Table 2 shows the simulated results for UMC90nm.

Table 2. The Worst Case Delay and Power Dissipation of Kogge-Stone Adder at Different Process Corners in UMC 90 nm

S.No.	Process corners	Temperature (^{0}C)	Power Dissipation ($*10^{-6}$W)	Worst case delay(ns)	Power-Delay-Product ($*10^{-15}$)
1	TT	27	0.30	49.05	14.72
2	SS	100	0.25	114.55	28.64
3	FF	0	1.85	13.55	25.07
4	SNFP	27	0.46	70.85	32.59
5	FNSP	27	0.47	64.05	30.10

5   Conclusion

In this paper, we have analyzed the 32-bit KS adder in sub-threshold region for the worst-case-delay and power in all five corners and also the corresponding power-delay product is calculated. To compare the performance of the adder, Spectre simulation in UMC180nm and UMC90nm technology was done. Monte-Carlo simulation is also done in UMC180nm for checking the reliability of the circuit. There was no error in the functionality but the delay of the combination circuit got increased from 1.16us to 1.35us.

Acknowledgments. The authors are grateful to the lab facilities (Oysters Lab) of Department of Electrical & Electronics Engineering at Birla Institute of Technology & Science (BITS), Pilani where most of the work has been carried out and is also thankful to the Department of Electronics & Communication Engineering of Mody Institute of Technology& Science, Lakshmangarh for the support to finish this work successfully.

References

1. Kwong, J., Chandrakasan, A.P.: Variation Driven Device Sizing for Minimum Energy Subthreshold Circuits. In: Proc. of the International Symposium on Low Power Electronics and Design, New York, USA, pp. 8–13 (2006)
2. Savari Rani, S., Ramasamy, S., Rajan, C.C.A., Harini, V.: 8-Bit Sub Threshold Adders in 32nm CMOS Technology for. In: International Conference on Computing Communication and Networking Technologies, pp. 1–6 (2010)
3. Mishra, B., Botteron, C., Farine, P.A., AI-Hashimi, B.M.: Ultra Low Power Multi -Operand Adder Architecture for Subthreshold Circuits. In: 54th International Midwest Symposium on Circuits and Systems, pp. 1–4 (2011)
4. Tran, A.T., Baas, B.M.: Design of an energy-efficient 32-bit adder operating at Subthreshold voltages in 45-nm CMOS. In: 3rd International Conference on Communications and Electronics, pp. 87–91 (2010)
5. Bagheri, M.R.: Ultra Low Power Sub-threshold Bridge Style Adder in Nanometer Technologies. Canadian Journal on Electrical and Electronics Engineering 2(7) (July 2011)
6. Ghobadi, N., Majidi, R., Mehran, M., Kusha, A.A.: Low Power 4-Bit Full Adder Cells in Subthreshold Regime. In: 18th Iranian Conf. on Electrical Engineering, pp. 362–367 (May 2010)
7. Rabaey, J.M., Chandrakasan, A., Nikolić, B.: Digital Integrated Circuits: A Design Perspective, 2nd edn. Prentice-Hall, New Jersey (2003)

Characterization of Logical Effort for Improved Delay

Sachin Maheshwari[1,*], Himadri Singh Raghav[2], and Anu Gupta[1]

[1]Department of Electrical and Electronics Engineering, BITS, Pilani
{sachin.mahe,himadri.singh.raghav}@gmail.com,
anug@pilani.bits-pilani.ac.in
[2]Faculty of Engineering and Technology, MITS Lakshmangarh, India

Abstract. In this paper, an effort has been made to improve the delay of a gate by skewing the gates by choosing proper sizing. The expression for skewed logical effort has been derived for universal logic gates namely NOT, NAND and NOR for minimizing the delay. The validations for minimum delay through simulation was done on a chain of inverters. The improved skewed gates showed 10% - 20% delay reduction on a chain of inverters as compared with normal skewed gate, high and low skewed gates, whereas, an improvement of 20% - 25% when compared to skewed gates favoring a particular transition. All simulations are done using Spectre in Cadence environment in UMC90nm CMOS technology at 1V power supply.

Keywords: Characterization, CMOS technology, delay, logical effort, skewed gate.

1 Introduction

Modeling and characterization of logic gates has been and still is the subject of numerous works as a critical issue either for delay characterization [1], [2], [3] and optimization [4] or to address the robustness related to random process variations in deep-submicron technologies. In [5], the authors presented an approach based on the method of logical effort for determining the minimum achievable delay of an implementation under optimal transistor sizing. While this is a useful metric, it is not sufficient to compare circuits sized to arbitrary (non-minimum) delay points.

In this paper, we have derived the expressions for logical effort of the universal logic gates, namely NOT, NAND and NOR for minimizing the delay. Before, we move forward, we have first found the mobility ratio of UMC90nm technology, which approximately comes out to be 2. Thus, the inverter used as the reference inverter is the one with balanced rise and fall drive strengths, so based on the simulation for equal rise and fall time width of the PMOS and NMOS transistors are chosen. Then, we explore the effect of shape factor (γ), and the mobility ratio (μ), on the logical effort of gates when to design a gate which favors the important transition. Finally, we have designed the skewed gates which gives the better delay as compared to

---

* Corresponding author.

M.S. Gaur et al. (Eds.): VDAT 2013, CCIS 382, pp. 108–117, 2013.
© Springer-Verlag Berlin Heidelberg 2013

the normal skewed gates, high skewed gates and low skewed gates. The validation for minimum delay was done through simulation on a chain of inverters. We have also compared our result with a chain of inverters which favors a particular transition.

2   Estimating Logical Effort and Sizing

The conductivity ratio between NMOS and PMOS transistors is defined as μ. The value of μ is calculated by simulating an inverter for equal rise and fall time. By keeping the width of NMOS to be constant and varying the PMOS width, a value of 2 approximately has been observed having equal rise and fall time. This becomes our reference inverter for calculating logical effort.

The logical effort of a gate is denoted by g, and is the average of the rising logical effort gu and the falling logical effort gd.

$$g = \frac{1}{2}(g_d + g_u)$$

(1)

The falling logical effort of a gate is determined by setting the width of the NMOS transistor to be equal to the reference inverter's, scaling the PMOS transistor size, and using the ratio of the input capacitance. For an inverter, ratio of PMOS and NMOS transistor is gamma (γ). We set the NMOS transistor size to be 1 and the PMOS transistor size to be γ. The falling logical effort is given by;

$$g_d = \frac{(1+\gamma)}{(1+\mu)}$$

(2)

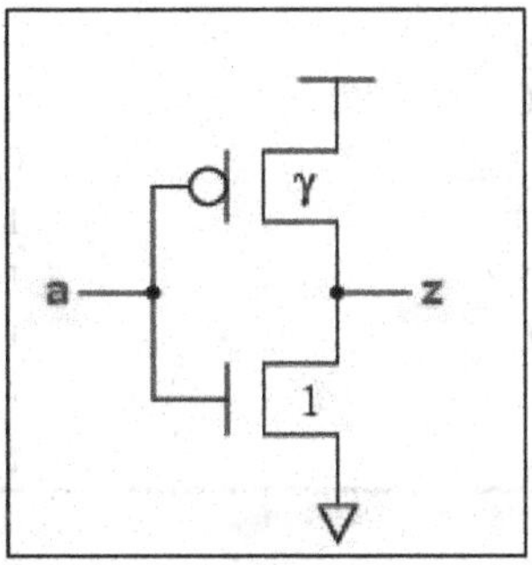

Fig. 1. Inverter for shortest falling delay

For the rising logical effort, the PMOS transistor size is set equal to μ which means that the NMOS transistor must be scaled down to μ/γ. This gives a rising logical effort of:

$$g_u = \frac{(\mu + \mu/\gamma)}{(1+\mu)}$$

(3)

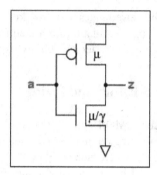

Fig. 2. Inverter for shortest rising delay

The logical effort g is then:

$$g = \frac{1}{2}\frac{(\gamma + 1 + \mu + \mu/\gamma)}{(1+\mu)} \tag{4}$$

In the UMC 90nm, $\gamma = 2$ has been chosen for the inverters because this represents a good compromise between speed and balanced rise and fall drive strengths, and also because it is simple and follows widely used industry practice.

Table 1. Logical Effort For Various Values Of Gamma (γ)

PMOS to NMOS ratio of γ	Logical Effort (g)
1.00	1.0000
1.20	0.9778
1.40	0.9714
1.50	0.9722
2.00	1.0000
2.25	1.0230
2.50	1.0500
3.00	1.1100
3.50	1.1700

2.1   How to Get the Fastest Inverter

The logical effort (g) varies as γ varies, and we can find the minimum value of g by differentiating with respect to γ and setting the differential to zero.

$$g = \frac{1}{2}\frac{(\gamma + 1 + \mu + \mu/\gamma)}{(1+\mu)}$$

$$\frac{dg}{d\gamma} = 1 - \mu/\gamma^2 = 0 \tag{5}$$

$$\gamma = \sqrt{\mu}$$

Thus, if μ=2, then the fastest inverter has γ=1.414 or approx. 1.4, which can be seen in table 1. This truth is further verified by simulations. The value of g here should satisfy the delay constraint to be smallest of its recent neighbors. The simulation results for falling and rising output delays are shown in table 2.

Thus, the value of γ for minimum delay of the inverter is 1.4. Using this the logical effort (g) of the inverter is 0.9714. The result thus obtained is also applied to test the validity to few other static circuits namely, 2-input NAND gate and 2-input NOR gate.

Table 2. Average Delay For Various Value Of Gamma (γ)

γ	Falling delay (ps)	Rising delay (ps)	Average delay (ps)
1.0	7.146	17.68	12.41
1.1	7.981	16.85	12.42
1.2	8.794	16.07	12.43
1.3	9.385	15.52	12.45
1.4	9.984	14.87	12.42
1.5	10.56	14.33	12.45
1.6	11.199	13.92	12.55
1.7	11.651	13.42	12.54
1.8	12.17	13.03	12.59
1.9	12.67	12.61	12.64
2.0	13.15	12.35	12.72

The result thus obtained is also applied to test the validity to few other static circuits. Here we consider only 2-input NAND gate and 2-input NOR gate.

2.2   NAND Gate

In order to calculate the logical effort of a NAND gate, we size the transistors so that their conductance is the same as the single transistors in a reference inverter. The PMOS transistors are in parallel so, this remains unchanged. But the NMOS transistors are in series, and must be increased in size so that they have the same conductance as a single NMOS transistor. We define the amount by which the transistor must be increased as K_N, the NMOS transistor conductivity coefficient.

In Logical Effort, Ohm's law is used so that K_N is 2 for a 2-NAND gate, 3 for a 3-NAND gate and 4 for a 4-NAND gate. The book recognizes that this is a simplification, because velocity saturation of the carriers means that series combinations of NMOS transistors are more conductive than a single one.

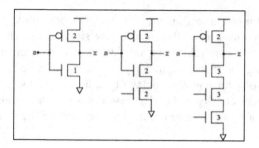

Fig. 3. Nand gates matching unit inverter

In a more general case where the NAND gate can have a PMOS and NMOS transistor ratio of γ; the NMOS and PMOS conductivity of μ; and the value for K_N of the NAND gates need not be equal to the number of series NMOS transistors. A 2-input NAND gate with the equivalent drive of an inverter with PMOS to NMOS ratio of γ : 1 has PMOS to NMOS ratio as γ : K_N. This matches the conductivity of the NMOS transistor of the reference inverter, so that the falling logical effort is given by;

$$g_d = \frac{(K_N + \gamma)}{(1 + \mu)} \tag{6}$$

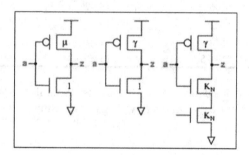

Fig. 4. Nand gates for shortest falling

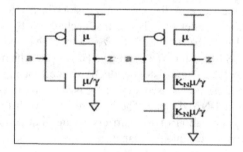

Fig. 5. Nand gate for rising delay

For the rising logical effort, we scale the PMOS transistor to μ and NMOS transistor to $K_N(\mu/\gamma)$, such that;

$$g_u = \frac{(\mu + K_N \mu/\gamma)}{(1+\mu)}$$

(7)

The logical effort g is then:

$$g = \frac{1}{2} \frac{(\gamma + K_N + \mu + (\mu/\gamma)K_N)}{(1+\mu)}$$

(8)

The fastest NAND gate is when

$$\frac{dg}{d\gamma} = 1 - K_N \mu/\gamma^2 = 0$$

(9)

$$\gamma = \sqrt{K_N \mu}$$

(10)

The way of checking the result is consider the value of $\gamma = 1.4$ (as obtained for the inverter) and then verifying the results for a K_N from the delay obtained. The model verified using simulation is shown in the table 3.

Table 3. Average Delay for various values of K_N

K_N	Falling delay (ps)	Rising delay (ps)	Average delay (ps)
1.00	14.27	18.22	16.25
1.17	12.62	19.34	15.98
1.33	11.35	20.33	15.84
1.40	11.01	20.66	15.83
1.50	10.28	21.32	15.80
1.67	9.35	22.24	15.79
1.83	8.56	23.08	15.82
2.00	7.89	23.89	15.89

It is quite evident from table 3 that at $K_N = 1.67 = 5/3$ the average delay is least. This value of K_N when applied to the formula of logical effort gives us the logical-effort of NAND gate which is 1.242.

2.3   NOR Gate

The calculation of the logical effort for NOR gates follows a parallel path to the one used for NAND gates. We size the series PMOS transistors so that their conductance is the same as the single transistors in a reference inverter. We define the amount by which the transistor must be increased as K_P, the PMOS transistor conductivity coefficient.

In Logical Effort, Ohm's law is used so that K_P is 2 for a 2-NOR gate, 3 for a 3-NOR gate and 4 for a 4-NOR gate. It recognizes that this is a simplification, because velocity saturation of the carriers means that series combinations of PMOS transistors are more conductive than a single one. However, the lower speed of holes compared to electrons means that the speed of the holes in a single PMOS transistor is not so subject to velocity saturation effects, so that K_P following Ohm's law is a more accurate approximation than it was for NAND gates.

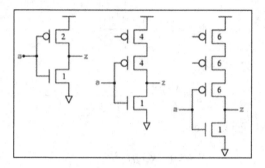

Fig. 6. NOR gate matching unit inverter

Proceeding in a very similar way, the NOR gate can have a PMOS to NMOS transistor ratio of γ; the NMOS to PMOS conductivity is μ; and the value for K_P of the NOR gates need not be equal to the number of series PMOS transistors. A 2-input NOR gate with the equivalent drive of an inverter with PMOS to NMOS is γ:1 has PMOS to NMOS as $K_P \cdot \gamma$:1. This matches the conductivity of the NMOS transistor of the reference inverter. Thus the falling logical effort is;

$$g_d = \frac{(1 + K_P \gamma)}{(1 + \mu)} \tag{11}$$

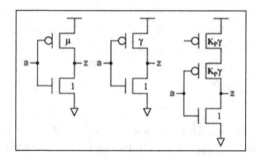

Fig. 7. NOR gate for shortest falling

For the rising logical effort, we scale the PMOS transistor of the equivalent inverter to PMOS equal to μ. The series PMOS transistors of the NOR gate are scaled to $K_P \cdot \mu$. Thus the rising logical effort is;

$$g_u = \frac{(K_P \mu + \mu/\gamma)}{(1 + \mu)} \tag{12}$$

The logical effort g is computed as:

$$g = \frac{1}{2} \frac{(K_P \gamma + 1 + K_P \mu + \mu/\gamma)}{(1 + \mu)} \tag{13}$$

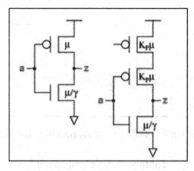

Fig. 8. NOR gate for rising delay

For UMC 90nm, the values used are μ=2, The values for K_P are empirical, and come from an analysis of the logical effort of NOR gates from various standard cell libraries. The fastest NOR gate occurs when;

$$\frac{dg}{d\gamma} = K_P - \mu/\gamma^2 = 0 \tag{14}$$

$$\gamma = \sqrt{\mu/K_P} \tag{15}$$

From simulations a similar result for K_P can be deduced, taking the $\gamma = 1.4$ (as of inverter). The delay values are shown in the table 4.

Table 4. Average Delay for various values of K_P

K_P	Falling delay (ps)	Rising delay (ps)	Average delay (ps)
1.000	12.16	25.96	19.06
1.125	13.09	24.56	18.83
1.250	14.00	23.35	18.68
1.375	14.81	22.27	18.54
1.500	15.55	21.34	18.45
1.625	16.28	20.60	18.44
1.750	16.97	19.89	18.43
1.875	17.65	19.14	18.39
2.000	18.30	18.62	18.46

The value of K_P comes out to be 1.875 (15/8). For this value the logical effort of a 2-input NOR gate is 1.2946.

3   Validation

For validating the above sizing, 5-stage chain of inverters was design at 500MHz using BSIM3 models of UMC90nm CMOS process in Cadence design environment at 1V power supply. Fig. 3 shows a chain of inverters favoring high transition.

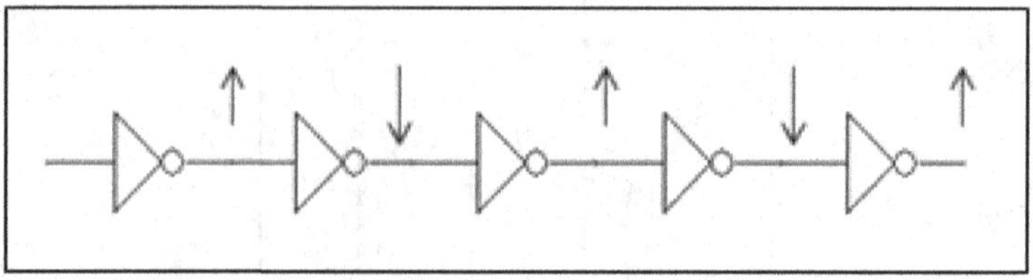

Fig. 9. Chain of inverters favoring high transition

Table 5. Delay Comparison

	Rising Delay (ps)	Falling Delay (ps)	Average Delay (ps)	Percentage Improvement (%)
Normal Skewed	65.90	72.60	69.25	---
High Skewed	86.20	102.80	94.50	-36.46
Low Skewed	61.80	54.90	58.35	15.74
Proposed High Skewed	60.00	63.40	61.70	10.90
Proposed Low Skewed	57.80	53.60	55.70	19.57

To get the better result various simulation were conducted and the results are tabulated in table 5 and table 6. First set consist of normal skewed chain-of-inverter with each inverter having 2:1 PMOS to NMOS width ratio, high skewed and low skewed chain of inverters and proposed high skewed and low skewed chain of inverters. Every path through a network of logic gate will experience alternating rising and falling transition and the results are tabulated in table 5, whereas, second set consist of alternate high and low skewed gates favoring a particular transition and the results are tabulated in table 6. The final output decides whether the transition is falling or rising.

Table 6. Delay Comparison of Favoring Transition

Favoring Transition	Rising Delay (ps)	Falling Delay (ps)	Average Delay (ps)	Percentage Improvement (%)
High	41.30	144.30	92.80	----
Low	135.50	40.70	88.10	----
Proposed High	49.50	89.90	69.70	24.89
Proposed Low	90.40	48.70	69.55	21.06

4 Conclusion

In this report a simple delay characterization using logical effort for inverter have been done using UMC90nm technology. The new logical effort values obtained for basic universal gates gives minimum delay when validated on a chain of inverters compared with the existing logical effort. From table 5, it is quite evident that the proposed skewed gate shows much improvement when compared with existing skewed logic and from table 6, the proposed skewed logic favoring a particular transition shows much improvement over existing skewed logic. Thus, we can conclude that to get minimum delay and reduced area one can use the proposed low skewed gate in designing a logic for minimum delay.

Acknowledgement. The authors are grateful to the lab facilities (Oysters Lab) of Department of Electrical & Electronics Engineering at Birla Institute of Technology & Science (BITS), Pilani where the work has been carried out.

References

1. Sutherland, D.H.I., Sproull, B.: Logical Effort: designing fast CMOS circuits. Morgan Kaufmann (1999)
2. Lasbouygues, B., Engels, S., Wilson, R., Maurine, P., Azémard, N., Auvergne, D.: Logical Effort Model Extension to Propagation Delay Representation. IEEE Transactions on Computer-Aided Design of Integrated Circuits and Systems 25(9) (September 2006)
3. Kabbani, A., Al-Khalili, D., Al-Khalili, A.J.: Delay analysis of CMOS gates using modified logical effort model. IEEE Trans. Comput.-Aided Des. Integr. Circuits Syst. 24(6), 937–947 (2005)
4. Dao, H., Oklobdzija, V.G.: Application of Logical Effort Techniques for Speed Optimization and Analysis of Representative Adders. In: 35th Asilomar Conference on Signals, Systems and Computers, California, vol. 2, pp. 1666–1669 (2001)
5. Raghav, H.S., Maheshwari, S., Gupta, A.: A Comparative Analysis of Power & Delay Optimize Digital Logic Families for High Performance System Design. In: International Conference on Electronic Systems, NIT Rourkela, India, pp. 174–177 (2011)
6. Rabaey, J.M., Chandrakasan, A., Nikolić, B.: Digital Integrated Circuits: A Design Perspective, 2nd edn. Prentice-Hall, New Jersey (2003)

A Dual Material Double-Layer Gate Stack Junctionless Transistor for Enhanced Analog Performance

Ratul Kumar Baruah and Roy P. Paily

Department of Electronics and Electrical Engineering
Indian Institute of Technology Guwahati, India
{r.baruah,roypaily}@iitg.ernet.in

Abstract. In this paper, we present a simulation study of analog circuit performance parameters of a dual material double-layer gate stack (high-k/SiO_2) (DM-DGS) symmetric double-gate junctionless transistor (DGJLT). The characteristics are demonstrated and compared with dual material gate (DMG) DGJLT and single material (conventional) gate (SMG) DGJLT. DMG DGJLT present superior transconductance (G_m), early voltage (V_{EA}) and intrinsic gain ($G_m R_O$) compared to SMG DGJLT. These parameters are further improved for DM-DGS DGJLT and it can be attributed to their better gate control on the channel region.

Keywords: Double-gate junctionless transistor (DGJLT), dual material double-layer gate stack (DM-DGS), intrinsic gain, unity gain frequency, workfunction.

1 Introduction

The nano scale conventional metal-oxide semiconductor field-effect transistors (MOSFETs) impose challenges such as enlarged gate leakage and added serious short channel effects (SCEs), with the continuous miniaturization of device sizes. Multiple gate FETs (Mug-FETs) have better scalability due to its superior controllability of the gates on the channel region. However, very abrupt source and drain junctions requirement put challenges in doping profile techniques and thermal budget. Junctionless transistor (JLT), which does not have pn junction in the source-channel-drain path has better short-channel effects (SCE) performance and therefore better scalability, greatly simplified process flow and low thermal budgets after gate formation [1]-[4]. However, JLTs suffer from lesser drain current and transconductance compared to inversion mode MOSFETs due to high doping concentration in the channel region [1],[5]-[6].

Dual-material gate (DMG) devices offer improved carrier transport efficiency, transconductance and the drain output resistance than conventional MOSFETs [7]-[14]. By adjusting the metal work functions, channel potential and electric field distributions along the channel can be controlled. Razavi *et. al.* have reported that a dual material gate stack, double-gate conventional MOSFET reduces the impact of hot carrier effect and threshold voltage roll-off [8]. Long *et. al.* had experimentally shown that DMG MOSFET offers simultaneous improvement of SCE as well as

M.S. Gaur et al. (Eds.): VDAT 2013, CCIS 382, pp. 118–127, 2013.
© Springer-Verlag Berlin Heidelberg 2013

transconductance [9]. Ghosh *et. al.* have shown by analytical modelling that dual metal gate stack surrounding gate MOSFET shows superior performance than conventional MOSFET [10]. Kasturi *et. al.* have reported that dual material gate silicon on Nothing (SON) MOSFET gives higher early voltage and reduced drain conductance thereby improving analog performance of the device [11]. They have also showed that the analog performance can be improved by dual material double-layer gate stack SON architecture [12]. The performance and stability of a transistor can be further improved using double-stacked active layers with proper material as gate oxide [13]. Low *et.al* reported that a dual material gate nanowire JLT offers improved transconductance and unity gain frequency compared to SMG JLT [7].

Combining the advantages of dual material gate along with double-layer gate stack, we propose a junctionless architecture called DM-DGS DGJLT in this paper. We have studied the analog circuit performance parameters viz. transconductance (G_m), transconductance to drain current ratio (G_m/I_D), early voltage (V_{EA}), output resistance (R_O), intrinsic gain (G_mR_O), and cut-off frequency (f_T) with the help of extensive device simulations.

2   Device Structure and Simulation

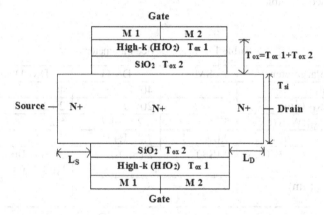

Fig. 1. Crosssectional view of n-type DM-DGS junctionless symmetric double-gate transistor (DGJLT)

The device structure for an n-type symmetric DM-DGS DGJLT is shown in Fig. 1. The operation of DGJLT is explained in [16] and [17]. An n-channel device   have an $N^+ - N^+ - N^+$ structure and uniform doping in the source, channel and drain region. In this work, P+ polysilicon gate is used. A dual material gate (DMG) DGJLT has two metal gates, denoted by M1 and M2, with different workfunction (W), 5.2 eV and 4.7 eV respectively. The first lateral gate is called control gate and the second one, the screening gate. Due to higher workfunction, the threshold voltage of M1, $V_{T(M1)}$ is greater than $V_{T(M2)}$. Single gate material (SMG) has a workfunction of 5.2 eV. Long *et. al.* reported that the relation between threshold voltage (V_T) and workfunction of the two gate materials can be expressed as [9]

$$\Delta V_T = S \ \Delta W \tag{1}$$

S=1 for silicon MOSFET. We define L_{M1} and L_{M2} as channel lengths for metal M1 and M2 respectively; and $L = L_{M1} + L_{M2}$ is the total channel length. The gate length ratio of the two metal gates and their workfunction difference affect the device characterises significantly [7]-[9], [11]-[12]. Recently, Lou *et. al.* have reported that in a DMG JLT, out of different combinations of L_{M1} and L_{M2}; $L_{M1}/ L =1/2$ and work function difference $\delta W = 0.5$ gives overall best characteristics of the device [7]. In this work, $L_{M1}:L_{M2} = 20$ nm: 20 nm is considered for both DM-DGS and DMG DGJLT. For DMG and SMG DGJLT, SiO_2 is used as a gate oxide material having thickness (T_{ox}) of 2 nm. For DM-DGS DGJLT, SiO_2 (oxide thickness = 1 nm) is stacked with high-k gate dielectric material (HfO_2) of equivalent oxide thickness (EOT) of 1 nm. All three devices namely, DM-DGS, DMG and SMG are optimized by adjusting channel doping concentration (N_{ch}) values such that each has a threshold voltage (V_T) of 0.31 V. Threshold voltage is defined as the gate voltage corresponding to constant drain current of 10^{-7} A at a drain voltage of 50 mV. The source and drain extensions $(L_S$ and $L_D)$ are taken as 10 nm. The process and device parameters used in this paper are summarised in Table 1.

Table 1. Process/Device Parameters

Parameter	SMG	DMG	DM-DGS
L (nm)	40	40	40
$L_{M1}:L_{M2}$ (nm)	—	20:20	20:20
$W_{M1}:W_{M2}$ (eV)	5.2 : —	5.2 : 4.7	5.2 : 4.7
N_{ch} (cm^{-3})	9.6 E+18	7.85 E+18	8 E+18
T_{ox} (nm) (EOT)	2 (SiO_2)	2 (SiO_2)	2(SiO_2:1nm, HfO_2:1nm)
T_{si} (nm)	8	8	8

Electrical characteristics for the devices are simulated using 2D ATLAS device simulator [18] with default parameter coefficients. For all simulations, uniform doping concentration throughout the channel and source/drain regions is assumed. The simulations are carried out using two carrier scheme, Fermi-Dirac model without impact ionization, doping concentration-dependent carrier mobility and electric field-dependent carrier model. Band gap narrowing model is included. Shockley-Read-Hall (SRH) recombination/ generation are employed in the simulation to account for leakage currents. The density gradient model is utilized to account for quantum mechanical effects.

3   Simulation Results

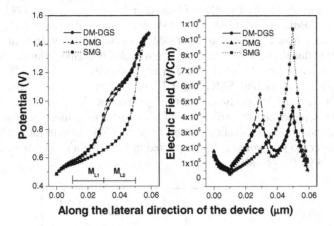

Fig. 2. Potential and Electric field of SMG, DMG, DM-DGS devices along the channel direction near the silicon-oxide interface at $V_{DS} = 1$ V for L =40 nm, T_{si} =8 nm and T_{ox} =2 nm

Fig. 2 shows the potential and electrical field distributions along the channel direction near the silicon-oxide interface for a drain voltage (V_{DS}) = 1 V and gate voltage (V_{GS}) of 1 V. The potential distributions of DMG and DM-DGS DGJLT have abrupt change at the workfunction transition point from W_{M1} to W_{M2}, whereas SMG DGJLT follows a monotonous trend from source to drain. This enhances the electric field of DMG and DM-DGS with two peaks, but for SMG DGJLT there is only one peak near the drain. Out of the three devices mentioned, DM-DGS has lowest peak near the drain, indicating that it suppresses SCE and hot carrier effect more effectively. This is due to better gate control of DM-DGS on the channel region. The electron velocity in the channel can be controlled by tailoring the first peak with proper workfunction of the metal gates [11].

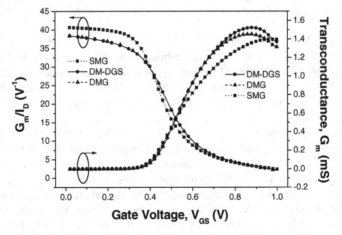

Fig. 3. Transconductance (G_m) and transconductance to drain current ratio (Gm/I_D) with respect to gate voltage for the devices at $V_{DS} = 1$ V for L =40 nm, T_{si} =8 nm and T_{ox} =2 nm

The transconductance, G_m $(=\partial I_D/\partial V_{GS})$ is a figure of merit which indicates how well a device converts a voltage to a current. Below the gate voltage of $V_{GS} \sim 0.55$ V, all three devices have almost similar value of G_m. After $V_{GS} = 0.7$ V, DM-DGS has highest G_m followed by DMG and SMG DGJLT as shown in fig. 3. Due to potential uplift at workfunction transition, G_m is increased for DM-DGS and DMG DGJLT. In JLT, drain current is mainly due the bulk current; and since its value is smaller, transconductance is inferior as compared to conventional inversion mode devices (not shown). The values of G_m for DM-DGS, DMG and SMG DGJLT are 1.52 mS, 1.45 mS and 1.37 mS respectively at $V_{GS}=0.9$ V. Transconductance generation factor is another important figure of merit representing the efficiency of a transistor to convert dc power into ac frequency and gain. It is also called transconductance/drain current ratio (G_m/I_D). The G_m/I_D with respect to gate voltage, V_{GS} is plotted in fig. 3 for a drain voltage, V_{DS} of 1 V. The values of G_m/I_D for SMG,

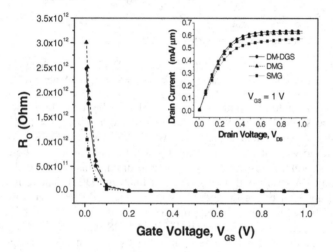

Fig. 4. Output resistance (R_O) with respect to gate voltage at $V_{DS} = 1$ V. Insight is drain current with respect to drain voltage at $V_{GS} = 1$ V for the devices. L =40 nm, T_{si} =8 nm and T_{ox} =2 nm

DMG and DM-DGS DGJLT are 39.92 V^{-1}, 36.94 V^{-1}, 36.82 V^{-1} respectively at $V_{GS}=0.2$ V. A smaller value of subthreshold slope (SS) for SMG implies its higher G_m/I_D value in the subthreshold region. G_m/I_D is mainly controlled by the body factor of the devices in weak inversion regime; however its value decreases in moderate/strong inversion regime due to the lower mobility at higher doping concentration [5].

Insight of Fig. 4 shows the drain current (I_D) with respect to drain voltage for the devices at $V_{GS} = 1$ V. DM-DGS has higher output current, followed by DMG and SMG DGJLT for aforementioned reasons. Fig. 4 also presents the output resistance (R_O) with respect to V_{GS}. DMG architecture offers slightly higher value of R_O in the subthreshold region due to smaller slope in I_D-V_{DS} characteristics as compared to DM-DGS, followed by SMG DGJLT as can be seen from the figure. However, the value of R_O is highest for DM-DGS followed by DMG and SMG DGJLT for gate voltage of ~ 0.5 V or higher. The values of R_O for DM-DGS, DMG and SMG DGJLT are 44.4 kΩ, 29.3 kΩ and 16.5 kΩ respectively at a gate voltage of 1 V.

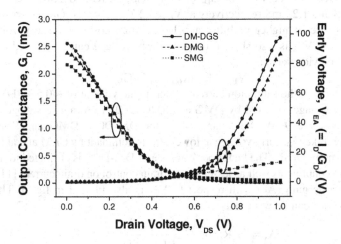

Fig. 5. Output conductance (G_D) and early voltage (V_{EA}) with respect to gate voltage for the devices at $V_{DS} = 1$ V for L =40 nm, T_{si} =8 nm and T_{ox} =2 nm

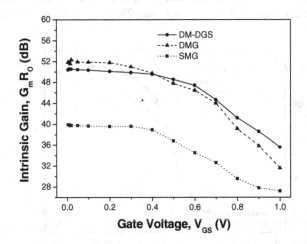

Fig. 6. Intrinsic gain (G_mR_O) with respect to gate voltage for the devices at $V_{DS} = 1$ V for L =40 nm, T_{si} =8 nm and T_{ox} =2 nm

Fig. 5 presents the output conductance G_D ($=\partial I_D/\partial V_{DS}$) variation of the devices with drain voltage, V_{DS} for a fixed value of V_{GS} =1 V. The DM-DGS DGJLT carries higher output current and hence output conductance compared to other two devices. At low V_{DS} (till ~ 0.55 V), output conductance is governed by channel length modulation (CLM) and at higher V_{DS}, it is governed by drain induced barrier lowering (DIBL), if impact ionization is not taken into account [11]. Thus, the curve brings out that DM-DGS architecture has lower values of CLM and DIBL compared to DMG and SMG DGJLT. The value of G_D for DM-DGS, DMG and SMG DGJLT are 1.42 mS, 1.4 mS and 1.25 mS respectively at $V_{GS}=0.2$ V. However, G_D decreases with gate voltage because of higher mobility and hence more collisions. Early voltage (V_{EA}) with respect to V_{GS} is also shown in fig. 5. Early voltage can be derived from output resistance and vice versa as

$$V_{EA} = R_O \, I_{D\,(sat)} \text{ or, } I_D/G_D \qquad (2)$$

Where, $I_{D\,(sat)}$ is the saturation current. After a gate voltage of ~ 0.5 V, DM-DGS has higher early voltage followed by DMG and SMG DGJLT. At a gate voltage of 1 V, the values of V_{EA} are 97 V, 86 V and 14 V for DM-DGS, DMG and SMG DGJLT respectively. Like G_D, early voltage at lower V_{DS} is dominant by CLM and at higher V_{DS}, it is dominant by DIBL. The better performance of DM-DGS is attributed to the superior vertical gate coupling as well as lesser lateral drain control on drain current [11].

The intrinsic gain (A_V) with respect to V_{GS} is also plotted in fig. 5. The intrinsic gain of a device can be written as

$$A_V = G_m R_O \text{ or, } G_m \left(\frac{V_{EA}}{I_{D\,(sat)}} \right) \qquad (3)$$

Dual metal gate devices offer higher A_V in comparison to single metal gate devices because of higher transconductance as well as output resistance for aforementioned reasons. The gain values for DM-DGS, DMG and SMG DGJLT are 50.1dB, 51.8 dB, 39.5 dB at $V_{GS}=0.2$ V; and 35.5 dB, 31.5 dB and 27.2 dB at $V_{GS}=1$ V respectively.

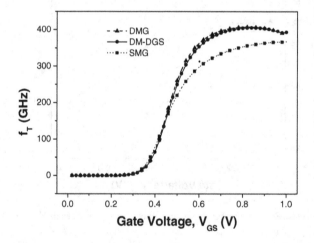

Fig. 7. Cut-off frequency (f_T) with respect to gate voltage for the devices at $V_{DS} = 1$ V for L =40 nm, T_{si} =8 nm and T_{ox} =2 nm

The unity-gain cut-off frequency (f_T) is another figure-of-merit useful for analog applications. It is given by [19]

$$f_T = \frac{G_m}{2\pi(C_{GS}+C_{GD})} \qquad (4)$$

Where, C_{GS} and C_{GD} are gate-to-source and gate-to-drain capacitances respectively. Fig. 7 shows the variation of f_T with V_{GS} for $V_{DS}=1V$. All the capacitances are extracted from the small-signal ac device simulations at a frequency of 1 MHz. At lower V_{GS}, till 0.45 V, the f_T is almost same for all the devices due to almost same values of transconductance.   The DM-DGS and DMG DGJLT posses almost same value of f_T for $V_{GS} > \sim 0.45$ V. However, SMG DGJLT presents lower f_T compared to other two devices at higher gate voltage.

The presented I_D-V_{GS} characteristics for SMG DGJLT are calibrated with Duarte's results [16] as shown in Fig. 8 for $L = 1$ μm, $T_{si} = 10$ nm, $T_{ox} = 7$ nm, $N_{ch} = 1 \times 10^{19}$ cm^{-3}, $L_S = L_D = 10$ nm, $V_{DS} = 50$ mV at room temperature.

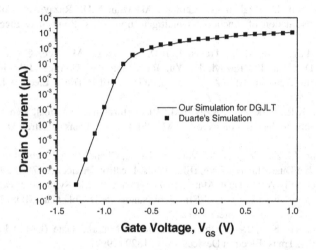

Fig. 8. Calibration of our simulation results for DGJLT with Duarte's simulation. I_D-V_{GS} characteristics at $L = 1$ μm, $T_{si} = 10$ nm, $T_{ox} = 7$ nm, $N_{si} = 1 \times 10^{19}$ cm^{-3}, $L_S/L_D = 10$ nm, $V_{DS} = 50$ mV

4   Conclusion

A dual material double-layer gate stack (DM-DGS) structure was incorporated in symmetric double-gate junctionless transistor (DGJLT), forming DM-DGS DGJLT. The device characteristics for analog applications were investigated and fair comparisons with DMG and SMG DGJLT were performed by setting the threshold voltage same for all the devices. DM-DGS offered superior transconductance, early voltage and intrinsic gain compared to DMG and SMG DGJLT. However, SMG DGJLT has higher G_m/I_D value as compared to the other two devices. Unity gain cut-off frequency was almost similar for DM-DGS and DMG DGJLT architecture at higher gate voltage. Using as germanium as substrate material, the conductivity can further be improved. The ON-state to OFF-state current ratio can be increased by incorporating high-k spacers on DM-DGS structure.

References

1. Colinge, J.P., Lee, C.W., Afzalian, A., Akhavan, N.D., Yan, R., Ferain, I., Razavi, P., O'Neill, B., Blake, A., White, M., Kelleher, A.M., McCarthy, B., Murphy, R.: Nanowire Transistors Without Junctions. Nature Nanotechnology 5, 225–229 (2010)
2. Lee, C.W., Afzalian, A., Akhavan, N.D., Yan, R., Ferain, I., Colinge, J.P.: Junctionless Multigate Field - Effect Transistor. Applied Physics Letters 94, 053 511-1–053 511-2 (2009)
3. Lee, C.W., Afzalian, A., Akhavan, R., Ferain, N.D., Yan, I., Razavi, P.R., Doria, R.T., Colinge, J.P.: Low Subthreshold Slope in Junctionless Multigate Transistor. Applied Physics Letters 96, 102106 (2010)
4. Lee, C.W., Ferain, I., Afzalian, A., Yan, R., Akhavan, N.D., Razavi, P., Colinge, J.P.: Performance estimation of junctionless multigate transistors. Solid-State Electronics 54, 97–103 (2010)
5. Doria, R.T., Pavanello, M.A., Trevisoli, R.D., de Souza, M., Lee, C.W., Ferain, I., Akhavan, N.D., Yan, R., Razavi, P., Yu, R., Kranti, A., Colinge, J.P.: Junctionless Multiple - Gate Transistors for Analog Applications. IEEE Trans. Electron Devices 58, 2511–2519 (2011)
6. Cho, S., Kim, K.R., Park, B.G., Kang, I.M.: RF performance and small signal parameter extraction of junctionless silicon nanowire MOSFET. IEEE Trans. Electron Devices 58(5) (2011)
7. Lou, H., Zhang, L., Zhu, Y., Lin, X., Yang, S., He, J., Chan, M.: A Junctionless Nanowire Transistor with a Dual-Material Gate. IEEE Trans. Electron Devices 59(7), 1829 (2012)
8. Razavi, P., Orouji, A.A.: Dual Material Gate Oxide Stack Symmetric Double Gate MOSFET: Improving Short Channel Effects of Nanoscale Double Gate MOSFET. In: Int. Biennial Baltic Electronics Conference (2008)
9. Long, W., Ou, H., Kuo, J.-M., Chin, K.K.: Dual - Material Gate (DMG) Field Effect Transistor. IEEE Trans. Electron Devices 46(5), 1829 (1999)
10. Ghosh, P., Haldar, S.R., Gupta, S., Gupta, M.: Analytical Modeling and Simulation for Dual Metal Gate Stack Architecture (DMGSA) Cylindrical/Surrounded Gate MOSFET. J. of Semiconductor Technology and Science 12(4) (2012)
11. Kasturi, P., Saxena, M., Gupta, M., Gupta, R.S.: Dual Material Double - Layer Gate Stack SON MOSFET: A Novel Architecture for Enhanced Analog Performance—Part I: Impact of Gate Metal Workfunction Engineering. IEEE Trans. Electron Devices 55(1), 372–381 (2008)
12. Kasturi, P., Saxena, M., Gupta, M., Gupta, R.S.: Dual Material Double-Layer Gate Stack SON MOSFET: A Novel Architecture for Enhanced Analog Performance—Part II: Impact of Gate - Dielectric Material Engineering. IEEE Trans. Electron Devices 55(1), 382–387 (2008)
13. Park, J.C., Lee, H.N.: Improvement of the Performance and Stability of Oxide Semiconductor Thin - Film Transistors Using Double-Stacked Active Layers. IEEE Trans. Electron Devices 33(6), 818–820 (2012)
14. Kumar, M., Chaudhry, A.: Two – dimensional analytical modelling of fully depleted DMG SOI MOSFET and evidence for diminished SCEs. IEEE Trans. Electron Devices 51(4), 569–574 (2004)
15. Chakraborty, S., Mallik, A., Sarkar, C.: Subthreshold performance of dual-material gate CMOS devices and circuits for ultralow power analog/mixed-signal applications. IEEE Trans. Electron Devices 55(3), 827–832 (2008)

16. Duarte, J.P., Choi, S.J., Moon, D.I., Choi, Y.K.: Simple Analytical Bulk Current Model for Long - Channel Double – Gate Junctionless Transistors. IEEE Electron Device Letter 32(6) (2011)
17. Sallese, J.M., Chevillon, N., Lallement, C., Iñiguez, B., Prégaldiny, F.: Charge-Based Modeling of Junctionless Double - Gate Field - Effect Transistors. IEEE Transactions on Electron Devices 58(8) (2011)
18. Atlas User's Manual: Device Simulation Software (2008)
19. Tsividis, Y.: Operation and Modeling of the MOS Transistor, 2nd edn. Oxford Univ. Press, New York (1999)

An Improved g_m/I_D Methodology for Ultra-Low-Power Nano-Scale CMOS OTA Design

Somnath Paul, Abhijit Dana, and Soumya Pandit

Institute of Radio Physics and Electronics, University of Calcutta, Kolkata India
sprpe@caluniv.ac.in

Abstract. This paper presents an improved g_m/I_D methodology for the design of low-power CMOS operational transconductance amplifier (OTA) circuit using nano-scale CMOS technology. This methodology takes into considerations the dependence of the Early voltage parameter with the bias points of a nano-scale MOS transistor. With such considerations, the DC voltage gain of the circuit can be controlled by adjusting the bias points of the transistors and keeping the channel length constant. The advantage of the improved methodology over the traditional methodology has been discussed and illustrated with simulation results.

Keywords: Nano-scale, g_m/I_D, Early Voltage, DIBL, OTA.

1 Introduction

The design of integrated circuits with ultra-low power dissipation is becoming an essential requirement considering the fact that most of the present day applications are battery operated [1]. In addition, with the scaling of transistor dimensions in nano-scale CMOS technology, it is becoming important to design with low supply voltage for better reliability of the integrated circuits. The main drawback associated with the scaling of supply voltage with technology generation is that the threshold voltage of MOS transistors do not scale as such with technology generation. Therefore, the design of nano-scale analog circuits with scaled supply voltage, is although an essential requirement, is extremely challenging. In the design of analog integrated circuits, the step of selecting device sizes and biases is crucial to enhance the final performance, power, and yield of the circuits. The g_m/I_D methodology [2,3] enables the designers to fix currents and transistors widths of CMOS analog circuits so as to meet specifications such as gain-bandwidth while optimizing attributes like low power and small area. The sizing method takes advantage of the transconductance g_m to drain current I_D ratio and makes use of either 'semi-empirical' data or compact models. The traditional g_m/I_D methodology does not explicitly consider the dependence of the Early voltage parameter upon the operating bias points of the transistor [4]. The Early voltage parameter is considered to be constant depending upon the chosen channel length of the transistor. Therefore, the gain specification is tried

M.S. Gaur et al. (Eds.): VDAT 2013, CCIS 382, pp. 128–137, 2013.
© Springer-Verlag Berlin Heidelberg 2013

to be satisfied by biasing the transistors in the weak inversion region and varying the channel length. But this in many cases, increase the area of the circuit.

This paper presents an improved g_m/I_D methodology where the explicit dependence of the Early voltage parameter on the operating bias points is taken into considerations. It has been shown through simulation results that this parameter significantly depends upon the drain bias for nano-scale MOS transistors. This is because of the combined effects of the channel length modulation and drain induced barrier lowering phenomenon. This dependence is utilized to obtain the desired gain, keeping the channel length constant. Thus the total area of the circuit is not unnecessarily increased. The bias voltages of the input transistors are determined automatically rather than to find out through trial and error method as done for the traditional methodology.

2   The Traditional g_m/I_D Methodology

The g_m/I_D based circuit sizing procedure is based on the relation between the ratio of the transconductance over dc current g_m/I_D and the normalized current $I_N = I_D/(W/L)$. The relation between the g_m/I_D parameter with the operating region of the transistor may be written as follows

$$\frac{g_m}{I_D} = \frac{1}{I_D}\frac{\partial I_D}{\partial V_{GS}} = \frac{\partial\left(\ln I_D\right)}{\partial V_{GS}} = \frac{\partial\left\{\ln\left[\frac{I_{DS}}{\left(\frac{W}{L}\right)}\right]\right\}}{\partial V_{GS}} \tag{1}$$

The maximum value of the g_m/I_D ratio is observed to be in the weak inversion region and the value decreases as the operating point moves toward strong inversion when V_{GS} is increased as shown in Fig. 1(a) It may be noted that the relationship between the g_m/I_D ratio and V_{GS} is independent of the transistor sizes. Therefore, this relationship is a unique characteristic for all transistors of the same type (n-channel MOS or p-channel MOS) in a given batch. This is shown in Fig. 1(b). The universal characteristic of the g_m/I_D versus I_N curve (shown in Fig. 2) is used to determine the aspect ratio of a transistor, which is then subsequently used to determine the channel width, assuming a fixed value of the channel length.

For a MOS transistor, the magnitude of the intrinsic voltage gain is given by

$$A_v = g_m r_0 = \left(\frac{g_m}{I_D}\right)(I_D r_0) = \left(\frac{g_m}{I_D}\right)V_A \tag{2}$$

where V_A is referred to as the Early voltage of the transistor. Assuming V_A to be constant for a particular channel length of a transistor, the intrinsic gain is determined by the g_m/I_D ratio. Therefore, the intrinsic gain of a MOS transistor is maximum in the weak inversion region and reduces as the operating point moves towards the strong inversion region. Therefore, an important guideline to get high gain for a MOS transistor, is to bias the transistor in the weak inversion region with as low V_{GS} as possible. Under weak inversion region very small

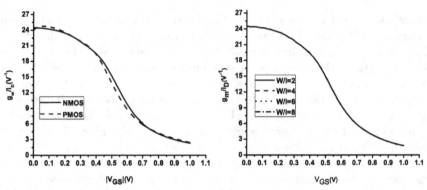

(a) Variation of g_m/I_D for n-channel and (b) Variation of g_m/I_D with different as-
p-channel MOS transistor.   pect ratio.

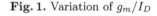

Fig. 1. Variation of g_m/I_D

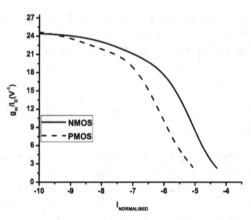

Fig. 2. Variation of g_m/I_D with normalized current

amount of drain current flows, which implies small amount of power dissipation. Therefore, by biasing the MOS transistor in the weak inversion region, it is possible to obtain high gain with very small power dissipation.

2.1   Shortcoming of the Traditional Methodology

An important shortcoming of the traditional g_m/I_D methodology is that it does not explicitly considered the dependence of the Early voltage V_A on the operating bias points (V_{DS}, V_{GS}) of the transistor. The Early voltage is considered to be constant depending upon the channel length. However, for nano-scale MOS transistors, the Early voltage is found to be significantly dependent upon the bias voltages. The intrinsic gain of a MOS transistor is dependent upon the Early voltage, which in turn can be controlled by the operating bias points.

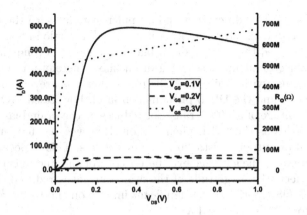

Fig. 3. Variation of drain current and output resistance with drain bias

Therefore, it is possible to control the gain of a MOS transistor within a moderate limit by controlling the bias points keeping the channel length constant.

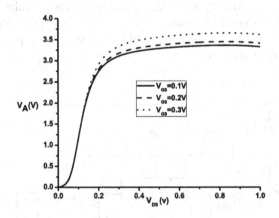

Fig. 4. Variation of Early Voltage with drain bias

3   The Improved g_m/I_D Methodology

This section presents the improved g_m/I_D methodology. The study of the variations of the Early voltage is discussed in the following sub-section, followed the description of the methodology.

3.1 Variations of the Early Voltage with the Operating Bias Points

The variations of the drain current and output resistance with the drain bias of an n-channel MOS transistor operating in the weak inversion region is shown in Fig. 3. It is observed that as the drain bias is increased beyond the saturation value, the drain current increases with drain bias. Therefore, the output resistance values reduce with drain bias. The physical causes are the channel length modulation effect and the DIBL phenomenon [5, 6]. For scaled MOS transistor, the threshold voltage of a MOS transistor reduces as the drain bias is increased. This is referred to as the DIBL phenomenon. However, as the gate bias is increases the fall of output resistance is somewhat less. This is because with the increase of gate bias, the gate achieves better control and due to carrier mobility degradation effect, the magnitude of the drain current is reduced. This physics of the scaled MOS transistor has significant impact on the Early voltage of the MOS transistor which is defined as

$$V_A = \frac{I_D}{\left(\frac{\partial I_D}{\partial V_{DS}}\right)} \tag{3}$$

The variations of the Early voltage with drain bias for different V_{GS} are shown in Fig. 4. It is observed that for scaled MOS transistor, the Early voltage does not remain constant with the operating bias points. Selection of suitable drain voltage is therefore, extremely important. In addition, the magnitude of the Early voltage also depends upon the gate bias to some extent. This characteristics of the Early voltage needs to be incorporated within the design procedure. This is discussed in the next section.

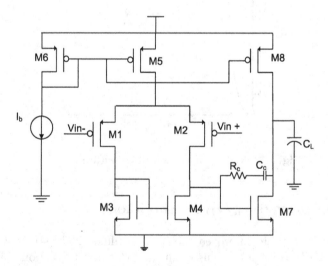

Fig. 5. Two-stage Miller OTA Circuit

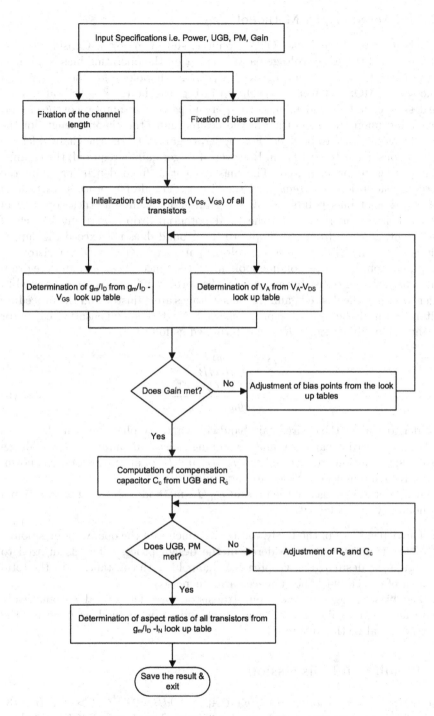

Fig. 6. Flow chart of the improved g_m/I_D methodology

3.2   Improved g_m/I_D Methodology

The chosen two stage Miller OTA circuit is shown in Fig.5. Considering the dependence of the Early voltage parameter V_A on the operating bias conditions of the MOS transistor, the improved g_m/I_D methodology for the design of a nano-scale CMOS OTA circuit is shown in Fig. 6. The input specifications are the desired gain, bandwidth, phase margin and power consumption of the circuit. Depending upon the magnitude of the desired gain, the channel length of the MOS transistors are to be fixed. For moderate gain $\simeq 60dB$, the channel length may be considered to be 100nm. However, if larger gain is required, the channel length needs to be increased. The bias current is fixed depending upon the power consumption requirement of the circuit. The design process starts with initialization of bias points for all the transistors such that these operate in the weak inversion region and the total potential drop across any branch of the circuit, starting from the supply to the ground does not exceed the supply voltage. The g_m/I_D and the Early voltage parameter V_A of each transistor are computed from the corresponding look up tables. Since the g_m/I_D and the drain current I_D of each transistor are known, the corresponding g_ms are computed.In order to satisfy the desired gain, the bias voltages are adjusted and the procedure is iterated until the desired gain is achieved. Next the compensation capacitor C_c and the nulling resistor R_c are determined as follows [7]

$$C_c = \frac{g_{m1}}{2\pi UGB} \tag{4}$$

$$R_c = \frac{1}{g_{m7}} \frac{C_c + C_L}{C_c} \tag{5}$$

In order to achieve the desired gain bandwidth and the phase margin, the values of the compensation capacitor and the nulling resistor are adjusted. Once all the desired specification are met and the g_m/I_D and I_D of all transistors are known, the corresponding aspect ratios are determined.

   The major advantages of the present g_m/I_D methodology over the traditional methodology are as follows

1. The dependence of the Early voltage parameter on the operating bias points of the transistor are considered in the design process. This is utilized to obtain the desired gain, keeping the channel length constant. Thus the total area of the circuit is not unnecessarily increased.
2. The bias voltages of the input transistors are determined automatically rather than to find out through trial and error method as done for the traditional methodology.

4   Results and Discussion

The desired specifications are (1) gain $A_v > 60dB$, (2) $UGB > 45KHz$, (3) $PM > 55^0$ and (4) power dissipation $P < 350nW$. The chosen CMOS technology is 45-nm with supply voltage of 1V. The circuits are simulated with BSIM4 compact model [8] and PTM model parameters [9] under HSPICE simulation environment.

The OTA circuit with the desired specifications is designed with the traditional methodology as well our methodology for comparison purpose. The SPICE simulation results as obtained from the traditional methodology are summarized in Table. 1.

Table 1. Simulation results for design by the traditional methodology L=100nm

Parameters	Specifications	Traditional
A_v	$> 60dB$	41.4dB
UGB	$> 45KHz$	56KHz
PM	$> 55^0$	86^0
CMRR		72dB
ICMR		0.065 V to 0.9 V
PSRR		80.4 dB @ (0.01 to 200)Hz
Slew rate		25V/ms
P	$< 350nW$	299nW

Table 2. Simulation results for design by our methodology in two iterations L=100nm

Parameters	1st iterations	2nd iterations
A_v	56.2dB	61.4dB
UGB	54KHz	50.4KHz
PM	60^0	60^0

Table 3. Simulation results for design by our methodology L=100nm

Parameters	Specifications	Our Method
A_v	$> 60dB$	61.4dB
UGB	$> 45KHz$	50.4KHz
PM	$> 55^0$	60^0
CMRR		67.7dB
ICMR		0.05 V to 1 V
PSRR		84 dB @ (0.01 to 200)Hz
Slew rate		29V/ms
P	$< 350nW$	299nW

It is observed that the desired gain could not be achieved with the traditional methodology considering the channel length to be 100nm. The traditional methodology under this circumstance demands increase of the channel length, which means increase of the consumed area.

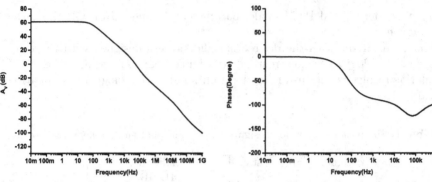

(a) Gain Plot of the design with our methodology..

(b) Phase Plot of the design with our methodology.

Fig. 7. Gain and Phase Plot

The OTA circuit is designed for the same specification and the channel length using the present methodology. The specifications are satisfied with two iterations. For these two iterations, the results are summarized in Table. 2. The AC analysis plots for the design with our methodology are shown in Fig.7(a), 7(b). The final simulation results are tabulated in Table. 3. It is observed that the design with our methodology satisfies all the desired specifications even at the channel length of 100nm.

5   Conclusion

The traditional g_m/I_D methodology does not consider the variations of the Early voltage of the transistor with the operating bias points. The Early voltage is kept constant for a particular channel length. However, in the nano-scale domain, the Early voltage significantly depends upon the drain bias due to the combined effects of channel length modulation and DIBL phenomenon. This has been extensively studied in the present work in the 45-nm CMOS technology. By taking this variation of the Early voltage with the operating bias points, into considerations an improved g_m/I_D methodology has been proposed. The methodology has been demonstrated with a numerical results.

References

1. Magnelli, L., et al.: Design of a 75-nW, 0.5V subthreshold complementary metal-oxide-semiconductor operational amplifier. Int. Journal Circuit Theory and Applications (2013)
2. Silveira, F., Flandre, D., Jesper, P.: A g_m/I_D-based Methodology for the Design of CMOS Analog Circuits and its Application to the Synthesis of a Silicon-on-Insulator. IEEE Journal Solid State Circuits 31, 1314–1319 (1996)

3. Cortes, F., Fabris, E., Bampi, S.: Analysis and design of comparators in CMOS 0.35 μm technology. Microelectronics Reliability 44, 657–664 (2004)
4. Ferreira, L., Pimenta, T., Moreno, R.: An ultra-low voltage ultra-low power CMOS Miller OTA with rail-to-rail input/output swing. IEEE Trans. Circuits and Systems-II 45, 843–847 (2007)
5. Taur, Y., Ning, T.: Fundamentals of Modern VLSI Devices. Cambridge Univ. Press (1998)
6. Tsividis, Y., McAndrew, C.: Operation and Modeling of The MOS Transistor, 2nd edn. Oxford University Press (2010)
7. Allen, P., Holberg, D.: CMOS Analog Circuit Design. Oxford University Press (2004)
8. Dunga, M., et al.: BSIM 4.6.0 MOSFET Model-User's Manual. Department of Electrical Engineering and Computer Sciences, University of California, Berkeley (2006)
9. Zhao, W., Cao, Y.: New Generation of Predictive Technology Model for Sub-45 nm Early Design Exploration. IEEE Transactions Electron Devices 53, 2816–2823 (2006)

An Efficient RF Energy Harvester
with Tuned Matching Circuit

Sachin Agrawal, Sunil Pandey, Jawar Singh, and P.N. Kondekar

PDPM-Indian Institute of Information Technology,
Design and Manufacturing Dumna, Khamaria P.O., Jabalpur, India-482005
{sachin.agrawal,sunilpandey,jawar,pnkondekar}@iiitdmj.ac.in

Abstract. Microstrip line with π matching circuits are very attractive because of high output power and good impedance matching which makes it an alternative over earlier matching circuit. This paper presents an RF energy harvester with microstrip line in series with tuned π-matching circuit that enables efficient power conversion at different RF input power under different load conditions. Matching circuit parameters were optimized for better efficiency. We have focused for specific input power range -15 to 10dBm for 3-stage, 5-stage and 7-stage of energy harvesting circuit. Optimum efficiency of approximately 80% is achieved at input power 0 to 10dBm for higher stages. Effect of load variation also shows that better efficiency is achieved for input power -10 to 10dBm for 3-stage, 5-stage and 7-stage of the harvesting circuit.

1 Introduction

In recent years use of wireless battery operated devices are increasing in broadcast and communication system. These devices continuously provide availability of free RF energy. The device like mobile phone, FM transmitter, AM and Wi-Fi operates at different frequency. The frequency spectra of these devices have different characteristics that depends on environmental conditions and surrounding locations for instance, humidity of the location. Energy harvesting circuits may be an atterative solution to provide sufficient voltage for driving low power electronic circuits, which requires power in microwatts or milliwatts[1]. Energy harvesting is a process of extracting ambient energy available from the environment converting them into usable electrical energy.

Some related work has been done on solar energy harvesting since it has the highest energy density among other choices. However, it has a drawback of being able to operate only when sunlight is present. Wireless battery charging system as discussed in[2], shows the concept of charging a cellular phone battery, using monopole antenna that gives 50% efficiency for commercial product. Main motivation behind this work is the demand for self powered devices is increasing day by day and it become an attractive choice for remotely deployed low voltage battery wireless sensors.

This paper focuses on improving the efficiency of RF energy harvester that uses Wi-Fi and mobile signal because the maximum power intensity lies within

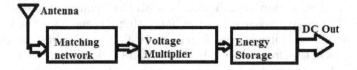

Fig. 1. Block Diagram of Energy harvesting circuit

the GSM bandwidth (890-915MHz and 935-960MHz), these signals carry maximum power but only a small amount can be harvested due to heat dissipation or absorption by other materials, so multiple stages of voltage multiplier are required to reach at appropriate level that can charge the wireless devices. Fig.1 shows the block diagram of a typical RF energy harvester circuit. The matching network composed of inductive and capacitive elements, ensures the maximum power delivery from antenna to voltage multiplier. The received RF power is converted into dc power by the voltage multiplier. The energy storage ensures smooth power delivery to the load, and as a reservoir for durations when external energy is unavailable[3].

Smaller number of the multiplier stages will make certain immediate charging of the capacitor, so the result is a small amount of the voltage generated that may be inadequate to operate sensor mote besides increasing the number of voltage multiplier stages, a slight change in the matching circuit parameter alters drastically the frequency range in which the efficiency of the energy conversion is maximum often by several MHz[3]. Hence, to design RF energy harvester involves a very essential part to choose the parameter of the circuit.

2 Design Methodology of Energy Harvesting Circuit

The incident RF energy need to be converted into usable dc power require an antenna with high directivity to receive more incident RF energy because the gain of the antenna is directly proportional to its directivity[11], a matching circuit to match the load impedance with the antenna impedance and rectifier circuit to develop the required voltage at the output, for this many approaches have been reported in the literature[4],[5],[6] and [7].

But according to Friis transmission equation[8]:

$$P_r = \frac{P_t G_t G_r \lambda^2}{(4\pi R)^2} \tag{1}$$

where
P_r = Received power
P_t = Transmitted power
G_t = Gain of the transmitted antenna
G_r = Gain of the receiver antenna
R = Distance between the transmitter and receiver antennas
λ = wavelength of the transmitted signal.

The received signal strength diminishes with the square of the distance and frequency. The main challenge faced in harvesting RF energy is the free-space path loss of the transmitted signal with distance[3], it requires special sensitivity considerations in the circuit design. In this section We describe a new circuit that is capable of harvesting energy with high efficiency. Beginning with the selection of the circuit components, we choose the Dickson topology as shown in Fig.2, in this configuration parallel capacitors in each stage reduces the circuit impedance and hence, makes the matching task simpler[3]. In the following, we describe the design strategies for efficient RF energy harvesting circuit and its performance.

2.1   Selection of Matching Circuit

One of the crucial requirement of energy harvesting circuit is to transfer the total received power from antenna to the rectifier circuit. This can be done by proper selection of matching circuit and its components parameters, due to non-linear dependence of the rectifier impedance on the frequency and power, broadband impedance matching network is essential for maximum power transfer. If RF circuit is not matched we get reflected power, this reflected power builds standing waves on the transmission line between the source and load. Depending on the phase between the forward and reflected waves can either subtract or add. Because of that on the line we can get places where the voltage is the sum of both voltages or eventually places where the voltage equals zero (maximum current). If the standing wave is positioned in such a way on the transmission line so that the maximum voltage or current is applied to the circuit, they can be destroyed. There are various type of matching topologies are available such as resistive matching network that include only one resistor, here matching will be achieved but it is not a desirable solution because in resistive matching most of the power will be lost in the resistor. Another topology is transformer matching, it converts source power from one voltage and current level to another voltage and current level. Disadvantage of transformer matching is that it can match only the real part of the impedance, if there is a large amount of reactance in the load, a transformer will not eliminate these reactive components. Transformers however, works poorly at microwave frequencies. The L type matching network

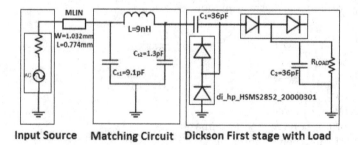

Fig. 2. Equivalent circuit of 1st stage harvester circuit

consists of series capacitor with shunt inductor or series inductor with shunt capacitor. The bandwidth obtained by a single L-C network is not sufficient, however it can be increased by adding another section that forms π matching network. Advantage of the π networks is that by using an extra element there is an extra degree of freedom to control the value of quality factor in addition to perform impedance matching.

2.2 Selection of Diodes

As the peak voltage of the ac signal obtained from the antenna is generally much smaller than the diode forward voltage drop[9]. So here is requirement to select the diode with very low turn on voltage. Since RF energy harvesting is done in GSM range, therefore the diode with very fast switching speed is required, schottky diode have metal semiconductor junction in which metal side acts as the anode and n-type semiconductor acts as the cathode of the diode, which fulfills the requirement of very fast switching and low forward voltage drop. Because of its low forward voltage drop, less energy dissipation makes it most efficient choice for applications sensitive to efficiency. In this paper, we use schottky diode HSMS-2852 from Avago Technologies that has the turn on voltage 150 mV, as the edges of the schottky contact are fairly sharp, high electric field gradient occurs around them which limits the reverse breakdown voltage, low forward voltage and fast recovery time leads to increased efficiency. Moreover saturation current is another parameter that affects the efficiency of diode, so for obtaining high efficiency it is desirable to have diodes with high saturation current, low junction capacitance, and low equivalent series resistance (ESR)[3].

2.3 Selection of Voltage Multiplier Stages

The number of multiplier stages has a major influence on the output voltage of the energy harvesting circuit. Since only one or two stages are not sufficient to provide a fix amount of voltage that is capable to operate a wireless device, so we have to increase the number of stages. The efficiency, output voltage and output power are directly proportional to the number of stages, which is shown in Fig. 3, 4 and 5. For example from Fig.3 it can be seen that when the voltage multiplier stage is 1 the maximum efficiency is around 50%. As we going to increases the voltage multiplier stages from 1 to 7, it increases gradually. In Fig.4 V_1, V_3, V_5 and V_7 are the output voltages of 1-stage, 3-stage, 5-stage and 7-stage respectively with different values that shows the effect of number of stages. Fig.3 shows the another effect that, as we increases the order of stages the peak of efficiency is shifted toward the higher input power region.

2.4 Selection of Load Impedance

Every electronic device has a standard condition to operate for a specific range of load impedance, below and above this particular range the device performance

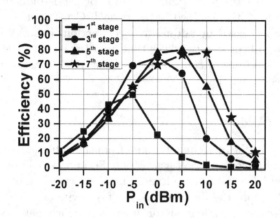

Fig. 3. Effect of number of stages on the efficiency of harvester circuit

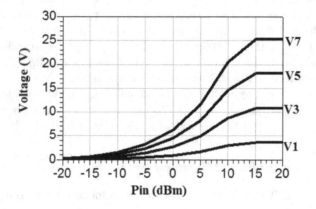

Fig. 4. Effect of number of stages on the output voltage of harvester circuit

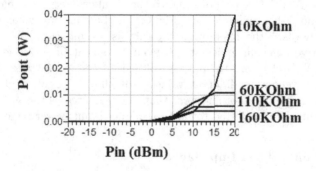

Fig. 5. Effect of load impedance variation on the output power of harvester circuit

is going to degrade. Energy harvesting circuits also have some specific range of load impedance that varied according to the number of stages, types of nonlinear device, and the choice of reactive component, therefore it is important to verify the selection of load impedance range and its impact on the circuit performance.

3   Simulation Results, Analysis and Discussion

Our aim is to calculate the steady state solution of nonlinear circuit or measurement of the various frequencies present in the system, so we use the harmonic balanced analysis (a frequency domain method). The another method so called transient analysis (time domain) is not used due to the reason that it must collect sufficient samples for the highest frequency component and it involves significant memory and processing requirement.

For simulation the values of inductor L, tuned capacitors C_{t1}, C_{t2} and stages capacitor are 31nH, 5.81pF, 0.66pF and 36pF repsectively. Width and length of microstrip transmission line is 1.032mm and 0.774mm respectively, here all simulations are performed at 915MHz.

We simulate the effect of load impedance on the output power and efficiency of the circuit with input power sweep -20 to 20dBm and load impedance sweep value 10-160kOhm for RF input power. Fig.5, 6, 7 and 8 shows the effects of load impedance. We examine that the circuit attains the highest efficiency at some particular load impedance. From Fig.6, 7 and 8 it is clear that the circuit gives highest efficiency in case of 60kOhm, it reduces drastically if the load value is too low or too high. In[10], for 0dBm input power at 950 MHz an efficient Periodic Steady State(PSS)-based power matching circuit gives 55.2% efficiency for RF to DC converter system. In[3], harvester circuit provides the highest efficiency 71%, the proposed circuit gives the maximum efficiency nearly equal to 80% for 3-stage, 5-stage and 7-stage which is shown in Fig.3. From Fig.6, 7 and 8 it is

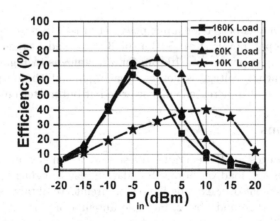

Fig. 6. Effect of load impedance on the efficiency of 3rd stage of harvester circuit

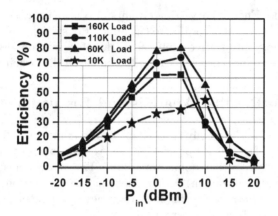

Fig. 7. Effect of load impedance on the efficiency of 5th stage of harvester circuit

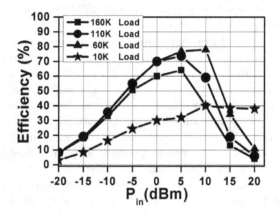

Fig. 8. Effect of load impedance on the efficiency of 7th stage of harvester circuit

shown that efficiency is better for input power -10 to 10dBm over[3]. Optimum efficiency is for input power -5 to 5dBm for 3-stage and 5-stage as shown in Fig.6, 7 and for input power 0 to 10dBm for 7th stage as in Fig.8. From Fig.4 it is clear that output voltage is nearly equal to[3], but the output power is increasing over[3] due to increased current arised at output terminal.

4   Conclusions

This paper introduces an RF energy harvester with tuned π-matching circuit for different stages and load variations. Simulation result of efficiency and power shows the improvement over existing harvester circuit. To obtain more improvement in output voltage and power, multiple antenna or array of antenna can be used but it will increase the size or cost of the circuit so for future work a feedback circuit can be proposed that will improve the power and efficiency.

References

1. Wright, M.: Harvesters gather energy from the ether, power lightweight systems. EDN (December 2006), http://edn.com/article/CA6399099
2. Harrist, D.W.: Wireless battery charging system using radio frequency energy harvesting, M.S. thesis, Univ. Pittsburgh, Pittsburgh, PA (2004)
3. Nintanavongsa, P., Muncuk, U., Lewis, D.R., Chowdhury, K.R.: Design Optimization and Implementation for RF Energy Harvesting Circuits. IEEE Journal on Emerging and Selected Topics in Circuits and Systems 2(1), 24–33 (2012)
4. Arrawatia, M., et al.: RF Energy Harvesting System at 2.67 and 5.8GHz. In: APMC 2010 (December 2010)
5. Barnett, R., et al.: Design of multistage rectifiers with low-cost impedance matching for passive RFID tags. In: 2006 IEEE RFIC Symp. (June 2006)
6. Wilas, J., et al.: Power harvester design for semi-passive UHF RFID Tag using a tunable impedance transformation. In: 9th Int. Symp. on Comm. and Info. Tech., ISCIT 2009 (September 2009)
7. Mazzilli, F., et al.: Design methodology and comparison of rectifiers for UHF-band RFIDs. In: 2010 IEEE RFIC Symp. (May 2010)
8. Pozar, D.M.: Microwave Engineering, 3rd edn. Wiley
9. Yan, H., Montero, J.G.M., Akhnoukh, A., de Vreede, L.C.N., Burghart, J.N.: An integration scheme for RF power harvesting. Presented at the 8th Annu. Workshop Semiconductor Advances Future Electron. Sensors, Veldhoven, The Netherlands (2005)
10. Arrawatia, M., Diddi, V., Kochar, H., Baghini, M.S., Kumar, G.: An integrated CMOS RF energy harvester with di erential microstrip antenna and on-chip charger. In: Proceedings of the IEEE International Conference on VLSI Design, Sister Conferences of DAC, Hyderabad, India (2012)
11. Balanis, C.A.: Antenna Theory: Analysis and Design, 3rd edn. John Wiley & Sons, Hoboken (2005)

A Modified Gate Replacement Algorithm for Leakage Reduction Using Dual-T_{ox} in CMOS VLSI Circuits

Surabhi Singh, Brajesh Kumar Kaushik, and Sudeb Dasgupta

Microelectronics and VLSI Group, Department of Electronics and Communication Engg.
Indian Institute of Technology Roorkee, Roorkee – 247667, India
surbhi_singh_1986@yahoo.com, {bkk23fec,sudebfec}@iitr.ernet.in

Abstract. This research paper presents different leakage mechanisms including the subthreshold and gate leakage current that occurs due to the aggressive scaling in nanoscale CMOS VLSI circuits. A novel algorithm is proposed based on the conventional gate replacement technique that is used to reduce the leakage current in CMOS VLSI circuits. This technique employs the stacking effect using dual-T_{ox} transistors. This approach is more effective for lower technology nodes wherein the gate leakage dominates the subthreshold leakage. The stacking effect, used with dual-T_{ox} transistors, efficiently reduces the gate and subthreshold leakage in both the standby and active mode. Apart from this, leakage current can be further reduced using the pin reordering technique. Using these techniques, the modified gate replacement algorithm is applied for technology nodes below 65nm that reduces the overall leakage current by 39.9% in standby mode.

Keywords: Leakage current, benchmark circuits, gate replacement, subthreshold leakage, gate leakage, dual-T_{ox}, VLSI.

1 Introduction

For the last few decades, CMOS devices have been scaled down to achieve higher packing density and improved performance. In order to maintain the power consumption under control, supply voltage (V_{dd}) of CMOS devices is scaled down. However, threshold voltage (V_{th}) has to be commensurately scaled to maintain a high drive current and to achieve an improved performance [1]. The reduced V_{th} results in substantial increment of leakage current of a CMOS VLSI circuit. Consequently, in order to keep the driving capability of gate at considerable level, it is desirable to reduce the gate oxide thickness (T_{ox}) that results in gate tunneling leakage. Therefore, gate and subthreshold leakage currents have significant contributions in power dissipation at nanoscale VLSI circuits [1, 2].

In nanometer regime, the leakage current is primarily dominated by the subthreshold, gate and reverse-biased *pn* junction leakage current [2]. In addition to these three major leakage components, gate-induced drain leakage, punch-through current and gate leakage due to hot-carrier injection also degrades the device performance with a negligible effect in current technology nodes [3].

M.S. Gaur et al. (Eds.): VDAT 2013, CCIS 382, pp. 146–152, 2013.
© Springer-Verlag Berlin Heidelberg 2013

Subthreshold leakage occurs due to the weak inversion region created between the drain and source terminals when the gate voltage is lower in comparison to the V_{th}. Gate leakage is the adverse effect of aggressive scaling of the oxide thickness that gives rise to higher electric fields. The high electric fields results in tunneling of electrons (or holes) from the substrate to gate through the gate oxide potential barrier. On the other hand, the reverse biased *pn* junction leakage can be referred as a continuum effect of higher electric fields across reverse-biased *pn* junction. It causes the tunneling of electrons from valence band of *p* region to the conduction band of *n* region. This leakage is negligible compared to the subthreshold and gate oxide leakages [2-6] for the technology nodes considered throughout the research paper.

This research paper primarily focuses on the reduction of leakage current by applying the gate replacement technique that uses dual-T_{ox} transistors. A novel algorithm is proposed using the modified technique that replaces the gates having higher leakage currents with the gates incorporating an extra sleep signal along with the dual-T_{ox} transistors [7]. Using this extra signal, it is observed that the functionality of the VLSI circuit is maintained in the active mode while the leakage is reduced both in the standby and active mode. Furthermore, pin reordering is applied that exhibits an inexpensive approach for leakage reduction [8, 9]. The organization of this paper is as follows: Section 1 introduces the briefs about the novel approach of leakage reduction mechanisms. The mechanisms of leakage reduction using conventional [5] and modified gate replacement techniques along with the dual-T_{ox} transistors are presented in section 2. Section 3 analyzes the HSPICE simulated results for different benchmark circuits at 45nm technology node. Finally, section 4 draws a brief summary of this paper.

2   Leakage Reduction Techniques

This section provides a detailed description of leakage reduction by using the gate replacement method. A logic gate can be considered at its worst leakage state (WLS) when its input state yields highest leakage current [5, 10, 11]. Using the gate replacement, a modified gate replacement technique is presented to reduce the leakages. This modified technique follows the conventional gate replacement mechanism using the stacking effect along with dual-T_{ox} transistors.

2.1   Basic Gate Replacement Technique

Using basic gate replacement technique, the logic gate at WLS is replaced by another gate containing an extra sleep signal. When the circuit is in active mode *i.e.* *SLEEP* = 1, this condition exhibits the correct functionality of the circuit. On the other hand, when the circuit is in standby mode, *i.e.*, *SLEEP* = 0, this condition reduces the leakage current of the replaced gate. This process may change the output of the replaced gate. This replacement technique may affect the leakage of other gates too, which are again considered for replacement [5].

2.2   Modified Gate Replacement Technique for Dual-T_{ox} Circuits

The conventional gate replacement technique [5] efficiently reduces the subthreshold leakage without considerable reduction in gate leakage. Theoretically, the probability of electron tunneling can be referred as a strong function of the oxide thickness (T_{ox}). Therefore, a small change in T_{ox} can have a tremendous impact on gate leakage. Using this concept, the transistors with higher gate leakage can be replaced by the transistors with higher T_{ox} values [7]. The different quantitative values of T_{ox} limits the application of this approach, thus, it is required to find a most appropriate value of T_{ox} that will effectively reduce the gate leakage with lesser delay penalty.

Input: $\{G_1, G_2, \ldots G_{n-1}, G_n\}$: gates in a circuit arranged in topological order

Output: a circuit of the same functionality in active mode along with lower leakage in standby

Modified gate replacement algorithm

```
1.   for each gate Gᵢ ∈ { Gₙ, Gₙ₋₁, Gₙ₋₂,………G₂,G₁}
2.      if (Gᵢ is at WLS and not marked )
3.         replace Gᵢ temporarily
4.            if (Total leakage reduces)
5.               Apply pin reordering
6.                  if (Total leakage reduces)
7.                     Make the changes permanent and move to next gate Gᵢ₊₁ at WLS
8.                  else go to next step
9.            else for each gate Gⱼ ∈ { Gᵢ₋₁, Gᵢ₋₂, Gᵢ₋₃,………Gₙ₋₁,Gₙ}
10.              if (Gⱼ is at WLS and not marked yet )
11.                 replace Gⱼ temporarily
12.                    if (Total leakage reduces)
13.                       Apply pin reordering
14.                          if (Total leakage reduces)
15.                             Make the changes permanent and move to next gate Gⱼ₊₁ at WLS
16.                          else go to next step
17.                    else mark and move to next gate in Gₘ till all gates in Gₘ are marked
18.              else move to next gate in Gₘ until all gates in Gₘ are marked
19.      else move to next gate in Gᵢ until all gates in Gᵢ are marked
```

Fig. 1. Pseudo code of the modified gate replacement algorithm

The increasing T_{ox} reduces the gate leakage while the overall propagation delay of the CMOS circuitry increases. One of the exciting solution to reduce the delay penalty is to increase the width of the transistor. Using this approach, a modified gate replacement technique can be applied after choosing some optimum value of T_{ox} on basis of the leakage and delay trade off. For an instance, the stacking effect of NMOS transistor in off state produces lower subthreshold leakage for a two-input NAND gate, whereas the PMOS transistors produces higher gate leakage if all the inputs are at higher potential. For this purpose, a 2-input NAND gate can be replaced using a

3-input NAND gate that substantially reduces the subthreshold leakage without considerable reduction in gate leakage. Therefore, it can be preferred to replace the PMOS transistors having lower T_{ox} by using the PMOS transistors having higher T_{ox}. It reduces the gate leakage as well as the subthreshold leakage of a two-input NAND gate. Apart from this, pin reordering is also referred as an effective technique for leakage reduction that can be applied after each replacement of gate.

The conventional mechanism [5] has used the technique to replace a gate at WLS in topological order. Using this approach, the outputs of the replaced gates have been changed that affects the leakages of fan out gates which are again considered for replacement. While moving towards the lower technology nodes, the gate leakage substantially dominates the subthreshold leakage that affects the fan in gates. Therefore, it is required to consider the leakage of fan out as well as fan in gates for replacement. Thus, using the modified algorithm as depicted in Fig. 1, the replacement has to be done for the gates from output towards the input by considering the effect of leakage on fan in gates.

3   Analysis of Leakage Currents

Using the above mentioned gate replacement algorithm, this section analyzes the reduction in leakage currents for different oxide thickness (T_{ox}), transistor widths (w) and benchmark circuits.

3.1   Analysis of Leakage Current for Different Oxide Thickness

The gate oxide leakage is primarily referred as a strong function of gate oxide thickness. Therefore, the variation of oxide thickness results in tremendous impact on the gate leakage current. The higher oxide thickness in noncritical paths reduces the gate leakage along with the subthreshold leakage while the lower oxide thickness in critical paths maintains the performance of the circuit. The variation of normalized leakage and delay for different oxide thickness is shown in Fig. 2(a). To reduce the complexity of the approach, an appropriate value of T_{ox} is selected among the set of values presented in Table 1. From these values, it is observed that the leakage current reduces with a slight delay penalty. For analysis, the value of T_{ox} for a PMOS transistor is selected as 2nm. To overcome delay penalty, width of the PMOS transistor is varied in the range of 135nm to 140nm for a fixed value of $T_{ox} = 2$nm. Figure 2(b) exhibits the normalized leakage and delay for different widths of PMOS transistors. Using the data presented in Table 2, the suitable value of the width for a PMOS transistor can be selected as 137nm. This quantitative value significantly reduces the delay with a negligible effect on the leakage of the circuit as presented in Fig. 2(b).

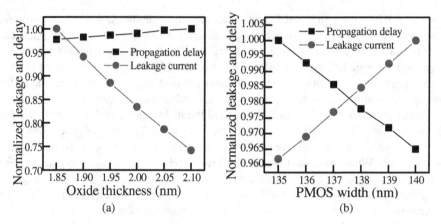

Fig. 2. Variation of propagation delay and leakage current with (a) oxide thickness and (b) width of PMOS transistor

Table 1. Variation of leakage current and propagation delay for different T_{ox} of a PMOS transistor

T_{ox} variation (nm)	Leakage current (nA)	Propagation delay (ns)
1.85	8.582	0.0987
1.90	8.069	0.0991
1.95	7.594	0.0996
2.00	7.156	0.1001
2.05	6.748	0.1007
2.10	6.370	0.1014

Table 2. Variation in leakage current and propagation delay for different widths of PMOS transistor at T_{ox} = 2nm

Width of PMOS transistor (nm)	Leakage current (nA)	Propagation delay (ns)
135	7.1557	0.1001
136	7.2129	0.0994
137	7.2702	0.0987
138	7.3275	0.0980
139	7.3847	0.0978
140	7.442	0.0967

3.2   Analysis of Leakage Current for Gate Replacement Using Dual-T_{ox} Transistors

Once the value of T_{ox} has been chosen, the modified gate replacement algorithm is applied wherein the gates can be replaced with another gate. This replaced gate incorporates an extra sleep signal along with PMOS transistors with higher value of T_{ox}. As presented in Table 3, while the variation of T_{ox} is applied to a circuit, it will not reduce the leakage of the circuit for all input states. Thus, the modified gate replacement approach can be applied wherein a two input NAND gate is replaced with three input NAND gates having higher value of T_{ox} for PMOS transistors. It is observed that when the sleep signal is low, circuit is in the standby mode. Using this mode, a drastic reduction in leakage current is observed along with the functionality of the circuit that is maintained in active mode without significant increase in leakage current.

Table 3. Leakage current for different input states for a two input NAND gate using T_{ox} variation and stacking effect along with dual-T_{ox} transistors

Input states	Initial Leakage(nA)	Leakage using T_{ox} variation(nA)	Leakage using stacking along with dual-T_{ox} transistors (nA)	
			Sleep=0	Sleep=1
00	0.786	0.772	0.929	1.104
01	13.262	13.255	0.717	12.391
10	4.850	4.843	0.690	7.432
11	17.161	14.309	6.502	17.052

3.3   Analysis of Leakage Current for Benchmark Circuits

This sub section analyzes the minimum leakage finding technique by using the modified gate replacement along with dual-T_{ox} PMOS transistors. Different benchmark circuits of ISCAS and ITC'99 [12, 13] series are used to find the minimum leakage current. It is observed that the overall leakage of the benchmark circuits is reduced by 39.9% in standby mode as presented in Table 4 and Fig. 3.

Table 4. Leakage reduction using modified replacement technique for benchmark circuits

Benchmark circuits	Initial leakage (nA)	Final leakage (nA)	% reduction
C17	61.407	31.604	48.5
B01	606.140	407.66	32.7
B02	439.828	271.20	38.3
B06	902.301	540.77	40.1

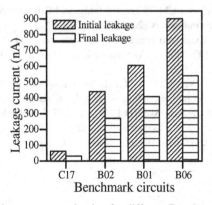

Fig. 3. Leakage current reduction for different Benchmark Circuits

4   Conclusion

This research paper introduces a modified gate replacement algorithm that uses the concept of dual-T_{ox} transistors. Using this approach, the normalized delay and leakage current is analyzed for varying T_{ox} and width of a PMOS transistor. Moreover, the approach is applied to different ISCAS and ITC'99 benchmark circuits that exhibit an overall reduction in leakage current by 39.9% as compared to the initial leakage.

References

1. Singh, S., Kaur, B., Kaushik, B.K., Dasgupta, S.: Leakage Current Reduction using Modified Gate Replacement Technique for CMOS VLSI Circuit. In: Proc. IEEE CODIS 2012, Kolkata, pp. 464–467 (2012)
2. Roy, K., Mukhopadhyay, S., Mahmoodi-Meimand, H.: Leakage current mechanisms and leakage reduction techniques in deep-sub micrometer CMOS circuits. Proc. of IEEE 91, 305–327 (2003)
3. Mukhopadhyay, S., Roy, K.: Accurate Modeling of Transistor Stacks to Effectively Reduce Total Standby Leakage in Nano-Scale CMOS Circuits. In: IEEE Int. Symp. VLSI Circuit Digest, pp. 53–56 (2003)
4. Abdollahi, A., Fallah, F., Pedram, M.: Leakage current reduction in CMOS VLSI circuits by input vector control. IEEE Trans. Very Large Scale Integration Systems (VLSI) 12, 140–154 (2004)
5. Yuan, L., Qu, G.: A Combined Gate Replacement and Input Vector Control Approach for Leakage Current Reduction. IEEE Trans. Very Large Integration (VLSI) Systems 14, 173–182 (2006)
6. Jayakumar, N., Khatri, S.P.: A Simultaneous Input Vector Control and Circuit Modification Technique to Reduce Leakage with Zero Delay Penalty. ACM Transactions on Design Automation of Electronic Systems (TODAES) 16, 9:1–9:20 (2010)
7. Sultania, A.K., Sylvester, D., Sapatnekar, S.S.: Gate oxide leakage and delay tradeoffs for Dual-T_{ox} circuits. IEEE Trans. Very Large Integration (VLSI) Systems 13, 1362–1375 (2005)
8. Rabaey, J.M., Chandrakasan, A., Nikolic, B.: Digital integrated circuits. Prentic Hall, New Jersey (2002)
9. Kang, S.-M., Leblebici, Y.: CMOS Digital Integrated Circuits: Analysis and Design, 3rd edn. Tata McGraw-Hill Publishers (2002)
10. Gao, F., Hayes, J.P.: Exact and heuristic approaches to input vector control for leakage power reduction. IEEE Trans. Computer-Aided Design of Integrated Circuits and Systems 25, 2561–2574 (2006)
11. Chen, Z., Johnson, M., Wei, L., Roy, K.: Estimation of standby leakage power in CMOS circuits considering accurate modeling of transistor stacks. In: IEEE Int. Symp. Low Power Electronics and Design (ISLPED 1998), pp. 239–244 (1998)
12. http://www.cad.polito.it/downloads/tools/benchmarks.html
13. http://www.ece.uic.edu/~masud/resources.html

Impact of Fin Width and Graded Channel Doping on the Performance of 22nm SOI FinFET

Jose Joseph and Rajendra Patrikar

Department of Electronics Engineering
Visvesvaraya National Institute of Technology, Nagpur-440010
josejosephpala@gmail.com, rmpatrikar@ece.vnit.ac.in

Abstract. The potential impact of fin width and graded channel doping on the analog performance of 22nm n-channel FinFET are studied using well calibrated 3D TCAD simulations. It is ascertained that for FinFETs, lesser the fin width, better the characteristics. But limitations in lithography process curb the fin width to be scaled beyond 10nm. Stability of the fins patterned beyond 10nm width is to be viewed with suspected eyes. It is observed that Graded doping of the channel will improve threshold voltage and hence the ratio of I_{on} to I_{off} will also increase, which is desired for enhanced performance in analog applications.

Keywords: FinFET, graded doping, fin width, TCAD.

1 Introduction

FinFET is one of the emerging CMOS devices that use an ingenious architecture allowing better control over short-channel effects (SCE) with the aid of 3D geometry [1]. The use of metal gates help to adjust the threshold voltage and prevents gate depletion and dopant penetration that frequently appear in the conventional polysilicon gate architecture [2]. Traditionally, fin channel is selected as undoped to avoid the device mismatches.

Pertaining to electrostatic integrity of FinFETs, the ratio of the minimum gate length to the minimum fin width should be larger than 1.5 [3]. Therefore, it could be said that the minimum feature size in FinFET technology is the fin width, not the gate length [4]. Narrow fin width devices exhibits better immunity to SCEs and reduced Subthreshold slope [5]. The absence of body contact for the SOI FinFET puts limitations for threshold voltage tuning and can be accomplished either by complicated gate metal work function engineering or by channel doping [6]. Doped-channel FinFETs are suitable for system-on-chip applications requiring multiple threshold voltages on the same die [7]. In this paper, we try to analyze the performance variations of 22nm FinFET subjected to different fin widths and graded doping conditions. Critical device attributes like I_{on}, I_{off}, V_T, DIBL, Subthreshold slope etc. are investigated as a function of fin width and graded doping conditions.

M.S. Gaur et al. (Eds.): VDAT 2013, CCIS 382, pp. 153–159, 2013.

2   Device Structure and Simulations

A novel 22nm FinFET was simulated using well calibrated Sentaurus TCAD 3D simulations. The device structure was formed with the aid of Sentaurus Structure Editor in the TCAD package [10]. Device parameters chosen for simulation are as given in Table 1. In industry standard <100> Si wafers, mesa etch results in <110> fin side walls. Since the mobility in <100> plane and <110> plane are different, a double gate operation has been ensured by keeping a thick oxide layer of 20nm the top surface of the fin [8]. Hence the structure becomes double gate and the problem of different current conduction and mobility on two crystallographic planes were solved.

Table 1. Nomenclature and values of the parameters used in the simulated device

Parameter	Value	Parameter	Value
Gate Length	22nm	Side oxide thickness	1.1nm
Fin Height	40nm	Top oxide thickness	20nm
S/D Extension	40nm	S/D extension doping	1E+19 cm^{-3}
S/D HDD length	50nm	S/D HDD doping	2 E+20 cm^{-3}
S/D HDD width	56nm	Gate metal thickness	20nm

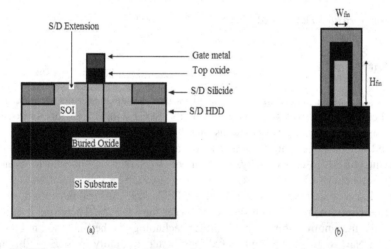

Fig. 1. FinFET structure used in simulations: (a) cross section along the length of channel and (b) cross section along the width of the channel

The gate metal work function is selected as 4.5eV and resistivity as 5.44E-6 Ω.cm, which corresponds to the material properties of Tungsten [9]. To improve the speed of the device, S/D silicides with resistivity of 2E-6 Ω.cm are employed. In spite of their positive impact on the speed of the device, silicides provide high temperature stability and excellent process compatibility with standard Si technology. Heavily doped

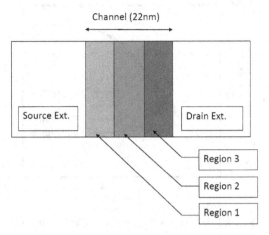

Fig. 2. 2-D Schematic diagram of graded doping profile used for simulations

Source/Drain (HDD) and abrupt box shaped Source/Drain extensions have been defined analytically. Device cross sections along the length and width of the fin are illustrated schematically in Fig. 1(a) and Fig. 1(b) respectively.

Fig.2 portrays the doping profile selected for graded doping simulations. The channel is partitioned into 3 regions of equal length. Simulations were carried out by assigning heavy doping near to source and gradually reducing to drain and vice versa. The results of these simulations were compared with those of constant channel doping of 1E+16.

Mobility models including doping dependence, high-field saturation (velocity saturation), and transverse field dependence are specified for all the simulations. '*BandGapNarrowing (OldSlotboom)*' is the silicon bandgap narrowing model which is employed for determining the intrinsic carrier concentration [10]. Drift-Diffusion equations coupled with Continuity and Poisson's equations were solved for the device structure shown in Fig.1, using Sentaurus Device from the TCAD package.

3   Results and Discussion

3.1   Impact of Fin Width

Width of the fin has been varied from 10nm to 16nm in steps of 2nm, keeping all the other device parameters constant. For the simulations in this section, undoped channel is selected. As expected the devices with lower fin widths are exhibiting reduced SCEs, but reducing the fin width increases the S/D resistance, which as shown in Fig. 3, leads to the reduction of normalized drain current.

It can be noted from Fig. 4 that the ratio of I_{on} to I_{off} is decreasing as we increase the fin width. When the width of fin is increased from 10nm to 16nm, approximately two orders of decrease in magnitude for I_{on}/I_{off} have been observed and it will affect the performance of FinFET for analog applications. Threshold voltage was also decreasing as we increase the fin width. Similar variations for threshold voltage is demonstrated in [15] for higher fin width devices.

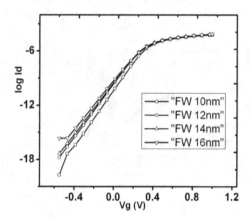

Fig. 3. Log I_d versus V_g curves for different fin widths

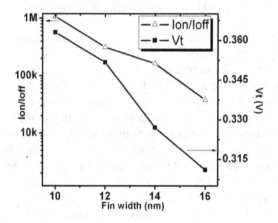

Fig. 4. Variation of I_{on}/I_{off} and threshold voltage with respect to fin width

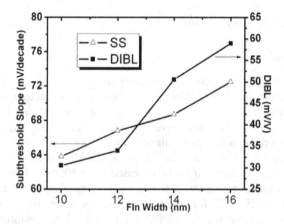

Fig. 5. Fluctuation of Subthreshold slope and DIBL with fin width

As shown in Fig. 5, Subthreshold slope increases linearly whereas DIBL was found increasing in discontinuous steps. Both these trends testify that for better performance, one should keep the fin width as low as possible. AC small signal simulation at 50GHz reveals that gate capacitance C_{gg} increases linearly as we augment the fin width. Transconductance will also build up with the fin width as shown in Fig. 6.

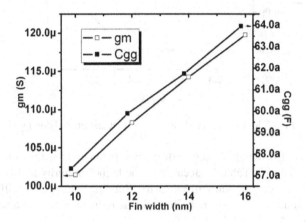

Fig. 6. Effect of fin width on transconductance and gate capacitance

All the parameter variations observed here are in closer agreement with those proposed in [11] for long channel devices devices.

3.2   Impact of Graded Channel Doping

Asymmetric channel devices have been studied thoroughly by many authors [12] [13]. In all those works, the channel is divided into two regions and heavy doping is assigned near to Source allowing the channel region near Drain to act as a Lightly Doped Drain (LDD). In this work, we, for the first time, investigated the performance variation of 22nm FinFET under two different graded channel conditions. Table 2 shows the doping profiles selected for these simulations.

Comparison of I_d-V_g characteristics for constant doping with GC1 and GC2 is elucidated in Fig. 7. It is to be noted that in this section, constant doping refers to a Boron channel doping of value 1E16 cm-3, unless otherwise specified.

Table 2. Graded channel profiles selected for simulations

Nomenclature	Region 1	Region 2	Region 3
GC1	1E18 cm^{-3}	1E16 cm^{-3}	1E14cm^{-3}
GC2	1E14 cm^{-3}	1E16cm^{-3}	1E18cm^{-3}

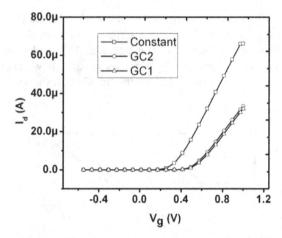

Fig. 7. Id-Vg characteristics of constant and graded doping

The variation of different device performance parameters with respect to channel doping type are listed in Table 3. Because of the higher impurity scattering in graded channel device, the conduction current in the Subthreshold region will come down and hence threshold voltage will rise. Remarkable reduction in I_{off} is also observed in both GC1 and GC2.

Table 3. Device performance parameters with different doping types

Doping Type	V_T (V)	SS (mV/decade)	I_{on}/I_{off}	gm (S)	C_{gg} (F)
Constant	0.351	66.79	3.15E5	1.082E-4	5.990E-17
GC1	0.564	62.89	2.28E8	7.210E-5	5.203E-17
GC2	0.549	63.51	1.95E8	7.239E-5	5.274E-17

It can be certified that for deep sub-micron technology nodes, GC1 offers advantages in analog performance than GC2, which is in closer agreement with the work explained for long channel SOI devices in [13]. Employing lesser doping near the Drain reduces the electric field and hence the total number of carriers generated by impact ionization will also be reduced. Since the channel is too short, the confinement of doping to the regions as depicted in Fig. 2 cannot be guaranteed as such in actual fabrication scenario and the device may tend to behave like a heavily doped one which puts limitation in adopting channel engineering for the deep sub-micron technology nodes. AC simulations at 50GHz show that gate capacitance C_{gg} is lowest for GC1 than GC2 or constant doping conditions.

It is also worth noting that the effect of GC1 on the transconductance is not so prominent. Since transconductance has a direct dependency on the mobility of carriers, variation in mobility is also negligible. On the other hand, the ratio of I_{on} to I_{off} is increasing by two orders of magnitude which is a striking advantage of the graded channel devices for analog applications.

4   Conclusion

Performance variation of 22nm n-channel FinFET subjected to different fin widths and channel graded doping have been analyzed in this work. For better performance, one needs to scale the fin width down to 10nm or lesser, taking the stability of the as formed fin into consideration. Graded doping in the channel helps one to improve the performance of FinFET for analog applications.

Acknowledgement. Authors wish to acknowledge INUP, IIT-Bombay for providing access to Sentaurus TCAD for this work.

References

1. Magnone, P., et al.: Matching Performance of FinFET Devices with Fin Widths Down to 10 nm. IEEE Electron Device Letters 30(12) (December 2009)
2. Cho, H.J., et al.: Fin Width Scaling Criteria of Body-Tied FinFET in Sub-50 nm Regime. IEEE
3. Colinge, J.P., et al.: FinFETs and Other Multi-Gate Transistors. Springer (2008)
4. Lee, D.H., et al.: A Guideline for the Optimum Fin Width Considering Hot-Carrier and NBTI Degradation in MuGFETs. IEEE Electron Device Letters 32(9) (September 2011)
5. Lederer, D., et al.: Dependence of FinFET RF performance on fin width. IEEE (2006)
6. Lin, C.-H., et al.: Channel Doping Impact on FinFETs for 22nm and Beyond. In: IEEE Symposium on VLSI Technology Digest of Technical Papers (2012)
7. Akarvardar, K., et al.: Impact of Fin Doping and Gate Stack on FinFET (110) and (100) Electron and Hole Mobilities. IEEE Electron Device Letters 33(3) (March 2012)
8. Dixit, A., et al.: Analysis of Parasitic S/D Resistance in Multiple-Gate FETs. IEEE Transactions on Electron Devices 52(6) (June 2005)
9. Lide, D.R., et al.: CRC Handbook of Chemistry and Physics, 90th edn. CRC Press, Boca Raton
10. Sentaurus TCAD User Manual, http://www.synopsis.com
11. Tuinhout, H.P., et al.: Effects of Gate Depletion and Boron Penetration on Matching of Deep Submicron CMOS Transistors. IEEE (1997)
12. Ma, W., et al.: Study of RF Performance for Graded-Channel SOI MOSFETs. IEEE
13. Pavanello, M.A., et al.: Graded-channel fully depleted Silicon-On-Insulator nMOSFET for reducing the parasitic bipolar effects. Pergamon Solid-State Electronics 44, 917–922 (2000)
14. The International Technology Roadmap for Semiconductors, http://www.itrs.net
15. Pei, G., et al.: FinFET design considerations based on 3-D Simulation and analytical modeling. IEEE Transactions on Electron Devices 49(8) (August 2002)

Power Reduction by Integrated Within_Clock_Power Gating and Power Gating (WCPG_in_PG)

Debanjali Nath[*], Priyanka Choudhury, and Sambhu Nath Pradhan

Department of ECE, NIT Agartala, Agartala, Tripura-799055, India
{nath.debanjali,priyanka.choudhury22,sambhu.pradhan}@gmail.com

Abstract. Leakage and switching power of circuit can be minimised in FSM based power gating technique by partitioning and encoding of FSM. Depending on the state of machine, at a time one sub-FSM is in power gated mode, but other one is in active mode which continues to dissipate power. In active sub-FSM, it is possible to reduce leakage, if the clock period is larger than the critical path delay of the sub-FSM, then there is a certain portion within the clock period which is idle and in this period power gating may be used. The objective of the paper is to reduce leakage power of active sub-FSM and to reduce leakage and switching power of inactive sub-FSM. So, this paper presents a new architectural technique, called WCPG_in_PG to minimize the overall power. WCPG_in_PG architecture of ISCAS89 benchmark circuit has been implemented and simulated in CADENCE VLSI tool at 45nm technology.

Keywords: Architecture, finite state machine (FSM), partitioning, encoding, power gating, within-clock, custom implementation, low power.

1 Introduction

Power dissipation has become an important consideration as performance and area for VLSI Chip design. Many techniques have been developed over the past decade to address the continuously aggressive power reduction requirements of most of the high performance VLSI systems. To reduce power, clock gating is one of the low power techniques which disables some portions of the circuitry so that its flip-flops do not change state; their switching power consumption goes to zero. The clock gating technique based on finite state machine decomposition for low power has been reported in [1]. In this clock gating technique leakage power is quite insignificant as compared to the dynamic power. But in today's technology leakage power consumption is becoming high with respect to the total power consumption of the circuit. To reduce leakage power, power gating is one of the effective low power technique by shutting down the power supply of inactive block.

1.1 Power Gating (PG)

This section briefly describes the power gating technique. Power gating is used to reduce the overall leakage power of the chip by temporarily turning off the circuit blocks that are not in use. When circuit blocks are required for operation, once again

---

[*] Corresponding author.

M.S. Gaur et al. (Eds.): VDAT 2013, CCIS 382, pp. 160–168, 2013.

they are activated to 'active mode'. Thus goal of power gating is to minimize leakage power by temporarily shutting down power supply to selective blocks that are not required in that mode. To reduce leakage power in power gating technique, high_V_T (high threshold voltage) PMOS transistor (sleep transistor) is used as header switches to shut off power supplies to parts of a design in standby or sleep mode. NMOS footer switches can also be used as sleep transistors.

Power gating structure for reduction of peak current and voltage glitch in system-on-chip environment is presented in [2]. The author of [3] presented multi way circuit partitioning strategy using genetic algorithm. Synthesis of finite state machine for low power dissipation including circuit partitioning and state encoding based on genetic algorithm (GA) has been reported in [4]. The author of [5] presented the state partitioning and state encoding strategy targeting low power Finite State Machine (FSM) decomposition based on GA approach to reduce leakage power as well as average power. In [6] authors have implemented new probabilistic power model of the power gated design of FSM and also GA is used to solve the problem of bi-partitioning and encoding of FSM. But in [6] authors did not implement circuit level architecture, they only implemented hypothetical architecture of PG, modelled the power and partitioned FSM to two sub-FSMs and encoded the states based on GA using power gating technique to save power. Here, new generic architecture of FSM based power gating technique has been proposed and multilevel realisation also have been done for saving power. A FSM is partitioned into two sub-FSMs and states are encoded based on genetic algorithm (GA) which is described in [6]. Proposed PG architecture is implemented in CADENCE virtuoso spectre at 45 nm technology. In this technique at a time only one sub-FSM is in power gated mode and other one is in active mode, so total power dissipation is less than the no power gating technique.

1.2   Within_Clock_ Power_Gating (WCPG)

FSM based power gating technique is used to reduce standby leakage and dynamic power by shutting down the power supply of the inactive block of the circuit but the active blocks continues to dissipate power. Leakage power of this active block also can be minimized by applying power gating within the clock cycle during the idle period if the clock period is larger than the critical path delay of the combinational part. Basic principle of this sub-clock power gating technique has been described in [7]. Author of [7] presented the sub-clock power gating technique to minimizing leakage power during active mode of combinational logic by concurrently frequency scaling and voltage scaling whereas traditional power gating technique applied in idle period. By frequency scaling leakage power reduces because if circuit operates at maximum operating frequency then there is no idle time within the clock period but if circuit operates at less than the maximum frequency then there is idle time present. As there is no switching in this idle period, leakage power reduces. In [7], actual implementation of PG architecture in circuit level is not done properly. In [8], the proposed technique, termed as within clock power gating (WCPG) technique has been implemented for minimizing leakage and total power of the sequential circuits during active mode of operation.

This paper proposes a new architecture which is termed as within_clock_ power_gating inside power gating (WCPG_in_PG) to reduce leakage power of active sub-FSM and overall power (leakage and dynamic) of inactive sub-FSM. Leakage power and average power results by frequency scaling for different input combination are reported in this paper.

The contributions of this paper as follows:

1. Here, multi-level implementation has been considered but in [5, 6] the power estimation is done targeting two-level circuit implementation only.
2. The final two-level PLA circuit after bipartition in [5, 6] has been taken as the input circuit in this work for its actual power gated implementation.
3. The idea of within_clock_ power_gating technique which has been described in [7, 8] has been implemented in active sub-FSM of FSM based power gating technique.
4. Full custom approach has been adopted for designing each logic block and after customizing in terms of area, power and noise margin, they are integrated in the environment of WCPG_in_PG circuit.
5. In [5, 6], power is estimated at algorithmic level and it only consider dynamic power of combinational logic but does not care the power of sequential logic. Here, leakage and dynamic power of all the parts of the architecture such as-combinational block, sequential blocks, latches and enable logics are considered.
6. Low power Hybrid latch Flip-Flops which is used as state register, state enable logic and latch with enable signal, 2:1 multiplexer have been designed. In [5, 6], all these logic are not implemented.
7. Leakage and average power results after simulating the proposed architecture in CADENCE virtuoso spectre at 45 nm technology for different frequency and input combinations have been reported separately and the results of this architecture are compared with FSM based power gating technique, within_clock_ power_gating and no power gating technique.

Rest of paper is organised as follows: proposed architecture and working principle of WCPG_in_PG are presented in section 2, design flow of this technique is shown in section 3, experimental results are reported in section 4 and conclusion and future scope of this work are described in section 5.

2   Proposed Architecture and Working Principle of WCPG_in_PG

In this section the proposed architecture for the implementation and working principle of within clock power gating inside power gating is explained. The proposed architecture of WCPG_in_PG is shown in Fig.1. Here, A FSM is partitioned into two sub-FSM and states of the FSM are encoded using GA algorithm to achieve power saving. After partitioning FSM into two sub-FSMs, some states are present in upper sub-FSM and some states are present in lower sub-FSM. At a time only one of these sub-FSM is active and the power supply of the other sub-FSM can be cut off for power saving. A high_V_T PMOS is connected between VDD and each of the sub-FSM for achieving low leakage power which is used to power gate each sub-FSM. Inner transitions occur within each sub-FSM and Cross transition occurs between the sub-FSMs. When one sub-FSM is in power gated mode then other sub-FSM is in active mode. At that time in active sub-FSM, within_clock_ power_gating concept has been used to reduce leakage power of active sub-FSM. Power will be reduced in active sub-FSM and power gated sub-FSM so that overall power will be reduced in this proposed architecture. Depending upon MSB bit of next state code, two enable signals are set in such a way that at a time one enable signal power gates one sub-FSM and at that moment other enable signal turns-on other sub-FSM within the clock period at the negative edge of clock.

Works in [5, 6] present partitioning and encoding technique based on genetic algorithm to divide the states into sub-FSM and to encode the states.

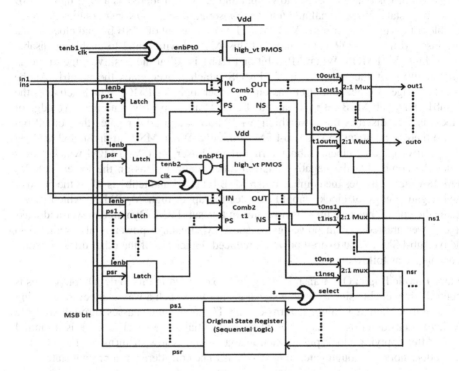

Fig. 1. Proposed architecture of WCPG_in_PG

For indicating the partition in which a particular state is present, each of state is encoded [6] in such a way that if MSB bit is '0', then state is present in upper sub-FSM (comb1) and if MSB bit is '1' then state is present in lower sub-FSM (comb2). Sleep transistor is used to power gate each sub-FSM depending on the MSB bit of state. Inputs are given to both the combinational block. Outputs of the both combinational blocks are fed into the 2:1 multiplexer. MSB bit of state code is considered as a select line of multiplexer to select the output from active sub-FSM. Initially, s is considered as a low input which is given externally. MSB bit of next state and s are fed to the OR gate, output of which is the select line of multiplexer. If MSB bit is '0' then it selects the outputs of comb1 because at that time comb1 is in active mode and comb2 is in power down mode and if MSB bit is '1' then it selects the outputs of comb2 which is in active mode. Similarly, when MSB bit is '0' then it selects the next states of comb1 otherwise it selects the next states of comb2. All the next states propagate through the original state register at the positive edge of clock and becomes the present states for the combinational logic after passing through the latch present between original state register and combinational logic. Present states are inserted into the number of latches, some of them are connected to the comb1 and the rest are connected to the comb2. Latch enable signal (lenb) enables and disables the latch depending upon the MSB bit of the state. When lenb signal is low i.e. MSB bit is '0' then it enables the latches which are connected to the comb1 and disables remaining latches which are connected to the comb2. Similarly, reverse process is applicable when MSB bit is '1'. Initially tenb1 is considered as a low input and tenb2 considered as a high input. MSB bit of next state, clock signal and tenb1 are inserted into the OR gate, output of which enables or disables upper high_V_T PMOS. Inverted output of MSB bit and clock signal are inserted into the OR gate, output of this ANDed with tenb2 to enable or disable lower high_V_T PMOS. When MSB bit and tenb1 is '0' at the positive edge of clock, enbpt0 turns-off the upper high_V_T PMOS which power gates the comb1. At the negative edge of clock, enbpt0 turns-on the upper high_V_T PMOS which activates the comb1 and when MSB bit is '0' and tenb2 is '1' at the positive and negative edge of clock, enbpt1 disables the lower high_V_T PMOS which power gates the comb2 because there is no states in this sub-FSM. Similarly, When MSB bit and tenb2 is '1' at the positive edge of clock, enbpt1 turns-off the lower high_V_T PMOS which power gates the comb2. At the negative edge of clock, enbpt1 turns-on the lower high_V_T PMOS which activates the comb2. When MSB bit is '1' and tenb1 is '0' at the positive and negative edge of clock, enbpt0 disables the upper high_V_T PMOS which power gates the comb2 because there is no states in this sub-FSM. Dynamic power and leakage power are reduced in power gated sub-FSM. Leakage power is also reduced in active sub-FSM so that overall power is reduced. Functions of the other different components are as follows:

State Enable Logic. One transmission gate (TG) is used in this logic. Output of this is controlled by enable signal. Enable signal is chosen in such a way that before applying clock pulse when it is high, it turns-on the TG then, input passes through the gate which is considered to be as a present state at initial stage because there is no initial state After applying clock pulse when enable signal is low, it turns-off the TG then input does not pass trough gate, so next state is to be considered as a present state.

2:1 Multiplexer. Multiplexer is used to select output from active sub-FSM. MSB bit is to be considered as select line. When MSB bit is '0', then it selects output from comb1 because at that instant that machine is in active mode. Similarly when MSB bit is '1', then it selects output from comb2.

Latch with Enable Signal. At the positive edge of clock signal latch changes its output. Enable signal decides whether state will pass from input to output. Here, MSB bit of next state is considered to be enable signal. When it is high then it passes the states otherwise, it disables the latch.

3   Design Flow

Step 1: The circuit in FSM format is taken as input of this architecture. FSM form of dk27 benchmark circuit is

.i 1

.o 2

.p 14

.s 7

0 START state6 00

0 state2 state5 00

0 state3 state5 00

0 state4 state6 00

0 state5 START 10

0 state6 START 01

0 state7 state5 00

1 state6 state2 01

1 state5 state2 10

1 state4 state6 10

1 state7 state6 10

1 START state4 00

1 state2 state3 00

1 state3 state7 00

Step 2: Boundary depth of the circuit is determined.

First, steady state probability of each state is calculated using [6]. Boundary depth is taken as 2 for dk27 circuit.

Step 3: Targeting power gated implementation probabilistic power model is developed.

Step 4: FSM is partitioned and encoded together using Genetic Algorithm taking cost function developed at step 3.

Step 5: Two, 2-level PLA – t1 and t2 are obtained after step 4.

After encoding and partitioning, dk27 benchmark circuit is divide into two PLA file in SIS tool:

.t0 PLA file-		.t1 PLA file-	
.i 4		.i 4	
.o 5		.o 5	
.p 4		.p 4	
0011	11000	-110	00010
1000	00100	-1-1	01000
10-1	00010	11--	00100
-000	10001	-1--	10000
.e		.e	

Step 6: Run ESPRESSO [6] for t1 and t2 to get area optimized PLA.

Step 7: Synthesis t1 and t2 in SIS [6] using *lib2-genlib* to get multi-level circuits.

Net list of two PLA file circuit using *lib2-genlib* of SIS [6] tools are obtained. The net list consists of basic cells- INVERTER, NAND, NOR and DFF.

Step 8: Library development for basic cells like INVERTER, NAND, NOR and DFF using transistors at TSMC 45nm technology.

Step 9: Basic cells are connected to form F1 (from t1) and F2 (from t2) with the associated logic for power gated (PG) design.

Step 10: Within_clock_ power_gating concept which is described in [8] is developed in FSM based power gated design.

Step 11: Within_clock_ power_gating technique inside power gating (WCPG_in_PG) architecture is implemented in this paper.

The architecture of WCPG_in_PG design of dk27 circuit is shown in Fig. 2. This architecture is designed and simulated in Cadence Virtuoso Spectre at 45 nm technology.

Step 12: Simulate the WCPG_in_PG architecture in Cadence Virtuoso Spectre using 45nm TSMC technology.

Step 13: Estimate leakage and dynamic power of combinational and sequential blocks.

Steps 1 to 5 are executed as in [6]. These steps are followed in the FSM level targeting power gated design and power is estimated but not actual circuit level implementation. To get the circuit level implementation of the hypothetical architecture developed in [6], the architecture is modified as in this paper and steps 6 to 9 are followed. Circuit level implementation of within_clock_ power_gating concept is developed inside power gating technique and architecture of WCPG_in_PG is implemented in Fig 2 and steps 10 to 13 are followed.

4   Experimental Result of WCPG_in_PG

The technique of WCPG_in_PG is implemented taking dk27 benchmark circuit. The circuit has been designed and simulated in CADENCE virtuoso spectre at 45 nm TSMC technology. Supply voltage (VDD) is taken as 1V. Efficiency has been established by comparing the results with the no power gating, FSM based power gating (PG) and within_clock_ power_gating technique (WCPG).

After creating symbols of all the gates they are integrated to build the complete schematic of dk27 circuit without WCPG_in_PG and dk27 circuit with WCPG_in_PG design (Fig. 2).

Leakage power saving is influenced by shutting down power supply of the inactive block and operational frequency. As the clock period is larger, the idle time of the combinational logic becomes more because the difference between evaluation time and clock period increases and hence, greater leakage power saving is achieved. During evaluation time transitions occur, whereas, no transitions occur during idle time. Leakage power and average power are calculated for different input combination at 0.1MHz, 0.05MHz, 0.03MHz, 0.025MHz frequency and also the power results of WCPG are compared with the results of PG and no power gating(no PG) technique at 0.1 MHz frequency. In this WCPG_in_PG technique leakage power is calculated at the positive part of clock cycle. Depending on MSB bit at a certain time one sub-FSM is in power gated mode at both edge of clock and other active sub-FSM is in power gated mode at positive edge of clock and it is in active mode at negative edge of clock.

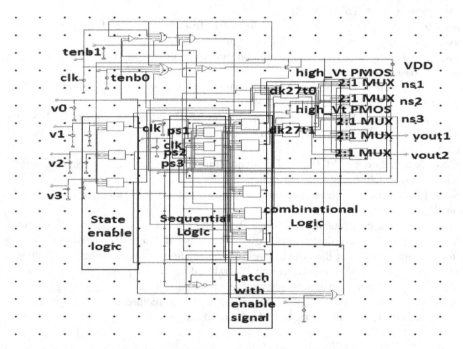

Fig. 2. Schematic of dk27 circuit with WCPG_in_PG designed in CADENCE virtuoso spectre

Here, result of WCPG_in_PG, WCPG and PG in % saving are compared with no PG. In no PG technique, leakage power is calculated at the negative edge of clock during idle period. In PG technique, at a time one sub-FSM is in active mode and other one is in power gated mode. Leakage power is calculated during the period where no transition occurs. In WCPG technique, leakage power is calculated at the positive edge of clock during idle time and at the negative edge of clock it evaluates the states.

Leakage power and average total power (dynamic + leakage) of WCPG_in_PG for few input combinations with different frequency are tabulated in Table 1 and 2 respectively. Table 1 and 2 show that with the decrease of frequency as clock period increase, leakage power and average total power consumption decreases. Average power (switching and leakage) and average leakage power saving of WCPG_in_PG, WCPG, and PG with respect to no PG at 0.1MHz frequency have also been noted in Table 3. Table 3 shows that, on the average 90% saving in leakage and around 80% saving in total power are obtained compared to the no power gating technique at 0.1MHZ.

Table 1. Leakage power of WCPG_in_PG

| Input | | | | Leakage power (nw) of WCPG_in_PG | | | |
| | | | | Frequency(MHz) | | | |
IN1	IN2	IN3	IN4	0.1	0.05	0.03	0.025
0	0	1	0	2.04	2.05	2.10	1.93
0	1	1	0	1.14	1.10	1.03	0.40
0	0	0	0	1.5	1.04	0.75	0.67
0	1	0	0	1.02	0.87	0.85	0.68
0	0	1	1	1.16	0.86	0.84	0.83
Average Leakage power				1.16	0.99	0.93	0.76

Table 2. Average total power (dynamic + leakage) of WCPG_in_PG

Frequency(MHz)	0.1	0.05	0.03	0.025
Average of total power (nw) of WCPG_in_PG	2.27	2.23	2.2	2.18

Table 3. Average leakage power and average power saving

| Frequency | Average Leakage saving with respect to no PG | | | Average power saving with respect to no PG | | |
	PG	WCPG	WCPG_in_PG	PG	WCPG	WCPG_in_PG
0.1 MHz	16.23%	75.00%	90.00%	53.60%	56.00%	80.95%

5   Conclusion

This paper presents the architecture implementation of WCPG_in_PG technique in CADENCE Virtuoso Spectre at 45nm technology. Leakage power and total power saving are reported in this architectural approach. Results confirm that average leakage power and as well as total power saving are more in this technique than no PG, PG, WCPG technique. It is also observed that leakage power and average total power reduces with down scaling of frequency. However, the reported circuit is small.

For larger circuit custom implementation of WCPG_in_PG architecture is not feasible for high complexity. WCPG_in_PG design of large circuit may be done by designing proposed WCPG_in_PG architecture in RTL level by HDL coding, simulation, synthesis and then generating layout in Cadence/Synopsys CAD tool.

References

1. Monteiro, J.C., Oliveira, A.L.: Finite State machine Decomposition for Low Power. In: Proc. of Design Automation Conference, pp. 758–763 (1998)
2. Kim, S., Kosonocky, S.V., Knebel, D.R., Stawiasz, K., Heidel, D., Immediato, M.: Minimizing Inductive Noise in System-On-a-Chip with Multiple Power Gating Structures. In: Proc. of the 29th European Solid-State Circuits Conference, pp. 635–638 (2003)
3. Gill, S.S., Chandel, R., Chandel, A.: Genetic Algorithm Based Approach to Circuit Partitioning. International Journal of Computer and Electrical Engineering 2(2), 1793–8163 (2010)
4. Chaudhury, S., Rao, J.S., Chattopadhyay, S.: Synthesis of Finite State Machines for Low Power and Testability. In: IEEE APCCAS, Singapore, December 4-7 (2006)
5. Kumar, M.T., Pradhan, S.N., Chattopadhyay, S.: Power-gated FSM Synthesis Integrating Partitioning and State Assignment. In: IEEE TENCON, Hyderabad, November 18-21 (2008)
6. Choudhury, P., Pradhan, S.N.: An Approach for Low Power Design of Power Gated Finite State Machines Considering Partitioning and State Encoding Together. Journal of Low Power Electronics 8, 1–12 (2012)
7. Mistry, J.N., Al-Hashimi, B.M., Flynn, D., Hill, S.: Sub-Clock Power-Gating Technique for Minimising Leakage Power During Active Mode. In: Design, Automation and Test in Europe, Grenoble, France, March 14-18. ACM/IEEE (2011)
8. Pradhan, S.N., Nath, D., Choudhury, P., Nag, A.: Within-Clock Power Gating Architecture Implementation to Reduce Leakage. In: 5th International Conference on Computers and Devices for Communication (CODEC 2012), Kolkata, December 17-19 (2012)

Design and Analysis of a Novel Noise Cancelling Topology for Common Gate UWB LNAs

Mohd Anwar[1], Syed Azeemuddin[1], and Mohammed Zafar Ali Khan[2]

[1] Center for VLSI & Embedded Systems Technology, IIIT, Hyderabad
mohd.anwar@research.iiit.ac.in, azeemuddin.s@iiit.ac.in
[2] Department of Electrical Engineering, IIT, Hyderabad
zafar@iith.ac.in

Abstract. In this paper, we present a noise cancellation technique for common gate ultra wide band (UWB) low noise amplifiers (LNAs) which not only reduces the noise but also increases the gain. On implementing this technique in one of the existing UWB LNAs significant reduction of noise figure (NF) compared to same LNA without noise cancellation technique was observed. Noise cancellation of the most dominating thermal noise source viz. the input matching device with theoretical analysis is presented in this paper. Simulation results with TSMC 0.18 μm CMOSRF technology shows a peak gain of 28 dB and base NF of 3.16 dB for a 6.6 GHz (2.4-9 GHz) band LNA with noise cancellation when compared to peak gain of 21 dB and base NF of 4.09 dB without noise cancellation. Both theoretical analysis and simulation results are in good agreement.

Keywords: Low noise amplifier, Noise cancellation, Ultra wide band, High gain, Noise Contribution.

1   Introduction

In wireless receiver systems, effect of noise of all the subsequent stages is reduced by the gain of LNA whose noise injects directly into the receiver. Thus, it is necessary to boost the desired signal power while adding as little noise and distortion as possible so that the retrieval of this signal is possible in the later stages in the system. Recent demonstrations show that UWB LNAs ranging from few MHz to 10 GHz are included to wireless receivers which uses single LNA for contiguous broadband signal processing [1-3]. There are various techniques to design UWB LNA such as design using common source (CS) configuration and common gate (CG) configuration. CS configuration with inductive degeneration LNA provides good input matching for UWB range but requires a passive network at the input which consist large number of high Q inductors. Moreover, LNA of this configuration shows good noise performance for narrow band (NB) applications but not at corner frequencies for UWB applications [4]. However, CG LNA provides ultra wide band input matching due to its low input impedance resulting in an improved reverse isolation and therefore provides better stability. In contrast, noise figure of CG LNA is considerably large when compared to CS LNA but it can be improved by using g_m boosting technique which trades off with gain [5].

M.S. Gaur et al. (Eds.): VDAT 2013, CCIS 382, pp. 169–176, 2013.

Recently, few topologies implementing noise cancellation techniques have been reported. The thermal noise cancellation technique which uses resistive feed forward CS configuration was implemented for an LNA operating below 2 GHz [6]. However, this technique was extended to higher frequencies by using inductive peaking which shows reduction in noise figure in 3.1-10.6 GHz frequency range [7]. In addition, various other noise cancellation techniques has been reported in literature such as simultaneous noise and third order distortion cancellation technique in CG-CS cascade LNA operating till 2.1 GHz [8] and resistive feed forward noise cancellation technique in two stage differential transconductance LNA operating till 4.5 GHz [9]. Hence it is evident that noise cancellation techniques usually do not consider much about gain improvement.

In this work, we propose a noise cancellation technique which not only reduces the noise but also improves the gain and is novel to best of our knowledge. In order to cancel the dominant noise, we analyzed the noise contributions from both active and passive components in CG UWB LNA reported in ref. [10]. The input matching device viz. first CG transistor was identified as the most dominant noise source. The technique is based on combining two paths one with reversed phase noise signal and the other with non-reversed phase noise signal, simultaneously the RF signals in the two paths will be in phase. The two parallel paths were designed by symmetrical cascade combination of CG-CS and CS-CG stages. Theoretical model of noise cancellation is presented along with the derived equation of overall noise figure and implementation is done using TSMC 0.18 μm CMOSRF technology on Cadence Spectre RF tool.

2   Noise Analysis

A three stage UWB LNA as shown in Fig. 1 is taken for detailed analysis of noise sources [10]. First stage is a CG stage followed by cascode CS stage and resistive feed forward cascode CS stage with a buffer at the output. Major noise contribution of this UWB LNA is from the CG transistor (M1) which is approximately 42% over the entire range of 3.1-10.6 GHz shown in Fig. 2, extracted from noise simulation results. Second stage CS transistor (M2) contributes 22% for the entire range and its noise contribution is more near the corner frequencies. This is due to the restriction of narrow band characteristics of CS amplifier while CG amplifier shows WB characteristics and its noise contribution is almost equal (2.8 ± 0.3) dB for the entire range of UWB as shown in Fig. 3. Third stage noise contribution is negligible as it receives the amplified signal from the earlier two stages. Therefore, it is desirable to suppress the noise contribution of M1.

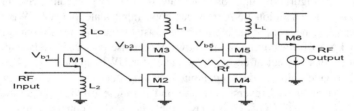

Fig. 1. UWB LNA without noise cancellation

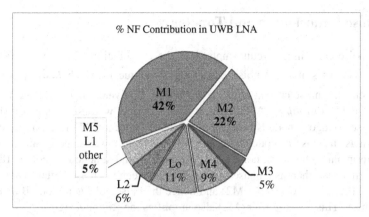

Fig. 2. Noise contribution by UWB LNA components for entire range of 3.1-10.6 GHz

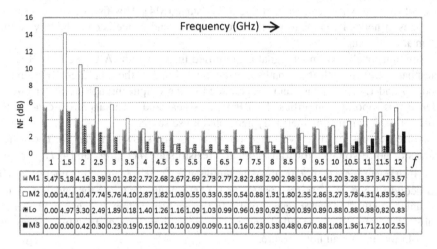

	1	1.5	2	2.5	3	3.5	4	4.5	5	5.5	6	6.5	7	7.5	8	8.5	9	9.5	10	10.5	11	11.5	12
M1	5.47	5.18	4.16	3.39	3.01	2.82	2.72	2.68	2.67	2.69	2.73	2.77	2.82	2.88	2.90	2.98	3.06	3.14	3.20	3.28	3.37	3.47	3.57
M2	0.00	14.1	10.4	7.74	5.76	4.10	2.87	1.82	1.03	0.55	0.33	0.35	0.54	0.88	1.31	1.80	2.35	2.86	3.27	3.78	4.31	4.83	5.36
Lo	0.00	4.97	3.30	2.49	1.89	0.18	1.40	1.26	1.16	1.09	1.03	0.99	0.96	0.93	0.92	0.90	0.89	0.89	0.88	0.88	0.88	0.82	0.83
M3	0.00	0.00	0.42	0.30	0.23	0.19	0.15	0.12	0.10	0.09	0.09	0.11	0.16	0.23	0.33	0.48	0.67	0.88	1.08	1.36	1.71	2.10	2.55

Fig. 3. Noise figure contribution of UWB LNA major components at all frequencies

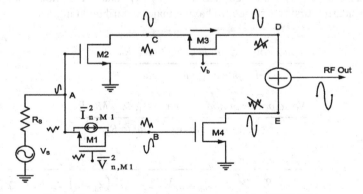

Fig. 4. Proposed noise cancellation concept for UWB LNA

3   Noise Cancellation and Topology

Proposed noise cancelling circuit emphasizes the cancellation of noise generated by M1. Fig. 4 shows simplified noise cancelling technique in which $\overline{I}^2_{n,M1}$ is thermally generated channel noise current equal to $4kT\gamma g_{m1}\Delta f$. Equivalent noise voltage $\overline{V}^2_{n,M1}$ at the gate of M1 is $4kT\gamma\Delta f/g_{m1}$. With respect to this source, we observe a phase shift of 180° in noise voltage at node B because of CS stage (source of M1 is common terminal) while it is in phase at node A because of source follower stage (drain of M1 is common terminal). Therefore, noise voltage at node A and at node B becomes 180° out of phase. After that, there is a phase shift of 180° between the noise voltages at node A and node C because of CS stage (M2) and hence the noise voltage at node B and node C are in phase. This CS amplifier (M2) also amplifies the RF input signal V_s.

The noise voltage generated by M1 is observed to be in phase at nodes C and D due to CG stage (M3) while the noise voltage at node E is 180° out of phase with respect to noise voltage at node B due to CS stage (M4). This finally results in noise voltages at nodes D and E to be 180° out of phase and hence is cancelled by adding them at the output.

Simultaneously, RF input signal is amplified through paths A-C-D and A-B-E and the phase shift in both these paths are identical. Finally, the amplified RF signal at node D and E are in phase and hence added at the output through an adder circuit. Hence this topology amplifies the RF input signal and simultaneously cancels the noise of most dominating thermally generated noise source.

Noise sources of first two stage components are shown in Fig. 5. Theoretical values of noise voltages for transistors and resistors are $4kT\gamma\Delta f/g_{mi}$ and $4kTR_i$. Where k is Boltzmann constant, T is absolute temperature, γ is transistor parameter, g_{mi} is transconductance of ith transistor, R_i, and X_i are equivalent resistor and impedance associated with i^{th} inductor respectively. In the analysis below, it is assumed that the noise of M1 is being cancelled and remaining components of first two stages are contributing to overall noise figure.

Let F_z and $F_{z'}$ are noise factors at two different output nodes z and z' as shown in Fig 5. Equations (3), (4) and (6) are derived for F_z, $F_{z'}$ and overall noise factor of the circuit considering first two stages are having major contribution in noise:

$$F_z = 1 + \frac{\text{Noise power at node } z \text{ due to } R_o, R_2, R_4, M_4}{\text{Noise power at node } z \text{ due to } R_s} \tag{1}$$

$$F_{z'} = 1 + \frac{\text{Noise power at node } z' \text{ due to } R_1, M_2, M_3, R_2}{\text{Noise power at node } z' \text{ due to } R_s} \tag{2}$$

$$F_z = 1 + \frac{R_o}{\left(g_{m1}X_o\right)^2 R_s} + \frac{R_2}{4R_s} + \frac{R_4}{\left(g_{m1}g_{m4}X_oX_4\right)^2 R_s} + \frac{\gamma}{\left(g_{m1}X_o\right)^2 g_{m4}R_s\alpha_1^2\alpha_4^2} \tag{3}$$

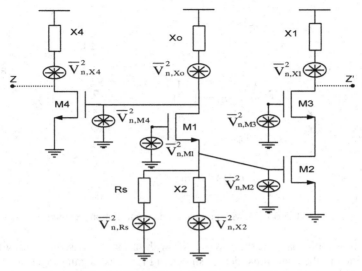

Fig. 5. Major noise sources of UWB LNA

$$F_{z'} = 1 + \frac{R_1}{R_s \left(g_{m2} X_1 \right)^2 \alpha_2^2} + \frac{\gamma}{g_{m2} R_s \alpha_2^2} \tag{4}$$

$$F = 1 + (F_z - 1) + (F_{z'} - 1) \tag{5}$$

$$F = 1 + \frac{R_2}{4R_s} + \frac{R_o}{\left(g_{m1} X_o \right)^2 R_s} + \frac{R_4}{\left(g_{m1} g_{m4} X_o X_4 \right)^2 R_s} + \frac{\gamma}{\left(g_{m1} X_o \right)^2 g_{m4} R_s \alpha_1^2 \alpha_4^2}$$
$$+ \frac{R_1}{R_s \left(g_{m2} X_1 \right)^2 \alpha_2^2} \tag{6}$$

Equations (7) and (8) describe the noise of M1 at z and z' respectively. The factor r is defined as the ratio of these two noise factors as given in (9). For the condition of complete noise cancellation, the value of r should ideally be equal to 1. Thus, the factor r signifies the fraction of noise of M1 cancelled at the output.

$$\textit{Noise factor of M1 at } z = \frac{\left(\dfrac{4kT\gamma}{g_{m1}} \right) \left(-\dfrac{g_{m1} X_o}{1 + g_{m1} \left(R_s \parallel X_2 \right)} \right)^2}{\left(g_{m1} \left(X_o \parallel r_{o1} \right) \right)^2 4kTR_s} \tag{7}$$

$$\textit{Noise factor of M1 at } z' = \frac{\left(\dfrac{4kT\gamma}{g_{m1}} \right) \left(\dfrac{X_2 \parallel R_s}{R_s \parallel X_2 + 1/g_{m1}} \right)^2}{4kTR_s} \tag{8}$$

$$r = \frac{\textit{Noise of M1 at } z}{\textit{Noise of M1 at } z'} \tag{9}$$

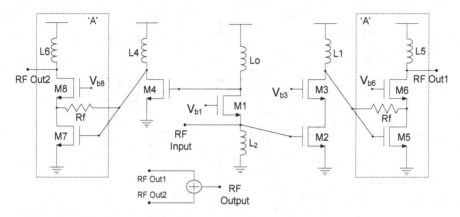

Fig. 6. UWB LNA with proposed noise cancellation technique

Fig. 6 shows schematic of the UWB LNA with proposed noise cancelling topology. In addition to the conceptual design shown in Fig. 4, extra gain stages i.e. resistive feed forward cascode CS stage marked by 'A' are added to improve the overall signal gain and bandwidth of amplifier. Noise cancellation is achieved by combining the outputs of these gain stages.

4   Results and Discussion

The proposed noise cancelling topology is designed for UWB LNA operating from frequency range 2.4 GHz to 9 GHz. Small size of M1 transistor demonstrates wideband input matching characteristic. Transconductance (g_{m1}) of M1 transistor is fixed at 20 mS for 50 Ω input matching with bias current of 1.8 mA and L2 is 4.44 nH, which keeps input reflection coefficient well below -10 dB over the entire range of 2.4 GHz to 9 GHz. The g_m of M2 (43.53 mS), M3 (43.56 mS) and M4 (47.55 mS) are decided by considering the radio frequency circuit design tradeoffs and cancellation of the noise of M1 at output. Simulated noise figures, which are optimized at 6 GHz for UWB LNA with and without noise cancellation technique, are shown in Fig. 7 and report approximately 1 dB reduction. Minimum noise figures of 3.16 dB and 4.09 dB are noted with and without noise cancellation respectively.

Fig. 8 shows the circuit simulated power gain of 24.24 dB (average) in the frequency range of 2.4 GHz to 9 GHz and 17.7 dB (average) in the frequency range of 3.1 GHz to 10.6 GHz for UWB LNA with and without noise cancellation technique respectively. Fig. 9 compares simulated and theoretical noise figures, which shows an excellent noise performance at 3 GHz and lower corner frequency. Simulated noise figure value increases towards upper corner frequency due to the noise contribution of components that were not considered during NF analysis and are not included in (6). However, in this paper an UWB LNA is designed which exploits thermal noise cancellation of its first stage CG transistor (M1). Equation (6) is used to get the plot for theoretical noise figure as shown in Fig. 9, which in turn is compared with the simulated noise figure plot and they are found to be in close agreement near a frequency of 3 GHz. Table I compares the performance of UWB LNA with and without noise cancelling technique.

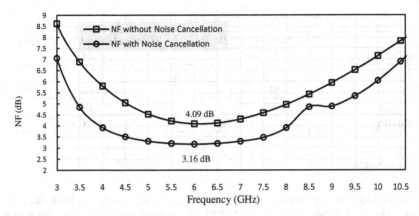

Fig. 7. Simulated noise figure plots for UWB LNA with and without noise cancellation

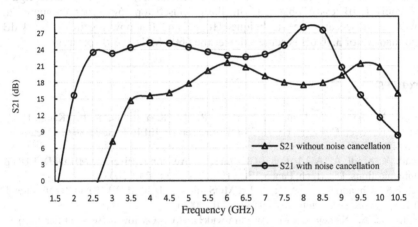

Fig. 8. Simulated power gain plots for UWB LNA with and without noise cancellation

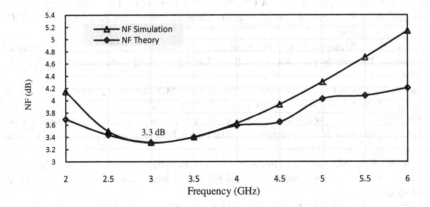

Fig. 9. Simulated and theoretical noise figure plots for UWB LNA with noise cancellation

Table 1. UWB LNA Performance Comparison

	With Noise Cancellation	Without Noise Cancellation
Frequency (GHz)	2.4 ~ 9.0	3.1 ~ 10.6
S11 (dB)	< -10	< -10
S21 (dB)	24.24 (average)	17.70 (average)
NF (dB)	3.16	4.09
Technology	0.18 μm CMOS	0.18 μm CMOS

5   Conclusion

A noise cancelling topology for CG UWB LNA in 2.4-9 GHz range has been demonstrated in a standard TSMC 0.18 μm CMOSRF technology and analysis of all noise contributing sources is performed. Significant reduction (33.17%) in noise figure approximately 1 dB less is obtained with the proposed topology when compared to LNA without noise cancelling technique. Higher and flat power gain of 24.24 dB (average) and NF of 3.16 dB is achieved over the 6600 MHz UWB spectrum.

References

1. Razavi, B., Aytur, T., Lam, C., Yang, F.-R., Li, K.-Y., Yan, R.-H., Kang, H.-C., Hsu, C.-C., Lee, C.-C.: A UWB CMOS transceiver. IEEE J. Solid-State Circuits 40, 2555–2562 (2005)
2. Ismail, A., Abidi, A.: A 3.1- to 8.2-GHz direct conversion receiver for MB-OFDM UWB communications. Dig. Tech. Papers IEEE ISSCC, pp. 208–209 (2005)
3. Lee, F.S., Chandrakasan, A.P.: A BiCMOS ultra-wide-band 3.1–10.6-GHz front-end. IEEE J. Solid-State Circuits 41(8), 1784–1791 (2006)
4. Bevilacqua, A., Niknejad, A.M.: An ultra wideband CMOS low-noise amplifier for 3.1–10.6-GHz wireless receivers. IEEE J. Solid-State Circuits 39(12), 2259–2268 (2004)
5. Shekhar, S., Li, X., Allstot, D.J.: A CMOS 3.1-10.6 GHz UWB LNA employing stagger-compensated series peaking. In: Proc. IEEE Radio Frequency Integrated Circuits (RFIC) Symp., p. 4 (2006)
6. Bruccoleri, F., Klumperink, E.A.M., Nauta, B.: Wide-Band CMOS Low-Noise Amplifier Exploiting Thermal Noise Cancelling. IEEE Journal of Solid-State Circuits 39, 275–282 (2004)
7. Liao, C.-F., Liu, S.I.: A broadband noise-cancelling MOS LNA for 3.1–10.6-GHz UWB receiver. IEEE J. Solid-State Circuits 42(2), 329–339 (2007)
8. Chen, W.H., Liu, G., Zdravko, B., Niknejad, A.M.: A highly linear broadband CMOS LNA employing noise and distortion cancellation. In: IEEE Radio Freq. Integrated Circuits Symp. Dig., pp. 61–64 (2007)
9. Chen, X., Silva-Martinez, J., Hoyos, S.: A CMOS Differential Noise Cancelling Low Noise Transconductance Amplifier. In: IEEE Dallas, Circuits and Systems Workshop, pp. 1–4 (2008)
10. Lu, Y., Yeo, K.S., Cabuk, A., Ma, J., Do, M.A., Lu, Z.: A novel CMOS low-noise amplifier design for 3.1-to-10.6-GHz ultra-wideband wireless receiver. IEEE Trans. Circuits Systems 53(8), 1683–1692 (2006)

A Combined CMOS Reference Circuit
with Supply and Temperature Compensation

Madhusoodan Agrawal and Alpana Agarwal

Thapar University, Patiala, India
vashu13jan@gmail.com, alpana@thapar.edu

Abstract. In this paper, a Combined CMOS Reference Circuit is proposed in UMC 180 nm standard CMOS Process. It consists of a start-up circuit, a current generator, and a voltage generator. This circuit achieves a nominal value of 50.11 μA and 776.4 mV for current and voltage respectively, from a 1.8 V supply voltage. The line sensitivity of 285 ppm/V and 347 ppm/V for current and voltage is achieved respectively, under the ±10 % variation in supply voltage. The temperature coefficient for current and voltage are 93 ppm/°C and 295 ppm/°C respectively in temperature ranges −40 °C to 125 °C.

Keywords: Beta Multiplier, Current reference, Oscillators, Temperature compensation, Voltage Reference.

1   Introduction

In most Mixed Signal circuits, Reference Circuit is a key component in the design of many analog and mixed signal applications including PLL, Analog-to-Digital Convertor (ADC), Voltage Regulators, Digital to Analog Convertor (DAC) and many other measurement and control systems. The Reference Circuit is required to be insensitive to supply and temperature variations.

Many current reference and voltage reference circuits have been reported [1–3]. The references are used individually for generating fixed value of current or voltage for the particular use in mixed signal design [4, 5] . These individual current and voltage reference circuits fail, when there is a requirement of both fixed current and voltage in any circuit, *e.g.* a oscillator circuit requires both current and voltage reference. So the main aim of this work is to offer a design methodology for a combined reference circuit, which provides both current as well as voltage with a better supply and temperature independency.

The paper is organized as follows. Section 2 presents about the basic building blocks of the proposed combined reference circuits. Section 3 describes the simulation and various results of proposed reference circuit, which is followed by discussion and conclusions in Section 4.

M.S. Gaur et al. (Eds.): VDAT 2013, CCIS 382, pp. 177–184, 2013.

2   Proposed Circuit

The combined reference circuit is illustrated in Fig. 1.The circuit consists of mainly three blocks. The first block is start-up circuit. The next block is current generator and the last block provides a voltage generator.

2.1   Start-Up Circuit

A start-up circuit is used to set the desired operating point of the circuit. Once the desired state is reached, the start-up circuit should not interfere with the circuit. The start-up circuit is shown in Fig. 1.

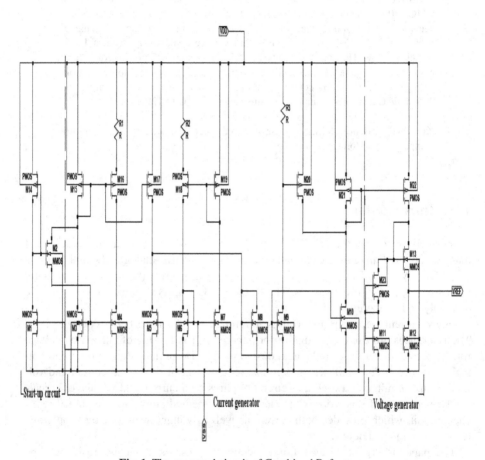

Fig. 1. The proposed circuit of Combined Reference

2.2   Current Generator

The current generator, is used in the proposed circuit is marked in Fig. 1. In previous work [4], the supply dependency is high, so to reduce the supply dependency at lower technology the following circuit is to be shown here. It gives the current, which is almost insensitive to supply and temperature variations. In Fig. 1 two beta multipliers generate currents I_1 and I_2 respectively. Now the common terminology in this circuit is that, when two parallel lines will subtract with different magnitude, then we get a straight line. So these two currents I_1 and I_2 are applied to a sub-tractor circuit and a current is generated, which must be supply independent [4].

The output of Beta-Multiplier is given as

$$I_1 = \frac{2}{\mu_p C_{ox}(W/L)_P} \frac{1}{R^2} \left\{ \left(1 - \frac{1}{\sqrt{K_1}}\right)^2 \right\} \tag{1}$$

&

$$I_2 = \frac{2}{\mu_p C_{ox}(W/L)_P} \frac{1}{R^2} \left\{ N\left(1 - \frac{1}{\sqrt{K_1}}\right)^2 \right\} \tag{2}$$

Now these current pass through the sub-tractor circuit and the final current is given as

$$I_S = \frac{2}{\mu_p C_{ox}(W/L)_P} \frac{1}{R^2} \left\{ \left(1 - \frac{1}{\sqrt{K_1}}\right)^2 - N\left(1 - \frac{1}{\sqrt{K_1}}\right)^2 \right\} \tag{3}$$

The supply insensitive current I_S has a positive temperature coefficient. So the temperature sensitivity is also compensated by using a simple current subtraction.

2.3   Voltage Generator

The voltage generator is also shown in Fig. 1. It simply consists of four transistors. The first two transistors work as potential divider. And the next two transistors biased by I_S. Here maximum portion of current pass through last two transistors. Here we use a Active potential divider circuitry instead of passive circuit by using two transistors. So this improves the overall performance of reference circuit.

The output voltage V_{REF} of the circuit is given by

$$V_{REF} = V_{SGM23} + V_{GSM21} - V_{GSM13} \tag{4}$$

By using the current-voltage characteristic of a MOS transistor and neglecting the channel length modulation effect, the value of reference voltage is given as

$$V_{REF} = V_{th} + \left\{ \left(1 + \sqrt{\frac{K_{M21}}{K_{M23}}} \right) - \sqrt{\frac{(W/L)_{M12}}{(W/L)_{M13}}} \right\} \cdot \sqrt{\frac{2.I0}{K_{M21} + K_{M12}}} \qquad (5)$$

Where $K_i = \mu_i.C_{ox}$, $V_{th} = |V_{thM23}| + V_{thM21} - V_{thM13}$, μ is the mobility of electron in the channel, C_{ox} is the oxide capacitance per unit area, V_{th} is the threshold voltage, and W and L are the channel width and length respectively [5].

3   Simulation and Results

The proposed combined reference circuit is implemented in 0.18 μm CMOS 1.8 V technology. Fig. 2 and Fig. 3 show the characteristics of current and voltage reference for supply variation from 1.62 to 1.98 V for Pre and Post simulation.

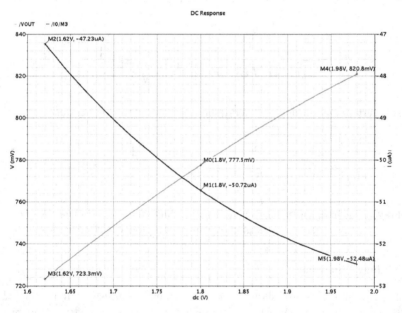

Fig. 2. Pre-Simulated behavior of the Combined Reference with Supply Variation

The Pre-Simulation average supply dependency for current is 285 ppm/V and for voltage is 348 ppm/V, while for Post-Simulation average supply dependency for current is 285 ppm/V and for voltage is 347 ppm/V. Fig. 4 and Fig. 5 show the Pre and Post Simulation results for current and voltage reference, while temperature ranges from –40 °C to 125 °C. The Pre-Simulation average temperature coefficients are 98 ppm/°C and 293 ppm/°C for current and voltage generator respectively, while for Post-Simulation average temperature coefficients are 93 ppm/°C and 295 ppm/°C for current and voltage generator. Fig. 6 shows the layout of the proposed Combined Reference Circuit.

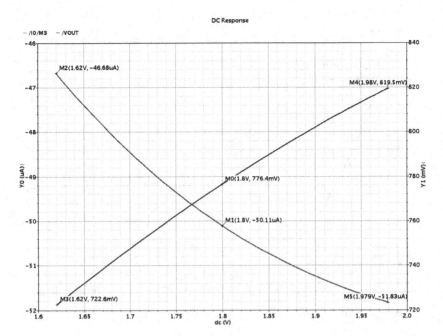

Fig. 3. Post-Simulated behavior of the Combined Reference with Supply Variation

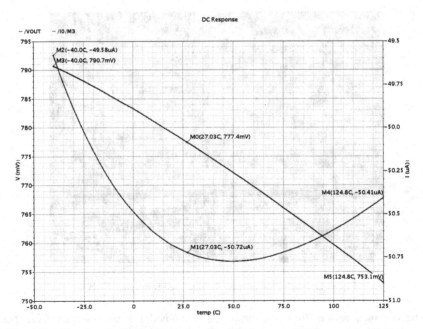

Fig. 4. Pre-Simulated behavior of the Combined Reference with Temperature Variation

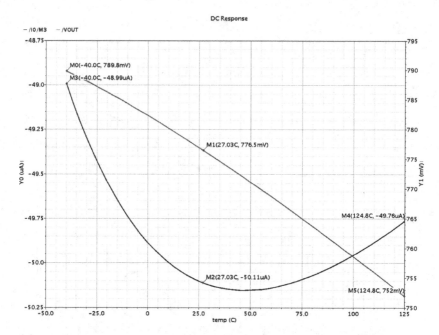

Fig. 5. Post-Simulated behavior of the Combined Reference with Temperature Variation

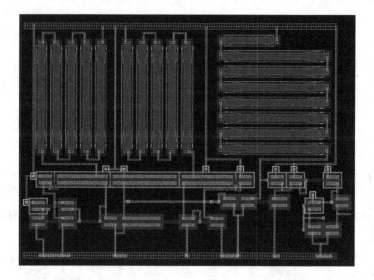

Fig. 6. Layout of the proposed Combined Reference Circuit

The obtained results from the proposed combined reference circuit have been compared with the available comparable references in Table 1.

Table 1. Comparison table of various reference circuits

References Parameters	[4]	[5]	This Work
Year	2011	2007	2013
CMOS Technology (μm)	0.09	0.25	0.18
Temperature Range (°C)	−40~125	0~120	−40~125
Supply Voltage (V)	1.6	3.3	1.8
V_{REF}(mV)	771	N/A	776.4
I_{REF}(μA)	N/A	10.45	50.11
Temperature Coeffi cient (TC)			
For Current Reference	7.5	720	93
For Voltage Reference (ppm/°C)	N/A	N/A	295
Supply Dependency			
For Current Reference	N/A	1700	285
For Voltage Reference (ppm/V)	N/A	N/A	347
Chip Area (mm^2)	0.03	0.002	0.002

4   Conclusion

A Combined Voltage and Current Reference Circuit has been proposed in standard 180 nm CMOS process that exhibits excellent supply and Temperature independency. The design of CMOS Current generator is by simply subtracting two current outputs with the same dependencies on the supply voltage and temperature. While for Voltage generator we used the Active load, which gives the fix value of voltage with variations in supply voltage and temperature. Achieved results show that developed Architecture of combined reference can be easily used for oscillators and many other mixed signal integrated circuits with better Supply and Temperature dependency.

References

1. Leung, K.N., Mok, P.K.T.: A sub-1-V 15 ppm/°C CMOS bandgap voltage reference without requiring low threshold voltage device. IEEE J. Solid-State Circuits 37, 526–530 (2002)
2. Tanaka, H., Nakagome, Y., Etoh, J., Yamasaki, E., Aoki, M., Miyazawa, K.: Sub-1V A dynamic reference voltage generator for battery operated DRAMs. IEEE J. Solid-State Circuits 29(4), 448–453 (1994)

3. Ueno, K., Hirose, T., Asai, T., Amemiya, Y.: A 1μW 600-ppm/°C Current Reference Circuit Consisting of Sub threshold CMOS Circuits. IEEE Transaction on Circuits and Systems-II: Express Briefs 57(9) (September 2010)
4. Yoo, C., Park, J.: CMOS current reference with supply and temperature compensation. Electronics Letters 43(25) (December 2007)
5. Samir, A., Girardeau, L., Bert, Y., Kussener, E., Rahajandraibe, W., Barthelemy, H.: 771mV, 173nA, 90nm CMOS resistorless trimmable voltage reference. In: IEEE 9th International New Circuits and System Conference (NEWCAS) (June 2011)

Convex Optimization of Energy and Delay Using Logical Effort Method in Deep Sub-micron Technology

Sachin Maheshwari, Rameez Raza, Pramod Kumar, and Anu Gupta

Department of Electrical and Electronics Engineering, BITS, Pilani, India
{sachin.mahe,rameez.alig,pramodkumarchennoju}@gmail.com,
anug@pilani.bits-pilani.ac.in

Abstract. Tradeoff between the power dissipation and speed is one of the major issues in modern VLSI circuit design. Improving the circuit speed methods typically lead to excessive power consumption. In this work, we explore the energy-delay design in CMOS circuits, to find gate sizes which produce the lowest possible energy and delay. Our analysis methods include delay minimization using logical effort, formulating energy relationship with logical effort model and then optimizing the energy-delay using optimization technique. Thus, we introduce the Energy-Delay-Gain (EDG) to measure the energy reduction rate for each delay increase that is acceptable by the designer. The simulation is done using Spectre in cadence environment in UMC90nm CMOS technology.

Keywords: convex optimization, delay, energy-delay-gain, logical effort, deep-sub-micron technology.

1 Introduction

The logical effort model is used commonly to estimate the delay of logic gates [1], [2],[3].But the model used will not provide proper energy performance of the digital circuits. Energy optimization can be achieved with equalization of sensitivities to sizing, supply and threshold voltage compared to the reference design sized for minimum delay [4].

In [5] a simple and yet accurate closed-form expression for power estimation has be developed for CMOS gates but the method does not incorporate the effect of parameters like change in library, rise and fall time of input, etc.

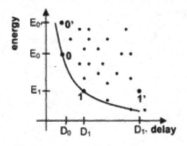

Fig. 1. Energy Efficient Curve

M.S. Gaur et al. (Eds.): VDAT 2013, CCIS 382, pp. 185–193, 2013.
© Springer-Verlag Berlin Heidelberg 2013

The energy efficient curve[6] which shows the optimal implementations in the energy-delay plane is shown in fig.1. By sizing the gates using logical effort we minimized delay to reach point 0. Although we get delay reduced but energy is increased, in order to reach the optimized point 1 we have to use certain optimization technique which will complete our goal.

In this paper, we proposed a model based on logical effort and optimization technique to get proper trade-off between energy and delay in digital CMOS circuits. Energy-Delay-Gain (EDG) is used to get the optimized value of energy and delay as in [6]. But in this paper, we developed a relationship between energy and logical effort model which is used for optimization. We used logical effort method to reduce the delay to minimum value but it will give larger power dissipation. To achieve proper trade-off between energy and delay we formulated a problem which can be solved using geometric programming.

The paper is organized as follows: Section 2, describes the method to obtain delay efficient design. Section 3, illustrates the dependence of power on logical effort (g) and electrical effort (h). In section 4, energy equation has been derived and the energy delay (EDG) model is introduced. Section 5, discusses the optimization technique. Finally, a conclusion is presented in the last section.

2   Delay Efficient Design

In order to get delay efficient circuit we sized the gates using logical effort technique. Logical effort is a design methodology for estimating the delay of CMOS logic circuits. The method also specifies the proper number of logic stages on a path and the best transistor sizes for the logic gates.

Using logical effort delay can be expressed as in [3] given by:

$$d = (gh + p)\,\tau \tag{1}$$

Where,
g = logical effort, h = electrical effort, p = parasitic delay, τ = basic delay unit

2.1   Calculation of Delay for Single Inverter

In the delay expression, to get the value of the electrical effort we require to find the input capacitance of an inverter

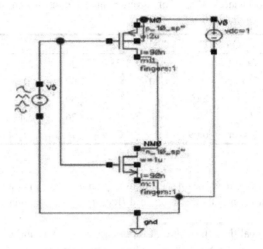

Fig. 2. CMOS inverter

From fig.2, C_{gdp}, C_{gdn} are contributing capacitances at input side as well as at the output as in [7], so by using miller effect the capacitance at the input side are;

$$C_{gdp}' = (1+Av)C_{gdp} \qquad (2)$$

$$C_{gdn}' = (1+Av)C_{gdn} \qquad (3)$$

Here the gain of an inverter (Av) is unity. Theoretically, the total input capacitance is given by;

$$C_{in} = C_{gsp} + C_{gsn} + 2C_{gdp} + 2C_{gdn} \qquad (4)$$

Here, we have taken the dimensions of an inverter as Wn=1um, Wp=2um and L=90nm. The value of oxide thickness was found to be 2.25nm for NMOS and 2.45nm for PMOS for UMC 90nm technology file. Based on oxide thickness values the oxide capacitance value, which is given by ε_{ox}/t_{ox}, is calculated for both NMOS and PMOS respectively. We found for UMC 90nm technology the oxide thickness values of NMOS and PMOS are found to be 2.25nm and 2.45nm respectively. Hence we get the oxide capacitances of NMOS and PMOS as:

$$Coxp = 14.087 \text{ mF/m}^2$$
$$Cox_n = 15.34 \text{ mF/m}^2$$

In order to calculate the input capacitances of an inverter different regions of operation of an inverter are considered and input capacitances in each case is calculated as in [7], and the values found are given in the table below:

Table 1. Input Capacitances (C_{in}) of inverter in different region of operations. All Capacitances are in femtofarad (fF).

S.No.	PMOS	NMOS	C_{gsn}	C_{gdn}	C_{gbn}	C_{gsp}	C_{gdp}	C_{gbp}	$C_{in,total}$
1	Linear	Cutoff	0	0	1.38	1.26	2.4	0	5.18
2	Sat.	Linear	0.69	1.30	0	1.69	0	0	3.69
3	Sat.	Sat.	2.07	0	0	1.69	0	0	2.60
4	Linear	Sat.	2.07	0	0	1.26	2.4	0	4.72
5	Cutoff	Linear	0.69	1.30	0	0	0	1.26	3.33

Finally, the theoretical value of the input capacitance, C_{in} is calculated by taking average of all input capacitances found in different regions of operation and is found to be 3.923 fF.

Now, in order to validate the value of input capacitances found theoretically, simulation is carried out using Spectre in cadence environment in UMC 90nm CMOS technology and the values found are given in the table 2.

Table 2. Simulated CMOS inverter junction capacitances for different gate voltages using Spectre in cadence environment in UMC 90nm CMOS technology

V_G	C_{gsn} (fF)	$2C_{gdn}$ (fF)	C_{gsp} (fF)	$2C_{gdp}$ (fF)	$C_{in,total}$ (fF)
0	0.376	0.667	2.038	1.261	4.33
0.1	0.425	0.680	1.970	1.265	4.341
0.2	0.511	0.742	1.755	1.270	4.278
0.3	0.615	0.736	1.510	1.277	4.138
0.4	0.685	0.730	1.311	1.280	4.004
0.5	0.770	0.728	1.111	1.283	3.888
0.6	0.851	0.727	1.000	1.286	3.855
0.7	0.950	0.725	0.770	1.290	3.753
0.8	1.120	0.724	0.740	1.292	3.876
0.9	1.157	0.723	0.670	1.297	3.824
1.0	1.172	0.722	0.630	1.30	3.824

Taking the average of the simulated value, the input capacitance comes out to be 4.077fF. Thus, the theoretical value calculated is approximately same as simulated value. To calculate delay for an inverter we require the value of τ and parasitic capacitance, p_{inv}. Thus, the delay of an inverter is calculated at different loads is shown in fig. 3.

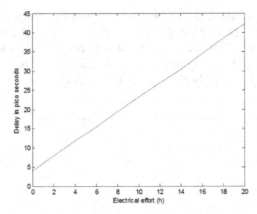

Fig. 3. Graph between Delay and electrical effort

We calibrated τ by measuring the delay of a logic gate as a function of delay and electrical effort and fitting straight line to the results. The slope of the above curve gives the τ for particular technology that is found to be equal to 1.92ps. The straight line intersect the h=0 axis at d= τ p_{inv}. Thus, the value of p_{inv} is found to be 2.1019.

Validation for the above values were done by calculating the value of delay theoretically for h=4, which comes out to be 11.715ps. At h=4, the simulated value is 11.815ps from fig.3. The percentage error is less than 1% for the above calculated values. Thus, from the above result, we finalized that the theoretical delay and practical delays are matched for an inverter.

2.2   Gate Sizing for Delay Minimization

Now, an inverter chain having 7 stages with load capacitance of 100fF is considered. The delay calculated without sizing the chain of inverter, by considering all inverter dimensions equal for all stages, was found to be 198.16ps.

Now, resizing the chain of inverters for minimum delay the logical effort method is used as in [3] and the widths of all the transistors are calculated for the load capacitance of 100fF.

After resizing the gates of inverter stages using logical effort technique, the delay of the inverter chain was found to be 116.044ps. Validation of this is done by simulating the inverter chain, for which the delay was found to be 113.9ps. The percentage error is less than 2% for the above calculated values. Thus, from the above result we finalized that the theoretical delay and practical delays are matched for an inverter chain.

3   Power Dependence on Logical Effort

To determine the dependence of power on the logical effort parameter 'g' we used two different inverter configurations, one having single NMOS and PMOS transistors and another having two NMOS and one PMOS transistors, to vary input capacitance so as to vary logical effort, g. The input capacitance, C_{in} changes as the width of the MOSFET's change, as a result the logical effort, g and electrical effort, h also changes. To keep the electrical effort, h value as constant so as to capture only the effect of logical effort, g the output load capacitance, C_{out} is also changed. Fig. 3 shows that Power, P is directly proportional to logical effort, g.

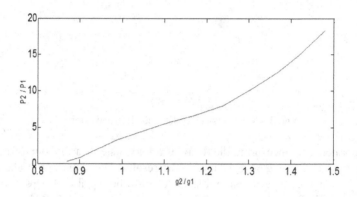

Fig. 4. Graph showing power and logical effort

Another factor which changes the power, P is the change in electrical effort, h. Hence, the effect of change of h is captured by changing the output load, C_{out} while the width of the MOSFET's is kept constant, which keeps input capacitance, C_{in} to be constant. With change in C_{out} the logical effort, g and parasitic, p remains constant and hence, the change in power is only due to the change in electrical effort value. Fig. 5 also shows that power, P is directly proportional to the electrical effort.

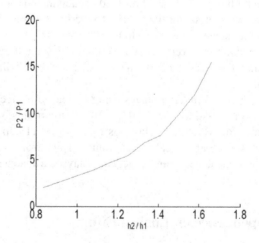

Fig. 5. Graph showing power and electrical effort

4   Analytical Model

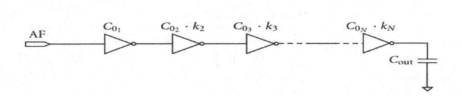

Fig. 6. Chain of Inverter

From the above section for single stage we found that;

$$P \propto gh \tag{5}$$

For multiple stage;

$$P = K[g_1 h_1 + g_2 h_2 + g_3 h_3 + \underline{\hspace{2cm}} + g_N h_N] \tag{6}$$

Where 'K' depends upon following factors

- Supply Voltage
- Rise time and Fall time of inputs
- Other MOS parameters like C_{ox} and mobility of transistors which depends upon the model libraries
- Sub threshold conduction

Further, Initial Energy, E_0 is given as

$$E_0 = K[AF_1 g_1 h_1 + AF_2 g_2 h_2 + AF_3 g_3 h_3 + \underline{\hspace{2cm}} + AF_4 g_N h_N] \tag{7}$$

After re-sizing gates by factor 'k_i' the final energy E_f comes out to be:

$$E_f = K \left[\sum_{i=1}^{N} AF_i \, k_{i+1} g_{i+1} + AF_{out} \prod h_i \, g_1 k_1 C_{in} \right] \tag{8}$$

Where,

- AF_i:activity factor (switching probability) of gate i
- AF_{out}:output activity factor of gate i
- g_i:logical effort of gate i
- p_i:parasitic delay of gate i
- k_i: sizing factor for gate i. The k's are used in the gate re-sizing process

When using the logical effort notation, the initial path delay D_0 is

$$D_0 = \Sigma \, g_i \, h_i + P \tag{9}$$

After re-sizing gates by factor 'k$_i$' the final delay D$_f$ comes out to be:

$$D_f = \Sigma_{i=1}^N g_i \frac{C_{i+1}k_{i+1}}{C_i k_i} + P \tag{10}$$

$$D_i = g_i \frac{C_{i+1}}{C_i} \tag{11}$$

Therefore,

$$D_f = \Sigma_{i=1}^N D_i \frac{k_{i+1}}{k_i} + P \tag{12}$$

We get the delay increase rate (d$_{inc}$) due to re-sizing of the gates as;

$$d_{inc} = \frac{\Sigma_{i=1}^N D_i \frac{k_{i+1}}{k_i} + P - D_0}{D_0} \tag{13}$$

Energy-Delay-Gain is the parameter used to optimize the power consumption of the circuit.

It is defined as follows;

$$EDG = \frac{\frac{E_0 - E_f}{E_0}}{\frac{D_f - D_0}{D_0}} \tag{14}$$

Where,

$$\text{Energy gain} = \frac{E_0 - E_f}{E_0} \quad \text{Delay gain} = \frac{D_f - D_0}{D_0}$$

5   Optimization Technique

In order to do optimization we formulated an Objective function using equation 8 and is given by;

$$f_0(k_1, k_2, k_3, - - - - - - - -, k_N) = K \left[\sum_{i=1}^N AF_i \, k_{i+1}g_{i+1} + AF_{out} \prod h_i \, g_1 k_1 C_{in} \right] \tag{15}$$

To get the Constraint goal we use (13) which will give

$$f_1(k_1, k_2, - - - - - - - - - - - k_N) = \sum_{i=1}^N \left(\left(\frac{D_i}{d_{inc}D_0 + D_0 - P} \right) \frac{k_{i+1}}{k_i} \right) \leq 1 \tag{16}$$

(15) and (16) forms the optimization problem, which we will solve using geometric programming problem technique. Geometric programming is an optimization technique applicable to non-linear programming problems involving mathematical functions called posynomials. This technique involves the use arithmetic mean-geometric mean inequality for any number of non-negative numbers.

6   Conclusion

We proposed a convex optimization model based on logical effort theory, extended to model energy and delay, to give the optimum energy-delay trade-off through gate sizing. The proposed model expresses switching energy of CMOS gates which reduces the mathematical complexity and gives a good insight about a circuit performance. The validation of the above model can be done either by solving mathematically and then simulating or using MATLAB programming.

Acknowledgments. The authors are grateful to the lab facilities (Oysters Lab) of Department of Electrical & Electronics Engineering at Birla Institute of Technology & Science (BITS), Pilani where the work has been carried out.

References

1. Cheng, C.W., Markovic, D.: Delay Estimation and Sizing of CMOS Logic Using Logical Effort With Slope Correction. IEEE Transactions on Circuits and Systems—II: Express Briefs 56(8), 634–638 (2009)
2. Tiwari, S.C., Gupta, A., Singh, K., Gupta, M.: Logical effort based automated transistor width optimization methodology. In: IEEE World Congress on Information and Communication Technologies, Trivandrum, pp. 1067–1072 (2011)
3. Sutherland, I.E., Sproull, B.F., Harris, D.L.: Logical Effort: Design fast CMOS circuits (1998)
4. Markovic, D., Stojanovic, V., Nikolic, B., Horowitz, M.A., Brodersen, R.D.: Methods for True Energy-Performance Optimization. IEEE Journal of Solid-State Circuits 39(8), 1282–1293 (2004)
5. Kabbanin, A.: Logical effort based dynamic power estimation and optimization of static CMOS circuits. Integral, the VLSI Journal 43, 279–288 (2010)
6. Aizik, Y., Kolodny, A.: Exploration of Energy-Delay Tradeoff in Digital circuit Design. In: IEEE (2008)
7. Kang, S.M., Leblebici, Y.: CMOS digital integrated circuits analysis and design (2003)
8. Mittal, K.V.: Optimization Methods in operations research and system analysis (2007)

A Cache-Aware Strategy for H.264 Decoding on Multi-processor Architectures

Arani Bhattacharya[1], Ansuman Banerjee[1], Susmita Sur-Kolay[1],
Prasenjit Basu, and Bhaskar J. Karmakar[2,*]

[1] Indian Statistical Institute
{arani89,prasenjit.basu}@gmail.com,
{ansuman,ssk}@isical.ac.in
[2] S3Craft Technologies
bhaskar@s3craft.com

Abstract. H.264-AVC is one of the most popular formats for the recording, compression and distribution of video. Encoders and decoders for the H.264 standard are widely in demand, and efficient strategies for enhancing their performance have been areas of active research. With the proliferation of many-core architectures in the embedded community, there has been a trend towards parallelizing implementations of encoders and decoders. In this paper, we present a run time heuristic which exploits macro-block level parallelism and efficient scheduling inside a H.264 decoder to reduce the number of cache misses and improve the processor utilization. Experiments on standard benchmarks show a significant speed-up over contemporary strategies proposed in literature.

1 Introduction

H.264/MPEG-4 Part 10 or AVC (Advanced Video Coding) is one of the most common video formats in recent times. H.264 provides much better compression ratios than most other video formats such as H.263 and MPEG-2. Encoders and decoders for the H.264 standard are widely in demand, and efficient strategies for enhancing their performance have been areas of active research.

Security applications typically involve widespread deployment of H.264. In the security context, videos are mostly intra-coded, i.e. all existent motion dependencies are within the same frame. Intra-coded videos have therefore been a subject of active research in both the academic and industrial setting.

With the proliferation of many core architectures in the embedded community, there has been a trend towards parallelizing implementations of encoders and decoders. In general, these proposals have focused on efficient exploitation of inherent parallelism (at the frame level, slice level or macro-block level) in the

* This work was started while Bhaskar J. Karmakar and Prasenjit Basu were at Texas Instruments, India. The authors would like to acknowledge the financial assistance received from Texas Instruments, and thank Dr. Mahesh Mehendale, Fellow, Texas Instruments for his continuous encouragement and support.

M.S. Gaur et al. (Eds.): VDAT 2013, CCIS 382, pp. 194–203, 2013.

video structure with an aim of achieving better decode performance by load balancing and distribution of workload among available processors, while honouring video dependency constraints as applicable.

For intra-coded videos, strategies exploiting macro-block level parallelism have been found to be more successful in general. The problem in this setting essentially is to identify the macro-block dependency structure inside a H.264 slice/frame, in order to process the macro-blocks in parallel (honouring dependencies as applicable) on the available processors in a multi-core setting, with an objective to minimize the end-to-end decode time. Both static and dynamic macro-block scheduling strategies have been proposed. Static scheduling strategies in general assume worst case dependency patterns among the constituent macro-blocks and often, equal processing times, irrespective of their types.

This paper has two important considerations. A static scheduling approach, which assumes uniform macro-block processing times, leads to poor processor utilization. In reality, macro-block processing times vary depending on the inputs and the dependency structure. Hence, it is possible to improve the effective processor utilization by adopting a dynamic scheduling approach that assigns macro-blocks to free processors as soon as they are ready, as opposed to a static solution that would normally schedule at pre-defined intervals. In addition to improving utilization, we also show that the effective speed-up obtained crucially depends on the cache interaction of the decode strategy in a multi-processor setting with a hierarchical (private L1, shared L2, DRAM) memory structure. Many of the existing decode strategies often do not consider the cache misses resulting from cache oblivious selection of the macro-blocks to be processed, which in turn leads to significant slowdown in decoder performance due to frequent accesses to the lower and slower memory levels.

Our work has two proposals for harnessing the effective power of parallel computation in a multi-core setting. On one hand, we propose a cache-aware [5] scheduling strategy to minimize the number of cache misses, by carefully selecting the macro-blocks to be considered next, keeping in view the chance of a macro-block it depends on, getting evicted from the cache due to capacity or conflict misses. On the other hand, we attempt to improve the number of macro-blocks available for processing at every time point, which in turn implies better processor utilization and hence, improvement in speedup.

We implemented our schedule heuristic and evaluated it on a number of standard benchmarks. Experiments have shown significant speed up as compared to methods that currently exist.

2   Background and Related Work

A H.264 video [1, 6] consists of a sequence of frames. A frame is an array of luma samples and two corresponding arrays of chroma samples. Each frame is further divided into spatial units called slices. A slice consists of blocks of 16 x 16 pixels, known as macro-blocks (MB). A macro-block contains type information describing the choice of methods used to code the macro-block and prediction

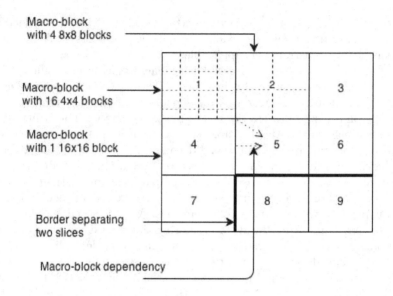

Fig. 1. A 3x3 H.264 frame

information such as intra prediction mode information and coded residual data. Within a macro-block, luma samples may be coded as one of the three types of block sizes, namely 4x4, 8x8 or 16x16 pixels. Chroma samples are commonly coded as blocks of 8x8 pixels.

Reconstruction is an important step in the decoding an H.264 video frame. Reconstruction of a decoded macro-block involves obtaining the data from neighbouring macro-blocks based on which motion prediction had been made by the encoder. This cannot be done independently, but only after fetching data of neighbouring macro-blocks. In an intra-coded video frame, all dependencies are in the same frame of video. In addition, a MB includes a variable amount of residual information that cannot be inferred from previous MBs.

Attempts to parallelize the reconstruction step have been done at frame-level, slice-level and macroblock-level. At the frame level, different frames are decoded by different cores. However, this leads to too much pressure on the memory system. Since there are no dependencies among macro-blocks across slices, slice-level parallelism places much lower demands on the memory system. However, since the number and dimensions of the slices are variable, it leads to poor load-balancing. Thus, macro-block level parallelism is the most commonly used technique to implement parallel H.264 decoders. [3] presents an excellent survey of approaches to H.264 decoder parallelization proposed in literature.

The 2D wavefront approach [3] for parallel H.264 decoding exploits macro-block level parallelism and computes a static schedule and a processor allocation strategy. This has been quite successful in practice and proved to be an efficient solution in a multi-processor setting. Figure 2 shows a snapshot of this method

1A	2A	3A	4A	5A	6A	7A	8A	9A	11A	13A
3B	4B	5B	6B	7B	8B	9B	11B	13B	15A	17A
5C	7C	7C	8C	9C	11C	13C	15B	17B	19A	21A
7D	8D	9D	11D	13D	15C	17C	19B	21B	23A	25A
10D	12D	14D	15D	17D	19C	21C	23B	25B	27A	29A
14C	16D	18D	19D	21D	23C	25C	27B	29B	31A	32A
18C	20D	22D	23D	25D	27C	29C	31B	32B	33A	34A
22C	24D	26D	27D	29D	31C	32C	33B	34B	35A	36A
26C	28D	30D	31D	32D	33C	34C	35B	36B	37A	38A

Fig. 2. 2D wavefront in action

in action on a frame with 99 MBs, in a 4 processor setup. A, B, C, and D are
the 4 processors. Each MB is labelled with the processor to which it is assigned.
Also, the number associated with each MB denotes the cycle at which the MB
will be processed. For example, the topmost leftmost MB (labelled as 1A) will
be processed in the first cycle on processor A. The next MB to its right, being
dependent on it (1A), cannot start till it finishes, and hence, is assigned to time
unit 2 in the same processor. The entire frame is processed in 38 time units on
4 processors, in the schedule as mentioned as labels on the MBs in Figure 2.
In order to improve scalability, this has been further extended to 3-dimensional
approach (3D wavefront), where two or more frames are decoded simultaneously
depending on the number of idle cores in the multiprocessor system [2].

3   Motivation and Objectives

Our work has several important considerations that makes it different from those
proposed in literature. Static approaches to parallelize decoding [3], in general,
assume, a regular dependency structure for a MB and equal processing times,
i.e. each MB is dependent on all its four neighbours [1] (top left, top, top right,
and side left), depending on which of these are actually present according to its
position (the top row MBs excepting the leftmost one, for example, only have
left dependency edges). However, in reality, there is a lot of input-dependent
variation, and in practice, the dependencies vary across MBs. In effect, a MB
can actually turn out to depend on one / two / three / all /none of its neighbours,
a fact that can lead to improvement in decode performance in a parallel setting.
This motivates a dynamic run-time schedule strategy.

Secondly, static methods often schedule MBs at uniform intervals on all cores,
assuming all MBs have equal processing times. This is not true in H.264. This
forces some of the cores to remain idle. For example, in Figure 2, if processor
A finishes processing MB 15A early, it has to wait for other cores. We assume

variable processing times, and also attempt to improve on processor utilization through our MB selection method.

Finally, most of the techniques for parallel decoding do not consider cache misses. Consider the working of the wavefront strategy as shown in Figure 2. The gray shaded MBs are the ones needed in the processor cache for processing the yellow ones (since worst case 4-neighbour dependency is assumed). For example, for processing the MB marked 15A in core A, the processor needs to load the MBs 9A, 11A, 13A and 13B in the local cache. Since the MB marked 13B is being processed in core B, this means, we need to fetch its data present in core B of L1 through L2. An important consideration that can reduce cache misses is to avoid the same MB being reloaded into cache. This can be done by giving priority to MBs whose parents have a chance of being expelled due the cache replacement policy. In our schedule heuristic, we keep this under consideration.

4   Cache-Aware Heuristic

In this section, we present the details of our MB scheduling and processor allocation strategy in a multi-processor setting with a private L1 cache, a shared L2 cache and DRAM. We assume the following about the processor model.

- Every cache uses Least Recently Used (LRU) replacement policy.
- All caches are assumed to follow multi-level inclusion policy, i.e., if some data item is present in L1 cache, then it is also present in L2 cache and DRAM. Similar policy is also followed for L2 cache. However, the data present in DRAM may be obsolete.
- L1 cache is assumed to use write-through policy. L2 cache is, however, assumed to use write-back policy.
- Write-invalidate is used at L2 cache to ensure memory consistency. In other words, when some data is written to the L1 cache of some processor, that data is immediately invalidated at all other L1 caches, and the updated data is brought in from L2.
- Bus arbitration of L2 cache is done on First Come First Serve (FCFS) basis.

We further assume that all frames are fully accommodated in the main memory. Thus, there is no need for disk access at any point of time. We now define the concept of *cache flush time*, a key element of our schedule heuristic.

Definition 1. *The cache flush time τ of a node u is the number of cache misses for which the node will be present in the cache.*

Since we assume a LRU replacement policy, the cache flush times can be obtained from the LRU counters in a modern architecture. The MB scheduling problem is modelled as a scheduling problem on a task graph, where the MBs form the nodes and for each dependency relation between a pair of MBs (u, v), there is a directed edge from u to v if the MB for v depends on u. We call such a task graph that is used to model this problem as a frame task graph. A node (i.e. a MB) of the frame task graph is labelled with three components.

- Macro-block type: Indicates the type of block size present, i.e. 4x4/8x8/16x16.
- Position of macroblock dependency in memory hierarchy: For each dependency of a macro-block, the position in the memory hierarchy (L1 cache, L2 cache or DRAM) where the dependency macroblock is present.
- Cache flush time: For each dependency of a macroblock, the value of τ.

4.1 Proposed Algorithm

Our heuristic method uses simple priority-based scheduling. It has a ready queue A of macro-blocks that can be accessed by any processor. A processor that becomes idle accesses the ready queue, calculates the priority value of each macro-block present in the queue using the algorithm described below and then chooses the one having the highest priority for decoding. Priority of a macro-block depends on the position of the macro-blocks in memory, their cache flush times and the number of available macro-blocks in the ready queue. While assigning priority, we take into account the following factors:

- Minimum cache flush time of L2 among all nodes (CFT_{L2}): We examine each node in A, one or more of whose parents reside in the L2 cache. For each node, we compute the parent with minimum τ value (i.e. has the most chance of being evicted), and find that node in A whose parent has the highest chance of being evicted, i.e, the minimum τ value – we call this CFT_{L2}. We have a threshold value t_{L2}, which we compare with CFT_{L2}. If CFT_{L2} is greater than the threshold value, then we know that there are no nodes in the L2 cache that are at risk of being flushed. So, we are then free to choose which node will be selected depending on other constraints. On the other hand, if CFT_{L2} is less than or equal to the threshold value, then we need to ensure that those nodes which are about to be flushed are accessed quickly by the decoder. The scheduler, therefore, needs to schedule the children of nodes about to be flushed from L2 cache as quickly as possible.
- Minimum cache flush time of L1 among all nodes (CFT_{L1}): As with L2, we similarly use the threshold value t_{L1} to compare with CFT_{L2}.
- Memory access time of L1 and L2: We know that L1 has a much lower memory access time as compared to L2. When there is no danger of any required node to be flushed from L1 or L2, we assign higher priority to nodes whose parents are in L1. The higher the number of parents in L1, the higher is the priority of a node.
- Number of free nodes in the ready queue: One of our objectives is to ensure that idle time of processor cores is reduced. So we aim to have enough nodes in our available list so that processor cores remain busy in processing nodes. When fewer nodes are present in the available list, we give more priority to nodes that have more outgoing edges.
- For source nodes, i.e, nodes with no incoming edges, we give weightage to the number of neighbours that have been processed. This ensures adjacent nodes are processed at approximately similar times to maintain temporal locality.

Algorithm 1. CalculatePriority

1: $p_{data} \leftarrow CalculateDataPriority(A)$
2: $p_{available} \leftarrow CalculateAvailablePriority(A)$
3: **for all** node n $\in$ A **do**
4:     $p[n] \leftarrow \frac{1}{p_{data}} + \frac{p_{available}}{x}$ // x is the number of available MB nodes in A
5: **end for**

Algorithm 2. CalculateDataPriority

1: $Q \leftarrow \bigcup\limits_{n \in A} parent[n]$
2: $CFT_{L2} \leftarrow \min\limits_{n \in Q \cap L2} \tau_{L2}[n]; CFT_{L1} \leftarrow \min\limits_{n \in Q \cap L1} \tau_{L1}[n]; cachePriority \leftarrow none$
3: **if** $CFT_{L2} < t_{L2}$ **then**
4:     $cachePriority \leftarrow L2$
5: **else if** $CFT_{L1} < t_{L1}$ **then**
6:     $cachePriority \leftarrow L1$
7: **end if**
8: **if** $cachePriority! = none$ **then**
9:     **for all** node n $\in$ A **do**
10:         $p_{data}[n] \leftarrow \min\limits_{p \in parent[n]} \tau_{cachePriority}[p]$
11:     **end for**
12: **else**
13:     **for all** node n $\in$ A **do**
14:         $p_{data}[n] \leftarrow (l * |nodes[L2] \cap parent[n]| + |nodes[L1] \cap parent[n]|)/|parent[n]|$
15:     **end for**
16: **end if**
17: **return** p_{data}

Algorithm 3. CalculateAvailablePriority

1: **for all** node n $\in$ A **do**
2:     $p_{outgoing}[n] \leftarrow$ no of outgoing edges from current available node
3:     **if** sn is source **then**
4:         $p_{source}[n] \leftarrow$ no of spatial neighbours of this node processed
5:         $p_{parallel}[n] \leftarrow k * p_{source}[n] + (1 - k) * p_{outgoing}[n]$
6:     **else**
7:         $p_{parallel}[n] \leftarrow p_{outgoing}$
8:     **end if**
9: **end for**
10:
11: **return** $p_{parallel}$

Algorithm 1 uses simple priority-based scheduling exploiting the factors discussed. There are two distinct priority components – p_{data} and $p_{parallel}$. p_{data} is calculated based on the position of a node's parents in the cache hierarchy. A node whose parent is in danger of being evicted from the L2 cache (obtained by comparing the parent node's CFT with t_{L2}) is given priority. If no parent is in danger of being evicted from L2 cache, we then perform the same process for L1 cache. The reason behind avoiding misses from L2 cache getting higher priority is that data that is expelled from L2 cache takes a much longer time to bring back compared to L1 cache. If we find that no parent node is in danger of being evicted from either L1 or from L2, we then calculate the average priority of each node, assuming that L1 has a higher priority than L2. This is done to ensure that memory access times are minimized. The other component, $p_{parallel}$, is used to assign priority depending on the number of outgoing edges. The higher the number of child nodes, the greater is the value of $p_{parallel}$. k denotes a scaling factor. For source nodes, this also includes the number of its spatial neighbours which have been processed. The total priority, p, is then calculated by assigning weightage to the two priority factors. The node having the highest priority is then processed by the core that executed the scheduler. If there is a tie among two processor who started the priority computation at the same time and ended up selecting the same MB, we resolve it arbitrarily in favour of any of the processors.

We now explain the working of our algorithm on Figure 2. We assume L1 can accommodate 2 macroblocks, and L2 can accommodate 8 macroblocks. Let us assume the macroblock labelled 15A is dependent on those marked 13B and 11A, while 15B is dependent on 11B and 13C. The first processor is idle and calls the scheduler. 11A is in L1 with τ value 1, 13B is in L2 with τ 5, 11B is in L2 with τ 4, whereas 13C is in L2 with τ value 8. The threshold values are 2 for L1 and 4 for L2. No MB in L2 is in the danger of being evicted (comparing τ values with the threshold), and hence, we look at nodes whose parents are in L1. Then, 15A is scheduled to be processed next using our algorithm, since its parent 11A will be flushed out of L1 cache before the threshold. If, however, 11A had a τ value of 2, and 13C had a τ value 3, then the macroblock marked 15B would have been selected.

5   Experimental Results

We implemented an architecture simulator to evaluate our proposed scheduling strategy in a multi-processor setting. Our implementation assumes a cache block size of 32 bytes, and fetching from DRAM in bursts of 256 bytes. We also assume that fetching one line of data requires 1 cycle for L1, and 8 cycles for L2. Our implementation uses efficient data structure for modelling the processors, the cache structure and the main memory. In this way, we are able to efficiently obtain the cache entries that are about to be flushed.

We ran our method on a set of standard test videos. We selected a set of 11 video clips which are widely used across the digital video domain for benchmarking the decoding, encoding and other pre/post processing algorithms. All the clips are of HD (720p) resolution and contain 150 frames. Most of them have high details and large variations within a frame; hence the intra coded frames are expected to have very good distribution of intra prediction modes (and hence the dependencies among macroblocks). Our goal was to generate an intra-only stream suite which has a good variation of dependency relations among the macroblocks.

We used the Joint Model reference software (JM) [4] version 17.2 for encoding the contents in order to generate our test suite consisting of all only intra-coded videos. The streams were then parsed with our in-house H.264 decoder and the task-graphs were generated. For our experiments, we used the value 4 for both the cache thresholds and 0.5 for k. Simulations were done on a 2GHz machine.

In order to obtain the number of cycles needed per macro-block, we note that a 1080p30 video has 1920 * 1080 pixels = 120 * 67 = 8040 macroblocks and a frame rate of 30 frames/s. Thus, 1 frame has to be decoded every 1/30 s. In other words, 1 macroblock has to be decoded every $1/(30 * 8040) = 4.145$ μs. Decoding of a frame is slowest when all macro-blocks are of 4x4 type. Assuming a 2 GHz machine with 15% margin, the machine can execute $1.7 * 10^9$ instructions every second. Thus, number of cycles required = $1.7 * 10^9 * 4.145 * 10^{-6} = 7046.5$ for one 4x4 macroblock. But only 2/3 of the cycles are used to process luma samples. Thus, number of cycles required for luma samples = 2/3 * 7000 = 4667 cycles. An 8x8 luma macroblock on an average requires 2/3 * 4667 = 3111 cycles. Therefore, one 16x16 luma macroblock requires 1/4 * 4667 = 1167 cycles. We use these values in our implementation to compute the speedup and execution time.

We compared the speedup obtained by our method over the 3D-wavefront approach, which is the most commonly used parallel approach currently available. We implemented the 3D-wavefront method in a multi-core setting assuming that the macroblocks to be assigned to each processor have been kept in separate queues, and this has been done before the actual decoding of macroblocks begin [3]. While implementing Algorithm 1, we assumed that there is a single shared queue (in L2) present for all ready macroblocks. The communication time for fetching the required residual data is considered while computing the speedup values. A processor that becomes idle executes the proposed heuristic to select the next macroblock to be decoded. The execution of our heuristic was found to take 40 cycles per macroblock present in the queue. Speedup values, measured as the ratio of the number of processor cycles used by us compared to that by 3D-wavefront are shown in Table 1. Each row of the table (between rows 2 to 12) represents the speedup obtained for a particular video clip when 4, 8, 16, 32 and 64 processors are present. The final three rows show the minimum, maximum and average speedup values. For most of the videos, our algorithm offers improvements (speedup > 1) or comparable performances. The ones, for which our method is slower than the wavefront method, the runtime overhead (graph extraction, dependency structure building, processing time calculation, scheduling overhead) turns out to slow down the decode process, in comparison to a simple-minded static strategy. We note that the speedup is minimum for 32-core processors. This can be explained by observing that the number of macroblocks in ready queue peaks at this point. Having fewer number of processors reduces the number of macroblocks actually being made available at each cycle, whereas having higher number of processors ensures that the macroblocks kept waiting are very few in number.

Table 1. Speedup over 3D-wavefront

Video	4-proc.	8-proc.	16-proc.	32-proc.	64-proc.
bus	1.12	1.08	1.08	0.9	1.05
crowdrun	1.52	1.57	1.68	1.43	1.72
duckstakeoff	1.78	1.98	2.31	2.11	2.94
intotree	1.31	1.24	1.19	0.95	1.43
night	1.25	1.24	1.31	1.039	1.105
oldtowncross	1.26	1.16	1.10	0.26	0.93
parkjoy	1.79	1.76	1.87	1.64	2.10
parkrun	1.39	1.26	1.33	1.08	1.12
shields	1.07	1.19	1.27	0.95	0.93
shuttlestart	1.12	1.06	0.94	0.72	0.68
stockholm	1.26	1.25	1.29	0.99	0.90
Maximum	1.79	1.98	2.31	2.11	2.94
Minimum	1.07	1.06	0.94	0.26	0.68
Average	1.35	1.23	1.39	1.10	1.35

6   Conclusion

In this paper, we present an efficient method for cache aware scheduling to improve the speedup of a H.264 decode algorithm in a multi-processor setting. We believe that a cache-oblivious strategy can benefit tremendously using the proposed modifications. We are currently addressing ways to extend similar ideas to the other compression standards.

References

1. Richardson, I.E.: The H. 264 advanced video compression standard. Wiley (2011)
2. Azevedo, A., Juurlink, B., Meenderinck, C., Terechko, A., Hoogerbrugge, J., Alvarez, M., Ramirez, A., Valero, M.: A highly scalable parallel implementation of H.264. In: Stenström, P. (ed.) Transactions on HiPEAC IV. LNCS, vol. 6760, pp. 111–134. Springer, Heidelberg (2011)
3. Juurlink, B., et al.: Scalable Parallel Programming Applied to H.264/AVC Decoding. Springer (2012) ISBN: 978-1-4614-2229-7
4. H.264/AVC JM software, http://iphome.hhi.de/suehring/tml/
5. Guan, N., et al.: Cache-aware scheduling and analysis for multicores. In: Proceedings of EMSOFT 2009, pp. 245–254 (2009)
6. Wiegand, T., et al.: Overview of the H. 264/AVC video coding standard. IEEE Transactions on Circuits and Systems for Video Technology 13(7), 560–576 (2003)

Random-LRU: A Replacement Policy for Chip Multiprocessors

Shirshendu Das, Nagaraju Polavarapu,
Prateek D. Halwe, and Hemangee K. Kapoor

Indian Institute of Technology Guwahati, Guwahati, India
{shirshendu,n.polavarapu,h.prateek,hemangee}@iitg.ernet.in

Abstract. As the number of cores and associativity of the last level cache (LLC) on a Chip Multi-processor increases, the role of replacement policies becomes more vital. Though, pure least recently used (LRU) policy has some issues it has been generally believed that some versions of LRU policy performs better than the other policies. Therefore, a lot of work has been proposed to improve the performance of LRU-based policies. However, it has been shown that the true LRU imposes additional complexity and area overheads when implemented on high associative LLCs. Most of the LRU based works are more motivated towards the performance improvement than the reduction of area and hardware overhead of true LRU scheme. In this paper we proposed an LRU based cache replacement policy especially for the LLC to improve the performance of LRU as well as to reduce the area and hardware cost of pure LRU by more than a half. We use a combination of random and LRU replacement policy for each cache set. Instead of using LRU policy for the entire set we use it only for some number of ways within the set. Experiments conducted on a full-system simulator shows 36% and 11% improvements over miss rate and CPI respectively.

Keywords: LRU, Pseudo-LRU, Tiled CMP, NUCA, Random-LRU.

1 Introduction

Chip Multiprocessors (CMPs) that contain multiple CPUs on the same die are the main components for building today's computer systems [1]. In the long run, it is expected that the number of cores in CMPs will increase and also accommodate large on-chip Last Level Cache (LLC).

CMP cache architectures are mainly of two types [1]: i) CMP with private LLC and ii) CMP with shared LLC. We assume L2 as LLC throughout this paper. Private L2 caches are relatively small and physically placed very near to the core, hence the cache access time is very less. But it has the capacity problem, since the cache size is small it causes several capacity misses. On the other hand shared L2 is comparatively very large and only a single copy of each data can store in it; all the requesting core will share the same data block and the cache storage can be dynamically allocate to the cores depending on their

M.S. Gaur et al. (Eds.): VDAT 2013, CCIS 382, pp. 204–213, 2013.

workloads. But shared LLC increases hit time, because of much larger cache size as compared to private LLC.

Replacement policy plays a major role in the performance improvement of CMPs last level caches [1]. The most efficient replacement algorithm for cache is to always discard the information that will not be needed for the longest time in the future. This optimal result is referred to as Belady's optimal algorithm [2]. But it is not implementable in practice because it is generally impossible to predict how far in future the information will be needed. Recent studies found that there is a huge performance gap between LRU and the Belady's optimal algorithm and the miss rate using LRU policy can be up to 197% higher than the optimal replacement algorithm [3] .

As mentioned in [4], the least-recently-used (LRU) policy has two major disadvantages: First, a cache block can remain long time in the cache even after its last use. This is because it takes a long time to make the block as LRU block. In this way the block is staying in the cache unnecessarily. Such types of blocks are called dead blocks [4]. The time gap between the death time (the time when the block is last used) and the replacement time of a block become worse as associativity increases. The second problem is that there can be some blocks in L2 which may never be reused in future; such blocks are immediately dead after loading into L2 cache. This is because of the spatial bursty reuse of different bytes of the same cache line which aggravates with increase in block size. The problem with such bursty reuse is that it makes the block MRU (most recently used) in L1 and accessed once in L2. Even the block is accessing rapidly in L1, it accessed in L2 only once. So the principle of temporal locality holds in L1 but not in L2. These blocks are called never-reused blocks [4]. Such dead and never-reused blocks are an unnecessary burden of LRU policy and degrade performance.

In case of highly associative LLC's, true LRU impose additional complexity and area overheads. That is the reason that most of the current processors in the market use pseudo-LRU replacement policy. Pseudo-LRU has lesser hardware complexity as compared to LRU and performs almost same as LRU. There are some other interesting proposals for cache replacement policies (discussed in Section 2). But most of them have complex mechanism and hardware overhead for maintaining aging bits, counters etc. LRU performs better in many applications having higher temporal locality [1]. Hence, instead of completely removing the concept of LRU, researchers proposed many innovative techniques to improve the performance of LRU based policies [3, 5–7]. In these proposals the concept of aging and temporal locality exists but improves the performance of LRU.

In this paper we proposed a mechanism called random-LRU to improve the performance of LRU in LLC with much lesser hardware cost than true LRU as well as some other LRU based policies. The cache using local replacement policies maintain separate replacement hardware for every set. In our proposed policy we have not implemented LRU policy for the entire set. We divide the ways of each set into two partitions: random partition (**RP**) and replacement partition (**LP**). We use LRU as replacement policy only for **LP**. A subset of ways (max 50%) can be the part of **LP**. Rest of the ways belongs to **RP** and uses a random replacement policy which requires no extra hardware. During the block eviction phase, the LRU block of **LP** is replaced by a randomly chosen block from **RP** and the newly incoming block is allocated to **RP**, in place of the random block. So ultimately the newly incoming block is placed in a randomly selected position of **RP** and the victim block in that position is moved into **LP**, replacing the LRU block of **LP**.

Since LRU policy is implemented only for a subset of ways (e.g., max 50%) the hardware cost is much lesser than true LRU. Also, instead of choosing the LRU block from the whole set as victim block, our policy selects the LRU block from a number of randomly chosen blocks as the final victim block. This can partially solve the two major issues of implementing LRU based scheme in LLC as discussed earlier. Note that our proposed replacement policy is for the LLC (here L2), the replacement policy for L1 can be any existing policy.

The rest of the paper is organized as follows. The next section presents the related works in CMP cache architectures and replacement policies. Section 3 describes our proposed cache replacement policy. Section 4 covers performance evaluation using full-system simulation. In the Section 5, we conclude the paper.

2   Related Work

Replacement policies have been well-studied in past [8, 9]. But emergence of larger sized LLCs in CMP, motivated researchers for more innovation in this field. It has been generally believed that some version of LRU based policy performs better than other replacement policies [1]. But multicore and hierarchical cache organizations affects the performance as well as the cost of LRU policies. The pros and cons of both local and global replacement policies are discussed in [10]. The author proposed several global replacement policies and compared them with local replacement policies. He found that global replacement policies are not always performing better than local replacement policies.

An MLP (memory level parallelism) based replacement policy has been proposed in [7] to consider both the fetching (from main memory) cost and recency into account during the replacement of a block. However counting and managing the mlp-cost for each block adds significant memory and hardware overhead.

As discussed in Section 1, dead lines and never-reused lines degrade the performance of LRU based policies. A counter based technique [4] has been proposed to deal with this issues. Though the proposed technique improves performance, using counter for each cache line is an extra overhead.

Cache replacement policy is a major area of research and there are many more innovative ideas already been proposed. Some resent papers in this area includes [6, 11–13].

All the LRU based policies described above perform better than LRU but most of them are more performance oriented than hardware cost. LRU is normally considered expensive in terms of hardware requirements. Also all the above proposals implemented their replacement policy for the entire set. In our proposal we have not implemented LRU policy for the entire set. We use random replacement policy, which has no additional hardware requirement, for some number of ways (min 50%) and LRU for the remaining ways in a set. Note that, any local replacement policy is implemented for each set separately and so is true in our case also.

3   Random-LRU

During the block eviction phase, a cache line from **RP** is randomly selected as the victim block (say V_1) and replaces it with the newly arrived block. But instead of removing the victim block (V_1) completely from the cache it is moved to **LP** and inserted into the MRU position. To move the victim block (V_1) into **LP**, a block from **LP** may need to be evicted. In such a situation the **LP** will select its own LRU block as victim block and replace it with the block V_1. Here the LRU block means the oldest block in **LP**. For example, in case of a 8-way set associative cache if we consider 4 ways for **RP** then the replacement algorithm applies only on the remaining 4 ways. When a block in **LP** accessed again, it is moved into **RP** and another random block from **RP** is moved into **LP**. In this way we always maintain the initial allocated size of both **RP** and **LP**. Moving the randomly selected victim block from **RP** to **LP** gives a high priority block another chance to remain in the cache. Also choosing a random block from **RP** partially solves the two major issues of LRU based policies (as discussed in Section 1).

Though the **LP** section can use any replacement algorithm in this work we only consider LRU as the replacement algorithm. The hardware cost of true LRU is relatively high but using LRU only for a subset of ways, we can able to reduce a huge amount of hardware cost. For the remaining discussion in this section we consider that the cache is N-way set-associative and out of N ways, LP_n ways are for **LP**. Let RP_n $(= N - LP_n)$ ways are for **RP**.

3.1   Logical Block Movement and LRU Implementation

As we mentioned earlier, in case of random-LRU the blocks may need to be moved between **LP** and **RP** within the same set. Such kind of physical movement of blocks can be done in the background without affecting the performance of the cache. But it consumes some additional energy. As our main intention is to reduce the energy and hardware complexity we use a concept of logical block movement. In this technique each way in a set has a bit ($isLP$) to indicate whether the way belongs to **LP** or not. For any cache line if $isLP$ bit is set to 1 then the block belongs to **LP** and otherwise belongs to **RP**. Initially for each set the $isLP$ bit of LP_n ways are set as 1 and RP_n ways as 0. The ways are randomly distributed over the two sections and they may not be contiguous. Whenever we want to move a block from **RP** to **LP**, we just set its $isLP$ bit as 1. Similarly whenever we want to move a block from **LP** to **RP** we reset its *isLP* bit to 0. In this way we are logically moving a block between **LP** and **RP** with just changing a bit value. Inserting, replacing or removing a block does not affect the *isLP* bit of the corresponding way. It has to be done separately.

In case of local LRU replacement policy, each set has different hardware to implement LRU policy for that particular set. In random-LRU, the LRU hardware needs to maintain records only for LP_n number of ways (for each set). But since there is no physical movement of blocks within the set, the ways belonging to **LP** section will change dynamically and the same is also true for the LRU hardware. For example, if the LRU hardware implements a data structure to maintain the LRU records then there will be LP_n number of nodes in the data structure and each node contains one aging variable and a pointer to indicate the way in which the corresponding block resides. The detail hardware based explanation of LRU policy is beyond the scope of this paper. We assumed that logical block movement does not add any extra hardware overhead for implementing LRU in **LP**.

4   Experimental Evaluation

4.1   Tiled Chip Multiprocessor

We used a 16 core Tiled CMP architecture [1] for experimenting all replacement policies. Each tile has a processor, a private L1-cache and an L2-cache. The tiles (or processor nodes) are connected to each other over a 2D mesh popularly known as network-on-chip (NoC). The L2-cache with each tile can be private, or shared among all processors on the chip. In this paper we assume a shared cache, where the slice located in each tile will be called a cache-bank. Each bank itself is a independent set-associative cache. All the experimental results shown in this section are for the entire LLC, combining the results of all the banks together.

4.2   Experimental Setup

In order to evaluate the proposed cache management technique, we performed simulations by running benchmarks on a multi-core simulator GEMS [14] with the help of a full-system functional simulator. GEMS has Ruby, which is a timing simulator of multiprocessor memory system. We used MESI_CMP based cache controller in GEMS. The configuration details of the processor, cache memory and main memory used in our experiments is given in Table 1. For calculating the latencies incurred at L1 caches, L2 banks and directories we used Princeton's Garnet [15] network simulator. The parameters used are listed in the Table 2.

We used six multi-threaded applications from PARSEC [16] benchmark suite for simulation. Note that, our proposed replacement policy is only applicable to L2 and the behavior of L1 caches remains unchanged.

Table 1. System Parameters

Component	Parameters
No. of tiles	16
Processor	UltraSPARCIII+
L1 I/D cache	64KB, 4-way
L2 cache bank	256KB 8-way
Memory bank	1GB, 4KB/page

Table 2. Network Parameters

Network Configuration	Parameters
Flit Size	16 bytes
Buffer Size	4
Pipeline Stage	5-stage
VCs per Virtual Network	4
Number of Virtual Networks	5

4.3 Simulation Results and Analysis

We compared our proposed method with baseline shared cache design (shared tiled CMP using true LRU). We ran each benchmark up to its termination with 16 parallel threads. As mentioned in the documentation of PARSEC distribution, we only measured the performance of ROI (region of interest) section for each benchmark. The performance is analyzed for two different configurations: (a) 50% LP (b) 25% LP. Below we discuss the performance analysis of each configuration separately.

50% LP. In this configuration, we consider that the **LP** takes 50% ways (4 ways out of 8) from each set. Other important parameters are mentioned in table 1. Figure 1 shows the performance comparison of our proposed method with the baseline design. Each graph in the figure shows the results of different performance metrics normalized to the baseline design value.

Figure 1(a) shows that random-LRU gets 21%-58% reduction in miss rate with an average of 36.0%. Reduced off-chip traffic due to lesser misses results in lesser network usage. Hence network power consumption also reduces. Figure 1(b) shows the performance comparison in terms of cycle per instruction (CPI). It shows that in case of random-LRU, CPI improves between 3.5%-47.8% with an average improvement of 11.4%. Table 3 shows the performance improvement in terms of both miss rate and CPI for each benchmark.

25% LP. In this configuration, we consider that the **LP** takes 25% ways (2 ways out of 8) from each set. Figure 2 shows the performance comparison of our proposed method with the baseline design.

Table 3. Performance improvement (in %) chart for Random-LRU (25% LP) with baseline design

Benchmark Name (short name)	CPI	Miss Rate
fluidanimate (fluid)	3.54 %	49.81 %
x264 (x64)	47.80 %	39.61 %
ferret (fert)	14.24 %	21.59 %
freqmine (freq)	20.30 %	33 %
bodytack (body)	5.56 %	26.29 %
vips (vips)	8.20 %	58.76 %
Geometric mean	11.40 %	36 %

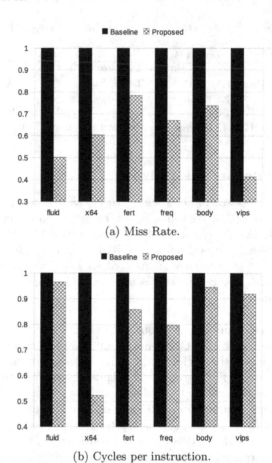

(a) Miss Rate.

(b) Cycles per instruction.

Fig. 1. Normalized performance comparison of Random-LRU (50% LP) with baseline design

Figure 2(a) shows that random-LRU gets -4.7% to 24.8% reduction in miss rate with an average of 9.29%. The improvements in terms of CPI is shown in Figure 2(b). It shows that random-LRU improves performance (CPI) between -8.0% to 46.0% with an average of 5.0%. We can see that the improvement in 25% LP is not as satisfactory as 50% LP. This is because, in case of 25% LP, 75% ways (6 ways) from each set follows random replacement policy and only 25% ways are follows LRU policy. From Figure 2 we can see that random-LRU (25% LP) degrades performance of the benchmarks having higher temporal locality.

Analysis. As explained in Section 1 the applications having more number of dead and never-reused blocks cause higher miss rate in case of LRU replacement policy. On the other hand a completely random replacement policy can

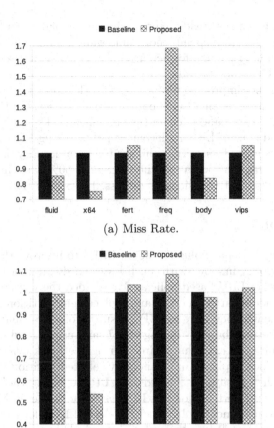

(a) Miss Rate.

(b) Cycles per instruction.

Fig. 2. Normalized performance comparison of Random-LRU (25% LP) with baseline design

replace dead or never-reused blocks early but it may also choose MRU block (or other frequently used blocks) as victim block. So in case of these two replacement policies, the advantage of one is the disadvantage of other. In our proposed replacement policy a randomly selected victim block from **RP** is placed in **LP**. Now if the selected victim block is a frequently used block then very soon it will be requested again and hence moved from **LP** to **RP**. Otherwise the block will be eventually removed from the cache. In this way our policy takes the advantage of both LRU and random replacement policy. Hence it improves the miss rate as well as the CPI.

Normally reduction in miss rate results in higher improvement of CPI. But in our experiments some benchmarks show exceptional behavior, where the improvement in CPI is not as expected even when there is a large reduction in the miss rate. This is because of the non-deterministic thread management by the operating system for multithreaded applications; as explained in [17]. It may be possible that an application spends more time waiting in an idle loop of operating system or in a loop waiting for acquiring a lock. In such cases the miss rate will improve but CPI may degrade.

Since 25% LP is not improving performance for the applications having higher temporal locality, using it for LLC is not a valuable choice. On the other-hand, 50% LP improves performances for all the six benchmarks and it perfectly balances the pros and cons of LRU replacement policy. Using LRU policy for 50% ways helps a benchmark to satisfy its higher temporal locality demand. On the other hand, using random policy for the remaining 50% ways helps to remove the basic drawbacks of LRU policies as discussed in Section 1.

5   Conclusion

We proposed a replacement policy "random-LRU" to improve the performance of the true LRU policy in LLC, with much lesser hardware cost than true LRU as well as some other LRU based policies. We divided the ways of each set into two partitions: random partition (**RP**) and replacement partition (**LP**) and used LRU as replacement policy only for **LP**. A subset of ways (max 50%) can be the part of **LP**. Rest of the ways belong to **RP** and uses a random replacement policy which requires no extra hardware. During the block eviction phase, the newly incoming block is placed in a randomly selected position of **RP** and the victim block in that position is moved into **LP**, replacing the LRU block of **LP**. Also the newly inserted block in **LP** has to be made as MRU block. In other words the replacement policy in **LP** selects LRU block as victim block and insertion policy in **LP** inserts a newly incoming block into MRU position. Since LRU policy is implemented only for a subset of ways the hardware cost is much lesser than true LRU. Also instead of choosing the LRU block from the whole set as victim block our policy selects the LRU block from a number of randomly chosen blocks as victim block. This can partially solve the major issues like dead lines and never-reaccessed lines of pure LRU based scheme in LLCs. Experiments conducted on a full-system simulator shows 36% and 11% improvements over miss rate and CPI respectively. Reduction in CPI and miss rate together guarantees performance improvement.

References

1. Balasubramonian, R., Jouppi, N.P., Muralimanohar, N.: Multi-Core Cache Hierarchies. Morgan & Claypool Publishers (2011)
2. Belady, L.: A study of replacement algorithms for a virtual-storage computer. IBM Systems Journal 5(2), 78–101 (1966)
3. Wong, W., Baer, J.L.: Modified lru policies for improving second-level cache behavior. In: Proceedings of the Sixth International Symposium on High-Performance Computer Architecture, HPCA-6, pp. 49–60 (2000)
4. Kharbutli, M., Solihin, Y.: Counter-based cache replacement and bypassing algorithms. IEEE Trans. Comput. 57(4), 433–447 (2008)

5. Qureshi, M.K., Jaleel, A., Patt, Y.N., Steely, S.C., Emer, J.: Adaptive insertion policies for high performance caching. SIGARCH Comput. Archit. News 35(2), 381–391 (2007)
6. Jain, A., Shrivastava, A., Chakrabarti, C.: La-lru: A latency-aware replacement policy for variation tolerant caches. In: 2011 24th International Conference on VLSI Design (VLSI Design), pp. 298–303 (2011)
7. Qureshi, M.K., Lynch, D.N., Mutlu, O., Patt, Y.N.: A case for mlp-aware cache replacement. SIGARCH Comput. Archit. News 34(2), 167–178 (2006)
8. Belady, L.: A study of replacement algorithms for a virtual-storage computer. IBM Systems Journal (1966)
9. Wong, W., Baer, J.L.: Modified lru policies for improving second-level cache behavior. In: Proceedings of the Sixth International Symposium on High-Performance Computer Architecture, HPCA-6, pp. 49–60 (2000)
10. Zahran, M.: Cache replacement policy revisited. In: The Annual Workshop on Duplicating, Deconstructing, and Debunking (WDDD) Held in Conjunction with the International Symposium on Computer Architecture (ISCA) (June 2007)
11. Fricker, C., Robert, P., Roberts, J.: A versatile and accurate approximation for lru cache performance. In: 2012 24th International Teletraffic Congress (ITC 24), pp. 1–8 (2012)
12. Morales, K., Lee, B.K.: Fixed segmented lru cache replacement scheme with selective caching. In: 2012 IEEE 31st International Performance Computing and Communications Conference (IPCCC), pp. 199–200 (2012)
13. Juan, F., Chengyan, L.: An improved multi-core shared cache replacement algorithm. In: 2012 11th International Symposium on Distributed Computing and Applications to Business, Engineering Science (DCABES), pp. 13–17 (2012)
14. Martin, M.M.K., Sorin, D.J., Beckmann, B.M., Marty, M.R., Xu, M., Alameldeen, A.R., Moore, K.E., Hill, M.D., Wood, D.A.: Multifacet's general execution-driven multiprocessor simulator (gems) toolset. SIGARCH Comput. Archit. News 33(4), 92–99 (2005)
15. Agarwal, N., Krishna, T., Peh, L.S., Jha, N.: Garnet: A detailed on-chip network model inside a full-system simulator. In: IEEE International Symposium on Performance Analysis of Systems and Software, ISPASS 2009, pp. 33–42 (April 2009)
16. Bienia, C.: Benchmarking Modern Multiprocessors. PhD thesis, Princeton University (January 2011)
17. Alameldeen, A., Martin, M., Mauer, C., Moore, K., Xu, M., Hill, M., Wood, D., Sorin, D.: Simulating a $2m commercial server on a $2k pc. Computer 36(2), 50–57 (2003)

Analysis of Crosstalk Deviation for Bundled MWCNT with Process Induced Height and Width Variations

Jainender Kumar, Manoj Kumar Majumder,
Brajesh Kumar Kaushik, and Sudeb Dasgupta

Microelectronics and VLSI Group, Department of Electronics and Communication Engg.
Indian Institute of Technology Roorkee, Roorkee – 247667, India
{jainenderkumariitr,manojbesu}@gmail.com,
{bkk23,sudeb}fec@iitr.ernet.in

Abstract. Process variation is an important design concern in current nanoscale regime. This research paper analyzes the effect of process induced height and width variations for a multi-walled carbon nanotube (MWCNT) bundle interconnects. For different bundle heights and widths, the average deviation in crosstalk delay is analyzed for bundles having MWCNTs with different number of shells. A capacitively coupled interconnect line is used to analyze the crosstalk delay by using the Monte Carlo simulations with 100 different samples. Using Gaussian distributed widths and heights, a bundle having MWCNTs with higher number of shells exhibits least deviation in crosstalk.

Keywords: Carbon nanotube (CNT), Multi-walled CNT (MWCNT) bundle, crosstalk deviation, process variation, VLSI interconnects.

1 Introduction

Carbon nanotubes (CNTs) have aroused lot of research interests for their applicability as VLSI interconnects [1]. CNT possess superior electrical properties as compared to Cu or other interconnect materials due to the unique band structure of graphene that leads to zero effective mass of electrons and holes [2]. In deep submicron and nano scale regime, conventional interconnect materials such as Al and Cu suffers from electromigration [3, 4], skin effect, resistive parasitic [5-7] etc. CNTs can be constructed with length-to-diameter ratio of up to 132,000,000:1 [8], which is significantly larger than any other material. The sp^2 bonding in graphene is stronger than the sp^3 bonds in diamond [2] that makes graphene the strongest material. CNTs have large current carrying capability [9], long ballistic transport length, higher thermal conductivity [10] and mechanical strength [11].

Structure of CNTs depend on chiral indices (n,m) that represents the rolling up direction of graphene sheets. CNTs can be either metallic or semiconducting in nature depending on their chiral indices. Based on the number of concentrically rolled up graphene sheets, CNTs are categorized as single- (SWCNT) and multi-walled CNTs (MWCNTs). MWCNTs consist of several concentric shells with different diameters

M.S. Gaur et al. (Eds.): VDAT 2013, CCIS 382, pp. 214–222, 2013.

due to which each shell exhibits different physical and electrical properties. MWCNTs having diameter greater than 20nm are conductive in nature as they exhibits band gap lesser than the thermal energy at room temperature ($E_G < k_{BT} \approx$ 0.0258eV) [2]. The number of conducting channels and mean free path increases for higher diameters of MWCNTs [8] that exhibits an improved performance as compared to the SWCNTs. MWCNT bundle can be preferred over single MWCNT or bundled SWCNT as it provides more number of conducting channels. Specific arrangements of MWCNT bundles can be obtained by using a technique known as atomic force microscopy (AFM) [8].

Advancement in current technology results in shrinking device dimensions that requires more sophisticated technological tools. There is always a certainity in achieving these small device dimensions. In this research paper, these certainties are considered for process induced bundle width and height variations. Variation in bundle width and height offers more deviation in outputs as compared to any other process or parameter variations. The research paper is organized in four different sections: Section 1 introduces a recent research scenario and briefs about the works carried out. Using the geometry and bundle arrangements, section 2 presents an analytical model of bundled MWCNT. A detailed analysis of Monte Carlo simulations by using capacitively coupled interconnect lines is presented in section 3. The impact of bundle height and width on average crosstalk deviation is analyzed in section 4. Finally, section 5 draws a brief summary of this paper.

2   Interconnect Model

This section presents an analytical model of MWCNT bundle that depends on the arrangements of MWCNTs. Initially, an equivalent *RLC* model of single MWCNT is presented by considering the effects of shell diameter and conducting channels. Finally, this model extends to describe a distributed *RLC* network that provides a detailed analysis for different interconnect parasitics of bundled MWCNT.

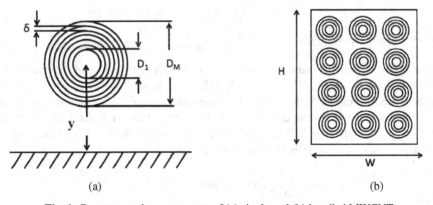

Fig. 1. Geometry and arrangements of (a) single and (b) bundled MWCNT

2.1   Geometry of Single and Bundled MWCNT

MWCNT consists of several concentric rolled up graphene sheets as shown in Fig. 1(a) where the distance between each shell is approximately equivalent to the Vander-Waal's gap (δ) ≈ 0.34nm [12]. Inner and outer diameters are represented as D_i and D_M respectively, where M denotes the number of shells in an MWCNT. The distance between the center of MWCNT and ground plane is denoted as y. Outer diameter of MWCNT depends on the number of shells and can be expressed as [13]

$$D_M = D_1 + 2 \times \delta \times (M - 1) \tag{1}$$

Figure 1(b) presents an MWCNT bundle (height=H and width=W) that consists of different number of MWCNTs having similar number of shells. Therefore, the total number of MWCNTs in a bundle can be expressed as [4]

$$n_{MWCNT} = n_W n_H - (n_W/2) = n_W n_H - [(n_W - 1)/2] \tag{2}$$

(if n_H is an even and odd number respectively)

where $\qquad n_W = W/(D_M + \delta) \qquad$ and $\qquad n_H = H/(D_M + \delta) \tag{3}$

2.2   Equivalent *RLC* Model for MWCNT Bundle

MWCNT consists of numbers of cylindrical shells that can be viewed as several shells in parallel. It is seemed to be similar to an SWCNT bundle that consists of several nanotubes in parallel; but in fact, it has significant differences with SWCNT bundle. For an MWCNT, the number of conducting channels depends on the shell diameters. The interconnect parasitics such as resistance, inductance and capacitance are modeled based on the total number of conducting channels that accounts for the effect of spin degeneracy and sub-lattice degeneracy of carbon atoms. Using the assumption of one third shells as metallic, the average number of conducting channels for a particular shell in MWCNT can be expressed as [15]

$$\begin{aligned} N_i(D_i) &\approx k_1 T D_i + k_2, & D_i &> d_T/T \\ &\approx 2/3 & D_i &\leq d_T/T \end{aligned} \tag{4}$$

where D_i represents the diameter of ith shell in MWCNT, k_1 and k_2 are equivalent to 2.04×10^{-4}nm^{-1}K^{-1} and 0.425 respectively [15]. The thermal energy of electrons and gap between the sub-bands determines the quantitative value of d_T which is equivalent to 1300nmK at room temperature (T=300K) [15]. Thus, the total numbers of conducting channels in an MWCNT bundle can be calculated using the summation of conducting channels (N_i) of each shell in an MWCNT [15]

$$N = n_{MWCNT} \sum_{i=1}^{p} N_i \; ; p = \text{total number of shells in a MWCNT} \tag{5}$$

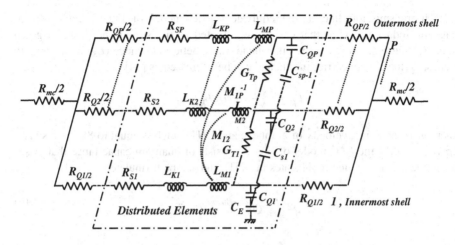

Fig. 2. Equivalent *RLC* model of MWCNT having *p* number of shells

Since all the interconnect parasitics of different shells vary in MWCNTs, the potentials of different shells cannot be assumed to be equal as in the case of SWCNT bundle. Therefore, a shell-to-shell coupling capacitance is introduced that arises due to the small separation between two adjacent shells. The per unit length (*p.u.l.*) shell-to-shell coupling capacitance (C_S) can be expressed as [13]

$$C_S = \frac{2\pi\varepsilon}{\ln(D_p/D_{p-1})} = \frac{2\pi\varepsilon}{\ln\left[D_p/(D_p-2\delta)\right]} \tag{6}$$

Based on the aforementioned analysis, Li *et al.* [13] proposed a distributed *RLC* model for MWCNT interconnects as presented in Fig. 2. The resistance of each shell in Fig. 2 can be defined as (1) quantum resistance R_Q, (2) scattering resistance R_S and (3) imperfect metal-nanotube contact resistance R_{mc}. The scattering resistance (R_S) occurs if the length of the nanotube is larger than the mean free path (*mfp*) of electrons. R_Q and R_S are intrinsic, and the value of R_{mc} depends on the fabrication process. The interconnect parasitics of MWCNT bundle is calculated using the equivalent *RLC* model of Fig. 2 where each parasitic is modeled using the total number of conducting channels in MWCNT. Therefore, the total resistance (R_{total}) can be determined as [13]

$$R_{total} = R_Q + R_S = \frac{h}{2e^2 N} + \frac{h}{2e^2 N \lambda_{mfp}} \tag{7}$$

where $h/2e^2 \sim 12.9 k\Omega$, λ_{mfp} and N are the *mfp* and total number of conducting channels respectively. The *mfp* is calculated using the diameter of each shell in MWCNT. Apart from this, the imperfect metal-nanotube contact resistance R_{mc} exhibits a value ranging from zero to hundreds of kΩ depending on the different growth process [13]. Moreover, the tunneling conductance (G_T) depends on the diameter of each shell in MWCNT [13].

Each transmission line in the equivalent *RLC* model of Fig. 2 comprises of magnetic inductance (L_M) that can be represented as the stored energy for a given amount of current flow. On the other hand, the kinetic inductance (L_K) arises mainly because of the charge carrier inertia and can be expressed as [14]

$$L_K = \frac{L_{K0}}{N}; \quad where\, L_{K0} = \frac{h}{2e^2 v_F} \tag{8}$$

where v_F is the Fermi velocity of graphene and CNT which is equal to 8×10^5 m/s [13]. Apart from this, the *RLC* model of Fig. 2 consists of quantum capacitance that arises due to the density of electronic states in CNTs and can be formulated as [14]

$$C_Q = N.C_{Q0}; \quad where\, C_{Q0} = \frac{2e^2}{hv_F} \tag{9}$$

3   Simulation Setup

This section analyzes the propagation delay under the influence of crosstalk for bundled MWCNT having different numbers of shells at interconnects lengths of 100μm. The equivalent *RLC* model of bundled MWCNT represents the capacitively coupled interconnect lines as shown in Fig. 3. Simulation setup uses CMOS driver at 32nm technology node in which the technology parameters (length and width) for NMOS is taken as 32nm and 640nm and for PMOS, these parameters are taken as 32nm and 1280nm, respectively. Using the process induced bundle height and width variations, the average deviation in crosstalk is analyzed for different bundled MWCNT by invoking the Monte Carlo simulations with 100 different samples. The interconnect line is terminated by a load capacitance $C_L = 10$fF.

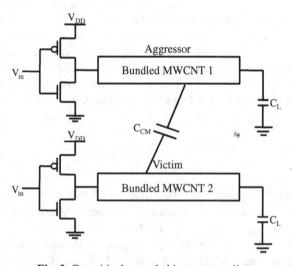

Fig. 3. Capacitively coupled interconnect lines

4   Performance Analysis

This section provides a detailed insight of crosstalk delay using Gaussian distributed bundle widths and heights. Performance is analyzed for a bundle having MWCNTs with different numbers of shells. To analyze the average crosstalk deviations, the minimum and maximum dimensions of an MWCNT bundle are presented in Table 1. The average crosstalk deviation is investigated for the bundles having MWCNTs with 5-, 10- and 15-shells.

Tables 2 and 3 summarizes the variation in interconnect parasitics for bundled MWCNTs for different bundle heights and widths respectively. The different interconnect parasitics includes the total number of MWCNTs in bundle, total number of conducting channels, quantum resistance, scattering resistance, kinetic and magnetic inductance, quantum capacitance, electrostatic capacitance and coupling capacitance. It is observed that the total number of conducting channels increases for maximum bundle width and height which is due to the higher number of MWCNTs in bundle. The higher number of conducting channels significantly lowers the resistive and inductive parasitics whereas capacitive parasitics are increased as directed from expressions (7) to (9). Thus, a MWCNT bundle with minimum dimension exhibits higher parasitic values as compared to the maximum dimension of the bundle.

Table 1. Variation in bundle dimension

Parameters	Nominal value	Variation	Minimum value (nm)	Maximum value (nm)
Width (W)	45nm	10%	40.5	49.5
Height (H)	81nm	10%	72.9	89.1

Table 2. Interconnect parasitics of a bundled MWCNT for process induced bundle heights at 100µm interconnect length

Parameters	5 shell		10 shell		15 shell	
	Min	**Max**	**Min**	**Max**	**Min**	**Max**
n_{CNT}	179	221	50	61	21	28
$N_{channel}$	424	524	336	410	274	365
$R_Q\,(\Omega)$	11.8	9.52	8.14	6.7	6.82	5.11
$R_S\,(\Omega)$	1175	952	814	667	682	511
$L_K\,(\text{nH})$	1.88	1.53	2.66	2.18	3.1	2.32
$L_M\,(\text{nH})$	0.102	0.102	0.09	0.09	0.082	0.082
$C_Q\,(\text{pF})$	8.19	10.11	6.48	7.91	5.3	7.04
$C_E\,(\text{fF})$	11.95	11.95	7.45	7.45	5.423	5.423
$C_M\,(\text{fF})$	19.2	23.71	13.95	17.1	12.2	16.3

Table 3. Interconnect parasitics for a bundled MWCNT for process induced bundle widths at 100μm interconnect length

Parameters	5 shell		10 shell		15 shell	
	Min	Max	Min	Max	Min	Max
n_{CNT}	162	219	45	55	18	25
$N_{channel}$	384	519	302	369	235	326
$R_Q (\Omega)$	13	9.61	9.04	7.39	7.9	5.7
$R_S (\Omega)$	1299	961	904	740	795	573
$L_K (nH)$	2.1	1.54	2.96	2.42	3.61	2.59
$L_M (nH)$	0.102	0.102	0.896	0.896	0.0821	0.0821
$C_Q (pF)$	7.41	10.02	5.83	7.13	4.53	6.3
$C_E (fF)$	9.78	13.035	6.205	7.446	4.07	5.423
$C_M(fF)$	21.56	21.56	15.505	15.505	14.231	14.231

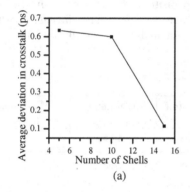
(a)

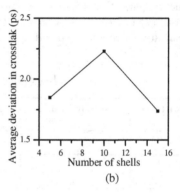
(b)

Fig. 4. Average crosstalk deviation for Gaussian distributed bundle (a) height and (b) width

Figure 4(a) presents the average crosstalk deviation for Gaussian distribution of MWCNTs in different bundle heights. It is observed that the average crosstalk deviation reduces for the bundle having MWCNTs with higher number of shells. For 10% deviation in heights, there are lesser number of 15-shell MWCNTs that are accommodated in comparison to the bundle having 10- and 5-shell MWCNTs as presented in Table 2. It causes lesser effect of capacitive coupling between two bundled MWCNTs (Table 2). Therefore, a bundle having MWCNTs with 15-shells exhibits lower crosstalk deviation as compared to the bundles having MWCNTs with 10-shell and 5-shell respectively.

Figure 4(b) demonstrates the average crosstalk deviation for Gaussian distribution of MWCNTs in different bundle widths. For the bundle dimension of (45nm × 91nm), it is observed that the average crosstalk deviation increases for the bundle having MWCNTs with 10-shells whereas reduces for the bundle having MWCNTs with 15-shells. The primary reason behind this effect is the difference between minimum and maximum number of conducting channels in a bundled MWCNT. For the bundle having MWCNTs with 5-shells, the difference between minimum and maximum number of conducting channels is lesser in comparison to the bundle having MWCNTs with 5- and 15-shells as observed from Table 3. The minimum difference in conducting channels reveals to the minimum difference in interconnect parasitics for the bundle having MWCNTs with 10-shells. Therefore, the bundle having MWCNTs with 10-shells exhibits higher crosstalk deviation in comparison to the bundle having MWCNTs with 5- and 15-shells.

5   Conclusion

This research paper presented an analytical model of bundled MWCNT that uses the total number of conducting channels to model the interconnect parasitics. To analyze the crosstalk delay, the equivalent RLC line of bundled MWCNT has been used to represent the capacitively coupled interconnect lines. Monte Carlo simulations are performed to analyze the average crosstalk deviation for process induced bundle heights and widths variations. Using Gaussian distributed bundle widths and heights, it has been observed that the average crosstalk deviation reduces for the bundle having MWCNTs with higher number of shells.

References

1. Ijima, S.: Helical microtubules of graphite carbon. Nature 354, 56–58 (1991)
2. Li, H., Xu, C., Srivastava, N., Banerjee, K.: Carbon Nanomaterials for Next-Generation Interconnects and passives: Physics, Status, and Prospects. IEEE Trans. Electron Devices 56(9), 1799–1821 (2009)
3. Srivastava, N., Banerjee, K.: A comparative scaling analysis of metallic and carbon nanotube interconnects for nanometer scale VLSI technologies. In: Proc. Int. VLSI Multilevel Interconnect Conf., pp. 393–398 (2004)
4. Srivastava, N., Banerjee, K.: Interconnect challenges for nanoscale electronic circuits. TMS J. Mater. 56(10), 3–31 (2004)
5. International Technology Roadmap for Semiconductors (2005),
   http://public.itrs.net
6. Im, S., Srivastava, N., Banerjee, K., Goodson, K.E.: Scaling analysis of multilevel interconnect temperatures for high performance ICs. IEEE Trans. Electron Devices 52(12), 2710–2719 (2005)
7. Steinhogl, W., Schindler, G., Steinlesberger, G., Traving, M., Engelhardt, M.: Comprehensive study of the resistivity of copper wires with lateral dimensions of 100 nm and smaller. J. Appl. Phys. 97(2), 023706-1–023706-7 (2005)
8. Dadgour, H., Cassell, A.M., Banerjee, K.: Scaling and variability analysis of CNT-based NEMS devices and circuits with implications for process design. In: Proc. IEEE IEDM Tech. Dig., pp. 529–532 (2008)
9. Wei, J.Q., Vajtai, R., Ajayan, P.M.: Reliability and current carrying capacity of carbon nanotubes. Appl. Phys. Lett. 79(8), 1172–1174 (2001)
10. Collins, B.G., Hersam, M., Arnold, M., Martel, R., Avouris, P.: Current saturation and electrical breakdown in multiwalled carbon nanotubes. Phys. Rev. Lett. 86(14), 3128–3131 (2001)

11. Berber, S., Kwon, Y.K., Tomanek, D.: Unusually high thermal conductivity of carbon nanotubes. Phys. Rev. Lett. 84(20), 4613–4616 (2000)
12. Rossi, D., Cazeaux, J.M., Metra, C., Lombardi, F.: Modeling crosstalk effect in CNT bus architecture. IEEE Trans. Nanotechnol. 6(23), 133–145 (2007)
13. Li, H., Yin, W.Y., Banerjee, K., Mao, J.F.: Circuit Modeling and performance Analysis of Multi-Walled Carbon Nanaotube Interconects. IEEE Trans. Electron Devices 55(6), 1328–1337 (2008)
14. Burke, P.J.: Luttinger Liquid Theory as a Model of the Gigahertz Electrical Properties of Carbon Nanotubes. IEEE Trans. Nanotechnol. 1(3), 129–144 (2002)
15. Pu, S.N., Yin, W.Y., Mao, J.F., Liu, Q.H.: Crosstalk Prediction of Single- and Double-Walled Carbon-Nanotube (SWCNT/ DWCNT) Bundle Interconnects. IEEE Trans. Electron Devices 56(4), 560–568 (2009)
16. Majumder, M.K., Pandya, N.D., Kaushik, B.K., Manhas, S.K.: Analysis of MWCNT and Bundled SWCNT Interconnects: Impact on Crosstalk and Area. IEEE Electron Devices Letts. 33(8), 1180–1182 (2012)

Congestion Balancing Global Router

Shyamapada Mukherjee[1], Jibesh Patra[2], and Suchismita Roy[2]

[1] Dr. B.C. Roy Engg. College, Durgapur, India
[2] National Institute of Technology, Durgapur, India
{shyamamukherji,jibesh.patra}@gmail.com,
suchismita27@yahoo.com

Abstract. A novel algorithmic approach for a global routing solution for VLSI circuits is proposed in this paper. Instead of following the traditional Steiner tree approach towards global routing, we have used a congestion sensing path laying approach. We introduce the concept of detouring of net segments running through heavily congested edges. The technique brings down the congestion of edges, to meet the constraints of edge capacity, by detouring the net segments through sparsely populated edges. Our approach has been implemented and tested on the ISPD 98 benchmark circuits and has achieved results comparable to other global routers when congestion minimization and wire length minimization are taken into consideration.

Keywords: Global Routing, Detouring, Steiner Tree.

1 Introduction

Routing is one of the traditional VLSI physical design automation area along with placement and synthesis. With exponentially growing demand of nano-circuits, shrinking size of integrated circuits which in turn increases chip density, and on chip communication, the challenges for current global routers are more than ever before. During the global routing phase, the planning of a provisional path between the interconnects, in various routing regions on the chip takes place. Global routing techniques in recent years have improved significantly with the introduction of ISPD1998 [1], ISPD2007 [2], and ISPD2008 [3] global routing benchmark circuits.

The approaches of solving global routing problem can be grouped into two broad categories: sequential and concurrent techniques. In sequential routing approaches, nets are first ordered according to their routing importance followed by each net being routed separately. However, once a net has been routed it may block other nets which are not yet routed. As a result, this approach is very sensitive to the order in which the nets are considered for routing. In this approach, routes for nets routed early can be easily found while the nets routed at a later stage might be difficult to route or become unroutable. Sequential algorithm was first introduced by Lee [4] and it became the basis for the maze runner algorithms. Several approaches have been proposed to extend these algorithms to

M.S. Gaur et al. (Eds.): VDAT 2013, CCIS 382, pp. 223–232, 2013.
© Springer-Verlag Berlin Heidelberg 2013

multi-terminal nets. While extending these algorithms for multi terminal nets the common feature has been the construction of Steiner tree for each net [5–11]. The popularity of sequential techniques has risen recently, because of their ability to handle large problem instance. The popular sequential techniques, usually order the nets according to their criticality, half-perimeter wire length, and number of terminals [12]. For example, some nets might be timing critical and hence would require to be routed early. Various techniques has been devised to minimize the effect of net ordering. These techniques include rip-up & reroute schemes, heirarchical methods, simulated annealing and a myriad other heuristics based methods. The traditional approach is to route each net, without taking congestion into account and then identify heavily congested areas. These heavily congested areas are then decongested by local rerouting of net segments. NTHU-Route [13] is an example of GR using iterative rip-up and reroute technique that uses a history-based cost function to distribute overflow, followed by identification of congested regions to specify the order in which rip-ups are performed. [14] presents a global routing algorithm that performs layer assignment before routing. This algorithm is based on a new flow for multi-layer routing, and uses bounding box of the nets to estimate the congestion, and distributes them to different layer pairs based on the aim of even congestion. The Archer router [15] employs a spectrum of point-to-point routing techniques, ranging from relatively cheap operations to expensive but flexible procedures (e.g., traditional maze routing). For a given 2-pin connection, the specific technique used depends on congestion histories. Steiner trees are modified dynamically using a novel Lagrangian formulation for topology optimization. Fairly Good Router (FGR) [16] extends the PathFinder router originally developed for FPGAs [17] to handle the scale and sophistication of an ASIC environment with multiple routing layers. It offers several technical novelties, such as a particular function for congestion penalty, and closely linked algorithmic innovations, such as sharing in conjunction with continual net restructuring, and fast layer assignment followed by a 3D clean-up. With respect to runtime, FastRoute [18] remains one of the more competitive solvers to date. It uses a congestion map to warp the structure of a Hanan grid during Steiner tree generation, followed by edge shifting and a form of pattern routing. DpRouter [19] is based upon a congestion aware algorithm that combines two principal techniques: a dynamic pattern routing method to achieve optimal routing solutions for two-pin nets, and a segment move technique to extend its search space. Two elementary edge-based operations -extreme edge shifting and edge retraction- form the high-level operations of MAIZEROUTER [20]. These techniques are supported by an underlying foundation of interdependent net decomposition, in which routing solutions are implicitly maintained by at collections of intervals. Rather than operate on entire nets, individual segments are manipulated one-at-a time, enabling support for cheap incremental operations.

Concurrent global routing methods find routes for all nets in a circuit simultaneously. Doing so, helps in avoiding the net ordering problem faced by the sequential approaches. On account of unavailability of efficient polynomial algorithms for concurrent global routing, integer programming (IP) methods have been suggested. Integer programming can be formulated in a number of ways.

The [21], solves the GR problem, using IP where GR constraints are combined to find the best wiring layput of a circuit. New modeling techniques are used to solve the routing problem formulated as an integer programming problem. The LP problem is solved by an interior point algorithm that finds a near optimal wiring in polynomial time without perfoming randomized rounding. Few, IP based GR are SideWinder [22], BoxRouter [23], and GRIP [24]. The common approach of IP based routers is the decomposition of multi pin nets into two pin nets using FLUTE. After decomposition, different router uses different ILP formulations to solve the global routing problem. Given the routing graph and a set of Steiner trees for each net, the goal of this technique is to select one Steiner tree for each net, such that, the total wire length is minimized and the channel capacity constraints are not violated. [25] presents an efficient approach to global routing that takes spacing-dependent costs into account and provably finds a near-optimum solution including these costs. [26] presents a parallel global routing algorithm that concurrently processes routing subproblems corresponding to rectangular subregions covering the chip area. The algorithm uses at it core an existing integer programming (IP) formulation both for routing each subproblem and for connecting them. GRIP [24] is another global routing technique via integer programming. GRIP optimizes wirelength and via cost directly. By using integer programming in an effective manner, GRIP obtains high-quality solutions. The paper [27] presents a collaborative procedure for multiobjective global routing that takes independently generated multiple GR solutions as input and performs multi objective optimization based on Pareto algebra to generate quick multiple GR solution.

This paper introduces a novel approach of reducing total overflow with focus on keeping wire length and signal delay in check. This paper makes the following contributions:

1. This algorithm does not follow traditional steiner tree construction approach, rather a congestion sensing algorithm has been developed for this.
2. For load adjustment a congestion balancing algorithm has been designed that takes signal delay and wire length into consideration.
3. Tree augmentation has been applied to the remaining of the the nets with atleast one congested edge few iterations of congestion balancing algorithm.

The rest of the paper is organized as follows. While the next section describes the congestion estimation and minimization technique, section 3 presents the experimental results and comparisons with some existing global routers. The conclusion of the paper is provided in section 4.

2   Congestion Estimation and Minimization

During global routing, pins with the same electric potential are connected using wire segments. The final design should reflect fully connected nets. While making

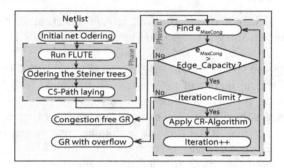

Fig. 1. Flow chart depicts the working steps to balance congestion

the net connections, same tracks of a circuit might get used by many nets. This in turn can lead to congestion of the tracks. Traditional global routing techniques does not employ any out of the box congestion minimization techniques and depends upon cumbersome maze routing techniques to achieve this. It is customary to map a global routing problem to a grid graph and then solve it. The technique depicted here uses grid formulation of the global routing and then tries to minimize congestion by following a two step approach. The sequence of operations or the steps are clearly defined by the flowchart shown in Fig. 1. In the first step, the technique tries to keep the congestion in control while laying out the paths of the circuit using *Congestion Sensing Path Laying* technique. Once the paths are laid, the second step uses heuristics to minimize congestion further while keeping the nets connected.

Algorithm 1. *CongestionSensing*

Input: Two steiner points $a(x_1, y_1) \& b(x_2, y_2)$ where $(x_1 \neq x_2) and (y_1 \neq y_2)$

Output: Connected path between two steiner points using grid edges considering grid edge congestion meanwhile.

A virtual box B is assumed with $(x_1, y_1), (x_1, y_2), (x_2, y_1), (x_2, y_2)$ corner points
Repeat the steps 3 to 10 until $a == b$
Select two incident edges $\overline{ap_i}$ and $\overline{aq_i}$ towards b within B;
if $(CapCongRatio(\overline{ap_i}) \leq \overline{aq_i}))$ **then**
    $Lock(ap_i)$;
    $a=p_i$
else
    $Lock(aq_i)$;
    $a=q_i$
end if

2.1 Congestion Sensing during Path Laying

This section describes the congestion minimization technique used while laying paths of nets. Initially Steiner minimal trees are generated using FLUTE [28]. FLUTE provides two pin tree segments of one or more edge lengths. The next step is to select the grid edge for laying the paths. At this juncture while laying out the edges, we make sure such that the same edge does not get selected repeatedly. Doing so helps to keep congestion in control and the heuristic applied

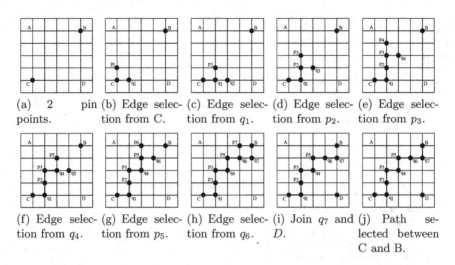

(a) 2 pin points. (b) Edge selection from C. (c) Edge selection from q_1. (d) Edge selection from p_2. (e) Edge selection from p_3.

(f) Edge selection from q_4. (g) Edge selection from p_5. (h) Edge selection from q_6. (i) Join q_7 and D. (j) Path selected between C and B.

Fig. 2. Path laying between C and B using *CongestionSensing* algorithm

in the second step becomes more feasible. The congestion should be minimized so that the electric load on one channel is reduced, since more wires or more current flow through one channel may increase the heat and sometime damage the circuit. Hence the focus is on congestion minimization rather than wire length minimization.

The internal working principle of the *CongestionSensing* algorithm is described in Algo 1. Fig. 2(a) shows the FLUTE generated bi-pins B and C to be connected. Our task is to create a connection between these two pins and the algorithm senses congestion while making this connection and subsequently adjusts the laying out of path. In this context congestion represents the number of Steiner trees that have used the edge for laying their path. A virtual box ABCD is conceptualized to bound the path between B and C. While laying out path from the lower pin C, the algorithm senses the congestion(use) of the two possible edges $\overline{cp_1}$ and $\overline{cq_1}$ and then chooses the least used edge. This process continues until the two pins get connected, as shown in Fig. 2(a) to 2(j). This is to ensure that one particular edge does not get chosen over and over again, thereby keeping congestion to a minimum.

2.2 Congestion Minimization by Rerouting the Most Congested Edge

This section describes the second step of congestion minimization technique that uses rerouting of the tree segment having path through the most congested grid edge, to minimize congestion. This phase does not focuses only on overflow reduction but also controls the wire length of each individual net and hence the signal delay. Most of the existing technique controls congestion and wire length, but some nets become lengthy and increase their signal delay. Initially the the

---

Algorithm 2. *CongestionReduction*
Input: Most congested edge e in the graph
Output: Less congested edge e

```
Find the set of trees T_e = {t_0, t_1, t_2, ...} having path through e;
while (Capacity(e) < |T_e|) do
    t_i = MaxWireLength(T_e);
    if (e is vertical edge) then
        V ≡ Left, P ≡ Right;
    end if
    if (e is horizontal edge) then
        V ≡ Up, P ≡ Down;
    end if
    if (Atleast two horizontal or vertical incident edges on opposite sides of e) then
        e_1 = e; e_2 = e;
        Repeat
        {
        e_1 = e_1.V, e_2 = e_2.P;
        if (!Marked(e_1) & Cong(e_1) ≤ Cong(e_2) & Bound(e_1)) then
            e_new = Lock(e_1);
            Break;
        else if (!Marked(e_2) & Bound(e_2))) then
            e_new = Lock(e_2);
            Break;
        else if (!Marked(e_1) & Bound(e_1))) then
            e_new = Lock(e_1);
            Break;
        else if (!Bound(e_1) & Bound(e_2))) then
            Break;
        end if
        }
    else if (only V side horizontal or vertical incident edge(s) on one side of e) then
        e_1 = e;
        Repeat
        {
        e_1 = e_1.V;
        if (!Marked(e_1) & Bound(e_1)) then
            e_new = Lock(e_1);
            Break;
        end if
        }
    else if (only P side horizontal or vertical incident edge(s) on one side of e) then
        e_1 = e;
        Repeat
        {
        e_1 = e_1.P;
        if (!Marked(e_1) & Bound(e_1)) then
            e_new = Lock(e_1);
            Break;
        end if
        }
    end if
    new path for e through e_new is set up
    Remove t_i from T_e;
end while
Mark e;
```

---

edge with maximum congestion is selected and further *CongestionReduction* Algorithm 2 is applied to this edge until the congestion comes down to the edge capacity. In some cases it may not be so and hence the algorithm might keep running on and on. For such cases, a check of preset limit on the number of iteration is made. Whenever this iteration goes beyond the limit, the algorithm moves on to the next net. The final output of this procedure is either a congestion free routing or routing with overflow. The selection of most congested edge as mentioned above is made irrespective of the edge being vertical or horizontal. Fig. 3(a) to 3(g) show all possible position of a congested vertical edge and corresponding new layout for the tree segments running through that edge, after the proposed technique is applied. Analogous procedure can be applied for reducing congestion of horizontal edges. Possible scenarios of congested edges with the possible tree structures are shown. Fig. 3(a) shows a net containing a congested edge $\overline{AB}$. Since, for this particular net, there are two horizontal edges

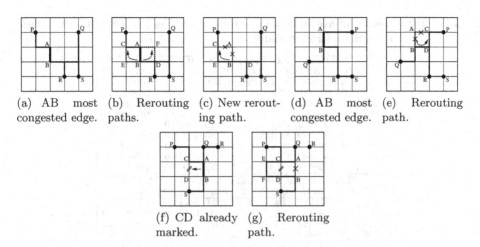

(a) AB most congested edge.

(b) Rerouting paths.

(c) New rerouting path.

(d) AB most congested edge.

(e) Rerouting path.

(f) CD already marked.

(g) Rerouting path.

Fig. 3. Congestion minimization using *CongestionReduction* algorithm

$\overline{CA}$ and $\overline{BD}$ incident on $\overline{AB}$. The two options for the tree detouring will be either through $\overline{CE}$ or $\overline{FD}$ as shown in Fig. 3(b). Among them, the edge with minimum existing congestion is selected for rerouting the net segment $\overline{AB}$. In the figure, we assume, $\overline{CE}$ has less congestion than $\overline{FD}$ and thereby detour our net through this edge as depicted in Fig. 3(c). After detouring we check whether the edge $\overline{AC}$ is part of the net under consideration and if found to be part of the original net $\overline{AC}$ is retained else removed. The depiction in the above figure assumes $\overline{AC}$ to be not a part of the original net, and hence has been removed. Similarly some other situation may happen with the most congested edge and a different net structure. Fig. 3(d) shows a net containing a congested edge $\overline{AB}$. Since, for this particular net, the horizontal edges are incident only from right side, we detour the net through $\overline{CD}$ as shown in Fig. 3(e). The next step is to check for $\overline{AC}$ being part of the net. If the removal of $\overline{AC}$ makes no effect to the connected net under consideration, remove it. We assume, it is not part of the net and subsequently remove it. For the third case, we assume $\overline{CD}$ was previously congested edge, which gets uncongested now, after applying our technique and marked, is shown in Fig. 3(f). The figure also shows that a segment of a net is passing through the most congested edge $\overline{AB}$ in the grid graph in this moment. Since, for this particular net, the horizontal edge is incident only from left we try to detour this net through $\overline{CD}$. But, $\overline{CD}$ being already marked the detouring does not takes place and we move forward to the adjacent edge $\overline{EF}$ and on finding it unmarked, detour our net through this edge.

3 Experimental Results

All experiments were performed on a Linux workstation with AMD A8 2.2Ghz CPU and 4GB memory. ISPD98 2D benchmark circuits have been used to implement our algorithms. The circuits are given in the form of grid graph along with number of nets, defined by terminal or pin coordinates in the graph.

Table 1. The results of five state-of-the-art global routers and CSaCB on ISPD'98 benchmark. The runtimes for each router are given in seconds.

Circuit	BoxRouter 2.0			FastRoute 2.0			FGR		
	TOF	WL	CT	TOF	WL	CT	TOF	WL	CT
ibm01	0	62659	32.8	31	68489	0.72	0	63332	10
ibm02	0	171110	35.9	0	178868	0.93	0	168918	13
ibm03	0	146634	17.6	0	150393	0.6	0	146412	5
ibm04	0	167275	115.9	64	175037	1.88	0	167101	29
ibm06	0	277913	47.4	0	284935	1.36	0	277608	18
ibm07	0	365790	85.9	0	375185	1.6	0	366180	20
ibm08	0	405634	90.1	0	411703	2.36	0	404714	18
ibm09	0	413862	273.1	3	424949	1.92	0	413053	20
ibm10	0	590141	352.4	0	595622	2.79	0	578795	92

Circuit	NTHU-Route 2.0			MaizeRouter			CSaCB		
	TOF	WL	CT	TOF	WL	CT	TOF	WL	CT
ibm01	0	62498	2.4	0	63720	NA	58	65012	2.6
ibm02	0	169881	3.3	0	170342	NA	36	170132	5.3
ibm03	0	146458	2.5	0	147078	NA	21	148338	2.7
ibm04	0	166452	5.9	0	170095	NA	122	170556	6.2
ibm06	0	277696	5.5	0	279566	NA	42	281124	6.2
ibm07	0	366133	6.4	0	369340	NA	84	366890	6.2
ibm08	0	404976	5.9	0	406349	NA	40	405684	6.8
ibm09	0	414738	5.7	0	415852	NA	18	416214	7.4
ibm10	0	579870	12.3	0	585921	NA	51	585654	15.3

Table 2. List machines used by other routers

Router	CPU	Memory
BoxRouter 2.0	Intel Pentium 4 2.8Ghz	2 GB
FastRoute 2.0	Intel Pentium 4 3.0 GHz	2 GB
FGR	AMD Opteron 2.4 Ghz	4 GB
NTHU-Route 2.0	AMD Opteron 2.2Ghz	8 GB
MaizeRouter	Dual-core 2.8-GHz AMD Opteron	16 GB

To empirically evaluate the performance of our *Congestion Sensing and Congestion Balancing*(CSaCB) technique, we compare it to six recent popular state-of-the-art academic global routers: FastRoute 2.0 [18], BoxRouter [23], FGR [16], NTHU-Route 2.0 [13], and MaizeRouter [20]. We compare the results in terms of total overflow, wirelength, and CPU time. The column heads "TOF", "WL", and "CT" denote the total overflow, total wire length, and CPU time required, in Table 1. All the existing router achieve 0 overflow for all nine circuits except FastRoute 2.0 which achieve 0 overflow for six out of nine circuits. The wirelength of NTHU-Route 2.0 is the least among all the routers. Our proposed technique CSaCB also achieves fairly good results with some overflow. Being an ongoing work, CSaCB requires few improvements and we hope the proposed technique will work well if we are able to incorporate these improvements. Table 2 shows the list of machines used by each router.

4   Conclusion

In this paper, we have presented the design and architectural details of a novel re-route based global routing, CSaCB. The technique based on two phases, viz. Congestion sensing path laying and congestion reduction, using net segment detouring procedure. While the first phase takes care of keeping congestion in control upto a certain extent, the second further reduces the congestion level and also keeps the wire length to a minimum value.

References

1. Ispd 1998 benchmark suite (1998),
   http://cseweb.ucsd.edu/~kastner/research/labyrinth/
2. Ispd 2007 benchmark suite (2007), http://archive.sigda.org/ispd2007/
3. Ispd 2008 benchmark suite (2008), http://archive.sigda.org/ispd2008/
4. Lee, C.Y.: An algorithm for path connections and its applications. IRE Transactions on Electronic Computers EC-10(3), 346–365 (1961)
5. Alpert, C.J., Hrkić, M., Hu, J., Kahng, A.B., Lillis, J., Liu, B., Quay, S.T., Sapatnekar, S.S., Sullivan, A.J., Villarrubia, P.: Buffered steiner trees for difficult instances. In: Proceedings of the 2001 International Symposium on Physical Design, ISPD 2001, pp. 4–9. ACM, New York (2001)
6. Chiang, C., Wong, C., Sarrafzadeh, M.: A weighted steiner tree-based global router with simultaneous length and density minimization. IEEE Transactions on Computer-Aided Design of Integrated Circuits and Systems 13(12), 1461–1469 (1994)
7. Areibi, S., Xie, M., Vannelli, A.: An efficient rectilinear steiner tree algorithm for vlsi global routing. In: Canadian Conference on Electrical and Computer Engineering, vol. 2, pp. 1067–1072 (2001)
8. Cong, J., Kahng, A., Leung, K.S.: Efficient algorithms for the minimum shortest path steiner arborescence problem with applications to vlsi physical design. IEEE Transactions on Computer-Aided Design of Integrated Circuits and Systems 17(1), 24–39 (1998)
9. Cong, J., Madden, P.: Performance-driven routing with multiple sources. IEEE Transactions on Computer-Aided Design of Integrated Circuits and Systems 16(4), 410–419 (1997)
10. Hu, J., Sapatnekar, S.: A timing-constrained simultaneous global routing algorithm. IEEE Transactions on Computer-Aided Design of Integrated Circuits and Systems 21(9), 1025–1036 (2002)
11. Kastner, R., Bozorgzadeh, E., Sarrafzadeh, M.: An exact algorithm for coupling-free routing (2001)
12. Sherwani, N.A.: Algorithms for VLSI Physical Design Automation. Kluwer Academic Publishers, Netherlands (1999)
13. Chang, Y.J., Lee, Y.T., Wang, T.C.: Nthu-route 2.0: A fast and stable global router. In: IEEE/ACM International Conference on Computer-Aided Design, ICCAD 2008, pp. 338–343 (November 2008)
14. Hsu, C.H., Chen, H.Y., Chang, Y.W.: Multilayer global routing with via and wire capacity considerations. IEEE Transactions on Computer-Aided Design of Integrated Circuits and Systems 29(5), 685–696 (2010)

15. Ozdal, M., Wong, M.: Archer: A history-based global routing algorithm. IEEE Transactions on Computer-Aided Design of Integrated Circuits and Systems 28(4), 528–540 (2009)
16. Roy, J., Markov, I.: High-performance routing at the nanometer scale. IEEE Transactions on Computer-Aided Design of Integrated Circuits and Systems 27(6), 1066–1077 (2008)
17. McMurchie, L.E., Ebeling, C.: Pathfinder: A negotiation-based path-driven router for fpgas. In: Proceeding of the International Symposium on FPGAs. ACM/IEEE (February 1995)
18. Xu, Y., Zhang, Y., Chu, C.: Fastroute 4.0: Global router with efficient via minimization. In: Asia and South Pacific Design Automation Conference, ASP-DAC 2009, pp. 576–581 (January 2009)
19. Cao, Z., Jing, T., Xiong, J., Hu, Y., He, L., Hong, X.: Dprouter: A fast and accurate dynamic-pattern-based global routing algorithm. In: Asia and South Pacific Design Automation Conference, ASP-DAC 2007, pp. 256–261 (January 2007)
20. Moffitt, M.: Maizerouter: Engineering an effective global router. In: Asia and South Pacific Design Automation Conference, ASPDAC 2008, pp. 226–231 (March 2008)
21. Behjat, L., Vannelli, A., Rosehart, W.: Integer linear programming models for global routing. INFORMS Journal on Computing 18(2), 137–150 (2006)
22. Hu, J., Roy, J.A., Markov, I.L.: Sidewinder: A scalable ilp-based router. In: Proceedings of the 2008 International Workshop on System Level Interconnect Prediction, pp. 73–80. ACM (2008)
23. Cho, M., Lu, K., Yuan, K., Pan, D.Z.: Boxrouter 2.0: A hybrid and robust global router with layer assignment for routability. ACM Trans. Des. Autom. Electron. Syst. 14(2), 1–32 (2009)
24. Wu, T.H., Davoodi, A., Linderoth, J.: Grip: Global routing via integer programming. IEEE Transactions on Computer-Aided Design of Integrated Circuits and Systems 30(1), 72–84 (2011)
25. Muller, D.: Optimizing yield in global routing. In: IEEE/ACM International Conference on Computer-Aided Design, ICCAD 2006, pp. 480–486 (November 2006)
26. Wu, T.H., Davoodi, A., Linderoth, J.T.: A parallel integer programming approach to global routing. In: 2010 47th ACM/IEEE Design Automation Conference (DAC), pp. 194–199 (June 2010)
27. Shojaei, H., Davoodi, A., Basten, T.: Collaborative multiobjective global routing. IEEE Transactions on Very Large Scale Integration (VLSI) Systems PP(99), 1
28. Chu, C., Wong, Y.C.: Flute: Fast lookup table based rectilinear steiner minimal tree algorithm for vlsi design. IEEE Transactions on Computer-Aided Design of Integrated Circuits and Systems 27(1), 70–83 (2008)

CMOS ASIC Design of a High Performance Digital Fuzzy Processor That Can Compute on Arbitrary Membership Functions

Anirban Guha and Shubhajit Roy Chowdhury

Center for VLSI and Embedded Systems Technology
International Institute of Information Technology, Hyderabad - 500032, India
anirban.guhaug08@students.iiit.ac.in, src.vlsi@iiit.ac.in

Abstract. The paper presents the CMOS ASIC design of a digital fuzzy processor, that can compute on arbitrary membership functions. The architecture exploits pipelining and parallelism to reduce the inferencing delay. The processor has been designed to operate at a frequency of 2 GHz using a power supply of 1 V. For a system with 256 active rules, the circuit has delay of 1285 ns and power dissipation of 70.5 mW. The set of common antecedents for a group of rules are stored separately, leading to reduction in delay and power dissipation. The performance of the proposed circuit has been compared with state of the art RISC and CISC processor architectures, and found to dissipate much less power and has much less delay.

Keywords: Fuzzy processor, Membership function, Antecedents, Rules.

1   Introduction

Fuzzy processors are commonly used in different control systems such as heating and air conditioning systems, automobile braking, washing machines, industrial automation etc. Fuzzy systems take the uncertainties in data into considerations while making decisions. The hardware implementation of fuzzy logic has been investigated in several works, with the first proposal coming from Togai and Watanabe [1]. The usage of general purpose processors in fuzzy logic computations has been mentioned in [2-5]. However, these are not suitable for real time applications where high speed infencing is needed, within hard real time deadline. Hardware dedicated for fuzzy computations has been developed for high speed applications [6-13]. However the use of FPGA based architectures adds flexibility in implementing the fuzzy system on chip [14]. Roy Chowdhury and Saha have proposed a high performance FPGA based fuzzy processor based on parallel-pipelined architecture in [15].

The current research is aimed at the ASIC design of a digital fuzzy processor. The processor has been designed to compute on arbitrary membership functions. This leads to better accuracy in results. The set of common antecedents for a group of fuzzy rules are stored separately in memory. This leads to reduction in memory space, delay and power dissipation.

M.S. Gaur et al. (Eds.): VDAT 2013, CCIS 382, pp. 233–241, 2013.
© Springer-Verlag Berlin Heidelberg 2013

The paper is organized as follows. Section 2 describes the processor architecture. Section 3 describes the simulation and results. Conclusion is presented is section 4.

2   Architectural Design of Processor

Fig. 1 depicts the fuzzy processor architecture. The processor has a controller, eight detection units (DU), eight antecedent units (AU), eight rule units (RU), a defuzzifier, antecedent memory, α-memory and an input buffer, whose details are given in the following subsections. Pipelining and parallelism have been employed in the architectural design to speed up the computation and increase throughput.

The number of fuzzy variables, n_F used in the architecture is 16 and the number of linguistic variables, n_L is 16. The maximum number of rules, n_R is 256, with each rule having one consequent. Each of the fuzzy variables is 16 bits wide. Thus the universe of discourse, d_U is 65536 values. The number of membership degrees, n_T for the linguistic sets is 256. The fuzzy sets taken into consideration are convex.

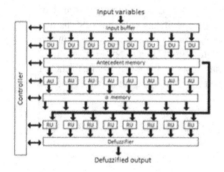

Fig. 1.   Processor Architecture

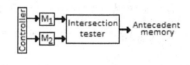

Fig. 2. Detection Unit

2.1   Detection Unit

The detection unit is used for finding the antecedents with a positive degree of truth i.e. having non-null intersection with the fuzzy input variables. The detection unit gets the input variables from the input buffer.

Intersection or overlap between the respective supports of the fuzzy sets is checked. Let F_{ik} be the fuzzy set for the kth ($k = 1,2, ..., n_L$) linguistic variable of the input X_i ($i = 1,2, ..., n_F$) . The indicator variable a_{ik} gets the value 1 or 0 depending on whether overlap exists or not between F_{ik} and the input fuzzy set X_i, and gets stored in the antecedent memory.

Fig. 2 shows the architectural design of the detection unit. Each detection unit has two memories M_1 and M_2. M_1 is used to store the supports for the linguistic variables and M_2 stores the supports for the fuzzy inputs. Since the fuzzy sets are convex, the supports can be represented by the left and right end-points. Both the end-points of a fuzzy set are stored in one word. M_1 contains 32 words, each having a width of $16*2 = 32$ bits. M_2 contains 2 words having same width as M_1.

2.2   Antecedent Unit

The antecedent unit is used for finding the degrees of truth for the antecedents. To find the degree of truth, it is necessary to store the membership functions for the fuzzy sets. The membership functions need not have linear edges and have to be approximated for storing them. They are approximated with piece-wise linear segments as shown in Fig. 3. The approximation has been done in such a way that the ordinates of the end-points of the linear-segments are multiples of Y and need not be stored. The abscissas of the end-points of the linear segments are stored. For each membership function there are 8 abscissas.

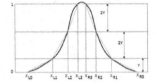

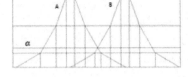

Fig. 3. Membership Function   **Fig. 4.** Intersecting membership functions

For a particular truth value α, it is necessary to calculate the α-cut. It is possible to know the segments that α intersects with, depending on the ordinates of the segment end-points between which α lies. The left and right end-points of the α-cut can then be calculated as

$$X_L(\alpha) = X_{Lni} + p_{Lni}(\alpha - Y_{ni}) . \tag{1}$$

$$X_R(\alpha) = X_{Rni} - p_{Rni}(\alpha - Y_{ni}) . \tag{2}$$

Where

$$p_{Lni} = \frac{X_{Ln(i+1)} - X_{Lni}}{Y_{n(i+1)} - Y_{ni}} . \tag{3}$$

$$p_{Rni} = \frac{|X_{Rn(i+1)} - X_{Rni}|}{Y_{n(i+1)} - Y_{ni}} . \tag{4}$$

The truth space of the antecedents is represented by 8 bits. The degree of truth for an antecedent is calculated by finding the maximum value of α for which the α-cut of the antecedent and input has a non-null intersection. This is done by first identifying the segments of the membership functions which intersect followed by finding the intersection point of these segments. In Fig. 4, are given 2 membership functions A and B, whose intersection point needs to be found out. To identify the intersecting segments, the first step is to find out the membership function nearer to the origin. Depending on that, the upper end-points of the intersecting segments will satisfy one of the equations

$$X_{RA} \leq X_{LB} \text{ (A is nearer to the origin) or } X_{RB} \leq X_{LA} \text{ (B is nearer to the origin) .} \tag{5}$$

To find the intersection point (supposing A is nearer to the origin), the following condition is tested:

$$X_{LBni}(\alpha) \le X_{RAni}(\alpha) . \tag{6}$$

$$\Rightarrow X_{LBni} + p_{LBni}(\alpha - Y_{ni}) \le X_{RAni} - p_{RAni}(\alpha - Y_{ni}) \quad \alpha \in [Y_{ni}, Y_{n(i+1)}] . \tag{7}$$

$$\Rightarrow (\alpha - Y_{ni})(p_{LBni} + p_{RAni}) \le X_{RAni} - X_{LBni} \quad \alpha \in [Y_{ni}, Y_{n(i+1)}] . \tag{8}$$

$$\Rightarrow (\alpha - Y_{ni})\, p \le \Delta X \quad \alpha \in [Y_{ni}, Y_{n(i+1)}] . \tag{9}$$

Equation 9 is tested using the binary-search algorithm, given below.

```
α = Yni + Yn(i+1) ;
        2
ΔY = Yn(i+1) - Yni ;
          2
Yp = ΔY * p ;
while ( ΔY != 1 )
{
    ΔY = ΔY ;
         2
    If ( Yp ≤ ΔX )
    {
        α = α + ΔY ;
        Yp = Yp + ΔY *p ;
    }
    else
    {
        α = α - ΔY ;
        Yp = Yp - ΔY *p ;
    }
}
```

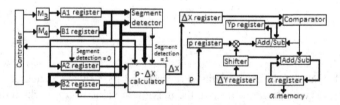

Fig. 5. Antecedent Unit

Fig. 5 shows the architectural design of the antecedent unit. Each antecedent unit has 2 memories M_3 and M_4. The abscissas of the end-points of the linear segments for the membership functions are stored in these memories. M_3 contains the antecedent membership functions while M_4 contains the input membership functions. Each membership function requires 8 memory locations. Thus M_3 has $32 * 8 = 256$ words while M_4 has $2 * 8 = 16$ words. Both the memories are 16 bits wide.

The *segment detector* is used to identify the intersecting segments. Registers A1 and B1 store the upper end-points while the registers A2 and B2 store the lower end-points. If an intersection is found, the contents of the registers are transferred to p-ΔX *calculator*. Otherwise the contents of A1 and B1 are transferred to A2 and B2 respectively and A1 and B1 get the upper end-points of the next segments from M_3 and M_4 respectively. p and ΔX are used in the search algorithm to find the intersection point.

2.3 Rule Unit

The rule unit is used for rule activation. There are 8 rule units for parallel inferencing of the fuzzy rules. The architectural design of the rule unit is shown in Fig. 6. Each unit has 3 memories M_5, M_6 and M_7. M_5 and M_6 store the antecedents of the rules and the consequents are stored in M_7.

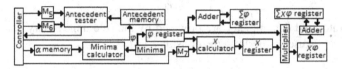

Fig. 6. Rule Unit

Usually a group of fuzzy rules have a set of common antecedents. The set of common antecedents for the group of rules are stored in M_5 and the varying antecedents are stored in M_6. This leads to savings in memory space, computation time and power dissipation. The total number of rules is 256. M_5 contains 8 words, each 24 bits wide. The first 16 bits are used to indicate the fuzzy variables which are common over a group of rules. The next four bits show the linguistic element and the last 4 bits give the number of rules in that group. Each group on an average has 4 rules. M_6 has 32 words each 20 bits wide. The first 16 bits indicate the uncommon fuzzy variables and the next 4 bits show the linguistic element.

The consequent of each rule is a membership function. Similar to the antecedent membership functions, the output membership functions are approximated using piece-wise linear segments. Each membership function has 7 linear segments. The abscissas of the endpoints are stored in M_7, with the ordinates fixed and known. Thus each consequent requires 8 memory words. M_7 has therefore $32 * 8 = 256$ words, each being 16 bits wide.

The process of rule activation involves minimization of the truth degrees of the antecedents. If the degree of truth for some antecedent is null, then that rule becomes inactive and is skipped. A word from memory M_5 is read and each antecedent is checked for its degree of truth in the *antecedent tester*. This is done by reading the corresponding indicator variable a_{ik} from the antecedent memory. If the indicator variable is zero, then the degree of truth for that antecedent is zero and as a result all the rules in that group are inactive. The control then passes onto the next word of M_5 (next group of rules). If the indicator variable is 1, then that antecedent has a positive degree of truth. The truth value is read from the α-memory and sent to the *minima calculator*.

This process gives us the minimum truth degree for all the common antecedents of a group. Similar steps are then performed over the varying antecedents of each of the rules in a group (stored in M_6), with one of the degrees of truth being the minima obtained for the common antecedents. If the degree of truth for a particular antecedent is null, then the rule is skipped and the next rule is read. The minimum truth degree obtained for a rule is stored in the φ register. The X calculator uses the output membership function from M_7 and φ to get X. φ and X for each of the rules are then combined to get $\sum_i \varphi_i X_i$ and $\sum_i \varphi_i$.

2.4   Defuzzifier

The defuzzifier is used for the defuzzification of the combined consequences. Yager's defuzzification method [16] is used for calculating the defuzzified output Z_o.

$$Z_o = \frac{\sum_i \varphi_i X_i}{\sum_i \varphi_i} . \tag{10}$$

The numerator and denominator are provided by the rule unit. Binary restoring division algorithm is used to perform the division.

2.5   Controller

The controller has been implemented as a hardwired controller and modeled as a finite state machine. The state diagram of the controller is shown in Fig. 7.

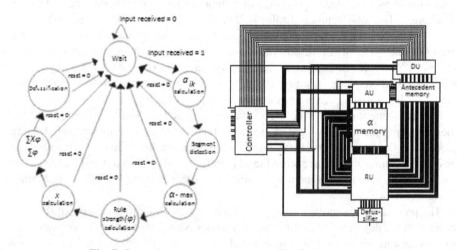

Fig. 7. Controller   **Fig. 8.** Processor schematic

The controller starts from the *wait* state. Once the input variables are received, the controller goes to the a_{ik} calculation state. After the indicator variables are calculated and stored in the antecedent memory, the *segment detection* state starts, where the intersecting segments of the membership functions are detected. The next state is the

α-*max calculation* state, where the intersection point of the segments is calculated. The intersection points are stored in the α-memory. Rule activation is performed in the *rule strength calculation* state. The rule strength is stored in the φ register, which is then used in the *X calculation* state to obtain the consequence X. In the next state, φ and X, for each rule are multiplied and accumulated to get $\sum_i \varphi_i X_i$ and $\sum_i \varphi_i$. The controller then passes onto the *defuzzification* state, which performs Yager's defuzzification to get the crisp output Z_o.

3   Simulation and Results

The circuit has been designed in 45 nm using NCSU PDK and OSU standard cell library. RTL synthesis has been done using the Cadence Encounter RTL Compiler. The simulations have been performed in Cadence Virtuoso Spectre Circuit Simulator. The circuit for the processor is shown in Fig. 8.

The circuit is designed to operate at a frequency of 2 GHz using a power supply of 1 V. Kogge-Stone adders have been used in the design. The power and delay of the circuit with respect to the number of active rules are presented in Table 1. As the number of active rules increases, the computation time and the energy dissipation of the rule unit increase. Thus there is an increase in delay with the increase in number of active rules. The computation time and the energy dissipation of detection unit, antecedent unit and defuzzifier are independent of the number of active rules. The contribution of these three units to average power dissipation decreases with the increase in delay, since the average is calculated over delay. Thus lesser delay results in higher average power dissipation. Thus the power dissipation increases with the decrease in number of active rules.

Table 1. Power and delay of circuit

No. of active rules	Power (mW)	Delay (ns)
8	123.9	260
16	104.7	355
32	86.5	545
64	84.4	605
128	71.7	1045
256	70.5	1285

Table 2. Comparison of the processors

Fuzzy processor	Power (W)	Delay (ns)
Proposed ASIC	0.124	260
ARM 922T	0.5	2500
Pentium IV	71.8	60000

The performance of the proposed ASIC has been compared with the performances of fuzzy processors based on RISC (200 MHz ARM 922T) and CISC (2 GHz Pentium IV) architectures [15] for 8 active rules in Table 2. The proposed circuit has much less power dissipation and delay compared to the general purpose processors.

4   Conclusion

The current work describes the ASIC design of a high speed fuzzy processor. The processor can work on different membership functions. The architecture exploits pipelining and parallelism to reduce the inferencing delay. The processor has been designed to operate at a frequency of 2 GHz using a power supply of 1 V. For a system with 256 active rules, the circuit has delay of 1285 ns and power dissipation of 70.5 mW. Storing the set of common antecedents for a group of rules separately leads to reduction in delay and power dissipation. The circuit has lesser power dissipation and delay compared to state of the art RISC and CISC architecture processors.

Acknowledgments. The authors would like to acknowledge the support lent by the Department of Science and Technology, Govt. of India and the Ministry of Human Resource Development, Govt. of India for providing the necessary fund and resources needed to carry out the research work.

References

1. Togai, M., Watanabe, H.: Expert System on a Chip: An Engine for Real-Time Approximate Reasoning. IEEE Expert Systems Magazine 1(3), 55–62 (1986)
2. Lim, M.H., Takefuji, Y.: Implementing fuzzy rule-based systems on silicon chips. IEEE Expert Systems Magazine 5(1), 31–45 (1990)
3. Zadeh, L.A.: Outline of a New Approach to the Analysis of Complex Systems and Decision Processes. IEEE Transactions on Systems, Man and Cybernetics 3(1), 28–44 (1973)
4. Zadeh, L.A.: Fuzzy logic, neural networks and soft computing. ACM Transactions on Computing 37(3), 77–84 (1994)
5. Surmann, H., Ungering, A.P.: Fuzzy rule-based systems on general purpose processors. IEEE Micro 15(4), 40–48 (1995)
6. Watanabe, H., Detloff, W.D., Symon, J.R., Yount, K.E.: VLSI fuzzy chip and inference accelerator board systems. In: Fuzzy Logic for Management of Uncertainty, pp. 211–243. Wiley, New York (1992)
7. Nakamura, K., Sakashita, N., Nitta, Y., Shimomura, K., Tokuda, T.: Fuzzy inference and fuzzy inference processor. IEEE Micro 13(5), 37–48 (1993)
8. Manzoul, M.A., Tayal, S.: Systolic VLSI array for multi-variable fuzzy control systems. International Journal of Systems and Cybernetics 21(1), 27–42 (1990)
9. Jaramillo-Botero, A., Miyake, Y.: A high speed parallel architecture for fuzzy infer-ence and fuzzy control of multiple processes. In: Proceedings of IEEE 1994 World Congress on Computational Intelligence, vol. 3, pp. 1765–1770 (1994)
10. Orsila, H., Kangas, T., Salminen, E., Hamalainen, T.D., Hannikainen, M.: Automated memory-aware application distribution for Multi-processor System-on-Chips. Journal of Systems Architecture 53(11), 795–815 (2007)
11. Samoladas, V., Petrou, L.: Special-purpose architectures for fuzzy logic controllers. Microprocessing and Microprogramming 40(4), 275–289 (1994)
12. de Salvador, L., Gutierrez, J.: A multilevel systolic approach for fuzzy inference hardware. IEEE Micro 15(5), 61–71 (1995)

13. Raychev, R., Mtibaa, A., Abid, M.: VHDL Modeling of a Fuzzy Co-Processor Architecture. In: Proceedings of International Conference on Computer Systems and Technologies, pp. I. 2.1–I. 2.6 (2005)
14. Aranguren, G., Barron, M., Arroyabe, J.L., Garcia-Carreira, G.: A pipe-line fuzzy controller in FPGA. In: Proceedings of IEEE Conference on Fuzzy Systems, vol. 2, pp. 635–640 (1997)
15. Roy Chowdhury, S., Saha, H.: A High-Performance FPGA-Based Fuzzy Processor Architecture for Medical Diagnosis. IEEE Micro 28(5), 38–52 (2008)
16. Yager, R.R., Filev, D.P.: SLIDE: A simple adaptive defuzzification method. IEEE Transactions on Fuzzy System 1(1) (1993)

Variation Robust Subthreshold SRAM Design with Ultra Low Power Consumption

Saima Cherukat and Vineet Sahula

Department of Electronics & Communication Engineering,
National Institute of Technology, Jaipur, India
saimacherukat@gmail.com, sahula@ieee.org

Abstract. Continued scaling of CMOS technologies has resulted in process variations emerging as a critical design concern. The power consumption requirement in portable devices is even more strictly constrained for extending the battery operating lifetime. In this work, we propose an asymmetrical Schmitt trigger based SRAM cell, suitable for ultra low power applications. It addresses the fundamental conflicting design requirement of read versus write operation of conventional 6T cell. A built-in feedback mechanism proposed for the cell, makes it more robust against process variations. Usually, a Schmitt trigger cell configuration has been used in literature for improving stability of inverter-pair. We propose asymmetrical cell-configuration as modification over this usual Schmitt-trigger based configuration so that the design becomes more tolerant of mismatch in neighboring transistors. Simulation results show that proposed bitcell operates on a very low leakage current and with much less power dissipation compared to 6T cell.

Keywords: Low voltage/Subthreshold SRAM Design, Low power SRAM, Process variation, Schmitt trigger.

1 Introduction

It is expected that more than 90% of the die area in future systems-on-chip (SoCs) will be occupied by SRAM and the requirements of higher density and low power SRAMs are increasing exponentially. The main sources of power consumption in digital Complementary Metal Oxide Semiconductors (CMOS) circuits are logic transitions, short circuit currents that flow directly from supply to ground when both n and p sub network conducts simultaneously and leakage current that accounts for static power dissipation. The active power dissipation in the switching parts of the circuit increases with improved performance and increased density with each technology generation. Leakage mainly consists of gate leakage and subthreshold leakage. The magnitude of leakage current is no longer negligible and it plays a significant role in total power consumption at lower technology nodes. For portable devices developed for 65nm technology node, it is estimated that subthreshold leakage power will account for about 50 percent of the total power consumption [1]. Ultra low power design is always on demand as it can meet the requirement of

M.S. Gaur et al. (Eds.): VDAT 2013, CCIS 382, pp. 242–248, 2013.
© Springer-Verlag Berlin Heidelberg 2013

extending battery life of portable electronic devices like smart phones, digital cameras, biomedical chips etc.

Different power reduction techniques like voltage scaling, pipelining, device & interconnect sizing and switching activity reduction have been implemented at device/circuit/architectural level. Among these, supply voltage scaling has remained one of the first choice of designers. The dynamic power can be reduced quadratically and leakage power linearly to first order by reducing supply voltage [2].

In a given process technology, the process constraints such as gate oxide limits the maximum supply voltage (V_{max}) for transistor operation and for a given performance requirement, the minimum supply voltage (V_{min}) is limited by increased process variation and sensitivity. With technology scaling, the V_{max} increases while the V_{min} increases. Therefore for low power operation, the V_{min} has to be lowered further to increase the SRAM bitcell operation range.

1.1   Process Variation

The major roadblock that designers face is process variation, as high performance processors move to sub 45nm technologies. The process parameter variation results in variation in maximum operating frequency and power consumption in fabricated dies [3]. Process variation can be due to variation in parameter, voltage and temperature. Inability to precisely control the fabrication process at nanometre technologies, results into parameter variation. Parameter variations can be mainly classified in to two categories- (i) Die to Die (D2D) variations, which affects all the transistors in a lot or wafer equally and (ii) With-in die (WID) variations, consisting of systematic and random components, causes electrical characteristics to vary across a die [4]. For a given design, both, power supply and temperature vary from chip to chip and within chip. Voltage variation can be caused by IR drops in the supply networks or by LdI/dt noise under changing load. Spatially and temporally varying factor causes temperature variations. All these variations cannot be tolerated as technology scales to smaller feature sizes.

In ultra low power designs, the sensitivity of circuit parameters increases with reduction in supply voltage. Memory cells are most sensitive to device variations causing device mismatch for several reasons. Therefore the process variation limit the circuit operation in sub threshold region, particularly in SRAM cells where minimum sized transistors are used. For several reasons memory cells are most sensitive to device variation which results in device mismatch. Usually the devices used in smallest memory cell for a given process, is smaller than the devices allowed elsewhere in the design [5].

1.2   Earlier Work on Process Variation Tolerant SRAM Bitcell

The 6 transistor (6T) cell which uses a cross-coupled inverter is the basic memory bitcell used in SRAM designs. Several SRAM bitcells have been proposed to meet different design goals such bitcell area, low voltage/ low power operation, timing specifications, bit density and reliability. To improve process variation tolerance, adaptive circuit techniques like source biasing and dynamic VDD have been proposed [6]. Different types of Single ended and differential operating bitcells have been proposed. For achieving improved read stability, different bitcell configurations use an extra sensing circuit for reading cell contents. Considering the fact that the stability of the inverter pair should be improved for stable SRAM operation at low supply voltages, Jaydeep P. Kulkarni et. al had proposed a Schmitt trigger based differential bitcell having built-in feedback mechanism for improved process variation tolerance [7].

The rest of this paper is organised as follows. In Section 2 the operation of basic SRAM cell, conflicting read vs. write design requirement and Schmitt trigger principle for cross-coupled inverter pair are discussed. Section 3 describes proposed SRAM bitcell. Section 4 covers the simulation results and paper concludes with Section 5.

2   Conventional 6T SRAM Bitcell

The basic static RAM cell is shown in Fig. 1. It consists of two cross-coupled inverters and two access transistors. Four of the transistors are used to make a pair of inverters – NOT gates, essentially. Each inverter requires a pair of transistors – if the input is 0, then the p-type transistor will be on, and the n-type off. This will connect the output to power, which is equal to logic 1. Otherwise, if the input is 1, the output will be connected to ground, or logic 0.

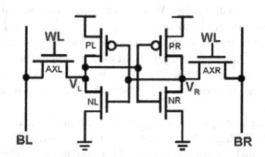

Fig. 1. Conventional symmetrical 6T bitcell

The two inverters are connected in a loop, with the output of one, the input of the other. The access transistors are connected to the wordline at their respective gate terminals, and the bitlines at their source/drain terminals. The wordline is used to select the cell while the bitlines are used to perform read or write operations on the cell. Internally, the cell holds the stored value on one side and its complement on the other side.

This arrangement has two stable states: we interpret these two states can be interpreted as 1 and 0. The other two transistors are used to control reading and writing. To read the contents of the RAM cell, the *word* line (WL) is set high, allowing the contents of the cell to be read out to the *bit* line say BL (and its inverse) to the *not bit* (BR) line. To write the cell, we again set the *word* line high, but this time we set the *bit* line (and its inverse) to the value we wish to store, forcing the cell into the appropriate state.

2.1   Conflicting Read vs. Write Design Requirement in 6T bitcell

For reliable read operation, the design requirement is such that the data should not be flipped. However during the write operation, the design requirement is such that the data should be flipped as easily as possible. This is the fundamental conflicting design requirement in the conventional 6T bitcell. This is because; the same pair of access transistors is used to initiate read/write operation in a 6T cell. Traditionally device sizing has been adopted to balance the read versus write design requirements. With increased process variations, satisfying the conflicting requirements during read-write operation is becoming very challenging [8]. This degrades the scalability of the SRAM cell as well. Moreover, device sizing is not effective for improving the cell stability at very low supply voltage [9]. Hence there arises a need for a novel design approach for successful low voltage operation of SRAM bitcells in nano-scaled technologies.

In order to resolve the read versus write conundrum in the 6T cell, Schmitt trigger principle for the cross coupled inverter pair had been proposed [10]. A Schmitt trigger is used to modulate the switching threshold of an inverter depending on the direction of the input transition.

3   Proposed Asymmetric SRAM Bitcell

Fig. 2 shows the schematics of proposed asymmetrical Schmitt trigger based bitcell. For maintaining the clarity of discussion, the bitcell configuration in [10] is termed as ST bitcell while the bitcell we proposed is termed as AST bitcell hereafter in this paper. The AST bitcell have 10 transistors, 2 wordlines (WLL /WLR) and 2 bit-lines (BL/BR). Transistors PL-NL1-NL2-NFL form ST- I inverter while PR-NR1-NR2-NFR form ST- II inverter. Feedback transistors NFL/NFR raise the switching threshold of the inverter during the 0→1 input transition giving the Schmitt trigger action.

Asymmetric cell (AST) differs from usual 6T and Schmitt trigger based SRAM cell in following manner.

- Read bitline (RBL) is separate from write bitline (WBL). This means that the read operation is performed independent of the right side bitline, unlike the traditional 6T/ ST cell which uses both bitlines simultaneously for read access and write operation.

- Read wordline (RWL) is separate from write wordline (WWL).This means that for read access the new cell only asserts RWL to enable the left switch pass transistor and the right pass transistor is kept off. This is opposite to conventional 6T/ST cell which uses both pass transistors by asserting common WL for read or write operation. Hence, the read access is performed only through the left side of the cell using RBL precharged high and then asserting the RWL. On the other hand, the write operation is accomplished only through the right side of the cell by enforcing the WBL to the desired value and then asserting the WWL, independent of the left side. With this structure the symmetric topology is no longer satisfied.

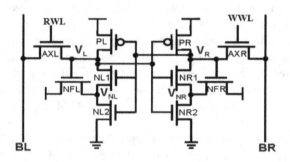

Fig. 2. Asymmetrical Schmitt Trigger Bitcell

4   Simulation Results

HSPICE simulations were performed using 45nm predictive technology model for MOS. Typical NMOS (PMOS) threshold voltage is 466mV (412mv).The conventional 6T bitcell and proposed AST bitcell are compared for various SRAM metrics. For 6T cell, transistor widths WPU/WAX/WPD are 80nm/160nm/240nm, respectively. For AST bitcell, extra transistors NFL/NL2 are of minimum width (80nm) while other transistors have the same dimensions as those of 6T cell.

The ST bitcells consumes approximately 2X area compared with the 6T cell. Hence, in order to estimate the operating conditions, it is only fair to compare the bitcells under Iso-area condition [7][10].

Fig. 3 compares the leakage current of AST with conventional 6T bitcell and ST. The results clearly demonstrate that, under Iso-area conditions, the leakage current of proposed cell is less compared to that of 6T cell and ST cell in subthreshold operation. Fig. 4 plots Iso- area power consumption vs. supply voltage (mV) of 6T, ST cell and proposed bitcell and it can be seen that the proposed AST consumes very less power compared to other in subthreshold operation making it a good choice in low power applications.

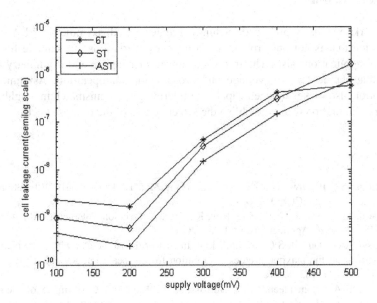

Fig. 3. Iso-area bitcell leakage current Comparison

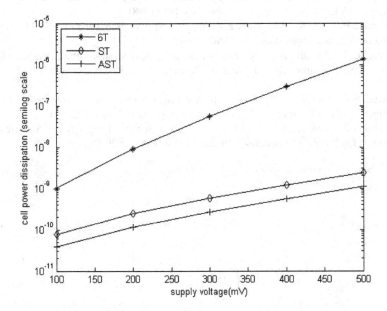

Fig. 4. Iso-area bitcell subthreshold power consumption comparison

5   Conclusions

In this work, we have proposed, Schmitt Trigger based asymmetric SRAM cell configuration that is not only robust against process variations but suitable for ultra low power applications also. The in-built feedback mechanism and asymmetry make it a suitable choice for low voltage and process tolerant operation. Asymmetrical configuration also makes this cell capable of tolerating more mismatch in neighboring transistors. Simulation results establish the effectiveness of the proposed cell.

References

1. Narendra, S., Blaauw, D., Devgan, A., Najm, F.: Leakage trends, estimation and avoidance. Tutorial ICCAD (2003)
2. Kulkarni, J.P., Kim, K., Park, S.P., Roy, K.: Process Variation Tolerant SRAM Array for Ultra Low Voltage Applications. In: DAC (2008)
3. Bowman, K.A., Duvall, S.G., Meindl, J.D.: Impact of die to die and within die parameter fluctuations on the maximum clock distribution for gigascale integration. IEEE J. Solid State Circuits 37, 183–190 (2002)
4. Bowman, K.A., Alameldeen, A.R., Srinivasan, S.T., Wilkerson, C.B.: Impact of Die to Die and Within- Die Parameter Variations on the Clock Frequency and Throughput of Multi-Core Processors. IEEE Trans. on VLSI Systems 17(12) (December 2009)
5. Heald, R., Wang, P.: Variability in sub-100nm SRAM Designs. IEEE (2004)
6. Kawaguchi, H., Itaka, Y., Sakurai, T.: Dynamic leakage cutoff scheme for low voltage SRAMs. In: VLSI Circuit Symposium, pp. 140–141 (1998)
7. Kulkarni, J.P., Kim, K., Park, S.P., Roy, K.: Process Variation Tolerant SRAM array for Ultra Low Voltage Applications. In: DAC (2008)
8. Yoshinobu, N., Masahi, H., Takayuki, K., Itoh, K.: Review and future prospects of low voltage RAM Circuits. IBM Journal of Research and Development 47(5/6), 525–552 (2003)
9. Calhoun, B.H., Chandrakasan, A.P.: Static noise margin variation for subthreshold SRAM in 65nm CMOS. IEEE Journal of Solid State Circuits 41, 1673–1679 (2006)
10. Kulkarni, J.P., Kim, K., Roy, K.: A 160mv Robust Schmitt Trigger Based Subthreshold SRAM. IEEE Journal of Solid State Circuits 42(10) (October 2007)

Modeling of High Frequency Out-of-Plane Single Axis MEMS Capacitive Accelerometer

Prashant Singh, Pooja Srivastava, Ram Mohan Verma, and Saurabh Jaiswal

Department of Microelectronics, IIIT-Allahabad, India
{psingh3688,poojasrivastava1405,rammohanverma15,
jaiswalsaurabh2009}@gmail.com

Abstract. The present paper deals with the modeling of high resonance frequency electrostatically actuated MEMS accelerometer having out-of-plane sensing axis. The accelerometer is based on folded beam support and comb structure configuration. Capacitance change phenomenon is used to determine the device acceleration. Effect of different structural parameters on the device performance is analyzed and the simulation is carried out on COMSOL Multiphysics, a strong 3D modeling software. The design is based on standard SOI-MUMP'S technology and with in-house fabrication capabilities. SOI-MUMP'S technology is preferred because of its outstanding performance and ease of fabrication.

1 Introduction

Micro electro mechanical (MEMS) accelerometer is one of the most popular miniaturized inertial sensor [1] used to measure displacement, velocity, acceleration/deceleration and vibration [2]. Miniaturized devices are advantageous in the way that they possess high frequency, small size, low power and low cost etc. The acceleration measures is in terms of g-value, the specific force acting in a body relative to some frame, g-value is zero for free falling body whereas g-value is very large for missile and navigation applications, the maximum value measured by accelerometer is 500g. Also the accelerometer is a device which is used to measure the acceleration producing forces, these force might be static such as constant force acting on a body or dynamic such as force varying with time. In present scenario MEMS accelerometer make its presence essential in all the applications where motion is involved [3-5]. Several approaches such as piezoelectric, piezoresistive, thermal, etc [6]. has been used for a long time in industry to design accelerometers but capacitive approach revolutionize accelerometer application and its market as such it replaces all other designing techniques. Capacitive accelerometer is the most fascinating device in the sense that it covers all the fields of application ranging from kids toys, motion sensor games [7], biomedical, military and navigation.

Capacitive accelerometer design is based on the measurement of change in capacitance value. MEMS structures are designed to sense the change of capacitance, an additional circuitry is required to convert change in capacitance into voltage value [8]. Capacitive accelerometer is designed on the basis of number of axis it sensed, the sensing axis can be one, two or three. Sensing is also based on the movement of

M.S. Gaur et al. (Eds.): VDAT 2013, CCIS 382, pp. 249–256, 2013.
© Springer-Verlag Berlin Heidelberg 2013

sensing structure relative to some frame of reference and it is two types either in-plane movement or out-of-plane [9]. The point should be noted that as the sensing axis increases the required additional circuitry increases and hence the device complexity. The model presents in this paper is based on out-of-plane sensing technique for low g applications. Advantage of capacitive design is that it can be used as both actuator and sensor. It has high sensitivity, high resolution, low noise and increased bandwidth etc.

2   Accelerometer Model

The basic accelerometer model consists of a spring mass damper model within a reference frame. Proof mass motion (X_m) lags to the frame motion (X_f) due to mass of inertia as shown in Fig 1.

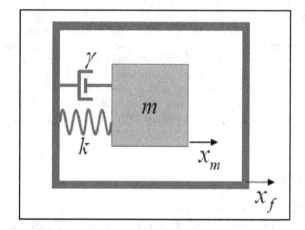

Fig. 1. Basic Accelerometer model

Where, 'm' is mass, 'k' is spring constant, 'γ' is damping constant. A force is applied on the mass results in displacement X_m, the equation of motion of proof mass is given by

$$m\frac{\partial^2 x_m}{\partial t^2} + \gamma\frac{\partial(x_m - x_f)}{\partial t} + k(x_m - x_f) = Fe \tag{1}$$

Where Fe is the actuating force acting on the mass, equation (1) can be simplified by subtracting $m\frac{\partial^2 x_f}{\partial t^2}$ from both sides leading to

$$m\frac{\partial^2(x_m - x_f)}{\partial t^2} + \gamma\frac{\partial(x_m - x_f)}{\partial t} + k(x_m - x_f) = -m\frac{\partial^2 x_f}{\partial t^2} + Fe \tag{2}$$

Here $(x_f - x_m)$ is the difference in reference frame and mass positions, now the equation can be further reduce as

$$m\frac{\partial^2 x}{\partial t^2} + \gamma\frac{\partial x}{\partial t} + kx = F \tag{3}$$

Where F is the summation of inertial and actuating forces $F = m\frac{\partial^2 x_f}{\partial t^2} - F_e$

3   Accelerometer Structure

The Accelerometer structure present in this paper is based on out-of-plane sensing where a pair of fixed-free folded beam support is attached to the proof mass, two pairs of comb structures are attached for capacitance sensing. 3-D structure of proposed structure is shown in Fig 2.

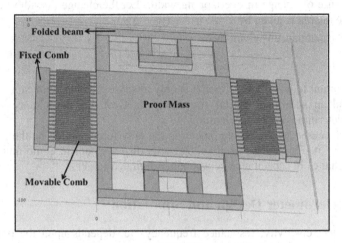

Fig. 2. 3-D structure of folded beam accelerometer

Proof mass, folded beam and comb fingers are the three basic components of the accelerometer structure. Comb structure form interdigited fingers between fixed and free comb where capacitance change is sensed shown in Fig 3.

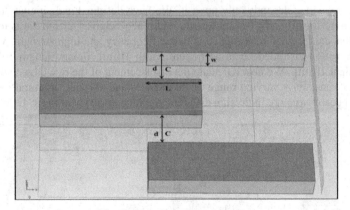

Fig. 3. Basic interdigited fingers

Capacitance formed by the structure at stationary position [10] is given by

$$c = \varepsilon \frac{A}{d}$$

Where 'ε' is the permittivity of the material between the fingers, 'A' is overlapping area and 'd' is the distance between the fingers. At stationary the capacitance value is maximum, its value decreases as there exist some oscillation or displacement. Finger overlapping area is given by

$$A = w * l$$

In the proposed model the overlapping length is always constant, change in area is always because of change in overlapping width. Let the change in width be Δw, and then change in area is given by $A' = l * (w - \Delta w)$

Changed capacitance is given by

$$C' = \epsilon \frac{l * (w - \Delta w)}{d}$$

It is important to note that the model is only to sense the change in capacitance, we need to add an additional digital circuitry to convert that capacitance value into voltage to determine proper acceleration.

The force sensed by the accelerometer is the only force applied on the proof mass that oscillates it. Proof mass oscillation results displacement in comb attached to it and hence change in capacitance between interdigitated fingers.

4   Accelerometer Design and Simulation

Accelerometer sensitivity, resonance frequency etc. depends upon the proof mass, comb structure and folded beam. In the present paper we are trying to design and simulate the structure to obtain high resonance frequency.

4.1   Folded Beam Design

Designing of folded beam is important in the terms that proof mass support and resonance frequency depends only upon it. We have designed and simulate the folded beam structure for different flexure length, width and height. Our motive is to obtain a structure that can provide maximum resonance frequency and high strength. We set the initial parameters of folded beam as flexure width 1[μm], flexure length 10[μm] and flexure height 1[μm]. We now calculate the displacement of the free edge that connects to the proof mass for a varying range of frequencies and varying structural parameters. The folded beam structure indicating different parameters is shown in fig 4.

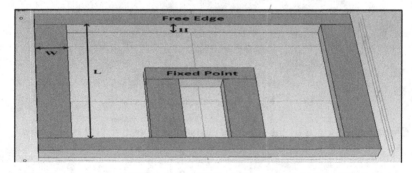

Fig. 4. Folded beam structure. 'H' is height, 'W' is width and 'L' is length of folded beam.

Frequency domain analysis is performed for frequency range 1MHz to 10 MHz, where total force of 1μN is applied at the free end of folded beam.

4.1.1   Effect of Structure Height on Free Edge Displacement

Variation in free end displacement is observed according to change in structure height for a range of 1[μm] to 15[μm] as shown in Fig 5.

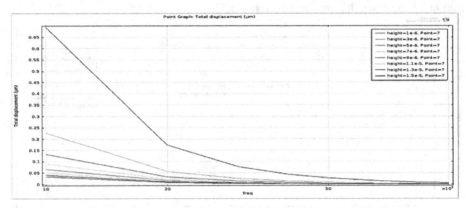

Fig. 5. Variation in folded beam free with change in structure height

Flexure width (1μm) and flexure length (10μm) is kept constant during analysis. It is observed from the graph that the displacement of free edge decreases exponentially with increase in the structure height.

4.1.2 Effect of Flexure Width on Free Edge Displacement

The folded beam flexure width varies for a range of 1μm to 20μm at a step size of 2μm. precaution is taken selecting the proper values so that the flexure length shall not less than 4 times the flexure width. Free end displacement for flexure length (80μm) and structure height (1μm) is shown in Fig. 6.

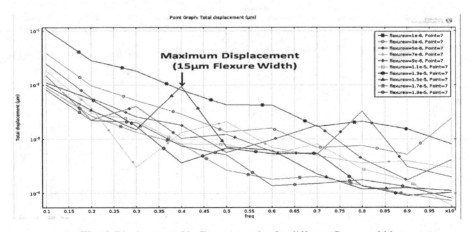

Fig. 6. Displacement Vs. Frequency plot for different flexure width

Only for some flexure width values the structure resonance frequency lies in the range of 1MHz to 10MHz, maximum displacement is obtained at 4 MHz frequency for flexure width of 15µm.

4.1.3 Effect of Flexure Length on Free Edge Displacement

Displacement of free end with change in flexure length at constant height [1µm] and constant flexure width [1µm] is shown in Fig. 7.

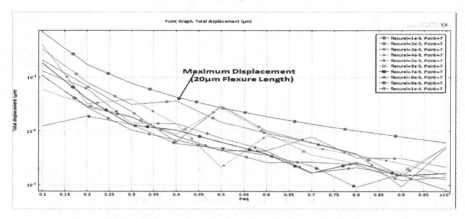

Fig. 7. Free end displacement with varying flexure length

Here we observe that the flexure length of 20µm give maximum displacement at 4MHz frequency. The flexure length to width ratio is 20:1 for 4MHz resonance frequency.

From the above simulations we have concluded that as the structure height increases the folded beam displacement decreases. There are many possibilities to construct an structure that provide resonance frequency of 4 MHz, for our design we have selected parameters as flexure length 46 µm, flexure width 10 µm and height 6 µm from the simulated structure whose response is shown in Fig. 8.

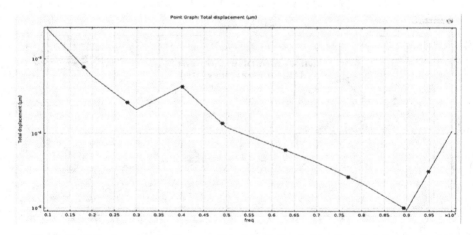

Fig. 8. Total displacement for flexure width=1.0e-5, flexure length=4.6e-5, height=6e-6

4.2   Accelerometer Design

The accelerometer design is based on the parameters obtained from the folded beam design shown in Table 1.

Table 1. Optimized design parameters for accelerometer

Parameters	Folded Beam (μm)	Proof Mass (μm)	Comb Structure (μm)
Length	-	100	-
Width	-	46	-
Flexure Length	46	-	-
Flexure Width	10	-	-
Number of fingers	-	-	10
Finger length	-	-	20
Finger Width	-	-	4
Finger Gap	-	-	2
Finger Overlap	-	-	15
Structure Height	6	6	6

4.2.1 Analytical Study

Based on the above parameters we have designed the accelerometer and performed analytical study to calculate total mass of the structure. The material is silicon having density 2329 Kg/m^3.

Total mass (excluding fixed fingers) = proof mas + mass of folded beam + mass of fingers

$Mass_{Total}= 64.2804*10^{-12} + 57.57288*10^{-12} + 22.3584*10^{-12}$

$Mass_{Total}= 144.21168*10^{-12}$ Kg

For the structure we performed frequency analysis to determine the proof mass displacement at different frequencies is shown in Fig. 9.

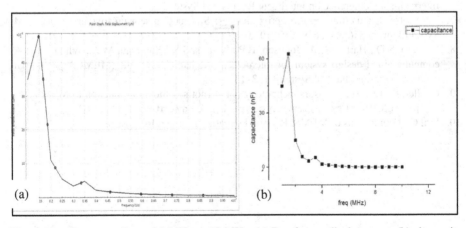

Fig. 9. For frequency range of 1 MHz to 10 MHz, (a) Proof mass displacement, (b) change in capacitance

When proof mass and comb structure get attached to the folded beam then the accelerometer resonance frequency decreases to 1.5 MHz. Proof mass displacement and capacitance between fingers decreases exponentially with frequency.

5   Conclusion

Single axis folded beam based capacitive accelerometer for high frequency application has been designed, beam support is modeled for a frequency of 4 MHz and the structure shows the resonance frequency of 1.5 MHz. Accelerometer having high resonance frequency find application in Navigation, missile guidance etc.

Acknowledgement. The authors would like to express their sincere thanks to Prof B.R. Singh, Project guide, Department of Microelectronics. IIIT Allahabad for their constant support and encouragement.

References

1. Beliveau, A., Spencer, G.T., Thomas, K.A., Roberson, S.L.: Evaluation of MEMS capacitive accelerometers. IEEE Design & Test of Computers 16(4), 48–56 (1999)
2. Yazdi, N., Ayazi, F., Najafi, K.: Micromachined Inertial Sensors. Proc. of the IEEE 86, 1640–1659 (1998)
3. MacDonald, G.A.: A review on low cost accelerometers for vehicle dynamics. Sensors and Actuators A21-A23, 303–307 (1990)
4. Legtenberg, R., Groeneveld, A.W., Elwenspoek, M.: A high-sensitivity z-axis capacitive silicon microaccelerometer with a torsional suspension. Journal of Microelectromechanical Systems 7, 192–200 (1998)
5. Legtenberg, R., Groeneveld, A.W., Elwenspoek, M.: Combdrive actuators for large displacements. Journal of Micromechanics and Microengineering 6, 320–329 (1996)
6. Luo, R.C.: Preparation of Papers in Two-Column Format for the IEEE/RSJ. In: International Conference on Intelligent Robots and Systems
7. Verplaetse, C.: Inertial proprioceptive devices: Self-motion-sensing toys and tools. IBM System Journal 35(3&4), 639–650 (1996)
8. Senturia, S.D., Harris, R.M., Johnson, B.P., Nabors, S.K., Shulman, M.A., White, J.K.: A computer-aided design system for microelectromechanical systems (MEMCAD). Journal of Microelectromechanical Systems 1, 3–13 (1992)
9. Chollet, F., Liu, H.: "Sensors technology" in A (not so) short Introduction to MEMS, ch. 2.5, p. 22 (2010), http://memscyclopedia.org/introMEMS.html
10. Liu, C.: Foundations of MEMS. Pearson Education Limited, India (2012)

CPK Based IO AC Timing Closure
to Reduce Yield Loss and Test Time

Sandip Ghosh and Rohit Srivastava

Freescale Semiconductor India Pvt. Ltd
Plot-18, Sector-16A, Flim City, Noida-201301, India
{sandip.ghosh,rohit.srivastava}@freescale.com

Abstract. With growing complexities of SoC, number of on-chip peripheral is also increasing and it is mandatory for SoC engineer to meet the I/O AC timing in Static Timing Analysis (STA). But, at times, it is found that I/O timing are failing or passing marginally, when Si is tested on Automated Testing Equipment (ATE). Failing of I/O AC specifications leads to extensive debugging of Si on ATE, resulting test time increase, yield loss & further revision of Si. This paper proposes a method whereby extra margin has been built on I/O AC timing closure of all peripherals in the design phase itself, keeping targeted Coefficient of Process Capability (CPK) in mind. It has been shown that using this approach, most of the peripherals meet ~ CPK of 2 when tested on different SoC. Consequently, ATE test time and yield loss is reduced.

Keywords: Co-efficient of process Capability, Static Timing Closure, Automated Testing Equipment, I/O AC Timing.

1   Introduction

Problem of I/O AC timing failure or having a less margin of different peripheral interfaces is inherent in many SoC. It is mandatory to close I/O AC timing in BCS and WCS for design sign-off. In BCS scenario, process is faster/less delay, voltage is kept high and temperature is low. Whereas in WCS, Si process is slower/lager delay, voltage is low and temperature is high. But, we tend to get failure or a less margin when Si is tested on ATE across process-voltage-temperature (PVT) condition. This could be due to various reasons, for example, I/O library characterization not accurately matching with Si behaviour, measurement uncertainty on ATE, interference or any parasitic effect, etc. Whatever may be the reason, the penalty is heavy in terms of time consumed on ATE to nail down the I/O AC timing failure and subsequent Si revision. Also, it leads to increase in ATE test time incurred due to running pattern on production which could have been removed if we had sufficient margin of I/O AC timing. There is huge push in semiconductor industry to reduce ATE test time as it has direct impact on product viability and gross margin. International Technology Roadmap for Semiconductor (ITRS) [6] has also given effort in this direction. There are various

M.S. Gaur et al. (Eds.): VDAT 2013, CCIS 382, pp. 257–266, 2013.
© Springer-Verlag Berlin Heidelberg 2013

approaches [7-12] to reduce the ATE test time. The approach proposed in this paper is another effort in this direction. It may also happen that, marginally passing AC I/O specification start to fail at some PVT condition on production during product life cycle resulting yield loss. Therefore, it is obvious that one should build sufficient margin on I/O AC timing in design phase of Si, so that it never fail on Si when tested on ATE. But, quantification of "how much margin" needs to be built is a difficult question to answer. In this paper, an attempt has been made to quantify the extra margin to be built on I/O AC timing closure based on required CPK on Si. CPK measures how close you are to your target and how consistent you are around your target. For example, a person may be performing with minimum variation, but he can be away from his target towards one of the specification limit, which indicates lower CPK. On the other hand, a person may be exactly at the target on an average, but the variation in performance is high. In such cases, CPK will be lower. CPK will be higher when you are meeting the target consistently with minimum variation. For any SoC qualification, every I/O AC specification needs to meet a particular CPK number. Here, a parallel hardware specification is created for different I/O interfaces with CPK value of 2, 1.67, 1.33 and 1. SoC designers are asked to meet I/O AC timing in STA for CPK=2 first. If I/O AC specification is more stringent at CPK=2 and unable to meet then, option for CPK=1.67 is considered. Similarly, if 1.67 is difficult to meet then 1.33, if not then option for CPK=1 is considered. In this way, a well defined directed approach has been followed to meet the I/O AC timing with required margin to be built on production.

The contents of the paper are organized as follows: Section 2 depicts a typical networking SoC architecture with different peripherals. In Section 3, basic of CPK is described to aid the understanding of this method. Section 4 focuses on how parallel hardware specification is made based on required CPK. Section 5 provides result of this approach on real Si. Section 6 lists the various challenges for implementing this method. Finally, section 7 concludes the paper.

2   Architecture of Networking SoC P1020

Fig.1 shows the architecture of P1020 SoC with different peripherals like dual data rate (DDR), enhanced local bus controller (eLBC), time division multiple access (TDM), serial peripheral interface (SPI), universal serial bus 2.0 (USB), etc. These digital peripheral interfaces communicate with the external world using their respective input/output (I/O) signal. Traditionally, SoC designer will meet the AC I/O timing for all these peripherals as per their hardware specification as depicted in Table 1 and Fig.2

Notes:

1. The symbols used for timing specifications follow the pattern of t(first two letters of functional block)(signal)(state) (reference)(state) for inputs and t(first two letters of functional block)(reference)(state)(signal)(state) for outputs. For e.g. tNIKHOV

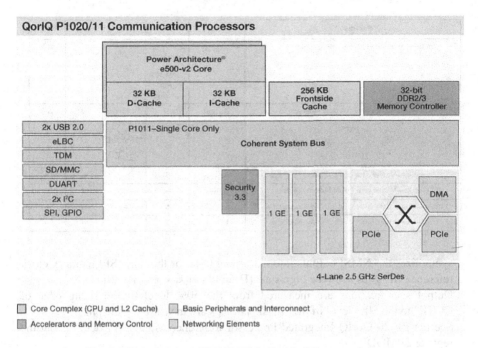

Fig. 1. Block diagram of P1020 [1] SoC with different peripherals

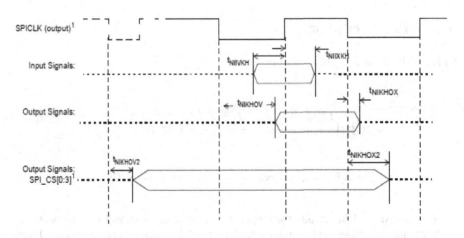

Fig. 2. SPI AC timing diagram in master mode (internal clock) of P1020 [1] SoC

Table 1. SPI AC Timing Specification of P1020 [1] SoC

Parameter	Symbol	Min	Max	Unit	Note
SPI outputs—Master data (internal clock) hold time	t_{NIKHOX}	0.5+(t_{PLAT} FOR M_CLK *SPMODE [HO _ADJ])	—	ns	2, 3
SPI outputs—Master data (internal clock) delay	t_{NIKHOV}	—	5.5+(t_{PLAT} FORM _CLK *SPMODE [HO_ ADJ])	ns	2, 3
SPI_CS outputs—Master data (internal clock) hold time	$t_{NIKHOX2}$	0	—	ns	2
SPI_CS outputs—Master data (internal clock) delay	$t_{NIKHOV2}$	—	6.0	ns	2
SPI inputs—Master data (internal clock) input setup time	t_{NIIVKH}	5	—	ns	—
SPI inputs—Master data (internal clock) input hold time	t_{NIIXKH}	0	—	ns	—

symbolizes the NMSI outputs internal timing (NI) for the time tSPI memory clock reference (K) goes from the high state (H) until outputs (O) are valid (V).
2. Output specifications are measured from the 50% level of the rising edge of CLKIN to the 50% level of the signal. Timings are measured at the pin.
3. See the P1020 QorIQ Integrated Processor Reference Manual for detail about the register SPMODE

As an example, Table 1 shows the I/O setup and hold time for SPI interface and Fig.2 depicts I/O data relationship wrt internal clock of SPI i.e. SPICLK.

3   CPK Description

CPK is calculated using the equation-

$$C_{pk} = \min[\frac{USL - \mu}{3\sigma} \; ; \frac{\mu - LSL}{3\sigma}] = \min[C_{pu} \; ; C_{pl}]$$

Fig. 3. Equation of Coefficient of Process Capability (CPK)

Where, USL & LSL stands for Upper & Lower Specification Limit respectively. μ & σ are the mean and standard deviation of the quality characteristic studied respectively.

Table 2. Standard Deviation, CPK & Yield relationship

Sl No	Standard Deviation	CPK	Yield /ppm (%)
1	3	1	99.73
2	4	1.33	99.9936
3	6	2	99.9999

The relation between CPK and yield/part-per-million (ppm) is given below –

4   Derivation of Parallel Hardware Specification Based on CPK

CPK is calculated by knowing mean value of measured data, USL & LSL and standard deviation of measured data as mentioned in Fig.3. To get the mean value of measured data (μ) for required CPK, one should know USL, LSL & standard deviation. There are two cases for deriving parallel hardware specification of any peripheral. One specification, for example, input setup time, should have value less than that specified in hardware specification document. For this case, USL should be taken for calculation of mean value of data. And the other specification should have value more than that specified in hardware specification document. In this case, LSL should be taken for calculation of mean value of data. Here, σ is taken from previous Si of same technology node when tested on ATE VERIGY 93K ATE [13]. Following are examples for calculating mean of data:

Case1: Input setup time calculation for CPK of 2.
  Input setup t_{NIVKH} (USL) =5ns
  Targeted CPK = 2
  Standard Deviation (σ) = 0.19 (for e.g.)
  CPK = (USL - μ)/3*σ
  μ = 3.85 ns
Therefore, targeted Design specification of input setup to meet CPK of 2 is 3.85ns.

Case2: Output hold time calculation for CPK of 2.
  Output hold time $t_{NIKHOX2}$ (LSL) = 0ns
  Targeted CPK = 2
  Standard Deviation (σ) = 0.19 (for e.g.)
  CPK = (μ - LSL)/3*σ
  μ = 1.14 ns

Therefore, targeted design specification of output hold time to meet CPK of 2 should be taken as **1.14ns.**

  For Output hold time $t_{NIKHOV2}$ (USL) = 6ns
  Targeted CPK = 2

Standard Deviation $(\sigma) = 0.19$ (for e.g.)

CPK = $(USL-\mu)/3*\sigma$

μ = 4.86 ns

Therefore, targeted design specification for maximum output delay to meet CPK of 2 should be taken as 4.86ns.

5   Case Study

This approach has been followed for SoC [1][2][3][4][5].

5.1   Parallel HW Specification for Different Peripherals

Table 3. : Parallel Hardware Specification of different interfaces for CPK of 2, 1.67, 1.33 & 1

Block	SPEC	Description	Value(ns)	Min / Typ / Max	Design Target for Different CPK				STA Numbers	CPK met
					2.00	1.67	1.33	1.00		
eSPI	t_{NIKHOX}	o/p delay	0.5	Min	1.25	1.00	0.83	0.71	1.35	2.00
	t_{NIKHOV}	o/p delay	4	Max	2.46	2.63	2.83	3.05	2.20	2.00
	t_{NIIVKH}	i/p setup	5	Min	2.91	3.12	3.38	3.68	3.20	1.33
	t_{NIIXKH}	i/p hold	-1	Min	-1.96	-1.69	-1.48	-1.32	-2.40	2.00
USB	t_{USIVKH}	i/p setup	4	Min	2.72	2.87	3.05	3.31	1.80	2.00
	t_{USIXKH}	i/p hold	1	Min	0.55	0.59	0.65	0.71	0.54	2.00
	t_{USKHOV}	o/p delay	7	Max	5.38	5.60	5.84	6.09	5.00	2.00
	t_{USKHOX}	o/p delay	2	Min	2.86	2.67	2.50	2.35	3.80	2.00
eLBC	t_{LBIVKH}	i/p setup	6	Min	4.38	4.58	4.81	5.06	4.20	2.00
	t_{LBIXKH}	i/p hold	1	Min	0.71	0.75	0.79	0.83	-2.50	2.00
	t_{LBIVKL}	i/p setup	6	Min	4.62	4.80	5.00	5.22	4.32	2.00
	t_{LBIXKL}	i/p hold	1	Min	0.77	0.80	0.83	0.87	-2.70	2.00
	t_{LBKLOV}	o/p delay	1.5	Max	0.78	0.84	0.93	1.02	0.60	2.00
	t_{LBKLOX}	o/p delay	-3.5	Min	-2.52	-2.65	-2.78	-2.93	-1.10	2.00
	$t_{SHSKHOX}$	o/p delay	3	Max	1.10	1.23	1.40	1.61	0.80	2.00
TDM	t_{DMIVKH}	i/p setup	3	min	1.88	2.00	2.14	2.31	1.00	2.00
	$t_{DMRDIXKH}$	i/p hold	3.5	min	2.19	2.33	2.50	2.69	1.60	2.00
	$t_{DMFSIXKH}$	i/p hold	2	min	1.25	1.33	1.43	1.54	0.75	2.00
	$t_{DMTKHOV}$	o/p delay	14	max	8.75	9.33	10.01	10.77	6.25	2.00
TDM	$t_{DMTKHOX}$	o/p delay	2	min	5.00	4.01	3.33	2.86	5.00	2.00
	$t_{DMFSKHOV}$	o/p delay	13.5	max	8.44	8.99	9.65	10.38	7.50	2.00
	$t_{DMFSKHOX}$	o/p delay	2.5	min	6.25	5.01	4.16	3.57	6.25	2.00

Table 3. (*Continued*)

	t_{NIKHOV}	o/p delay	6	max	3.75	4.00	4.29	4.62	3.90	1.67
	t_{NIKHOX}	o/p delay	0.5	min	1.25	1.00	0.83	0.71	0.40	1.00
QE SPI	t_{NEKHOV}	o/p delay	8	max	5.00	5.33	5.72	6.15	7.30	1.00
	t_{NEKHOX}	o/p delay	2	min	5.00	4.01	3.33	2.86	2.20	1.00
	t_{NIIVKH}	i/p setup	5	min	3.13	3.33	3.57	3.85	3.70	1.00
	t_{NIIXKH}	i/p hold	-1	min	0.00	0.00	0.00	0.00	-1.20	2.00
	t_{NEIVKH}	i/p setup	4	min	2.50	2.66	2.86	3.08	0.70	2.00
	t_{NEIXKH}	i/p hold	2	min	1.25	1.33	1.43	1.54	0.90	2.00
	t_{UEIVKH}	i/p setup	4	min	2.50	2.66	2.86	3.08	1.80	2.00
	t_{UEIXKH}	i/p hold	1	min	0.63	0.67	0.71	0.77	0.00	2.00
QE	t_{UEKHOV}	o/p delay	1	min	2.50	2.00	1.66	1.43	2.20	1.67
UTOPIA	t_{UEKHOV}	o/p delay	10	max	7.69	6.66	7.15	7.69	8.90	1.00
	t_{UIIVKH}	i/p setup	6	min	3.75	4.00	4.29	4.62	5.96	1.00
	t_{UIKHOV}	o/p delay	8	max	5.00	5.33	5.72	6.15	1.85	2.00

It can be seen from Table 3 that a parallel I/O AC timing is being made for different interface like eSPI, USB, eSDHC, TDM, JTAG, eLBIU/eLBC, QE UTOPIA & QE SPI under column "*Design Target for Different CPK*". IC Designer need to meet this timing instead of I/O AC specification mentioned in column "*Value*" in STA. Column "*SPEC*" provides the I/O AC specification of different interfaces. Details of each specification can be found in [1]. Under "Design Target for Different CPK" column, there are four sub columns for CPK of 2, 1.67, 1.33 & 1 for different I/O AC specification. Table 3 also gives the STA number under "*STA Number*" column. "*CPK met*" column indicates whether intended CPK is met in design phase or not.

5.2   Silicon Result for SoC P1020[1]

Table 4 gives the measured I/O AC specification of different interface mentioned under column "*Block*". I/O AC specification of different interfaces is mentioned in column "*Specification*". Details of each specification can be found in [1]. In "*Description*" column, meaning of different I/O specification has been described briefly. Value of different I/O specification is described in column "*P1020 HW spec (ns)*". Si data has been taken across different PVT condition, but, we have shown data here for temperature -45°C.

Different value across multiple die of Si were measured and put under column "*Min at -45°C*" meaning minimum measured value at -45°C. Similarly, column "*Mean at -45°C*" and "*Max at -45°C*" signifies mean and maximum value at -45°C. Last column "*CPK on Si*" of Table 4 provides the measured CPK value on Si. It can be seen from "*CPK on Si*" column that most of the peripherals I/O AC specification meeting CPK of 2 as expected during design phase.

Table 4. Si data of I/O AC Specification for SoC P1020 [1]

Block	Specification	Description	HW spec (ns)	Min/Max/Typ	Min value at -45°C	Mean at -45°C	Max at -45°C	CPK on Si
eSPI	t_{NIIVKH}	i/p setup	5	min	1.938	2.117	2.292	>=2
	t_{NIIXKH}	i/p hold	0	min	-1.710	-1.577	-1.264	<2
	$t_{NIKHOV2}$	o/p delay	6	max	1.154	1.394	1.946	>=2
	t_{NIKHOX}	o/p hold	0.5	min	0.722	1.059	1.211	>=2
USB	t_{USIVKH}	i/p setup	4	min	0.377	0.496	0.813	>=2
	t_{USIXKH}	i/p hold	1	min	0.281	0.349	0.531	>=2
	t_{USKHOV}	o/p valid	7	max	3.382	3.753	5.000	>=2
	t_{USKHOX}	o/p valid	2	min	2.559	2.813	3.078	>=2
eLBC	t_{LBIVKH}	i/p setup	6	min	2.750	3.057	4.421	>=2
	t_{LBIVKL}	i/p setup	6	min	2.125	2.428	2.743	>=2
	t_{LBIXKH}	i/p hold	1	min	-2.115	-1.939	-1.797	>=2
	t_{LBIXKL}	i/p hold	1	min	-2.490	-2.283	-2.080	>=2
	t_{LBKLOV}	o/p delay	1.5	max	0.657	0.774	1.004	>=2
	t_{LBKLOX}	o/p hold	-3.5	min	-0.572	-0.433	-0.322	>=2
TDM	$t_{DMFSIXKH}$	i/p hold	2	min	0.120	0.160	0.217	>=2
	$t_{DMFSKHOV}$	o/p valid	13.5	max	4.479	5.072	5.859	>=2
	$t_{DMFSKHOX}$	o/p hold	2.5	min	3.125	3.613	4.052	<2
	t_{DMIVKH}	i/p setup	3	min	0.570	0.707	1.096	>=2
	$t_{DMRDIXKH}$	hold	3.5	min	-0.185	-0.093	-0.024	>=2
	$t_{DMTKHOV}$	o/p valid	14	max	3.648	4.154	4.678	>=2
	$t_{DMTKHOX}$	hold	2	min	2.559	2.871	3.212	<2
QE SPI	t_{NIIVKH}	i/p setup	4	min	0.440	0.716	1.080	>=2
	t_{NIIXKH}	i/p hold	0	min	-0.300	-0.135	0.000	<2
	t_{NIKHOV}	o/p delay	6	max	4.080	4.546	5.100	<2
	t_{NIKHOX}	SPI o/p hold	0.5	min	3.600	3.923	4.260	>=2
	t_{NEIVKH}	i/p setup	4	min	0.000	0.114	0.160	>=2
	t_{NEIXKH}	i/p hold	2	min	0.100	0.163	0.240	>=2
	t_{NEKHOV}	o/p valid	9	max	4.480	5.248	6.040	>=2
	t_{NEKHOX}	o/p hold	2	min	3.620	4.101	4.560	>=2

Table 4. (*Continued*)

	t_{UEIVKH}	i/p setup	4	min	1.330	1.551	1.770	>=2
	t_{UEIXKH}	i/p hold	1	min	0.378	0.474	0.560	>=2
QE	t_{UEKHOV}	o/p valid	1	min	4.204	4.678	5.242	>=2
UTOPIA	t_{UEKHOV}	o/p valid	10	max	4.204	4.678	5.242	>=2
	t_{UEKHOX}	o/p valid	1	min	3.214	3.646	4.028	<2
	t_{UEKHOX}	o/p valid	10	max	3.214	3.646	4.028	<2
	t_{UIIVKH}	i/p setup	6	min	3.660	4.181	4.860	>=2
	t_{UIIXKH}	i/p hold	0	min	-0.740	-0.530	-0.400	>=2
QE	$t_{TUIKHOV}$	o/p hold	0	min	1.280	1.546	1.820	>=2
UTOPIA	$t_{TUIKHOV}$	o/p hold	8	max	1.280	1.546	1.820	>=2
	t_{UIKHOX}	o/p hold	0	min	0.440	0.873	1.100	>=2
	t_{UIKHOX}	o/p hold	8	max	0.440	0.873	1.100	>=2

6   Implementation Challenges

There are various challenges that need attention for implementation of this approach-

A. Standard deviation data from previous Si
Getting correct data from a previous Si of same technology node could be a challenge. There could be non-technical issues for getting this data from product engineering team, as it requires extra effort for churning huge data correctly.

B. Extra effort in I/O timing closure in STA
As design is more constrained due to this parallel hardware specification, extra effort is required to close I/O AC timing wrt traditional approach.

C. Changes in design for I/O AC timing closure
As a consequence of new hardware specification, it might happen that the logic which is responsible for meeting the I/O AC timing is not adequate with proposed approach to meet required CPK. Hence, we may have to change certain portion of logic to meet this requirement.

7   Conclusion

In this paper, we have proposed a CPK based approach to meet required I/O AC timing for different peripheral interface, taking standard deviation from previous Si of same technology node. This method has been applied to various SoC [1][2][3][4][5] and it has yield good result. As margin on this I/O specification is adequate, therefore, test engineer can confidently guarantee that this specification will never fail on Si as long as process doesn't shift, thus removing test pattern from production list. Hence, ATE test time is reduced. As chances of AC specification failure are comparatively less, so, there is an increase in yield of SoC. All these contribute to the increase of gross margin of SoC. As per our knowledge, this is the first proposal regarding CPK based I/O timing closure in STA for yield improvement and reduction of test time.

References

1. P1020 product descriptions and documentation, http://www.freescale.com/webapp/sps/site/prod_summary.jsp?code=P1020&fsrch=1&sr=1
2. P1022 product descriptions and documentation, http://www.freescale.com/webapp/sps/site/prod_summary.jsp?code=P1022&fsrch=1&sr=1
3. P1010 product description and documentation, http://www.freescale.com/webapp/sps/site/prod_summary.jsp?code=P1010&fsrch=1&sr=1
4. P1025 description, hardware specification, http://www.freescale.com/webapp/sps/site/prod_summary.jsp?code=P1025&fsrch=1&sr=1
5. PSC9131documentation, http://www.freescale.com/webapp/sps/site/prod_summary.jsp?code=BSC9131&fsrch=1&sr=1
6. The International Technology Roadmap for Semiconductors: Test and Test Equipment, 2011 edn. (2011), http://www.itrs.net
7. Poehl, F., Demmerle, F., Alt, J., Obermeir, H.: Production test challenges for highly integrated mobile phone SOCs-A case study. In: Test Symposium 2010, ETS, May 24-28, pp. 17–22 (2010)
8. Iijima, K., Akar, A., McDonald, C., Burek, D.: Embedded test solution as a breakthrough in reducing cost of test for system on chips. In: Test Symposium, November 18-20, pp. 311–316 (2002)
9. Deshayes, H.: Cost of test reduction. In: Proceedings of the IEEE International Test Conference, October 18-23, pp. 265–270. Conference Publications (1998)
10. Maxwell, P.: Principles and results of some test cost reduction methods for ASICs. In: IEEE International Test Conference, ITC 2007, October 21-26, pp. 1–5 (2007)
11. Sehgal, A., Iyengar, V., Krasniewski, M.D., Chakrabarty, K.: Test cost reduction for SOCs using TAMs and Lagrange multipliers. In: Proceedings of the DAC-2003, June 2-6, pp. 738–743 (2003)
12. Hashempour, H., Lombardi, F., Necoechea, W., Mehta, R., Alton, T.: An Integrated Environment for Design Verification of ATE Systems. IEEE Transactions on Instrumentation and Measurement 56(5), 1734–1743 (2007)
13. Verigy 93k, http://www1.verigy.com/ate/products/V93000/index.htm

Optimization of Underlap FinFETs and Its SRAM Performance Projections Using High-k Spacers

Pankaj Kr. Pal, Brajesh Kumar Kaushik, and Sudeb Dasgupta

Microelectronics & VLSI Group, Department of Electronics & Communication Engineering
Indian Institute of Technology-Roorkee,
Roorkee, Uttarakhand, India
pankajpal86@gmail.com, {bkk23fec,sudebfec}@iitr.ernet.in

Abstract. The undoped underlap region is unavoidable in devices with gate length 16nm or less to reduce SCEs. For the first time, this research paper addresses the complete underlap optimization analysis along with the spacer engineering from the device to circuit perspective. We elaborate the impact of underlap on drive current, leakage current and their ratio. The fringe capacitance component (included in total-gate capacitance) and the relative change in a drive current-to-capacitance is also investigated that helps to optimize circuit delay. Furthermore, the impact of underlap and spacer dielectric on various SRAM designs metric is investigated that mitigate read/write conflict. It has been observed that optimal underlap improves the SRAM stability and access times. For SRAM applications, underlap length near about 4nm provides superior performance improvements and thereafter, the cell designs metric degrades.

Keywords: Underlap FinFET, short channel effect (SCE), SRAMs, static noise margin (SNM), access-time, high-k spacers.

1 Introduction

As Intel progresses to use the 3D tri-gate transistors commercially in the 22nm technology node, a strong interest has emerged among semiconductor industries in forming 14nm and 10nm bulk FinFET. However, there are several challenges that need to be addressed. The undoped underlap region emerges as an attractive option to reduce leakage current and SCEs such as DIBL, GIDL, and subthreshold slope but at the expense of increased source/drain series resistance. Furthermore, increased source/drain (S/D) series resistance ($R_{S/D}$) degrades to drive current (I_{on}). For G-S/D underlap FinFET device; spacer engineering plays an important role. When the overlap is removed, the fringe field contribution modulates the source-drain channel conductivity. Along with the SCE-$R_{S/D}$ trade-offs, another trade-off found is in between $R_{S/D}$ and fringe capacitance C_{fr}, due to inner and outer fringe field lines. As the fringe capacitance increases, it accumulates more inversion charges in the undoped underlap region that reduces series resistance with improved SCEs. Therefore, the spacer material and the underlap length need to be carefully optimized [1].

From the circuit perspective, high-k spacers increase the fringe capacitance (C_{fr}) component of the total gate capacitance (C_{GG}) that worsens the circuit in terms of

M.S. Gaur et al. (Eds.): VDAT 2013, CCIS 382, pp. 267–273, 2013.
© Springer-Verlag Berlin Heidelberg 2013

delay. Several researchers over the past addressed gate-source/drain underlap. Yang *et al.* [1] demonstrated the device parameter comparison between overlap and underlap devices. Bansal *et al.* [2] reported the impact of gate underlap on gate capacitance and tunneling current. Trivedi *et al.* [3] described the source/drain series resistance and SCEs optimization for nanoscale underlap FinFETs. Pal *et al.* [4] demonstrated the dual-*k* spacers that optimize $R_{S/D}$-C_{fr} tradeoff. This paper primarily focuses on the complete analysis of underlap length with high-*k* spacers and optimization of underlap length for superior SRAM's performance.

This research paper is organized into five different sections. Section 2 describes the device architecture and the simulation setup. In Section 3, we present the electrostatics of underlap FinFET structure and the tradeoffs associated. Thereafter, we analyze the device characteristics such as drive current, leakage current and their ratio. Section 4 incorporates the underlap structure in the SRAM cell. The cell performance is evaluated based on SNMs (hold, read and write) and the read/write access times. It also shows the percentage improvement in SRAMs with varying underlap lengths and different spacer materials. Section 5 finally draws a brief summary.

2   Device Structure and Simulation Setup

The schematic cross-section of the underlap FinFET structure is shown in Fig. 1. The device dimensions are calibrated to meet the specification according to ITRS projections [5] summarized in Table 1. Work-functions of metal gates are tuned to 4.45eV for n-type and 4.77eV for p-type to achieve the requisite threshold [6]. Source/Drain extension region uses Gaussian doping profiles followed by a doping gradient of 3nm/decade, such that the dopant-segregation length (DSL) is 12nm. The channel and underlap regions are lightly doped with boron concentration of 1×10^{16} cm^{-3} to avoid random dopant fluctuations while providing high mobility [5]. The gate-electrode thickness (T_G) has kept nearly twice the L_G value [1]. Simulations were carried out with varying underlap length ranging from zero (non-underlap) to 16nm.

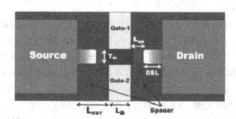

Fig. 1. 2D cross-sectional view of the underlap FinFET structure

Synopsys TCAD is used to carry out device and SRAM mixed mode simulations [7]. The quantum potential model is enabled to include the quantum confinement effect of inversion carriers in the thin body and also the direct tunneling model is included to take into account the gate leakages. The Lombardi mobility model has been activated that account for mobility degradation at the semiconductor-insulator interface.

Table 1. ITRS projections for high performance device in year 2017

Device Parameters	Abbreviations	ITRS Projections Value
Physical Gate Length	L_G	14 nm
Eq. Oxide Thickness	EOT	0.72 nm
Fin Thickness	T_{si}	9.4 nm
Supply Voltage	V_{DD}	0.75 V
Channel Doping	N_A	1×10^{16} cm^{-3}
Source/Drain Doping	N_D	1×10^{20} cm^{-3}
Threshold Voltage	V_{tsat}	220 mV

3   Device Characteristics with Underlap Length

The conduction band profile across the channel with an increasing underlap length as shown in Fig. 2(a) and 2(b) at $V_{DS}=0$, and $V_{DS}=V_{DD}$, respectively when $V_{GS}=V_{DD}$. Fig. 2(a) clearly depicts that the underlap barrier increases and hence $R_{S/D}$ with an increasing underlap length. It is also observed that the G-S/D underlap barrier is higher than the channel region barrier at $V_{DS}=0$V. With an increasing drain potential, the underlap barrier on the drain side reduces without affecting much the source side (G/S) underlap barrier as shown in Fig. 2(b). This source-side underlap barrier restricts the carriers to flow from source to drain. Introduction of the high-k spacer reduces underlap barriers to increased fringe coupling between gate and underlap region known as gate fringe induced barrier lowering (GFIBL) [8]. Therefore, the incorporation of optimal G-S/D underlap in nanoscale FinFETs is essential.

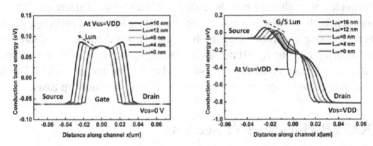

Fig. 2. Conduction band profile along the channel with increasing underlap length (a) at $V_{DS}=0$, and (b) $V_{DS}=V_{DD}$, when $V_{GS}=V_{DD}$

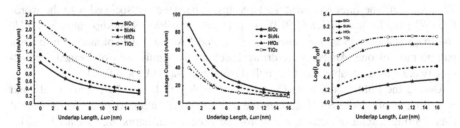

Fig. 3. Variation of (a) drive-current, (b) leakage current, and (c) drive-to-leakage current ratio for different spacer with varying underlap length (L_{un})

Strong fringe coupling on the undoped underlap region is observed by introducing high-k dielectric spacer. This helps in arranging the inversion charge carriers for which the extra parasitic series resistance is reduced that increases I_{on}. It is clear from Fig. 3 that, as the spacer-k increases, there is an improvement in device performance due to strong electric field coupling between a gate terminal and the underlap regions. Both, the I_{on} and the I_{on}/I_{off} parameter increases with an increasing spacer dielectric value due to an increased GFIBL effect [8]. The I_{on}/I_{off} ratio initially increases with the increase in underlap (Fig. 3(c)) and then becomes saturates after 4nm.

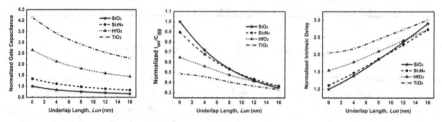

Fig. 4. Variation of the normalized (a) total gate capacitance, (b) drive current-to-total gate capacitance ratio (I_{on}/C_{GG}) and (c) the gate intrinsic delay for different spacer with varying underlap length (L_{un})

The variation in total gate capacitance (C_{GG}) with L_{un} for different spacer materials are shown in Fig. 4(a). The gate capacitance is normalized with the reference device with zero-underlap having low-k (SiO$_2$) spacer material. Clearly, the C_{GG} decreases with increasing underlap. Since, both the C_{GG} and the I_{on} decrease with the underlap therefore, performance will also change depending on their rate of decrease. The I_{on}/C_{GG} must be enough high to substantially reduce the delay. For zero underlap, the I_{on}/C_{GG} asset values decrease by introducing high-k spacers. Furthermore, it decreases with increasing underlap and for L_{un}=16nm underlap length; the I_{on}/C_{GG} is at minimum and same for different spacer materials. Fig. 4(c) indicates that the intrinsic delay through the circuit with high underlap will be more than that of a non-underlap case.

4   SRAM Performance Projections

This section provides the cell operation and methodology used in the underlap FinFET SRAM cell. The schematic of the tied-gate 6-T SRAM cell is presented in Fig. 5(a). The thick red and blue lines represent the large line capacitances associated with the word-line (WL) and bit lines (BL and BLB), respectively. The PMOS pull-up transistors (PU$_L$ and PU$_R$) and NMOS access transistors (PA$_L$ and PA$_R$) are of minimum size to set a pull-up ratio of one. Analyses are drawn based on the simulations performed for cell-ratio two, by using double-fin of the pull-down transistors (PD$_L$ and PD$_R$).

During the hold mode, node Q and QB store logic "1" and "0", respectively and word-line is off. Hold-SNM defines the stability in retention to preserve the stored data. During a read operation, the word-line access transistors are ON after the bit lines are precharged. The read-SNM is the metric used in read mode for reliable oper-ation [9]. For higher read stability, access transistor strength must be low. Read access time is the time period from 50% point of WL transition until 50-100mV voltage difference develops between the bitlines. To achieve a reduced read access time is another metric in read mode and depends on the maximum current flowing through the access and the pull-down transistors. In write operation, values "0" and "1" are applied to BL and BLB respectively with the access transistors turned on to flip the Q from "1" to "0". Similarly, write-margin and write access time are calculated for write operation. The write access time is measured between the time when WL reaches to 50% of V_{DD} and the time when a node QB reaches to switching threshold voltage of another inverter. To find SNM; the conventional method is used [10].

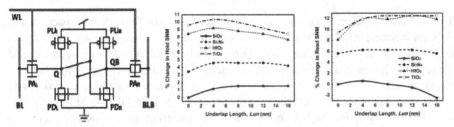

Fig. 5. (a) Conventional tied-gate 6T-SRAM cell configuration, (b) Percentage change in hold-SNM, (c) read-SNM as function of spacer material with varying underlap length (L_{un})

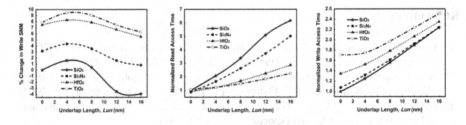

Fig. 6. Change in (a) write-margin, (b) read-access time, and (c) write-access time as function of spacer material with varying underlap length (L_{un})

Fig. 5(b), 5(c) and 6(a) shows the percentage change in hold, read and write noise-margins respectively, with respect to reference device as function underlap length and spacer materials. For low-k spacer material, a marginal change in hold and read SNMs are observed as an increase in underlap length. Incorporation of the high-k spacer material will enhance the SNMs up to 10-12% due to increased electrostatic integrity. The read and write access time variations are shown in Figs 6(b) and (c), respectively. It is observed that both read and write access time degrades because of reduction in the drive current with increasing underlap. The read access time degrades more rapidly with low spacer k value. However, write access time worsens more with high-k spacers due to increased gate-capacitance that enhance word-line capacitance. For SRAM applications, it is observed that for L_{un} near about 4nm provides superior performance improvements and thereafter, the cell designs metric degrades.

The other design concern with 6T SRAM cell is the read/write conflict, wherein a transistor sizing to enhance the read-stability degrades the write-ability and vice-versa. The measured result also shows that the use of high-k spacers can mitigate read/write conflict. The read/write stability is not directly dependent on the absolute value of I_{on} [11]. Apparently; SNM has a negative correlation with DIBL [12]. In agreement to this, it is observed that the SNMs are considerably improved using high-k spacers without affecting cell ratio and pull-up ratio.

5   Conclusion

This research paper presents the effect of underlap length for different spacer materials on device performance parameters such as drive-current, leakage current and their ratio. The fringe capacitance component (included in total-gate capacitance) and the relative change in a drive current-to-capacitance are also investigated that helps to optimize circuit delay. SRAM performance as a function of varying underlap and spacer materials are clearly depicted in the paper. Considering the SRAM discussion, we conclude that for high-k spacer and the underlap length near about 4nm provides superior performance improvements and thereafter, the cell designs metric degrades.

References

1. Yang, J.W., Zeitzoff, P.M., Tseng, H.H.: Highly manufacturable double-gate FinFET with gate-source/drain underlap. IEEE Trans. Electron Devices 54(6), 1464–1470 (2007)
2. Bansal, A., Paul, B.C., Roy, K.: Impact of gate underlap on gate capacitance and gate tunneling currents in 16nm DGMOS devices. In: IEEE SOI Conference, pp. 94–95 (2004)
3. Trivedi, V., Fossum, J.G., Chowdhury, M.M.: Nanoscale FinFETs with gate-source/drain underlap. IEEE Trans. Electron Devices 52(1), 56–62 (2005)
4. Pal, P.K., Singh, P., Anand, B., Kaushik, B.K., Dasgupta, S.: Performance analysis of dual-k spacer at source on underlap FinFETs. In: Proc. Annual IEEE India Conf., Kochi, India, pp. 915–919 (2012)
5. International Technology Roadmap for Semiconductors (2012), http://public.itrs.net
6. Choi, Y.K.: FinFET process refinements for improved mobility and gate work function engineering. IEDM Technical Digest, 259–262 (2002)
7. Sentaurus TCAD User Manual, Synopsys, Inc. (2010), http://www.synopsys.com
8. Sachid, A.B., Manoj, C.R., Sharma, D.K., Rao, V.R.: Gate fringe induced barrier lowering in underlap FinFET structures and its optimization. IEEE Electron Device Lett. 29(1), 128–130 (2008)
9. Rabaey, J., Chandrakasan, A., Nikolic, B.: Digital Integrated Circuits, ch. 10. Prentice-Hall, Upper Saddle River (2002)
10. Seevinck, E., List, F.J., Lohstroh, J.: Static-noise margin analysis of MOS SRAM cells. IEEE Journal of Solid-State Circuits 22(5), 748–754 (1987)

11. Kim, S.H., Fossum, J.G.: Design Optimization and Performance Projections of Double-Gate FinFETs with Gate–Source/Drain Underlap for SRAM Application. IEEE Trans. Electron Devices 54(8), 1934–1942 (2007)
12. Song, X., Suzuki, M., Saraya, T., Nishida, A., Tsunomura, T., Kamohara, S., Takeuchi, K., Inaba, S., Mogami, T., Hiramoto, T.: Impact of DIBL variability on SRAM static noise margin analyzed by DMA SRAM TEG. International Electron Devices Meeting, 3.5.1–3.5.4 (2010)

On-Chip Dilution from Multiple Concentrations of a Sample Fluid Using Digital Microfluidics*

Sudip Roy[1], Bhargab B. Bhattacharya[2],
Sarmishtha Ghoshal[3], and Krishnendu Chakrabarty[4]

[1] Indian Institute of Technology Kharagpur, India
sudipr@cse.iitkgp.ernet.in
[2] Indian Statistical Institute Kolkata, India
bhargab@isical.ac.in
[3] Bengal Engineering and Science University, Howrah, India
sharmi.bhatta@gmail.com
[4] Duke University, Durham, USA
krish@ee.duke.edu

Abstract. Preparing a sample with a specified concentration factor (CF) is an important step in automating biochemical laboratory protocols on a digital microfluidic biochip. In this paper, we address an open problem of sample preparation with a target CF in minimum number of mix/split steps when droplets of the same fluid are supplied with multiple CFs. We formulate this as a variant of the subset-sum problem and present a heuristic algorithm based on dynamic programming.

Keywords: Digital Microfluidics, Dilution, Mixing, Sample Preparation.

1 Introduction

A digital microfluidic (DMF) biochip is capable of manipulating nano- or pico-liter volume of discrete droplets by electrical actuation, on a two-dimensional electrode array of few square centimeters in size [1]. Recent years have seen a surge of interest in design automation methods for developing DMFs because of their applicability in implementing numerous biochemical laboratory protocols [1–4].

Automatic sample and mixture preparation is an important pre-processing step in designing a biochemical protocol. Since off-chip sample preparation poses a significant hindrance to the automation of a bioprotocol for high-throughput applications, several dilution and mixing algorithms have been proposed recently for on-chip sample preparation [5–15]. In this paper, we present, for the first time, a generalized dilution algorithm (GDA) for preparing a target droplet with a desired concentration factor (CF), when two or more arbitrary CFs of the same fluid are supplied. We formulate

* This work of S. Roy was supported by Microsoft Corporation and Microsoft Research India under the Microsoft Research India PhD Fellowship Award (2010-2014). The work of S. Ghoshal was supported in part by the Department of Science & Technology (DST) Women Scientists Scheme (WOS-A), 2009-2012. The work of K. Chakrabarty was supported in part by the US National Science Foundation under grants CCF-0914895 and CNS-1135853.

M.S. Gaur et al. (Eds.): VDAT 2013, CCIS 382, pp. 274–283, 2013.
© Springer-Verlag Berlin Heidelberg 2013

this as a subset-sum problem (SSP) and present a heuristic algorithm based on pseudo-polynomial time dynamic programming approach [16]. This solves an open problem posed by Thies et al. [6]. We report simulation results on a data set to demonstrate the efficiency of the proposed method for various objective functions.

The remainder of the paper is organized as follows. Section 2 provides the related prior work and motivation of our work. Section 3 deals with the scheme for generalized dilution from multiple (*two* or *more*) arbitrary concentrations of the same sample fluid. Finally, conclusions are drawn in Section 4.

2 Automatic Dilution and Mixing

In this paper, we consider the (1:1) mix-split model, in which a unit-volume droplet of a biofluid x_1 of $CF = C_1$ is mixed with a unit-volume droplet of another biofluid x_2 of $CF = C_2$ to produce a mixture of $CF = \frac{C_1+C_2}{2}$; it is then split equally into two unit-volume droplets. One (1:1) mix operation and a subsequent balanced split are together referred to as a *mix-split step*; the two droplets, thus produced, may be used in the next step or one of them is discarded as a *waste droplet* if not needed. A *dilution* or *mixing tree* is a binary tree where each leaf node represents an input fluid, and an internal node denotes a (1:1) mix-split step between two input (or intermediate) fluid droplets. If a target mixture with a certain ratio of its constituents is to be prepared from a supply of input fluids each with $CF = 1$, such that the error in each constituent CF does not exceed $\frac{1}{2^{d+1}}$, then a mixing tree of depth d is needed to depict the complete mix-split process. Dilution is a special case of mixing of only two input fluids (sample and buffer). A dilution tree of depth 5 that produces two target droplets (black nodes) of $CF = \frac{27}{32}$ from a sample ($CF = 100\%$) and a buffer fluid ($CF = 0\%$) is shown in Fig. 1(a). The intermediate and waste droplets, which are generated in the process, are also shown in different shades. The protocol to mix five input fluids with a ratio of 3:3:3:5:2 (all supplied with 100% CF), is depicted by a mixing tree of depth 4 as shown in Fig. 1(b).

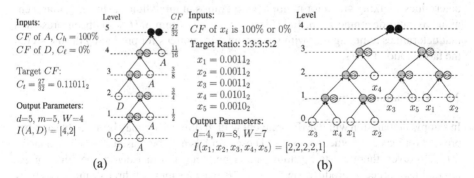

Fig. 1. (a) For target CF $C_t = 84.375\%$ ($\approx \frac{27}{32} \equiv 0.11011_2$), the dilution tree obtained by *twoWayMix* [6] using sample fluid A ($CF = 1$) and buffer D ($CF = 0$). (b) For target ratio 3:3:3:5:2, the mixing tree obtained by *Min-Mix* [6] using five input fluids all with $CF = 1$.

Let m be the total number of mix-split steps in a dilution/mixing tree. For a dilution tree, m is equal to d, whereas a mixing tree of height d can have at most $(2^d - 1)$ mix-split steps. A scheduled dilution/mixing tree provides the sequence of mix-split steps with timing assignment and the mixer allocation to its non-leaf nodes. Let M_{lb} be the number of mixers required for minimum-time (d time cycles) completion of executing a mixing tree as computed in [17]. After scheduling a mixing tree with M_{lb} mixers, the mixing tree can be executed in d time cycles, whereas with a fewer number of mixers it will take more time to complete. From Fig. 1 it is evident that for a dilution tree, $M_{lb} = 1$ and for a mixing tree, $M_{lb} > 1$. Let I be an array of integers denoting the total number of droplets of each input fluid required to produce two target droplets and W be the total number of waste droplets generated during dilution/mixing.

2.1 Prior Work

In the literature, there exist several dilution algorithms — GAG [5], twoWayMix [6], DMRW [7], IDMA [8], MTC [13], REMIA [14], and several mixing algorithms — Min-Mix [6], RMA [9], RSM [12] and MTCS [15]. Griffith et al. [5] proposed the first dilution algorithm GAG to determine a dilution graph for producing target droplets from the pure input fluids. Thies et al. [6] presented a dilution algorithm twoWayMix that represents the target CF C_t as a d-bit binary fraction to determine the dilution tree with an accuracy level of d (e.g., Fig. 1(a)). Two other dilution algorithms, namely DMRW [7] and IDMA [8], can be used to produce a desired target CF from two arbitrary concentrations of a sample. However, none of the existing algorithms is capable of producing a target concentration of a sample from three or more arbitrary concentrations of the same fluid. Other dilution algorithms presented in [13, 14] consider the problem of producing multiple target concentrations from the supply of two pure input fluids and do not discuss about generalized dilution from multiple arbitrary concentrations. Thies et al. [6] first proposed a mixing algorithm Min-Mix to determine the mixing tree of height d for a target ratio of N input fluids using N d-bit binary fractions (see Fig. 1(b)). Roy et al. [9] proposed a mixing algorithm RMA that determines the mixing tree for a target ratio using a ratio-decomposition based technique. Another mixing algorithm RSM [12] determines a mixing graph for multiple target ratios of input fluids using a similar technique as ratio-decomposition. In [15], a mixing algorithm MTCS has been presented that determines a mixing tree with some common subtrees for producing droplets with the target ratio of CFs.

2.2 Motivation of Our Work

In sample preparation with DMF, a reagent with multiple CFs may be available as a by-product (or waste) of other protocols. These droplets may be reused to produce a target CF. However, there exists no dilution/mixing algorithm that determines the correct mix-split sequence to produce the desired CF from a supply of three or more arbitrary CFs of the same fluid. This problem was mentioned as one of the open problems by Thies et al. [6]. This motivates us to formulate a more generalized dilution algorithm, which can be used for this purpose.

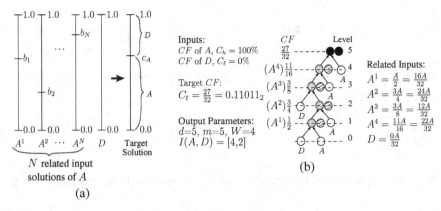

Fig. 2. (a) Related input and target CFs of same fluid in the scale 0 to 1. (b) An example of producing related input fluids as by-products of dilution process for $C_t = \frac{27}{32}$ by *twoWayMix* [6].

3   Dilution from Multiple Arbitrary CFs of the Same Fluid

In this Section, we present a scheme for generalized dilution of a sample fluid from the supply of multiple arbitrary concentrations (referred as *related* inputs) of the same fluid. The related inputs are the same fluid diluted with the same buffer solution to have different CFs. We formulate the generalized dilution problem as follows. **Inputs:** (a) N related inputs $A^1, A^2, \ldots, A^N$ ($N \geq 2$) of a biofluid A with CFs $b_1, b_2, \ldots, b_N$ are supplied, each diluted with the buffer solution D, where b_is are positive real numbers and $0 < b_i \leq 1$. (b) buffer solution D with $CF = 0$ is available in supply. Thus, the total number of related inputs including D is $(N + 1)$, where $(N + 1) \geq 3$. (c) desired CF C_A of the biofluid A, where C_A is a positive real number and $0 \leq C_A \leq 1$. (d) the integer d determines the accuracy level of C_A. Thus, the maximum error in C_A is bounded by $\frac{1}{2^{d+1}}$. **Output:** a dilution/mixing tree of depth d needed to produce droplets with target CF of fluid A as C_A.

If $C_A > \left(\max_i\{b_i\} + \frac{0.5}{2^d} \right)$ ($i = 1$ to $N+1$), the desired CF is not reachable from the inputs. Again, if C_A is in the range of $\left(b_i \text{ to } (b_i + \frac{0.5}{2^d}) \right)$ for any i ($i = 1$ to $N + 1$), then the desired CF is reachable and the input droplet with $CF = b_i$ can be treated as the target droplet. Otherwise, we need to solve this problem and the target droplet contains some part of fluid A coming from some of the N related inputs $A^1, A^2, \ldots, A^N$ along with a part of D and shown in Fig. 2(a). Hence, the CF of D in target droplets becomes $C_D = 1 - C_A$ (where C_D is a positive real number and $0 \leq C_D \leq 1$) and it may come from the related inputs only (as each of them are diluted with D) or it may require mixing of some additional amount of D.

We can have different optimization criteria to decide upon an optimal dilution/mixing tree as follows: (i) the total number of non-leaf nodes (m) in the dilution/mixing tree is minimized, or (ii) the height (d') of the dilution/mixing tree is minimized, or (iii) the lower-bound of number of mixers required for earliest completion, i.e., M_{lb} of the dilution/mixing tree is minimized.

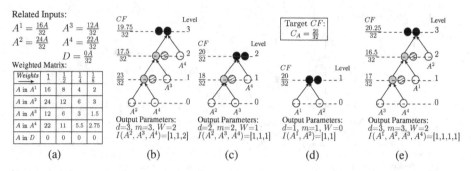

Fig. 3. (a) Weighted matrix for input CFs. (b)–(e) Four different dilution trees for $C_A = \frac{20}{32}$.

3.1 Examples of Generalized Dilution from Related Inputs

An example of producing four related inputs of fluid A (A^1, A^2, A^3 and A^4) as the by-products of dilution process for $C_t = \frac{27}{32}$ from pure sample and buffer fluids by *twoWayMix* [6] is shown in Fig. 2(b). Consider that we need to produce a target droplet with $C_A = \frac{20}{32}$ from the supply of these by-products (related inputs) and buffer solution D. Four different dilution trees for target CF $C_A = \frac{20}{32}$ are shown in Fig. 3(b)–(e). The best solution (dilution tree) among all these four solutions is shown in Fig. 3(d), as it takes minimum number of mix-split steps to produce the target droplet. However, if only three related inputs A^2, A^3 and A^4 are available after using A^1 is some other dilution process, then the dilution tree shown in Fig. 3(c) is the best solution, as it has less m and consumes less I than the dilution tree shown in Fig. 3(b).

A solution (dilution tree) can be envisaged with the help of some underlying data of the *weighted matrix* ($\mathcal{W}$) that is computed from the CFs of related inputs as shown in Fig. 3(a). For A^i, the portion of A contributed to the final concentration follows a geometric progression with a common ratio of $\frac{1}{2}$, depending on the level of tree at which it is used. For example, in Fig. 3(a) $\mathcal{W}$ has 24, 12, 6, 3 for A^2. In the dilution tree of Fig. 3(c), the contributions of A^2 and A^3 to the target CF are $\frac{6}{32}$ and $\frac{3}{32}$, respectively, as they are at depth 2 of the tree, whereas that of A^4 is $\frac{11}{32}$, as it is at depth 1 of the tree. This is easy to visualize from the basic principles of dilution. The selection of contributions from $\mathcal{W}$ for the target CF provides the binary fractions of the constituent fluids corresponding to a dilution/mixing tree. For example, the binary fractions of A^2, A^3 and A^4 for the dilution tree shown in Fig. 3(c) can be written as $0.01_2, 0.01_2$ and 0.10_2, respectively. A selection of numbers from $\mathcal{W}$ is *valid*, if a dilution/mixing tree can be constructed using *Min-Mix* from the binary fractions corresponding to the selection.

3.2 Problem Formulation and Proposed Algorithm

First, we represent b_i as $\frac{B_i}{2^d}$ (for all i) and C_A as $\frac{T}{2^d}$, where B_is and T are positive real numbers. For each input A^i, $(d + 1)$ geometric progression (G.P.) terms with the first term B_i and common ratio $\frac{1}{2}$, i.e., $B_i, \frac{B_i}{2}, \frac{B_i}{4}, \cdots, \frac{B_i}{2^d}$, are stored in an one-dimensional array $\mathcal{W}[i]$. A two-dimensional array $\mathcal{W}$ of size $(N + 1) \times (d + 1)$ stores the G.P. terms for all N inputs and D. Each element $\mathcal{W}[i, j]$ is associated with a weight $w_j = \frac{1}{2^j}$

and corresponds to the contribution $\mathcal{W}[i,j].w_j$ of fluid A^i, if it is at level $(d'-j)$ of the dilution/mixing tree of height d' to be determined. Next, a set Q is formed with all the elements of $\mathcal{W}$ except the elements of the row for D. The optimal dilution/mixing tree can be constructed by selecting some of the elements as a set R from Q (i.e., $R \subset Q$) and using some extra amount of D (if needed). While finding R from Q following parameters are computed: (a) the total weight of all the elements in R as $V = \sum_{\forall x,\, x \in R} w_j$, (b) the sum of all the elements in R as $T' = \sum_{\forall x,\, x \in R} x$, i.e., the target CF becomes $\frac{T'}{2^d}$, and (c) the height of the underlying dilution/mixing tree as $d' = max(j)$ such that for all i, j, $\mathcal{W}[i,j]$ is selected in R (hence, $0 < d' \leq d$).

Algorithm 1. $GDA\left(\langle b_1, b_2, \ldots, b_N \rangle, C_A, d\right)$

1: Set $b_{N+1} = 0$ (for buffer solution, D) and $\mathcal{T} = \Phi$.
2: Represent b_i as $\frac{B_i}{2^d}$ (for all i) and C_A as $\frac{T}{2^d}$, where B_is and T are positive real numbers.
3: **for** $i = 1$ to $N + 1$ **do**
4:    Set $\mathcal{W}[i][0] = B_i$.
5: Construct $\mathcal{W}$ by $(d+1)$ G.P. terms with $\mathcal{W}[i][0]$ as the first term and $\frac{1}{2}$ as the common ratio.
6: Obtain set Q with all the numbers (integers or reals) of $\mathcal{W}$ except the $(N+1)^{th}$ row.
7: For each number $x \in Q$, associate an weight $w_x = \frac{1}{2^j}$, if x is j^{th} G.P. term in $\mathcal{W}$.
8: Find R from Q, where $R \subset Q$ (Subset-Sum Problem), by using the pseudo-polynomial time dynamic programming approach [16]. A solution to this problem is a binary matrix $\mathcal{X}$ (i.e., R) denoting the selection of numbers from $\mathcal{W}$ (i.e., Q), such that $|T - T'| < 0.5$, where $T' = \sum_{\forall x,\, x \in R} x$. More than one solutions can be obtained.
9: **for all** the solutions **do**
10:    Compute $V = \sum_{\forall x,\, x \in R} w_x$.
11:    **if** $V \leq 1$ **then**
12:        The solution is valid.
13: **for all** the valid solutions **do**
14:    Compute $d' = max(j)$ s.t. $\mathcal{X}[i][j] = 1$, $\forall i, j$.
15:    Compute $m = |R| + \beta_{d'}(D) = \left(\sum_{\forall i,j} \mathcal{X}[i,j] - 1 \right)$, where $\mathcal{X}[N+1] = \left(1 - \sum_{i=0}^{N} \mathcal{X}[i] \right)$ and $\beta_{d'}(D) = \sum_{\forall j} \mathcal{X}[N+1][j]$, as $\mathcal{X}[i]$ is the binary fraction denoting selection of numbers from $\mathcal{W}$ for fluid A^i.
16:    Compute M_{lb}.
17:    Keep the optimal solution(s) depending on the optimality criteria.
18: Keep the binary matrix $\mathcal{X}$ for any one of the optimal solution(s).
19: Construct $\mathcal{T}$ from $\mathcal{X}$ using **Min-Mix** [6].

Note that, if $V > 1$, the underlying dilution/mixing tree cannot be constructed and hence the target is not reachable showing an *invalid* selection of elements in R, otherwise the target is reachable. Moreover, if $V = 1$, no extra buffer (D) droplet is required to achieve the target CF (i.e., $C_D = 0$), whereas if $V < 1$, extra buffer (D) is needed (i.e., $C_D \neq 0$). Let $\mathcal{B}[x.w_j]$ represent the binary fraction for the contribution of A^i, where $x \in R$ and $x = \mathcal{W}[i,j]$. The binary fraction for C_D can be represented as $\mathcal{B}[C_D] = \left(1 - \sum_{\forall x,\; x \in R} \mathcal{B}[x.w_j]\right)$ (obtained by binary addition and subtraction). Let $\beta_{d'}(D)$ be the number of 1s in a d'-bit binary fraction for buffer D, i.e., $\mathcal{B}[C_D]$.

Problem Statement: *Find a subset R from the set Q (i.e., $R \subset Q$), such that $(|R| + \beta_{d'}(D))$ is minimized, where $T' = \sum_{\forall x,\; x \in R} x$ and $|T' - T| \leq 0.5$ (i.e., $T' = T \pm 0.5$).*

We conjecture that this problem is computationally hard [18]. The subset-sum problem (SSP) [18] can be reduced to this problem, and we can obtain one or more solution(s) by using the pseudo-polynomial time dynamic programming approach [16]. A solution (optimal or suboptimal) to this problem provides a dilution/mixing tree of height d' and the corresponding selection of R can be represented with a binary matrix $\mathcal{X}$ of size $(N + 1) \times (d' + 1)$, where $\mathcal{X}[i,j] \in \{0, 1\}$. If $\mathcal{W}[i,j]$ is selected in R, $\mathcal{X}[i,j] = 1$, otherwise $X[i,j] = 0$. Hence, $\mathcal{X}[i]$ is a vector of $d' + 1$ bits representing the binary fraction for input A^i (with binary point between $\mathcal{X}[i][0]$ and $\mathcal{X}[i][1]$) and $\mathcal{X}[N + 1]$ represents the binary fraction for C_D, i.e., $\mathcal{B}[C_D]$. The time complexity of an algorithm to solve this problem depends on the size of input numbers, i.e., $\mathcal{O}(Nd.T)$, where $\mathcal{O}(N.(d + 1))$ is the total number of elements in Q and T is the desired sum.

The total number of mix-split steps (m) in the dilution/mixing tree for a valid solution (binary matrix) can be computed as $m = \left(\sum_i \sum_j \mathcal{X}[i,j] - 1\right)$. However, more than one valid solutions (binary matrices) can be obtained. Depending on the optimality criteria (minimization of m, d' or M_{lb}), several solutions (binary matrices) may be obtained. Any one of them can be used to construct a dilution/mixing tree (by arbitrarily breaking the ties). We present an algorithm (heuristic) *GDA* written as **Algorithm 1** to determine the dilution/mixing tree for generalized dilution. Here, we use *Min-Mix* [6] in Step-19 to construct the dilution/mixing tree from the binary fractions obtained in Step-18 of **Algorithm 1**. However, other algorithms like *RMA* [9], *RSM* [12] or *MTCS* [15] may also determine the tree from the target ratio after converting the binary fractions into a ratio of decimal integers.

For the example $\mathcal{W}$ of Fig. 3(a), four different selections of R from Q and the corresponding binary matrices are shown in Fig. 4. No tree can be constructed from the binary matrix of Fig. 4(b) indicating an invalid solution. The binary matrices of Fig. 4(c) and 4(d) may yield the trees as shown in Fig. 3(d) and (e), respectively. The binary matrix of Fig. 4(e) provides a suboptimal dilution tree with $d' = 3$ and $m = 3$.

3.3 Simulation Results

We have simulated the proposed algorithm for generalized dilution considering the target CF C_A within the range between 0 and $\max_i\{b_i\}$, $\forall i$ ($i = 1$ to N). The number of input CFs (expect buffer D) is varied from 3 to 6 and the input CFs are represented as $b_i = \frac{B_i}{2^d}$ with different d (4 and 6), where d is the accuracy level of target CF. Hence, C_A is represented as $C_A = \frac{T}{2^d}$. Let d' be the height of the dilution/mixing tree and m

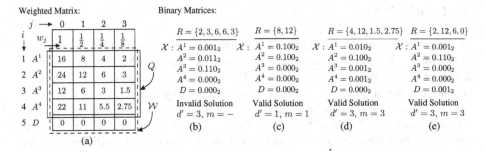

Fig. 4. (a) Weighted matrix shown in Fig. 3(b). (b)–(e) Different binary matrices obtained by finding R from Q for $C_A = \frac{20}{32}$.

Table 1. Results for Some Example Cases by *GDA* with Optimal d' or Optimal m

Example	$\langle B_1,\ldots,B_N,0\rangle$	T	d	Optimal d' $[d_1,\ldots,d_{N+1},T_d]$	$\langle d', m, I_{>1}, M_{lb}\rangle$	Optimal m $[d_1,\ldots,d_{N+1},T_d]$	$\langle d', m, I_{>1}, M_{lb}\rangle$
Ex.1	$\langle 7,14,15,0\rangle$	12	4	[2,2,1,0,T5]	$\langle 3,4,2,2\rangle$	[2,0,2,0,T4]	$\langle 3,3,2,1\rangle$
Ex.2	$\langle 1,4,61,0\rangle$	5	6	[3,2,1,2,T8]	$\langle 4,7,3,2\rangle$	[4,0,1,0,T5]	$\langle 4,4,3,1\rangle$
Ex.3	$\langle 3,6,9,12,15,0\rangle$	8	4	[2,1,1,1,1,0,T6]	$\langle 3,5,1,2\rangle$	[2,1,0,1,0,0,T4]	$\langle 3,3,1,1\rangle$
Ex.4	$\langle 4,6,8,9,12,15,0\rangle$	14	4	[0,0,1,1,1,3,0,T6]	$\langle 4,5,2,2\rangle$	[0,1,1,0,0,3,0,T5]	$\langle 4,4,2,1\rangle$
Ex.5	$\langle 1,3,52,0\rangle$	33	6	[2,1,1,2,0,T5]	$\langle 4,4,2,1\rangle$	[1,1,2,1,T5]	$\langle 3,4,1,2\rangle$

Table 2. Results for Some Example Cases by *GDA* with Optimal $I_{>1}$ or Optimal M_{lb}

Example	$\langle B_1,\ldots,B_N,0\rangle$	T	d	Optimal $I_{>1}$ $[d_1,\ldots,d_{N+1},T_d]$	$\langle d', m, I_{>1}, M_{lb}\rangle$	Optimal M_{lb} $[d_1,\ldots,d_{N+1},T_d]$	$\langle d', m, I_{>1}, M_{lb}\rangle$
Ex.1	$\langle 7,14,15,0\rangle$	12	4	[1,1,1,1,T4]	$\langle 3,3,0,1\rangle$	[2,2,0,1,T5]	$\langle 4,4,2,1\rangle$
Ex.2	$\langle 1,4,61,0\rangle$	5	6	[0,1,1,3,T5]	$\langle 4,4,0,1\rangle$	[3,3,1,0,T7]	$\langle 6,6,4,1\rangle$
Ex.3	$\langle 3,6,9,12,15,0\rangle$	8	4	[1,0,1,1,0,1,T4]	$\langle 3,3,0,1\rangle$	[3,1,0,1,0,0,T5]	$\langle 4,4,2,1\rangle$
Ex.4	$\langle 4,6,8,9,12,15,0\rangle$	14	4	[0,1,1,0,0,3,0,T5]	$\langle 4,4,2,1\rangle$	[0,1,1,0,0,3,0,T5]	$\langle 4,4,2,1\rangle$
Ex.5	$\langle 1,3,52,0\rangle$	33	6	[1,1,2,1,T5]	$\langle 3,4,1,2\rangle$	[2,1,2,0,T5]	$\langle 4,4,2,1\rangle$

be the total number of mix-split steps in the tree. The demand array $[d_1,\ldots,d_{N+1},T_d]$ denotes that the required number of droplets of fluid A^i is d_i, and T_d denotes the total number of input droplets required. Let $I_{>1}$ be the total number of extra (more than one) droplets of N different fluids (except buffer D) required as inputs in the tree, and let M_{lb} be the number of mixers required for minimum time completion of the dilution process. We present the results for several examples in Table 1 with the optimality criterion of minimizing d' or m. Table 2 provides the results with the optimality criterion of minimizing $I_{>1}$ and M_{lb} of the dilution/mixing tree.

4   Conclusions

In this paper, we have resolved an open problem of on-chip sample dilution using discrete droplets. For the (1:1) mixing model, we have developed a heuristic algorithm to handle this generalized dilution problem. The proposed algorithm determines a dilution/mixing tree of at most d height for producing the target droplet with a maximum error of $\frac{1}{2^{d+1}}$ in CF. Given an optimization criterion, the algorithm can be tuned to minimize either the height of the dilution/mixing tree (accuracy in CF), or the total number of mix-split steps (energy), or the number of input droplets used (cost). It can also be used to minimize the dilution time for a given number of on-chip mixers. Thus the scheme can be used for a wide range of biochip applications.

References

1. Chakrabarty, K., Xu, T.: Digital Microfluidic Biochips: Design and Optimization. CRC Press (2010)
2. Lin, C.C.Y., Chang, Y.W.: Cross-Contamination Aware Design Methodology for Pin-Constrained Digital Microfluidic Biochips. IEEE TCAD 30(6), 817–828 (2011)
3. Maftei, E., Pop, P., Madsen, J.: Routing-based Synthesis of Digital Microfluidic Biochips. Design Automation for Embedded Systems 16(1), 19–44 (2012)
4. Luo, Y., Chakrabarty, K., Ho, T.Y.: Error Recovery in Cyberphysical Digital Microfluidic Biochips. IEEE TCAD 32(1), 59–72 (2013)
5. Griffith, E.J., Akella, S., Goldberg, M.K.: Performance Characterization of a Reconfigurable Planar-Array Digital Microfluidic System. IEEE TCAD 25(2), 345–357 (2006)
6. Thies, W., Urbanski, J.P., Thorsen, T., Amarasinghe, S.: Abstraction Layers for Scalable Microfluidic Biocomputing. Natural Computing 7(2), 255–275 (2008)
7. Roy, S., Bhattacharya, B.B., Chakrabarty, K.: Optimization of Dilution and Mixing of Biochemical Samples using Digital Microfluidic Biochips. IEEE TCAD 29(11), 1696–1708 (2010)
8. Roy, S., Bhattacharya, B.B., Chakrabarty, K.: Waste-Aware Dilution and Mixing of Biochemical Samples with Digital Microfluidic Biochips. In: Proc. of the IEEE/ACM DATE, pp. 1059–1064 (2011)
9. Roy, S., Bhattacharya, B.B., Chakrabarti, P.P., Chakrabarty, K.: Layout-Aware Solution Preparation for Biochemical Analysis on a Digital Microfluidic Biochip. In: Proc. of the IEEE VLSID, pp. 171–176 (2011)
10. Hsieh, Y.L., Ho, T.Y., Chakrabarty, K.: On-Chip Biochemical Sample Preparation Using Digital Microfluidics. In: Proc. of the IEEE BioCAS (2011)
11. Hsieh, Y.L., Ho, T.Y., Chakrabarty, K.: Design Methodology for Sample Preparation on Digital Microfluidic Biochips. In: Proc. of the IEEE ICCD, pp. 189–194 (2012)
12. Hsieh, Y.L., Ho, T.Y., Chakrabarty, K.: A Reagent-Saving Mixing Algorithm for Preparing Multiple-Target Biochemical Samples Using Digital Microfluidics. IEEE TCAD 31(11), 1656–1669 (2012)
13. Mitra, D., Roy, S., Chakrabarty, K., Bhattacharya, B.: On-Chip Sample Preparation with Multiple Dilutions Using Digital Microfluidics. In: Proc. of IEEE ISVLSI, pp. 314–319 (2012)
14. Huang, J.D., Liu, C.H., Chiang, T.W.: Reactant Minimization during Sample Preparation on Digital Microfluidic Biochips using Skewed Mixing Trees. In: Proc. of IEEE/ACM ICCAD, pp. 377–384 (2012)

15. Kumar, S., Roy, S., Chakrabarti, P.P., Bhattacharya, B.B., Chakrabarty, K.: Efficient Mixture Preparation on Digital Microfluidic Biochips. In: IEEE DDECS, pp. 205–210 (2013)
16. Kleinberg, J., Tardos, E.: Algorithm Design. Addison Wesley (2005)
17. Luo, L., Akella, S.: Optimal Scheduling of Biochemical Analyses on Digital Microfluidic Systems. IEEE TASE 8(1), 216–227 (2011)
18. Garey, M.R., Johnson, D.S.: Computers and Intractability, A Guide to the Theory of NP-Completeness. W.H. Freeman and Company (1979)

Automatic Test Bench Generation and Connection in Modern Verification Environments: Methodology and Tool

Rohit Srivastava, Gaurav Gupta, Sarvesh Patankar, and Nandini Mudgil

Freescale Semiconductor Pvt Ltd.
rohit.srivastava@freescale.com

Abstract. Due to complex designs and time to market pressure verification closure is the bottleneck in ASIC/SoC design. Hence setting up a constrained random testbench environment seems to be a difficult task, especially when we consider that environments need to be flexible, scalable, and reusable. Although standard verification methodologies such as UVM [1], OVM [2] or VMM [3] help to an extent, but then creating testbench environment still consumes a lot of time. This calls for the need of testbench automation. There has been a lot of development in testbench automation techniques but still the problem of connectivity between the VIP interface and DUT remains unsolved which consumes considerable amount of time at SoC level. To solve this problem a novel technique has been proposed. The aim is to achieve a correct by construction technique to get the various existing components from IP level and make the automatic connection of the verification component with the design under test.

Keywords: SoC, Functional Verification, Testbench Automation, Verification Methodology, UVM, OVM, VMM.

1 Introduction

This paper presents a method to reduce time in testbench creation and setup of verification environment. Writing a new environment from scratch requires experience about the methodology and testbench environment, it may take anything from days to weeks depending upon the experience of the engineer. Nowadays SoCs are quite complex, typically they have multiple cores with hundreds of peripheral IPs and the interconnecting logic itself has very large number of interfaces. So, testbench bring up takes around 2-3 weeks for these SoC's. Apart from that, manual mistakes in the component connections at the later stage take many weeks to debug and fix.

According to an industrial survey [4] 32% time is consumed in debugging. Writing and Running test cases takes around 27% while around 28% of time is consumed in testbench development itself. If the time required for testbench development is reduced, then certainly the time to market for the product under development can be

M.S. Gaur et al. (Eds.): VDAT 2013, CCIS 382, pp. 284–293, 2013.
© Springer-Verlag Berlin Heidelberg 2013

shortened. Now the testbench development itself is a multi-step process: Following are the steps at IP level testbench creation:

1. Collect already available testbench components
2. Create template components for new interfaces
3. Connect verification IPs to make testbench
4. Connect various components with the design under test
5. Configure the verification IPs
6. Generate constrained random stimulus
7. Run sample test

The presented work automates the creation of all the above tasks and finally connects the testbench created with the actual design. The minimum required information related to interface connection and configuration is collected from user in the form of tabular data at block level. Based on this information, test environment is created, configuration is done, interface instances are connected to RTL design, meaningful random stimulus is generated and finally a top level testbench is created. At block level we use standard templates to produce new VIP components and table based input for connections etc where as at SoC level this methodology reuses the block level information to create and integrate the testbench. So this methodology is useful at both the levels.

At SoC Level where VIPs are used in verifying IPs, the real advantage is in collecting and connecting many such IP level environments from IP level to the SoC level. The previous information of block level can be reused. The user will just have to do hierarchical name changes in the previous database and design will automatically be connected to different VIP instances which save a lot of time in testbench creation. Simultaneously debugging time is also saved. Till date VIP instance connection to DUT is done manually, this is error prone and debugging connection related problem takes lot of time especially at later stage. Once the user has defined interface information in tabular format, connection is automatically done. If it runs successfully in a testbench, the information is made golden at block level. Every organization follows a standard directory structure. The need for organization specific tools and methodology arises because of specific market and product requirements. The tool set used are also not different. There are three parts of this work; process definition, current integration activities and enabling automation. Because of these requirements, methodology plays more important role in creating custom tools which integrate specific steps and processes and good practices to come up with a fully integrated testbench which can drive transaction into the DUT right within few hours both at block level as well as SoC level. The usage of this methodology has reduced testbench integration time considerably and also removed dependence on domain knowledge and experience.

2   Previous Related Work

The problem of testbench automation has been tackled in different ways. This section presents some of the relevant existing solutions and how the presented work is innovative in nature.

[5] Proposes an automated verification methodology (VeriSC2) that provides working testbenches during hierarchical decomposition and refinement of the design, even before the RTL implementation starts. This creates a running testbench but does not talk about interface connection and definition which remains the central idea of the paper.

[6] Deals with SoC design and testbench automation based on IP_XACT format. The Platform Verifier methodology creates a SoC level testbench but replaces the IP instances with empty modules and verification components. While the presented work connects different Verification IP's with the actual RTL/design without replacing IP instances.

Synopsys uvmgen tool creates an UVM [1] [7] based testbench based on certain inputs given by user. This approach is quite helpful at block level, but at SoC level this approach is not feasible and lacks the interface connection with actual RTL.

Here an automated UVM [1] based testbench is created while connecting the interfaces with the real design and most importantly re-using the IP level connection information at SoC level. The concept of standard directory structure and use of coding guidelines along with the use of central repository has been introduced in the presented work.

3   The Flow and Methodology

In this section, the flow of creating testbench around IP and SoC level has been discussed. The existing flow is presented in brief and more emphasis is laid on the new steps.

At IP level: As discussed in the section II the existing VIPs have to be fetched and new ones have to be written if they don't exist. After that the top level testbench has to be written which integrates all the VIPs together and comes up with top level test cases which have the hooks of the VIPs to exchange transaction details.

Based on certain inputs given by user on interfacing and configuration, a top-level testbench is created and integrated which is also connected to the actual RTL. The output of this step is a working testbench, which can be modified according to the requirements. From the user perspective, he/she just needs to specify the different VIP definitions. For an existing VIP we have the concept of central repository.

3.1   Use of Central Repository Database

It is assumed that different versions of standard Verification IPs used across various teams are kept in a common database. This approach aids in knowledge sharing and saves time in searching for the correct version of VIP.

Either a new VIP template is generated or existing VIP is fetched depending on the user input. The new VIP template classes are generated as discussed in [5,6], the templates used also impose coding guidelines for the testbench writers. Customization of VIP is important when VIP is reused and plugged in across different projects, hence is standardized according to the company's best practices.

To maintain stringent standards in terms of coding practices and guidelines the VIP has to undergo different checks to ensure quality. These checks can be of different categories like naming conventions, coding styles, file formats etc. This is done to make sure that the verification components used, also facilitate reuse and reduce the number of iterations during the verification cycle.

3.2   Importance of Directory Structure and Integration Tool

For large designs and equally large and complex testbenches, automation is needed at all levels of design and verification process. The automation proposed for integration is easy to implement only when there is standardization in SOC and IP data management. The process of design and testbench integration expects a complex and conditional file collection for large number of IPs and VIP data. This is facilitated by following a standard directory structure and disciplined naming conventions for all design and verification collaterals. The standard directory structure enables the reuse of standard IP blocks and portability of SOC data. Now after having all the VIPs in place the details given by the user are used to connect the VIPs and configure them. Sample test cases [5, 6] which use the VIPs to communicate with the design under test are also produced.

The next step is to integrate the VIPs with the DUT which is again done with the help of user given tabular inputs. But the aim is to get it correct by construction methodology. The connections are made based on manual inputs, thus can be error prone. So as to maintain quality and to ensure thoroughness, formal tools are used to verify connections.

3.3   Use of Formal Engine to Verify the Connection and Interface Coverage

The usage of formal methods to ensure quality and correctness of the connections has been proposed here. The source of error in connection information is either manual entry of the connection database or because of signal and port width mismatches. There could also be instances where port names or signal names are missing .All these discrepancies will be rectified here by running connectivity verification checks by using formal tools, thus ensuring completeness. For checking the missing port lists, options from the formal tool have been incorporated to show uncovered ports. As an input to the formal tool a dummy module is created with the port list comprising of the signals listed in the input CSV file. Connectivity assertions between corresponding pair of signals in the DUT top module and the dummy module created previously are generated. By following this, any error in the specification of the signals will be caught. This coverage driven connectivity checking provides strong basis at IP level leading to golden database creation.

So far IP level testbench creation has been discussed, SOC level poses different challenges; for example at SOC level although the need for writing of new VIPs is minimal as VIPs used at IP level already exist but the number of such VIPs to be connected is very large . A new methodology has been introduced to reuse the connectivity information of IP level at SoC level which simplifies the task of creating the testbench.

3.4   Re-use of Block Level Information at SoC Level

During IP level verifications users provide interface and configuration details for a specific VIP. This information is treated golden after successful verification. Interface related information includes name of protocol, instance name and various connection details. While creating SoC level testbench, this information can be updated by doing minimal changes related to hierarchy etc. Thus re-usability of information saves a lot of time both in testbench creation and debugging.

Configuration related information includes specific settings of a particular VIP, which are quite important for using any VIP. This can also be ported to SoC level. Figure 1 describes the flow of methodology at IP level. Followings are steps for automatic generation of UVM based testbench at IP level:

- Input the top level design for which testbench has to be made.
- Populate VIPs in your working area.
- Define the required information (interface connection and configuration) in tabular format.
- Invoke the ip_tb_gen tool.
- After this, a top level testbench will be made so start the verification process.
- Incase if there is any error in connection definition, update the tabular data.
- Repeat the process till connection definitions are clean.
- Once the verification closure is done, the definition is then made golden at IP level.

At this point a running IP level testbench is made. It is important to note that at SoC level test-bench integration, the VIP connections remain similar and only hierarchy of connections may change. Hence testbench integrator will reuse the connection information at SoC level. While doing so it not only eliminates the scope of manual error that is not caught by simulator compiler but also saves a lot of manual effort and time which would otherwise be spent in learning protocol and signals, doing manual integration and debugging wrong connection.

Figure 2, describes the flow at SoC level. The flow is similar as IP level with following changes: The connectivity information reused from IP level needs to be updated by testbench integrator. There will be multiple instances of protocols and hence multiple tabular definition files will be used as input by the tool.

Multiple projects will be able to share the connection information with few changes in the connectivity tabular database while the actual changes required in the testbench need large manual efforts. So finally the methodology delivers a fully functional testbench both at IP and SoC level.

This methodology adds value both at IP and SoC level testbench creation and integration.

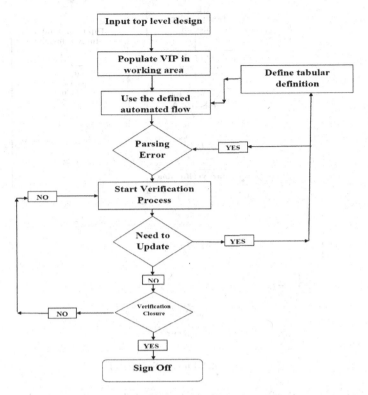

Fig. 1. Flow at IP level

4   ip_tb_gen Tool

Ip_tb_gen is a tool for automatic testbench generation. The verification methodology followed is UVM while currently it supports System Verilog as HVL. This language and methodology is chosen because this is the most adopted combination in the industry and all the major EDA vendors are supporting this. The configuration and connection is also quite easy without touching the underlying components.

The tool takes following as input:

- Name of the top level design block.
- VIP definition of a particular protocol which includes the name of VIP and following tabular definition files :
- Interface connectivity CSV: This will include interface connectivity information to DUT such as name of instance, name of testbench, input/output directions etc.
- Configuration settings CSV: This will include configuration settings related to VIP
- Mode of using VIP: either as master or slave.
- Type of VIP: Existing/Non-existing
- Name of top clock and reset signal.
- Name of simulator to be used.

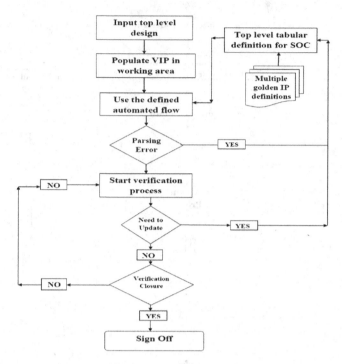

Fig. 2. Flow at SoC Level

This completes the information which is needed from the user side. Based on the above information given, tool will deliver a fully functional UVM based testbench.

Flow and working of tool:

Given the name of VIP, first it will look whether it is existing or non-existing. For existing ones, the tool will populate it from the central repository otherwise it will create complete VIP based on UVM which includes transaction item, sequence, sequencer, driver, monitor and agent. Now all the VIP blocks which were defined are in working area along with the top level design. The VIP instances will be automatically connected to DUT based on the tabular information specified. The interface definition using *uvm_config_db::set* will also be done so that lower level verification components will automatically get access to interface using *uvm_config_db::get* operation. Now the Environment class will be created which will instantiate different agents, build and connect them. Also tool has different sequences for each VIP which completes the requirement for creating a top level testbench class. Finally a UVM based testbench will be developed which will inherit environment and different sequence class. Different components will be built, configuration of VIP will be done and sequences will start on respective sequencer in run phase. Based on simulator choice, testbench will be simulated with proper command line arguments.

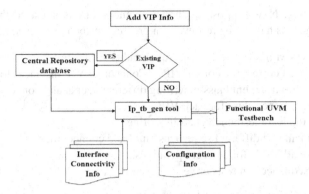

Fig. 3. Architecture of Tool

From the user's perspective both standard methodology and verification language i.e. UVM and System Verilog is used. So no extra learning is required in order to deploy this tool and methodology. Figure 3, explains the architecture of the tool. The inputs of the tools are mostly VIP definitions while the output is UVM based testbench. The tool also has the facility for creating VIP's which are non-existing, further which will be kept in central repository database.

5   Case Study

The ip_tb_gen tool methodology was applied for block level verification of IP based on Serial Communication Interface. The following section will make clear the understanding of both tool and methodology. For this UVM based testbench architecture is shown in Figure 4.The top level design is based on Serial Communication. There are four different VIP's namely UART, Register access, Clock driver and Interrupt Handler. Out of these Interrupt handler and clock driver

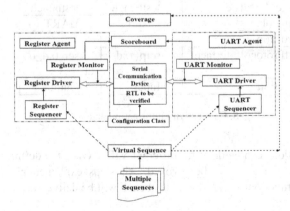

Fig. 4. Reference testbench architecture

were non-existing. Now suppose ip_tb_gen methodology is not used then in such a case following steps have to be followed for creating testbench environment.

- Create a UVM based VIP for Interrupt handler from scratch and test it.
- Search for all correct version of VIP's. Connect all VIP instances to DUT.
- Create an Environment class inheriting different agents and connecting them.
- Create a Sequence class for each VIP.
- Create a top level testbench class inheriting.
- Environment and different sequences build and connect them.
- Configure all VIP's for correct operations.
- Start all sequences on respective sequencer.

Following the ip_tb_gen methodology tabular definitions have to be given:

5.1   Interface Connectivity

For an example connectivity information for UART VIP is shown in Figure 5 In the pre-defined format:

- *IpTop:* Name of top level design.
- *Interface:* Name of VIP interface
- *Interface Instance Name:* Name of instance name of VIP interface.
- *Target Instance:* Name of target instance for DUT connection.
- *Protocol:* Name of the protocol used.
- *PortIPtop:* Name of the signal in VIP interface.
- PortProtocolInterface: Name of the corresponding signal in DUT.

IpTop	sci_dsc	sci_dsc
Interface	Uart_if	Uart_if
Interface Instance	uart_intf	uart_intf
Target Instance	testbench	testbench
Protocol	UART	UART
PortIPtop	rd	td
PortProtocolInterface	scip_rxd_ in	sci_txd_o ut
Direction	Input	Output

Fig. 5. Connectivity information data

Similarly VIP definitions can be done for different VIP's. Once the definitions for all the VIP's are made, the tool can be invoked. All steps explained above will be automated and fully functional UVM based testbench will be delivered.

6   Results

The proposed methodology was used to build and integrate IP level verification testbench around SCI [serial communication interface] which had 4 interfaces (as described above). The generated testbench was verified with Cadence IUS and Synopsys VCS simulators. As an initial step the integration time was reduced from around 2 days to half hour with case1 and case2 being true.

Case1: The integration related data was available for the tool to run.

Case2: The engineer has good knowledge of verification language.

Case3: The engineer has directory structure, Company's internal methodology knowledge to write interconnection and more important the minor details of the protocol. With case 2 and 3 the integration time without tool was around 1 day. So based on these results with all cases 1, 2 and 3 being true, the approximate connection time per interface is around 1.5 man hour without automation. Extrapolating this statistics for a medium sized SoC having around 65 interfaces , the testbench integration job would take approximately 3 Man weeks and with automation it can be cut down to few days, including the time needed for creating top level tabular data base.

7   Conclusion

The proposed work introduced a novel flow and methodology for testbench automation. The tool supporting methodology was also developed. The main aim of the idea was to reduce testbench creation time both at IP and SoC level. Initially some of the information obtained from user in tabular format for a specific protocol. The same information can be reused at SoC level by doing some minimal changes. The scope of manual error in making VIP instance connections to DUT is greatly reduced as this task is automated. The tool also develops VIP in case if it non-existing. Finally a fully functional UVM testbench is delivered. Application results have shown considerable amount of time saving in complete process of verification.

References

[1] UVM, https://verificationacademy.com/topics/verification-methodology

[2] OVM, https://verificationacademy.com/topics/verification-methodology

[3] VMM, http://www.synopsys.com/community/interoperability/pages/vmm.aspx

[4] Agile Soc, http://www.agilesoc.com/2012/05/07/wasted-effort-spent-in-verification/

[5] Da Silva, K.R.G., Melcher, E.U.K., Araujo, G., Pimenta, V.A.: An automatic testbench generation tool for a System C functional verification methodology. In: SBCCI 2004: Proceedings of the 17th Symposium on Integrated Circuits and System Design (2004)

[6] Cho, K., Kim, J., Jung, E., Kim, S., Li, Z., Cho, Y.-R., Min*, B., Choi, K.-M.: Reusable Platform Design Methodology for SoC Integration and Verification. In: International SoC Design Conference (2008)

[7] Synopsys uvmgen User Guide

A Methodology for Early and Accurate Analysis of Inrush and Latency Tradeoffs during Power-Domain Wakeup

Vipul Singhal, Ayon Dey, Suresh Mallala, and Somshubhra Paul

Texas Instruments (India), Bangalore, India
{Vipul,a-dey,suresh.mallala,wrik}@ti.com

Abstract. Power gating is used in almost all Low-power devices to lower leakage. In this power gating, the three important design parameters are the domain-wakeup latency (from sleep to active mode transition) time, the inrush-current when the power switches are turned on, and the voltage dip caused by the inrush current. Also, the analysis of these parameters has some uniqueness when there is an on-die power-supply system. In this paper we present a methodology for analyzing these parameters, followed by a case study involving analysis of all these parameters using circuit simulation (SPICE) for a wakeup latency critical low power SoC (System on a Chip).

Keywords: Power-domain, Wakeup-latency, Inrush-current, Power-management.

1 Introduction

Power-gating is a common power-saving feature in Low-power SoCs (System on a Chip). A typical low-power IC has a "Deep-Sleep" mode in which the power-supply to one or more parts of the design is gated-off by means of switches. Each such independently controllable part is called a Power-domain. During wake-up from the deep-sleep mode, the domain has to be charged to full rail-supply through the switches.

One of the well-known issues associated with un-gating a power-domain is that initially a large amount of current flows into the domain. This is known as "inrush current". As a result of the inrush current, the power-supply rail may see a sharp transient-drop in voltage. Since the power-rail is shared with other power-domains (which may be up and running), this drop can be fatal for their functionality. The usual solution is to slow-down the charging. This is achieved by using a switch-cell that consists of a strong-switch and a weak-switch (Fig 1.). The strong switches are used for operation in active mode, while weak switches are used to slowly charge-up the power domain, so that the inrush current is minimized. This concept is common in power-management-related literature [1].

Often, such Low-power SoCs are used in real-time system-control applications. Although the SoC may remain in standby mode or "deep-sleep" mode for a long time

M.S. Gaur et al. (Eds.): VDAT 2013, CCIS 382, pp. 294–303, 2013.
© Springer-Verlag Berlin Heidelberg 2013

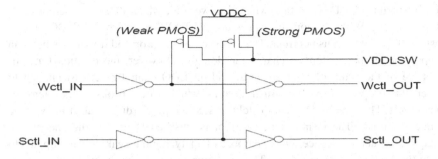

Fig. 1. Power-switch cell with weak and strong PMOS switches

when the system is dormant-state, but when a request for processing comes, it need to wake-up quickly from sleep to service the request. In the semiconductor-market, SoCs for control applications compete with each other on the time it takes them to wake-up from a standby mode. Since the wakeup–sequence requires charging one or more power domains to full-rail, the time required for the charging up the domain becomes a key parameter. In the rest of the discussion we will call this parameter as "domain charging latency" or just "latency" for short.

From the above discussion it is readily seen that designers are faced with two mutually contradictory requirements during domain-wakeup: If the domain-charging is too slow then the latency suffers, while if the domain charging is too fast then inrush current may cause a dip in the supply voltage, that could be fatal for already-ON and working domains. Designers need to strike a balance between the two requirements. The rest of the paper is dedicated to elaborating this issue in the context of low-power SoCs, and describing a methodology for an early analysis and resolution of this issue.

2   Power-Supply System in an SOC with on Die LDO

Many SoCs have a built-in on-die Low-drop-out (LDO) voltage regulator, which is the power supply for the various power-domains. Also, most LDOs use an off-die capacitor to stabilize their output (labeled 'C_0' in the fig 2. below).

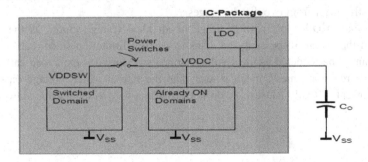

Fig. 2. Power-supply system with on-die LDO

In this picture, VDDSW is the switched power-rail, while VDDC is the constant-ON power-rail. When a domain wakes-up, VDDSW rises while VDDC sees a transient drop due to inrush current. The LDO senses the drop and it will slowly begin to supply additional current to charge the domain. However, the reaction times of LDOs are of the order of microseconds, and an LDO cannot react fast enough to counter the drop due to the inrush current which often peaks within tens of nanoseconds. Thus the LDO is completely ineffective in guarding against the voltage dip due to inrush. The instantaneous current is supplied by the on-die and off-die decoupling capacitors. Hence for the purpose of analyzing the peak voltage-dip due to inrush, the LDO is good as absent. This is shown in Fig 3 below, which also shows the charge transfer during domain-wakeup.

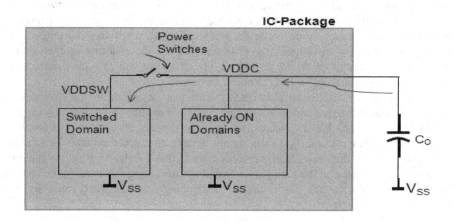

Fig. 3. Charge transfer during domain wake-up

3   Limitations of Currently Available Tools/Methodologies

Although several EDA tools are available in the industry to analyze inrush currents they mostly suffer from two disadvantages.

First, most EDA tools require usage of an ideal-voltage-source as the primary source in the circuit to be analyzed. This is a major limitation since real-life on-die LDOs cannot be modeled as ideal voltage sources because (as explained earlier) they have slow reaction-times : much slower than the rate at which voltage dips due to inrush current. Usually EDA tools do not provide a way to model this slow-reaction time.

Second, typical EDA tools that analyze inrush are not suitable for usage during Architecture stage or early design stages. This is because they require views like DEF and Timing analysis, which are available quite late in the product development cycle. On the other hand some information about best latency available is needed during product-definition/architecture or early-development stage. These limitations prompt us to find a simple solution that can overcome the two issues above.

4   Modeling

In this section we discuss a methodology for modeling the power-domain system. The first step is estimating the effective Gate-count (G_P) for each power-domain ("P"). Gate-count is the equivalent NAND-gates for the domain.

$$G_p = \sum_i \frac{A_i}{A_{NAND}} \tag{1}$$

where A_i is the area of the ith standard-cell in the power-domain P, and A_{NAND} is the area of the basic NAND cell in the library.

For simplicity let us assume that only one domain is switching at a time. Let us call the switching-on domain "S". The gate count (G_p) for this domain is designated as G_S. The next step is to arrive at an initial estimate on the number of switches "N_{PS}" in this power domain. Usually N_{PS} is derived from the peak-current considerations.

$$N_{PS} = \frac{I_{Peak(S)}}{I_{MAX\_SS}} \tag{2}$$

where $I_{Peak(S)}$ is the peak *Active-Mode* current requirement of the domain S, and I_{MAX_SS} is the maximum current that the strong-switch can supply across various process-temperature corners with a given (low) voltage drop across the switch.

While the domain S switches-ON, other domains which are already ON act as decoupling capacitors. The gate count of these already-ON domains can be estimated as -

$$G_{AON} = \sum_{p=1}^{p=L} G_p \tag{3}$$

where p is each domain among L domains that are already on when the domain 'S' is turning ON.

Thus, we now have a basic switching model for early analysis. The accuracy of this circuit can be improved by adding information about parasitic-elements like package-inductance (L_P) and package-resistance (R_P), as well as early estimates of resistance offered by the power grid-routing (R_{PR}). The circuit of fig 3 can now be elaborated as fig 4 below -

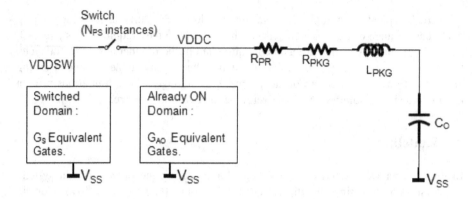

Fig. 4. Schematic circuit for domain-switching

5   Simulation

To make the model in figure above simulate-able in a circuit-simulator (like SPICE), we need to create a equivalent-circuit model for the logic-gates G_S and G_{AON}. The simplest model is a lumped capacitance whose value is estimated by multiplying the gate-count with a per-gate capacitance number, which in turn is derived by simulating simple gates. However this approach does not take into account several factors. First: logic-gates do not act as linear capacitors since the charge to voltage ratio varies with the voltage. Second: logic-charging may display significant short-circuit currents, not modeled by capacitors. Third: the effect of standard-cells being arranged in chains is also not captured by lumped capacitors. Thus lumped-cap models would-be an over-simplification and the results from those are not likely to be accurate at all. On the other hand, it is highly impractical to try to simulate a complete design-netlist in a circuit simulator, even if such a netlist is available at the early analysis stage.

As a middle-ground, we use multiple-instances of a standard-cell-chain as a more accurate model of logic in a domain. This may be a chain of randomly-picked logic gates, or (for simplicity) a chain of basic NAND2 gates may be used. For example if a chain of K nand-gates is used then, the GS Logic gates can be modeled by G_S/K instances of the nand-chain. Similarly the Already-On logic can be modeled by G_{AO}/K instances of the nand-chain. This is shown in Fig 5 below.

For a real design, this number of instances can still be too high to simulate in SPICE (or similar circuit-simulator) in any reasonable amount of time. To resolve this issue, a further simplification may be made with no loss of accuracy. The whole circuit of fig. 5 is "divided by" N_{PS} as shown in fig. 6 below. (When doing this, it is important to note that while on one hand the instance counts of switches and nand-chains as well as capacitance-value shall be divided by N_{PS}, on the other hand the resistor and inductor values should be *multiplied* by N_{PS}.) Now, the circuit has only

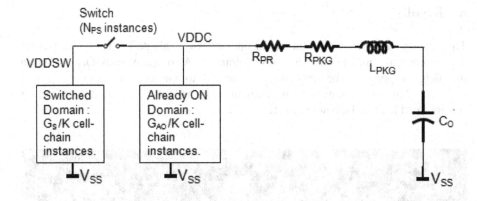

Fig. 5. Equivalent circuit for simulations

one switch-cell, as well as a drastically-reduced transistor-count. This helps make the SPICE simulation practical on a normal computing-machine.

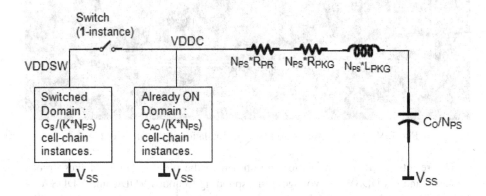

Fig. 6. Reduced Equivalent circuit for faster simulations

This circuit can now be simulated, by initializing the capacitance to the voltage before the domain switching, then closing the switch by switching the control-input of the switch-cell, and observing the transient response. The voltage-waveforms obtained from this circuit will be same as for the original circuit of fig. 5, while the current will have to ne multiplied by a factor of N_{PS} to get the actual value. Further, the current-waveform from this simulation can be input to LDO-simulation, to achieve a complete response including recovery to full rail voltage. This is demonstrated in the section below.

6 Results

This section shows analysis done on an SoC design. This design has a one power-domain charging-up, and one Already-ON domain. Also, the Already-ON domain in this deign happens to be very small compared to the charging-domain ($G_{AO} < 0.1 * G_S$). Multiple instances of a chain of 10-nand gates was used to represent standard-cell logic in both domains (K=10).

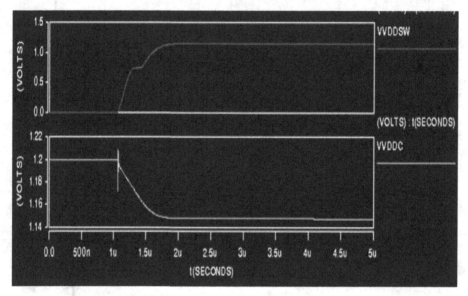

Fig. 7. Voltage waveforms from SPICE simulation of the circuit of Fig. 6

The results of SPICE-simulation are shown in the plots in fig-7. In these plots, VVDDC and VVDDSW are voltages corresponding to nodes VDDC and VDDSW of fig. 6. The switch is turned-ON at time t=1us. As the domain charges and VDDSW rises, the Already-ON domain and the external capacitor provide the charge, and consequently the voltage on the VDDC dips.

In this case the VDDC drops from 1.2V to about 1.15V which may be acceptable if the logic in the Already-ON domains has been designed to keep operating at 1.15V with process-temperature variation. This is an important result because this allows us to see whether the inrush is serious enough to impact active (already-ON) circuits, which was one of the stated goals of the exercise.

Another useful output is the waveform for the current through the external capacitor (Fig 8).

Note that the real instantaneous-values of the current are N_{PS} times the values in the plot (since our simulation was for a circuit reduced by a factor of N_{PS}.)

The simulation needs to be done at all process-temperature-voltage corners and the worst-case taken into consideration.

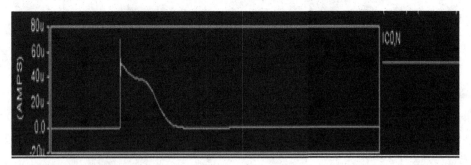

Fig. 8. Current from the external capacitor: from SPICE simulation of the circuit in Fig 7

Analog Simulation with LDO

The analysis described so far showed the dip in the voltage at VDDC and the current waveform, which is an important result. However it does not show the recovery back to the original voltage supplied by the LDO. To do this we need to bring the LDO back in the picture. The current waveform of Fig 8 is multiplied by a factor of NPS, and then replaced by an approximate piecewise-linear (triangular) waveform shown in the lower part of the figure below. This triangular waveform is then given as input into an analog simulation of the LDO. The bottom–graph in Fig 9 (marked *I(ma)*), shows this triangular current waveform. The LDO has been simulated across process-temperature corners, represented by different curves on the voltage graph in Fig 9.

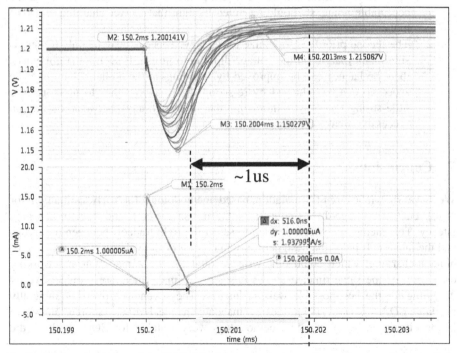

Fig. 9. Analog simulation of the LDO: The lower graph shows the current waveform applied, while the upper graphs show output voltage variations at various process-temperature corners

Key Observations

1. The output voltage dips by about 45mV. This is the same dip as seen from spice-simulation of figure 3. This confirms our earlier assertion that the LDO is too-slow to react to the initial dip.
2. It can also be observed that it takes about 1us for the system to get back to the original voltage. Hence it would not be advisable to start Active mode operations before 1us, since they typically tend to burn significant power, and can cause further dip. Thus 1us is the domain-charging latency for this implementation.

Usage of the Results in the Design
Having done this analysis, the design team will proceed as follows –

1. The first priority is to guard against functional failure due to voltage dip. If the voltage for the Already-ON domains (VDDC) dips fatally (below the min-voltage for which these domains have been designed), then this need to be fixed first. This will require slowing down the domain-charging, so that inrush-current is reduced. This can be achieved either by re-sizing the weak switches to make them still-weaker, or by adding delays between turning-on successive weak switches. After doing this, the analysis above should be repeated to confirm that the voltage-dip due to the new inrush current is the acceptable range. It should be noted though, that slower charging will cost higher latency.
2. The second priority is optimize for latency. This can be done only if there is significant margin on the voltage-dip due to inrush. If such a margin exists, then the latency can be improved by speeding-up the domain-charging. The speed-up can be achieved by re-sizing the weak-switches to make them a little-stronger, or by minimizing the delay (if any) between turning-on successive weak switches.

7 Conclusions

We have shown a circuit simulation based methodology for early estimation for inrush current, voltage-drop (induced by the inrush-current), and domain charging latency. This methodology can be used to select the right tradeoff between the inrush and the latency. It helps the designers stay in control of the voltage dip at the time of domain-charging, which could otherwise be fatal for the Already-On and working domains. At the same time, it allows designers to make their SoC competitive by designing for the best-possible wakeup latency. The advantages over commercially available EDA tools are – (1) It does not mandate an "ideal-voltage-source" anywhere in the circuit, thus making this methodology very suitable for SOCs with on-die

LDOs which are slow-reacting. (2) It does not require design views like DEF and timing-window information, so it can be used early in the design-cycle.

Reference

[1] Shi, K., Flynn, D.: Power Gating Design Tradeoffs and Consideration in Production Low-power Designs. In: Proc. of the IEC DesignCon (February 2009)

Fault Aware Dynamic Adaptive Routing Using LBDR

Rimpy Bishnoi, Vijay Laxmi, Manoj Singh Gaur, and Mohit Baskota

Department of Computer Engineering,
Malaviya National Institute of Technology, Jaipur, India
{rimpy,vlaxmi,gaurms,2009ucp853}@mnit.ac.in

Abstract. Network-on-Chip (NoC) is evolving as an efficient and scalable interconnect architecture for current and future CMP, MPSoC systems. An important challenge in NoC design is to choose an appropriate routing algorithm, as it impacts the NoC performance. As technology scales down to Deep-Submicron (DSM), on-chip networks are becoming increasingly prone to failures. At higher level these failures are handled by fault tolerant routing algorithms. Fault tolerant routing algorithms avoid faulty regions and route traffic through safe regions. Currently, routing algorithms are implemented as source or distributed routing. To handle faults, both source and distributed routing make use of routing tables. Algorithms implemented with routing tables do not scale well with network size. Scalable routing implementation, such as Logic Based Distributed Routing (LBDR) has been proposed for efficient and compact implementation of routing. LBDR handles faults without using routing table. In this paper we propose a fault tolerant routing scheme based on LBDR which aims to handle faults while at the same time addressing network congestion. Proposed method integrates deterministic and adaptive routing schemes to avoid congestion as well as faults that may be present in the network. Experimental results show the effectiveness of proposed method in case of single and multiple link failures.

Keywords: SoC, NoC, LBDR, DyAD, Fault tolerance.

1 Introduction

System on Chip (SoC) packages all complex heterogeneous components of a system on a single integrated circuit. Due to increasing transistor density, higher operating frequency driven by increasing computing demand, short time-to-market and reduced product life cycle have shifted the manufacturers to many-core processors [1]. In many-core systems large number of cores are assembled together on the same chip forming a SoC with complex functionality. Major challenge in many-core technology is to provide high performance while maintaining a low power budget [1].

One important component in these systems is the on-chip interconnect. A novel packet-switch interconnect, Network on Chip (NoC) [2] has been proposed for SoCs and chip multi-processors (CMPs) to deal with inefficient traditional interconnects (higher wire density of fully connected networks and scalability problems of buses) and to address the high communication demand of future many-core systems. Inspired from high-performance off-chip interconnects, NoC is a scalable, efficient, flexible and largely modular approach to interconnect various components [2]. Performance of NoC

M.S. Gaur et al. (Eds.): VDAT 2013, CCIS 382, pp. 304–311, 2013.

is affected by several design choices like topology, switching mechanism, and routing algorithms. In NoC, 2D mesh is the most common topology for constructing massively parallel multi-processors.

The routing algorithm [3] determines the path (sequence of channels) a packet should take to reach destination node. It can be deterministic where a fixed path is always chosen without considering the current network status or adaptive, where multiple paths can be generated and final path is selected based on current network status. Adaptiveness of a routing algorithm can used to handle the network congestion by avoiding the congested path. Most prominent characteristic of a routing algorithm is that it should be deadlock and livelock free. Recently, to handle faults present in on chip network, fault tolerance in routing algorithm is also considered as main issue to deal with [4]. Fault tolerance is the ability of the routing algorithm to work around the presence of failed components.

The primary focus of this paper is to address the fault tolerance in NoC using a fault tolerant routing algorithm. We propose a novel Fault Aware Dynamic Adaptive Routing using LBDR (FADAR-LBDR), an extension of Dynamic ADaptive (DyAD) routing algorithm [5]. Experimental results show the effectiveness of FADAR-LBDR algorithm even in presence of multiple link failures.

Rest of the paper is organised as follows: Section 2 discusses the related work in fault tolerance. Section 3 discusses DyAD approach. Section 4 shows Logic based Distributed Routing (LBDR), a routing implementation in NoC. Section 5 presents our proposed method. Experimental setup is presented in Section 6. Result analysis and future remarks are given in Section 7.

2 Related Work

In [6], Duato *et al* have shown how faults in the network affect the two main characteristic of the routing algorithm i.e freedom from deadlock and livelock. They also presented various definitions related to fault tolerant routing algorithm and defined common fault models use to design fault tolerant routing algorithm. Fault tolerant routing in SAF, VCT and Wormhole- switched networks is also presented in detail.

Glass and Ni [7] presented a method of designing dynamic fault-tolerant wormhole routing algorithms using turn model [8] without using virtual channels. They modified turn based negative first routing algorithm to use non-minimal paths and made it tolerate $(n - 1)$ faults in n-dimensional meshes. Ali *et al* [9] presented two most popular dynamic routing algorithms, Distance vector routing and Link state Routing from off-chip interconnects. Based on above routing algorithms author proposed one dynamic fault tolerant algorithm which is a modified version of link state routing.

Based on local information of faults Boppana and Chalasani [10] presented the issue of fault-tolerance into fully-adaptive and deterministic wormhole routing algorithms. They used block fault model where faults consist of rectangular region and fault rings and fault-chains are incorporated to route the messages around faulty-regions.

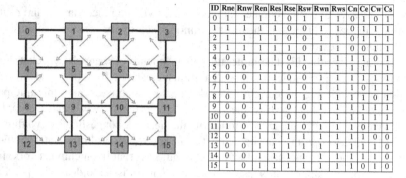

ID	Rne	Rnw	Ren	Res	Rse	Rsw	Rwn	Rws	Cn	Ce	Cw	Cs
0	1	1	1	1	0	1	1	1	0	1	0	1
1	1	1	1	1	0	0	1	1	0	1	1	1
2	1	1	1	1	0	0	1	1	0	1	1	1
3	1	1	1	1	1	0	1	1	0	0	1	1
4	0	1	1	1	0	1	1	1	1	1	0	1
5	0	0	1	1	0	0	1	1	1	1	1	1
6	0	0	1	1	0	0	1	1	1	1	1	1
7	1	0	1	1	1	0	1	1	1	0	1	1
8	0	1	1	1	0	1	1	1	1	1	0	1
9	0	0	1	1	0	0	1	1	1	1	1	1
10	0	0	1	1	0	0	1	1	1	1	1	1
11	1	0	1	1	1	0	1	1	1	0	1	1
12	0	1	1	1	1	1	1	1	1	1	0	0
13	0	0	1	1	1	1	1	1	1	1	1	0
14	0	0	1	1	1	1	1	1	1	1	1	0
15	1	0	1	1	1	1	1	1	1	0	1	0

Fig. 1. Routing restrictions and LBDR bits for XY

3   DyAD and LBDR: A Background

3.1   DyAD-Basics

Dynamic ADaptive Deterministic routing (DyAD) [5] is a novel routing scheme which integrates deterministic and adaptive routing algorithms by switching between them when needed. It switches according to the current congestion level at a particular router. Each router in the network, monitors its local congestion level. If the congestion is low it works in deterministic mode and enjoys low latency offered by the deterministic routing algorithm. On the other side it shifts to adaptive mode to avoid congested path when the congestion is high, resulting in high throughput.

3.2   LBDR-Basics

Logic Based Distributed Routing (LBDR) [11] is proposed as a new methodology for routing implementation in network on chip (NoC). LBDR aims to provide a simple, compact and flexible way to represent the topology and captures dynamics of a number of deadlock free routing algorithms without using routing tables.

To achieve compact and flexible representation of topology and routing algorithm, each router in the network is configured with three bits per router output port. For initial 2D mesh, it results in 12 bits for each router. These bits are computed off-line, and grouped into routing and connectivity bits. Routing bits represent the routing restrictions imposed by current routing algorithm for deadlock freedom. Connectivity bits are used to represent the current network topology.

These bits are computed off-line by analyzing current topology and applying routing restrictions to represent current routing algorithm. Figure 1 display routing restrictions corresponding to XY routing algorithm on 4 x 4 mesh and shows the corresponding routing and connectivity bits for XY routing. LBDR implements routing logic in two stages. In the first stage, a comparator compares the relative position of destination router from the viewpoint of the current router. In a second stage, it computes the routing decision using one logic unit with each output port.

LBDR is complemented with two extra bits per each input port. These bit implement a deroute option (they code an output port) in case the two previous phases fail in providing a valid output. These bit enable non-minimal paths to avoid internal failure inside the 2D mesh.

4 Proposed Method: FADAR-LBDR

Proposed method is motivated by DyAD [5] routing scheme. Similar to the previous scheme our approach integrates deterministic and adaptive routing schemes to avoid congestion. Deterministic and Adaptive routing algorithms are implemented with LBDR resulting in table less network even in presence of faults. Overview of our proposed method is shown in Figure 2.b.

- Deterministic and adaptive routing algorithms are selected such that they work together without creating deadlock and livelock situations.
- As the routing implementation is LBDR, routing and connectivity bits of each router are calculated and set prior to the normal operation. Deroute bits are also computed for the adaptive routing.
- Initial mode of a router is selected according to its congestion level. If it is low, it works in deterministic mode. But if congestion is low, and output port supplied by deterministic routing logic is faulty (connectivity bits corresponding to that output port is set to 0) then that port is rejected and routing mode shifts from deterministic to adaptive mode. If alternative minimal path generated by adaptive mode also encounters a failure, it will use deroute bit to avoid failures by routing packets non-minimally.
- If the congestion level of current router is high then it remains in adaptive mode and gives the output port which is not faulty and uses deroute bit when required.

4.1 Deadlock and Livelock Avoidance

FADAR algorithm combines two routing algorithms into one. Each routing algorithm is deadlock-free by itself as the channel dependence graph (CDG) is acyclic, however, the combination of both may introduce additional dependencies which could create cycles. For this reason, we need to restrict transitions between both algorithms. Proposed method uses two different sets of virtual channels (VC), one for deterministic routing and other for adaptive routing as shown in Figure 2.a. One way to use both algorithms is by relying on an acyclic escape path implemented by OE. In this sense, XY algorithm is used normally and when congestion is detected the message is injected into the OE virtual channel, following OE routing rules until the message reaches final destination. Therefore, transitions from OE to XY are not allowed. The overall algorithm is deadlock-free since the CDG of the OE layer is still acyclic. However, this restriction may affect performance as the OE layer can be overloaded. One way to relax the OE layer is to allow transitions to the XY layer. This can be achieved in networks with virtual-cut-through switching (VCT) and by guaranteeing the OE layer will be always available. That is, one message located in the OE layer can request both the XY virtual channel at the next hop and the OE virtual channel at the next hop. If the XY virtual channel is full, then the OE virtual channel can be selected. In wormhole, as messages can be blocked along multiple queues, transition to the XY layer should be prevented.

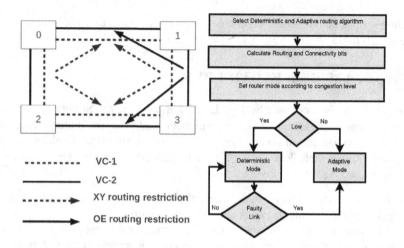

Fig. 2. (a) Deadlock Avoidance   (b) Proposed Method

Finally, in wormhole switched networks, some transitions to the XY layer can still be permitted not introducing deadlocks. This is the case when the routing restrictions of XY and OE coincide. Figure 2.a shows the routing restrictions for XY(dotted) and for OE (firm line). Notice that at switches 1 and 3, routing restrictions of XY and OE coincide and turns from X dimension to Y dimension are legal for both algorithms. Thus, in these locations, the transition from OE to XY can be allowed with no deadlock risk. Livelock situations are avoided by constraining packets to use only minimal path when it is available and use of Time to Live (TTL) in case non-minimal path is used.

5   Experimental Setup

We have used NoC simulator NIRGAM [12] [13] for simulation. NIRGAM is a SystemC based, discrete event cycle accurate simulator and provides an extensive environment to experiment various parameters like topology type, size, routing algorithms, buffer size and traffic pattern.

We have used XY for deterministic and Odd-Even for adaptive mode. Both XY and Odd-Even routing is implemented with LBDR. As routing restrictions used for deadlock freedom are different for deterministic and adaptive scheme, we used two sets of routing bits, one for XY and other for Odd-Even. Single set of connectivity bits is used for both schemes as topology is same for both schemes. All experiments are performed on a 2D mesh topology of size 4 × 4 under bursty traffic.

5.1   Experiment-1

In this experiment, node 4 is chosen as source node producing bursty traffic and node 15 is chosen as destination node. Figure 3 shows the topology along with failed links. Link failures are introduced one by one till the network survives. As there is currently a

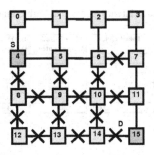

Fig. 3. Link Failure between source 4 and destination 15

single traffic flow so congestion level of network is assumed to be low. Table 1 shows the average latency per flit in presence and absence of failures. When there is no fault in the network and congestion is low, packets are routed using XY routing. When congestion remains same but fault occurs in XY path, routing mode shifts to adaptive. Table 1 shows that average latency remains same even in presence of multiple link failures. At low congestion, deterministic mode is shifted to adaptive mode in presence of failures on deterministic path. Network uses minimal path up-to 12 link failures. For 13th link failure, all minimal paths encounter faulty components and deroute bit at node 6 used for non-minimal path selection which results in increased latency.

5.2 Experiment-2

In this case multiple source destination pairs are chosen to analyze average latency in presence of faults. Node 0-15, 1-15 and 4-15 are chosen as source and destination nodes respectively. All source nodes generate bursty traffic. Link failures are same as experiment-1 shown in Figure 3. Network manages to deliver packets with some increased average latency 42.7843. It is increased due to faulty links as all paths use the same 3, 7 and 11 as intermediate nodes.

Table 1. Average Latency at low congestion level

Number of Failures	Failed Links	Packets Generated	Packets Received	Average Latency per flit
0	No link fail	1881	1881	16.4444
1	4-8	1896	1896	16.4444
2	4-8,5-9	1905	1905	16.4444
3	4-8,5-9,6-10	1932	1932	16.4444
4	4-8,5-9,6-10,8-9	1902	1902	16.4444
5	4-8,5-9,6-10,8-9,9-10	1875	1875	16.4444
6	4-8,5-9,6-10,8-9,9-10,10-11	1908	1908	16.4444
7	4-8,5-9,6-10,8-9,9-10,10-11,8-12	1899	1899	16.4444
8	4-8,5-9,6-10,8-9,9-10,10-11,8-12,9-13	1923	1923	16.4444
9	4-8,5-9,6-10,8-9,9-10,10-11,8-12,9-13,10-14	1887	1887	16.4444
10	4-8,5-9,6-10,8-9,9-10,10-11,8-12,9-13,10-14,12-13	1872	1872	16.4444
11	4-8,5-9,6-10,8-9,9-10,10-11,8-12,9-13,10-14,12-13,13-14	1917	1917	16.4444
12	4-8,5-9,6-10,8-9,9-10,10-11,8-12,9-13,10-14,12-13,13-14,14-15	1872	1872	16.4444
13	4-8,5-9,6-10,8-9,9-10,10-11,8-12,9-13,10-14,12-13,13-14,14-15, 6-7	1085	1085	31.5233

Table 2. Average latency(per flit) at high congestion level

Number of Failures	Failed Links	DyAD-Basic Average Latency	FADAR-LBDR Average Latency
0	No link fail	10.4444	10.4444
1	5-9	infinite	10.4444
2	5-9,9-10	infinite	10.4444
3	5-9,9-10,5-6	infinite	10.4444
4	5-9,9-10,5-6,1-5	infinite	10.4444
5	5-9,9-10,5-6,1-5,6-10	infinite	24.4444

5.3   Experiment-3

In this case node 1 and 10 is chosen as source and destination nodes respectively. This experiment is performed to show the case when basic DyAD scheme gives a single path for few source destination pair and when that path becomes faulty. As shown in Figure 3, there is only a single path for nodes present in even column destined for nodes present in next odd column. Table 2 shows the results when single path becomes faulty. As shown in Table 2, basic DyAD fails to generate any alternative path as it uses odd-even routing. On the other side, DyAD-LBDR uses deterministic mode where it uses XY routing to route the traffic through alternative path.

6   Result Analysis and Future Work

In this paper we have presented a Fault Aware Dynamic Adaptive Routing using LBDR (FADAR-LBDR) in NoC. The proposed method is implemented with LBDR without using routing table. Experimental results have shown the effectiveness of the proposed technique. Proposed method uses minimal path till there is at least one minimal path from source to destination. When there is no minimal path available, it uses deroute bit for non-minimal path selection. Results shown in Table 1 demonstrates that average latency and packet delivery ratio remains same in the presence of single and multiple link failures when atleast one minimal path is avaiable. When all minimal paths encounter faulty components, non-minimal path selection is used which results in increased latency as shown in last row of Table 1. 100% packet delivery ratio is observed in case of multiple source destination pair and multiple link failures with some increased average latency. Comparison of proposed method with basic DyAD scheme has shown in Table 2. Proposed method keeps the average latency same for cases where basic DyAD generates single path from source to destination. Proposed method is effective in sense that fault tolerance is achieved without using routing tables while maintaining the same performance. Deadlock freedom has been achieved using two virtual channels with limiting cases for transition. In future, we will be addressing the non-restriction switching of routing algorithm.

Acknowledgment. We would like to acknowledge support received from Indo-Spain DST project $DST/INT/Spain/P-35/11/1$. Authors would like to acknowledge the critical comments and inputs received from Dr. Jose Flich, DISCA, UPV, Spain for the above work.

References

1. Martin, G., Chang, H.: System-on-chip design. In: Proceedings of the 4th International Conference on ASIC, pp. 12–17 (2001)
2. Dally, W.J., Towles, B.: Route packets, not wires: on-chip interconnection networks. In: Proceedings of the Design Automation Conference, pp. 684–689 (2001)
3. Bjerregaard, T., Mahadevan, S.: A survey of research and practices of network-on-chip. ACM Comput. Surv. 38(1) (June 2006)
4. Marculescu, R., Ogras, U.Y., Peh, L.-S., Jerger, N.E., Hoskote, Y.: Outstanding research problems in noc design: System, microarchitecture, and circuit perspectives. IEEE Transactions on Computer-Aided Design of Integrated Circuits and Systems 28(1), 3–21 (2009)
5. Hu, J., Marculescu, R.: Dyad - smart routing for networks-on-chip. In: 41st Proceedings of the Design Automation Conference, pp. 260–263 (2004)
6. Duato, J., Yalamanchili, S., Ni, L.M.: Interconnection networks - an engineering approach. IEEE (1997)
7. Glass, C.J., Ni, L.M.: Fault-tolerant wormhole routing in meshes. In: The Twenty-Third International Symposium on Fault-Tolerant Computing, FTCS-23, Digest of Papers 1993, pp. 240–249 (1993)
8. Glass, C.J., Ni, L.M.: The turn model for adaptive routing. In: Proceedings of the 19th Annual International Symposium on Computer Architecture, pp. 278–287 (1992)
9. Ali, M., Welzl, M., Zwicknagl, M., Hellebrand, S.: Considerations for fault-tolerant network on chips. In: The 17th International Conference on Microelectronics, ICM 2005, p. 5 (2005)
10. Boppana, R.V., Chalasani, S.: Fault-tolerant wormhole routing algorithms for mesh networks. IEEE Transactions on Computers 44(7), 848–864 (1995)
11. Flich, J., Duato, J.: Logic-based distributed routing for nocs. Computer Architecture Letters 7(1), 13–16 (2008)
12. Jain, L., Al-Hashimi, B., Gaur, M.S., Laxmi, V., Narayanan, A.: Nirgam: A systemc based cycle accurate noc simulator (2010), http://www.nirgam.ecs.soton.ac.uk/
13. Nirgam, http://wiki.mnit.ac.in/mediawiki/index.php/Nirgam/

Architectural Level Sub-threshold Leakage Power Estimation of SRAM Arrays with its Peripherals

Nupur Navlakha, Lokesh Garg, Dharmendar Boolchandani, and Vineet Sahula

Malaviya National Institute of Technology,
Department of Electronics and Communication Engineering,Jaipur-302017
{nupurnavlakha,dbool6}@gmail.com,
lokesh_garg20@yahoo.co.in, sahula@ieee.org

Abstract. In this work, an analytical model for estimation of width scalable architectural level leakage current of the 6T Static Random Access Memory (SRAM), considering its peripherals is proposed in 45nm technology. Based on the mode of operation of SRAM (read, write and idle phase), the width dependent leakage current is estimated at an early stage which reduces design time and aid to power management. Finally, a SRAM structure (i.e. rows and columns) dependent model has been evaluated. Referring circuit simulator (HSPICE) as golden result, the proposed model shows a high accuracy with error margin less than 5%. The results are 143,127 and 330 times faster than that achieved by HSPICE simulation in idle, read and write phase respectively.

1   Introduction

A major portion of the processor design includes caches, block memories, predictors, state tables and other forms of on-chip memory. SRAM applications are wide in microelectronics, ranging from consumer wireless to high performance server processors, multimedia and System on Chip (SoC) applications. According to the International Technology Roadmap for Semiconductors (ITRS), it is projected that the percentage of embedded SRAM in SoC products will increase further from the current 84% to as high as 94% by the year 2014.Hence, its increasing demand requires its analysis at an early stage. Also, this is vital for enhancing various aspects of chip design and manufacturing.

Earlier, size reduction and better performance were the main concern for the design of ICs. With the reduction in the transistors size, along with the advances in portable computing and wireless communication, power dissipation is becoming more significant. Current trends show that static power dissipation is growing at a faster rate than dynamic power dissipation. It consumes about 30-50% of the total IC power consumption.

Leakage power is primarily the result of unwanted sub-threshold current in the transistor channel in its OFF state. In this paper, we have concentrated on sub-threshold leakage current.

M.S. Gaur et al. (Eds.): VDAT 2013, CCIS 382, pp. 312–321, 2013.

The sub-threshold current is given by equation (1):

$$I_{SUB-THRESHOLD} = k \times (W/L) \, e^{\frac{V_{GS}-V_{TH}}{nV_t}} (1 - e^{V_{ds}/V_t})$$ (1)

Here k and n are technology parameters, V_t is the temperature voltage, V_{th} is the threshold voltage, V_{gs} is the gate-source voltage and V_{ds} is the drain-source voltage. The equation shows that the leakage current is dependent on width. After estimating the leakage current, we can evaluate the static power using equation (2)

$$P_{STATIC} = V_{DD} \times I_{LEAKAGE} \cdot$$ (2)

The early estimation is useful for power management i.e., the power performance can be evaluated prior to the actual design of architecture. Moreover, end users can optimize their software as per the requirements. Thus, it is beneficial for design strategy.

Here, analytical models to estimate the leakage current as a function of width has been proposed. The derived equations depend on the structure (number of rows and columns) of SRAM. Also the evaluation is based on the mode of operation (read, write and idle phase).

2   Related Work

Since long time, static power estimation has been an area of research. Primarily, gate level estimation was the focus but now, estimation at higher level is given more attention. Butts and Sohi [2] proposed a generic model at micro-architectural level, whose design was based on a key design parameter, k_{design}. It captured device types, geometries and stacking factors based on the simulations. Zhang et al. [8] develop an architectural model for sub-threshold and gate leakage that captured temperature, voltage, gate leakage, and parameter variations. Mamidipaka et al. developed analytical models for subthreshold leakage estimation in memory arrays without spice simulation [10].They also estimated width dependent leakage current models [1]. A methodology for estimation of leakage power for micro-architectural components in interconnection networks was proposed by Chen et al. [3]. The results were based on the simulation of basic circuit components for varying input combination. Zhang et al. proposed a model for leakage power of SRAM considering temperature, supply voltage and bias voltage [9].

3   Proposed Work

In [1], width dependent leakage current of the SRAM was estimated in the form,

$$I_{LEAKAGE} = P \times W_{TRANSISTOR} \cdot \text{P is a constant}$$ (3)

In our work, we have used the curve fitting tool of MATLAB, to obtain the linear fitness equation for leakage current as a function of width. The equation, thus obtained is in the form,

$$I_{LEAKAGE} = P1 \times W_{TRANSISTOR} + P2 . \quad \text{P1 and P2 are constants} \quad (4)$$

The additional constant factor (p2) in the equation improvises the result over previous work.

The fitness equation of the leakage current for six different models (NMOS, PMOS and few stacked transistors) have been obtained, then these pre-characterized models are used to evaluate the leakage current for higher models.

In the design, the transistors in series results in lower leakage current than the sum of leakage current of the individual transistors. This is stacking effect which is taken into account by designing models for different combination of inputs. In [1], the stacking factor was estimated by the average of the values calculated using HSPICE whereas, in our work, the linear equations derived by curve fitting of the model is used .Earlier, it was taken as a constant irrespective of the width of the transistor ; therefore our work has an edge over previous obtained results.

Finally, the individual component's leakage current is summed up to obtain an analytical equation for the SRAM. These results have been verified by HSPICE simulations. Also, we have estimated the time required to calculate the leakage current through our work and also through HSPICE.

4   Analytical Models for Estimation of Leakage Current

SRAMs are the read/write memory which can retain its data till a sufficient power supply is provided. SRAM storage array, or core, is made up of simple cell circuits arranged to share connections in horizontal rows and vertical columns. SRAM core consists of memory cells, read column circuit, write column circuit, row and column decoders.

4.1   SRAM Cell

An SRAM cell is the SRAM component storing binary information, as shown in Fig. 1. The 6T memory cell basically uses two cross-coupled inverters forming latch and access transistors. Access transistors are enabled during read and write operation. True and complementary versions of the data are stored on cross-coupled inverters. The memory cell structure has been taken symmetrical (i.e. P1=P2, N1=N2, N3=N4), so the characteristics and geometry are same. Thus, they have the same leakage current. The phases of operation of SRAM are described as follows:

Idle Phase. In the idle phase, all the word lines are deselected and the bit lines are precharged to V_{dd}. The leakage current for bit=0 is same as for bit=1, replacing N3, N1 and P2 by N4, N2 and P1 respectively.

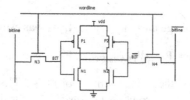

Fig. 1. T Memory Cell Schematic [1]

For single memory cell,

$$I_{IDLE\ 0/1} = I_{LN(N3/N4)} + I_{LP(P2/P1)} + I_{LN(N1/N2)} \cdot \tag{5}$$

$$I_{IDLE\_LEAKAGE} = 2 \times I_{LN} + I_{LP} \cdot \quad (for\ W_{N3}=W_{N1}) \tag{6}$$

For memory core with N_{ROWS} and $N_{COLUMNS}$,

$$I_{IDLE\ CORE\ 0/1} = N_{ROWS} \times N_{COLUMNS} \times (2 \times I_{LN} + I_{LP}) \cdot \quad (for\ W_{N3}=W_{N1}) \tag{7}$$

Read Phase. During Read operation, the bit lines are precharged to V_{dd} and the word line of that particular cell is selected by row decoder. When the word line is enabled, one of the bit lines connected to a "0" node is discharged through an NMOS transistor.
    For single memory cell,

$$I_{READ\ 0/1} = I_{LP(P2/P1)} + I_{LN(N1/N2)} \cdot \tag{8}$$

For memory core with N_{ROWS} and $N_{COLUMNS}$ (one cell will be in read phase and rest in idle mode),

$$I_{READCORE} = (N_{ROWS} - 1) \times N_{COLUMNS} \times I_{IDLE} + N_{COLUMNS} \times I_{READ} \cdot \tag{9}$$

Write Phase. In write phase, the cell selected to write data will have the leakage current as given by equation (11). The other cells that are unselected will have two conditions, either bitline $\neq$ bit or bitline=bit. Therefore, we take 50% probability for both the cases. Thus, the leakage current is given by,
    For single memory cell,

$$I_{WRITE\ CASE1} = I_{LP(P2/P1)} + I_{LN(N1/N2)} \cdot \quad (WL=1\ or\ WL=0;\ BIT=BL) \tag{10}$$

$$I_{WRITE\ CASE2} = I_{LP(P2/P1)} + I_{LN(N1/N2)} + I_{N3} + I_{N4} \cdot \quad (WL=0\ or\ Bit \neq BL) \tag{11}$$

For memory core with N_{ROWS} and $N_{COLUMNS}$ (one cell will be in write phase and rest in idle mode),

$$I_{WRITE\ CORE} = (N_{ROWS} - 1)N_{COLUMNS}(0.5 \times I_{WRITECASE1} + 0.5 \times I_{WRITECASE2}) + N_{COLUMNS} \times I_{WRITECASE1} \cdot \tag{12}$$

4.2   Decoders

For selection of row and column address, row and column decoder have been designed. The address decoders are controlled by an enable signal. For small single block memories, single stage row decoder architecture is efficient else multi-stage architecture is preferable. The above figure shows a 2×4 row decoder. For, higher order decoder this can be used as a basic block. Similarly, the tree based column decoders have been designed. The decoders are designed using dynamic circuits. Dynamic circuits suffer from charge leakage on the dynamic node. If the node is left floating after being precharged then the node will drift with time. Therefore, we use a keeper circuit that holds the output at static level.

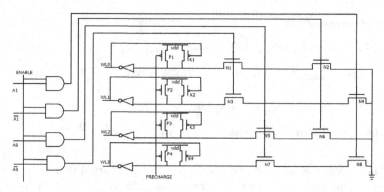

Fig. 2. Architecture of a 2×4 row decoder

The design includes stacked transistors whose leakage current has been evaluated using the models shown in Fig. 3,

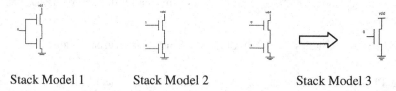

Stack Model 1   Stack Model 2   Stack Model 3

Fig. 3. Stack models to analyze leakage current in different modes of row decoder

The third stack model can be replaced by an NMOS in off state, as it results into same characteristics of leakage current.It maintains the accuracy and also reduces the time needed to characterise this model.

The leakage current differs with the input at enable and address bits.Based on this ,the lekage current for different input modes are summarised below:

$$I_{INV} = I_{PMOS} \qquad\qquad \text{for A0/A1=1} \qquad\qquad (13)$$

$$I_{INV} = I_{NMOS} \qquad\qquad \text{for A0/A1=0} \qquad\qquad (14)$$

$$I_{NAND/STACK} = I_{MODEL1} \qquad \text{for vin1, vin2 =00} \qquad (15)$$

$$I_{NAND/STACK} = I_{MODEL2} \qquad \text{for vin1, vin2 =10} \qquad (16)$$

$$I_{NAND/STACK} = I_{NMOS} \qquad \text{for vin1, vin2 =01} \qquad (17)$$

$$I_{NAND} = 2 \times I_{PMOS} \qquad\quad \text{for vin1, vin2 =11} \qquad (18)$$

$$I_{STACK} = I_{PMOS} + I_{KEEPER\ PMOS} \qquad \text{for vin1, vin2 =11} \qquad (19)$$

Therefore, the leakage current is given by equation (20),

$$I_{ROW\ DECODER} = \sum I_{INV} + \sum I_{NAND} + \sum I_{STACK}. \qquad\qquad (20)$$

4.3   Read Column Circuit

Read column circuit consists of bit line precharge logic, isolation logic, differential sense amplifier, and precharge logic for sense bit lines and buffers driving the data output as shown in figure 4.

In the idle phase, all the signals are deselected and the sense bit lines are at logic high. Therefore, the leakage current is due to the PMOS of buffers at the output and sense enable transistor. A model as shown above in fig 5 has been designed to analyze the leakage current due to sense enable transistor in idle state.

$$I_{\text{READ COLUMN IDLE}} = I_{\text{LN(READ COL-MODEL)}} + I_{\text{LP(OBUF1)}} + I_{\text{LP(OBUF2)}} . \tag{21}$$

During the read phase, the sense enable transistor is on, precharge logic is off and isolation logic is on for small period of time so that the bit line voltages are sampled by sense amplifier. Initially, both the bit lines are at high logic and then one discharges gradually according to the data that has to be read.

$$I_{\text{READ COLUMN READ}} = 2 \times I_{\text{LP-SPRE}} + I_{\text{LN(DSA)}} + I_{\text{LP(OBUF1)}} + I_{\text{LN(OBUF2)}} + I_{\text{LP(DSA)}} . \tag{22}$$

During write operation, all the signals in read column circuit are deactive. Bitline and Bitline_bar have complementary values but sense bit lines are at logic '1'.Therefore, the leakage current is given by:

$$I_{\text{READ COLUMN WRITE}} = 2 \times I_{\text{LP-PRE}} + I_{\text{LN(READCOL-MODEL)}} + I_{\text{LP(OBUF2)}} + I_{\text{LP(OBUF1)}} + I_{\text{LP(ISO)}} . \tag{23}$$

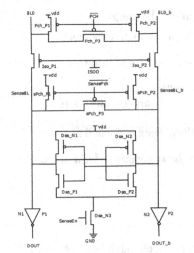

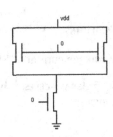

Fig. 5. Model used in read column circuit in the idle phase

Fig. 4. Schematic of Read Column Circuit.Pch denotes the bit line precharge logic, Iso the column isolation logic, SensePch the sense amplifier precharge logic, Dsa the Differential sense amplifier and SenseEn the enable signal. [1]

4.4   Write Column Circuit

The basic functionality of this circuit is to quickly discharge one of the bit lines from the precharge level to logic '0'.The circuit is enabled by write signal. For estimating the leakage current for write circuit, a model has to be designed with the stacked transistor including transistor N1, N3, N4 and write-enable as shown in figure 7.

In read and idle phase, the write enable signal is off. The bit lines are precharged to V_{dd} in these phases .The leakage current contribution is from the buffers and due to the model that has been characterized priory.

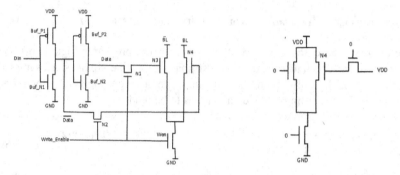

Fig. 6. Schematic of a Write Column Circuit [1]   **Fig. 7.** Model to analyze leakage current of write column in idle/read phase

$$I_{\text{WRITE COLUMN}\frac{\text{READ}}{\text{IDLE}}} = I_{\text{MODEL}} + I_{\text{LP(BUF1)}} + I_{\text{LN(BUF2)}}. \qquad (24)$$

In write phase, the write enable signal is on therefore, the main contributors of leakage current are the buffers.

$$I_{\text{WRITE COLUMN WRITE}} = I_{\text{LP(BUF1)}} + I_{\text{LN(BUF2)}}. \qquad (25)$$

The leakage current contribution by write column circuit in core memory is,

$$I_{\text{WRITE COLUMN READ/IDLE CORE}} = N_{\text{COLUMNS}} \times I_{\text{WRITECOLUMN-READ/IDLE}}. \qquad (26)$$

$$I_{\text{WRITE COLUMN-WRITE CORE}} = (N_{\text{COLUMNS}} - 1) \times I_{\text{WRITE COLUMN IDLE}} + I_{\text{WRITE COLUMN WRITE}}. \qquad (27)$$

Thus, the leakage current of SRAM structure have been estimated as:

$$I_{\text{LEAKAGE}} = I_{\text{SRAM-CELLS}} + I_{\text{WRITE COLUMNS}} + I_{\text{READ COLUMN}} + I_{\text{ROW DECODER}} + I_{\text{COLUMN DECODER}}. \qquad (28)$$

5   Results

At first, the curve fitting linear equations for the models have been obtained in the form, $I = p1 \times W + p2$ Where I is the leakage current, W width of the transistor, p1 and p2 are the coefficients with following values and with 95% confidence level:

Table 1. Coefficients of the linear equations with RMSE and correlation coefficient for different models

Model	P1	P2	Correlation Coefficient	RMSE
NMOS	0.1027	-1.032e-09	1	3.713e-12
PMOS	0.0687	-6.907e-10	1	3.015e-12
Read column Model	0.03677	2.8e-10	0.9901	3.258e-10
Write column Model	0.006145	-1.182e-10	0.9998	7.963e-12
Stack Model 1	0.002496	-2.394e-11	1	7.744e-14
Stack Model 2	0.03795	-3.794e-10	1	1.892e-12

Based on the above pre-characterized models the analytical equations for leakage current showing width dependency have been obtained. These values have been plotted to show the comparison of the previous results [1] and the golden results with our work.

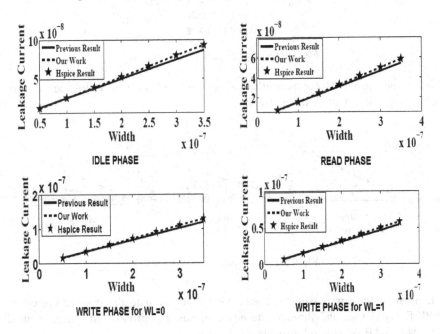

Fig. 8. Leakage current of SRAM cell in different phases

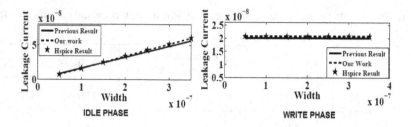

Fig. 9. Leakage current of write column

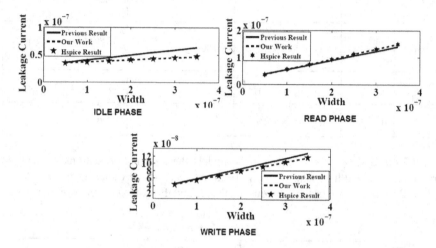

Fig. 10. Leakage current of read column

After the individual component's leakage current has been estimated we have analyzed the SRAM structure of size 4×1:

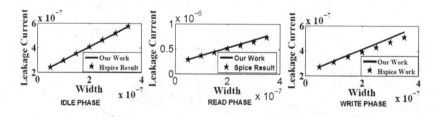

Fig. 11. Leakage current of 4×1 SRAM

Evaluating the time taken by a 4×1 SRAM to estimate the leakage current by HSPICE simulation and through the equation based approach (analytical method) using MATLAB we obtain following results:

Table 2. Comparison of estimated time for evaluating leakage current

Mode of Operation	Time taken by Hspice Simulator	Time taken by the proposed model	Improvement in speed by our model over HSPICE result
Idle Phase	1.062057 Sec	7.387 msec	143 times
Read Phase	0.706034 Sec	5.537 msec	127 times
Write Phase	1.455412 Sec	4.412 msec	330 times

6   Conclusion

In our work, we have estimated the width dependent leakage current of SRAM core at an early stage. We have proposed an analytical model of SRAM based on its mode of operation and structure .The proposed model have been compared with the design mentioned in [1] and the actual results (HSPICE simulation) .Our work shows higher accuracy than previous work with an error margin less than 5%.The timing analysis shows that our results obtained are many folds faster than the golden results.

References

1. Mamidipaka, M., et al.: Leakage Power Estimation in SRAMs. CECS Technical report, TR 03-32, UC Irvine (October 2003)
2. Butts, J.A., Sohi, G.S.: A static power model for architects. In: International Symposium on Microarchitecture, pp. 191–201 (2000)
3. Chen, X., Peh, L.: Leakage power modeling and optimization in interconnection networks. In: International Symposium on Low Power Electronics and Design (2003)
4. Jiang, W., Tiwari, V., Iglesia, E., Sinha, A.: Topological analysis for leakage prediction of digital circuits. In: VLSI Design 2002, pp. 39–44 (2002)
5. Mamidipaka, M., Khouri, K., Dutt, N., Abadir, M.: Idap: A tool for high level power estimation of custom array structures. In: International Conference on Computer Aided Design (2003)
6. SIA. International technology roadmap for semiconductors. Technical report, http://public.itrs.net/
7. Weste, N., Eshragian, K.: Principles of CMOS VLSI Design, A Systems Perspective. Addison-Wesley Publishing Company, Reading (1998)
8. Zhang, Y., Parikh, D., Sankaranarayanan, K., Skadron, K., Stan, M.: Hotleakage: A temperature-aware model of subthreshold and gate leakage for architects. Technical Report CS-2003-05, Univ. of Virginia (March 2003)
9. Zhang, F., Luo, R., Liu, Y., Wang, H., Yang, H.: Leakage Power Modeling Method for SRAM Considering Temperature, Supply Voltage and Bias Voltage. In: Proceedings of ICSICT 2006, Shanghai, China, October 23-26, pp. 1180–1182 (2006)
10. Mamidipaka, M., et al.: Analytical Models for Leakage Power Estimation of Memory Array Structures CODES+ ISSS 2004, September 8-10 (2004)

On Designing Testable Reversible Circuits Using Gate Duplication

Joyati Mondal[1], Debesh Kumar Das[1], Dipak Kumar Kole[2],
Hafizur Rahaman[3], and Bhargab B. Bhattacharya[4]

[1] Jadavpur University
{joyatimondal14,debeshkdas}@gmail.com
[2] St. Thomas' College of Engg. & Tech.
dipak.kole@gmail.com
[3] Bengal Engineering and Science University
rahaman_h@yahoo.co.in
[4] Indian Statistical Institute
bhargab.bhatta@gmail.com

Abstract. Design of reversible logic circuits has received considerable attention in recent times for their potential use in implementing quantum computers. In this paper, it is shown that in an $(n \times n)$ reversible circuit implemented with k-CNOT gates, addition of only two extra inputs along with at most 5 k-CNOT gates per gate can yield an easily testable design. The modified design admits a universal test set of size $(n + 2)$ that detects all SMGFs, PMGFs, and detectable RGFs in the circuit.

Keywords: Quantum computing, reversible logic, testable design.

1 Introduction

Management of energy loss has been an inherent problem in digital logic circuits, especially because of exponential growth in the number of transistors in integrated circuits [5]. According to Landauer's principle, irreversibility of information processing causes energy loss [1]. Reversible circuits, being information lossless, are likely to consume less energy. Also, with the advent quantum computing, synthesis of reversible circuits has drawn considerable attention in recent times [7-9].

Understanding of fault model and errors in a reversible circuit is an important concern from the viewpoint of dependability. Several fault models for these circuits were introduced in [2,6], namely Single Missing Gate Faults (SMGF), Partial Missing Gate Faults (PMGF), and Repeated Gate faults (RGF). In this paper, we propose a design-for-testability (DFT) technique to detect these faults. We make an $(n \times n)$ reversible circuit implemented with k-CNOT gates easily testable by adding only two extra input lines and some extra gates so that so that all such faults are detected by a universal test set of size $(n + 2)$. Our DFT scheme offers a significant reduction in quantum cost compared to an earlier work [4].

M.S. Gaur et al. (Eds.): VDAT 2013, CCIS 382, pp. 322–329, 2013.

2 Preliminaries

2.1 Reversible Gates

The basic CNOT type reversible gates used for synthesis are the following:
(i) (1×1)NOT$(x_1 \rightarrow x_1')$
(ii) (2×2) controlled NOT (CNOT) gate :$(x_1, x_2) \rightarrow (x_1, x_1 \oplus x_2)$
(iii) (3×3) Toffoli gate $(x_1, x_2, x_3) \rightarrow (x_1, x_2, x_1 x_2 \oplus x_3)$.
A generalized Toffoli gate has a set of control input C, a target input set T, and has
the form $TOF(C;T)$, where $C = (x_{i_1}, x_{i_2}, ..., x_{i_k})$ $T = \{x_j\}$ and $C \cap T = \phi$. It maps an
input vector $(x_1^0, x_2^0, ..., x_n^0)$ to $(x_1^0, x_2^0, ..., x_{j-1}^0, x_j^0 \oplus (x_{i_1}^0 . x_{i_2}^0 ..... x_{i_k}^0), x_{j+1}^0, ..., x_n^0)$.
This is called a k-CNOT gate and the line x_j is known as the target line. Thus, a NOT
gate is $TOF(x_j)$, a generalized Toffoli gate which has no control. The CNOT gate
$TOF(x_i, x_j)$, also known as Feynman gate is a generalized Toffoli gate with one control bit; The simple (3×3) Toffoli gate is a generalized Toffoli gate with two controls.
Any reversible function can be realized as a cascade of k-CNOT gates. Fig. 1 shows the
standard graphics symbol for some common CNOT based reversible gates.

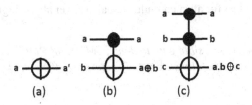

Fig. 1. Different types of CNOT based reversible gates: (a) NOT gate (b) CNOT gate (c) Toffoli
gate

2.2 Quantum Cost Analysis

The quantum cost of a gate G is the number of elementary quantum operations required
to realize the function given by G. Table I shows the required quantum cost $Q_c(n)$ in
the realization of Toffoli gate with n controls.

Table 1. Quantum cost of Toffoli gate with n controls

controls(n)	0	1	2	3	4	5	6	7	8
Quantum Cost$(Q_c(n))$	1	1	5	13	29	61	125	253	509

2.3 Reversible Logic

A reversible function has equal number of inputs and outputs, and simply induces a
permutation on the set of input vectors to produce an output vector. Further, in a circuit
implementation with reversible gates, no fanout is allowed.

2.4   Modeling of Faults and Their Detection

Several fault models for k-CNOT based reversible circuits were introduced earlier [6] as described below.

A *single missing gate fault* (SMGF) describes the removal of one k-CNOT gate from the circuit. Fig. 2(b) shows an SMGF for the circuit shown in Fig. 2(a). In the example of Fig. 2(b), if we apply (1,0,1,1) at the input of the circuit, the normal output in Fig. 2(a) would be (1,1,0,1), whereas in the presence of SMGF fault marked by the dotted box, the output in Fig. 2(b) will be (1,0,1,1).

The *repeated-gate fault* (RGF) model assumes that a gate in a circuit is repeated, i.e it shows up several times. Fig. 2(c) shows an an RGF fault.

The *multiple missing-gate fault* (MMGF) model assumes that several consecutive gates are missing. Fig. 2(d) shows an MMGF.

A partial missing-gate fault (PMGF) corresponds to removing m of the k control inputs of a k-CNOT gate, thus transforming it into a $(k - m)$-CNOT gate. The number m is called the order of the PMGF. Fig. 2(e) shows an PMGF with a box marking the position of the missing control. All k first-order PGMFs of a gate have detection conditions that conflict with each other and with the SMGF at the same gate; $k + 1$ test vectors are required to test for all such faults that also cover all the higher-order PMGFs at the same gate.

Lemma 1. *In an $(n \times n)$ reversible gate to detect SMGF, all PMGFs and all detectable RGFs involving this gate, the following set of vectors is sufficient.*

$$T = \begin{pmatrix} x_1 & x_2 & \cdots & x_n \\ 0 & 1 & \cdots & 1 \\ 1 & 0 & \cdots & 1 \\ \vdots & \vdots & \ddots & \vdots \\ 1 & 1 & \cdots & 0 \end{pmatrix}$$

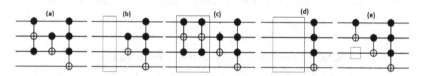

Fig. 2. (a) Fault-free circuit, (b) the same circuit with SMGF, (c) an RGF, (d) an MMGF, (e) a PMGF

3   Proposed Testable Design

Our goal is to design a DFT with a universal test set. The next result follows from Lemma 1.

Lemma 2. *A universal test set for detecting all SMGFs and all PMGFs in a general $(n \times n)$ reversible circuit, must include at least n test vectors.*

In our DFT design, we are using two additional input lines C_1 and C_2. For each gate G, some additional gates are introduced to maintain the same test set T to be applied to the next gate of G. We may skip the insertion of additional circuitry when G is the last gate in the original circuit. There may be three cases when G is not the last gate.

Case 1: The number of control lines (l)=0

G is duplicated in the same way as in [4]

Example 1: Consider the gate G_2 in Fig. 4. In its DFT design in Fig. 5, G_2 has been duplicated with an additional control on line C_1.

Case 2: $l \neq 0$ and $Con(G) \leq \lfloor n/2 \rfloor$, where n is the size of the original circuit.

For any gate G $(TOF(C,T))$ of Fig. 3(a) with control in the original circuit we are inserting a set of 4 k-CNOT gates $TOF(T,C_2)$ as G_1, $TOF(T,C_2)$ as G_2, $TOF(C_1,C_2,T)$ as G_3 and $TOF(C,C_2)$ as G_4, as shown in Fig. 3(b).

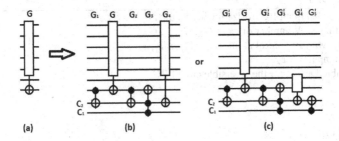

Fig. 3. Testing of gate G in the proposed DFT design

Example 2: G_3 and G_4 of Fig. 4 are the examples of such case. The set of additional 4 gates for these gates is shown in Fig. 5.

Case 3: $l \neq 0$ and $Con(G) > \lfloor n/2 \rfloor$.

For any gate G $(TOF(C,T))$ of Fig. 3(a) with control in the original circuit we are inserting a set of 5 k-CNOT gates $TOF(T,C_2)$ as G'_1, $TOF(T,C'_2)$ as G_2, $TOF(C_1,C_2,T)$ as G'_3, $TOF(n-C,C_2)$ as G'_4, and $TOF(C_1,C_2)$ as G'_5 as shown in Fig. 3(c).

Example 3: G_1 of Fig. 4 is the examples of case 3. The set of additional 5 gates for this gate is shown in Fig. 5.

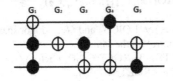

Fig. 4. A reversible circuit

This procedure is well described in the algorithm DFT that adopts 3 approaches in dealing with addition of extra circuitry to undo the change made by a gate so that the same universal test set can appear as input to every gate.

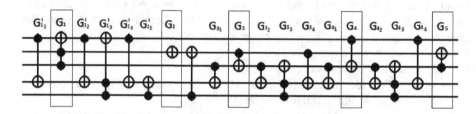

Fig. 5. Testable design for the reversible circuit of Fig. 4

Algorithm 1. DFT

Input: A reversible circuit RC of size n with depth N
consisting of N number of gates $G_1, G_2, ..., G_N$.
Gate G_i with its control at lines $x_{i_1}, x_{i_2}, ..., x_{i_l}$
gets an input $x_1, x_2, ..., x_n$.

Output: Testable Design for the reversible circuit RC

1: Introduce 2 control lines C_1, C_2.
2: **for** i=1 to N-1
    2.1. **if** ($Con(G_i) = 0$)
        {Con(G_i) is the number of control lines of gate G_i.}
        2.1.1. duplicate G_i with an additional
            control on C_1
    2.2. **if** ($Con(G_i) \neq 0$)
        2.2.1.**if** $(Con(G_i) \leq \lfloor n/2 \rfloor)$
            2.2.1.1. **if**$(Con(G_{i-1}) \neq 1$ OR G_i and G_{i-1} donot share
                target and control on the same line)
                2.2.1.1.1.Insert TOF(TARGET(G_i),C_2) before G_i
            2.2.1.2. Insert TOF(TARGET(G_i),C_2),
                TOF(C_1, C_2,TARGET(G_i))
                after G_i.
            2.2.1.3. **if**$(Con(G_i) \neq 1$ OR G_i and G_{i+1} donot share
                control and target on the same line
                ,$G_{i+1} \leq N - 1$)
                2.2.1.3.1.Insert TOF($x_{i_1}, x_{i_2}, ..., x_{i_l}, C_2$)
        2.2.2.**if**$(Con(G_i) > \lfloor n/2 \rfloor)$
            2.2.2.1.**if**$(Con(G_{i-1}) \neq 1$ OR G_i and G_{i-1} donot share
                target and control on the same line)
                2.2.2.1.1.Insert TOF(TARGET(G_i),C_2) before G_i
            2.2.2.2. Insert TOF(TARGET(G_i),C_2),
                TOF(C_1, C_2,TARGET(G_i)) and
                TOF($n - Con(G_i)$,C_2)
                after G_i.
3: **END**

Lemma 3. *Insertion of G_1, G_2, G_3, and G_4 for a gate G causes the same pattern to appear at the input of G and output of G_4 when $C_1=1$, $C_2=0$.*

Proof. m = input to target of G

$\quad G_1$ produces at $C_2 : m \oplus C_2 = m \oplus 0 = m$

$\quad G_2$ produces at $C_2 : m \oplus M$

$\quad$ where $M = m'$, when target flips the bit

$\quad\quad\quad\quad = m$, when target does not flip the bit

$\quad G_3$ produces at target line : $M \oplus C_1.C_2 = M \oplus 1.C_2 = M \oplus m \oplus M = m$

$\quad$ Thus in the Target line the output is restored the input value after G_3

$\quad G_4$ produces at $C_2 : C_2 \oplus x_{i_1}.x_{i_1}.....x_{i_l} = m \oplus M \oplus x_{i_1}.x_{i_1}.....x_{i_l}$ (1)

$M = m'$, $x_{i_1}.x_{i_1}.....x_{i_l}=1$

$\quad = m$, when $x_{i_1}.x_{i_1}.....x_{i_l}=0$

Thus at line C_2, we get either

$m \oplus m' \oplus 1$ or $m \oplus m \oplus 0$

In either case the value is 0

C_2 is restored to its original value after G_4.

In line C_1, there is no target thus the value is always retained.

Therefore it is possible to restore the same test pattern at the output level.

Lemma 4. *Insertion of G'_1, G'_2, G'_3, G'_4, and G'_5 for a gate G causes the same pattern to appear at the input of G and output of G_5 when $C_1=1$, $C_2=0$.*

Proof. m = input to target of G

Since the G'_1, G'_2 and G'_3 is same as G_1, G_2 and G_3 their output is also same.

$\quad G'_4$ produces at $C_2 : C_2 \oplus x_{i_1}.x_{i_1}.....x_{i_l} = m \oplus M \oplus x_{i_1}.x_{i_1}.....x_{i_l}$ (1)

$M = m'$, $x_{i_1}.x_{i_1}.....x_{i_l}=0$

$\quad = m$, when $x_{i_1}.x_{i_1}.....x_{i_l}=1$

Thus at line C_2, we get either

$m \oplus m' \oplus 0$ or $m \oplus m \oplus 1$ ....(2)

G'_5 produces at $C_2 : C_2 \oplus C_1 = C_2 \oplus 1 = m \oplus m' \oplus 0 \oplus 1$ or $m \oplus m \oplus 1 \oplus 1$ $\quad =0$

In either case the value is 0

C_2 is restored to its original value after G_4.

In line C_1, there is no target thus the value is always retained.

Therefore it is possible to restore the same test pattern at the output level.

Theorem 1. *The modified circuit derived by the proposed DFT method admits the following universal test set of length $(n + 2)$.*

$$S_U = \begin{pmatrix} x_1 & x_2 & \cdots & x_n & C_1 & C_2 \\ 0 & 1 & \cdots & 1 & 1 & 0 \\ 1 & 0 & \cdots & 1 & 1 & 0 \\ \vdots & \vdots & \ddots & \vdots & \vdots & \vdots \\ 1 & 1 & \cdots & 0 & 1 & 0 \\ 0 & 0 & \cdots & 0 & 0 & 1 \\ 0 & 0 & \cdots & 0 & 0 & 0 \end{pmatrix}$$

Proof. Notice that S_U includes T of Lemma 1 at the inputs $x_1, x_2, ..., x_n$. So the same test set T is always applied to each gate in the original circuit. Thus in the DFT design, the gates of the original circuit are becoming testable.

Now we look into the testing of the additional gates. G_1 and G_2 or G'_1 and G'_2 are 1-CNOT gates with control either at one of the input lines $x_1, x_2, ..., x_n$. G_4 or G'_4 is a k-CNOT gate with control on any improper subset of $x_1, x_2, ..., x_n$. Thus G_4 or G'_4 gets the test set T at its control lines, hence it is tested. The first n vectors of S_U provides test case for these 3 gates. For G_3 or G'_3 , we require (C_1, C_2) as (1,0) (1,1) and (0,1). There exist at least one test vector among the first n vectors in S_U, when the target of gate G is [not]flipped, In this case control line C_2 of gate G_3 (or G'_3) becomes [0]1, thus G_3 (or G'_3) gets (1,1)[(1,0)] at (C_1, C_2). The first two conditions are always achieved by the first n vectors in S_U, (1,1) is created on (C_1, C_2) by vectors which inputs 1 in all controls and (0,1) is developed by vectors which donot input 1 to all controls for a given gate, and The value (1,0) in (C_2, C_1) is achieved by the second last vectors in S_U. Test to detect fault in G'_5 is also present in S_U. Hence, all faults in the original as well as additional circuits are also detected.

Sometimes the second last vector in S_U becomes unable to produce (1,0) at (C_2, C_1) of G_3 or G'_3, in such case the work is done by the last vector in S_U. This situation arises due to the presence of 0 on C_1, as a result the additional gates fails to undo the changes made by the NOT gate. NOT gate produces 1 in the vector which causes other gates to act on the vector. Hence (0,0,......,0,1) fails to produce (0,1) at (C_2, C_1) of G_3 or G'_3. In such situation the work is done by the vector (0,0,...,0).

4 Experimental Result

We have synthesized several reversible benchmark circuits, the results of which are shown in Table 2. Columns 2 and 3 denote the circuit name, input size, and the gate

Table 2. Comparative results on quantum cost

Circuit	size	depth	% increment in Q.C	
			DFT[4]	Our design
5mod5d1	6	17	227.56%	100.54%
4_49d1	4	16	274.59%	274.46%
mod5adderd2	6	15	232.53%	161.45%
nth_prime6_inc	6	55	222.44%	95.95%
rd53d1	7	28	216.81%	107.75%
rd53d2	7	12	230.33%	130%
rd53d4	7	20	228.205%	135.899%
ham15d1	15	132	232.64%	150.55%
cycle10_2d1	12	19	204.75%	68.36%
hwb6d1	6	126	224.73%	103.34%
hwb7d1	7	289	216.29%	87.5%
hwb7d3	7	236	218.28%	98.99%
hwb7d4	7	331	237.69%	147.53%
hwb5d1	5	56	252.72%	203.83%

count respectively. The quantum cost of DFT design as designed by an earlier DFT method [4] and that by the proposed technique are shown in columns 4 and 5 respectively. For the circuits with a small number of 1-CNOT gates, our overhead is much less than that in [4]. In addition, the proposed universal test set detects all SMGF, all PMGFs, and all detectable RGF for all the gates in the circuit including those in the additional circuit in contrast to the earlier method [4] where the first order PMGF in the extra gate may remain undetectable. Further, in the earlier work [4], a replica of every gate was needed in order to make the circuit easily testable, and thus, the overhead had a uniform pattern. In contrast, in the proposed method, the quantum cost of the each additional gate depends on the number of control inputs of the original gate; thus, the overhead strongly depends on the circuit structure.

5   Conclusion

We have proposed a novel DFT technique for a reversible circuit to make it testable with a universal test set of length $(n + 2)$. Our design offers significantly reduced quantum cost for most of the benchmark circuits compared to earlier approaches [4].

Acknowledgement. The work was partly supported by CSIR grant (ref.-22(0590)/12/EMR II) and UGC MRP grant (ref.-41/620/2012(SR)).

References

[1] Landauer, R.: Irreversibility and heat generation in the computing process. IBM Research and Development 5, 183–191 (1961)

[2] Polian, I., Hayes, J.P., Fienn, T., Becker, B.: A family of logical faults models for reverrsible circuits. In: Proc. of the Asian Test Symp., Kolkata, India, pp. 422–427 (2005)

[3] Maslov, D.: Reversible Logic Synthesis. Ph.D Thesis, The University of New Brunswick, Canada (September 2003)

[4] Rahaman, H., Kole, D., Das, D.K., Bhattacharya, B.B.: On the detection of missing gate fault in reversible circuit by a universal test set. In: Proc. of the VLSI Design, pp. 163–168 (2008)

[5] Moore, G.E.: Cramming more components onto integrated circuits. Electronics Magazine, 114–117 (April 19, 1965)

[6] Polian, I., Hayes, J.P.: Advanced modeling of faults in reversible. In: Proc. of the East-West Design & Test Symposium, pp. 376–381 (2010)

[7] Soeken, M., Wille, R., Hilken, C., Przigoda, N., Drechsler, R.: Synthesis of reversible circuits with minimal lines for large functions. In: Proc. of the ASP-DAC, pp. 85–92 (2012)

[8] Duttagupta, S., Pathak, G.J.: Design and synthesis of reversible Logic. In: Proc. of the International Conference on VLSI Design (2013)

[9] Datta, K., Rathi, G., Sengupta, I., Rahaman, H.: Synthesis of reversible circuits using heuristic search method. In: Proc. of the International Conference on VLSI Design, pp. 328–333 (2012)

Circuit Transient Analysis
Using State Space Equations

Kai Chi Alex Lam and Mark Zwolinski

School of Electronics and Computer Science
University of Southampton
Southampton, UK SO17 1BJ
{kcal1g10,mz}@ecs.soton.ac.uk

Abstract. The method to rearrange the classic transient analysis circuit simulation algorithm is presented in this paper. The steps of transforming circuit equations into state variable equations are illustrated. Explicit fourth order Runge Kutta method written in C is selected to solve the transformed equations in order to break the time dependencies, and hence to permit parallel transient analysis. Results of implementing the new algorithm on non-linear example circuits are reported. This approach can obtain significant speedup as compared to the simulation on the same circuit using tradition method. The proposed ideas of extracting parallelism are also discussed.

Keywords: Circuit simulation, SPICE, Parallel Computing.

1 Introduction

Circuit simulation is an essential tool for predicting the behaviour of integrated circuits. As transistors decrease in size with each generation of CMOS technology, their variability is increasing, so there is a need to characterize digital systems at the circuit level. Conventional algorithms for transient analysis such as those used in SPICE, have many features that are inherently sequential and have proven very difficult to parallelize. With the speed of conventional processors limited to less than 4GHz, it is essential that parallel algorithms are found. A number of attempts to accelerate circuit simulation algorithms in some of the new computing architectures such as GPGPUs [1–3] , Multi-core CPUs or clusters [4–6] were published recently. However, they are based on the traditional methods as described in [7, 8]. Although the device evaluation phase can be naturally executed in parallel, matrix solution can not. Also there is barrier between these two phases. According to Amdahl's law [9], the barrier is the bottleneck for further speedup of the algorithm. A state space approach is therefore proposed to solve the circuit simulation parellization problem.

This paper first demonstrates the process of converting an MNA equation to an SV equation in section 2. Section 3 describes solving non-linear circuit blocks using the new method. Section 4 gives results of simulation of selected circuits and section 5 discusses the possibility of parallelizing transient analysis using the SV method. Section 6 has the conclusions.

M.S. Gaur et al. (Eds.): VDAT 2013, CCIS 382, pp. 330–336, 2013.

2   Converting from MNA to State Variable Form

State Variable analysis (SV) is a concise way to describe the behaviour of circuits, but SV formulation is non-trivial compared with MNA, and this has limited the use of SV in circuit simulation. Nevertheless, a method of transforming MNA to SV [10] addressed this problem. SV is formed by eliminating excess voltage and current variables in MNA. Hence, only capacitor voltages and inductor currents are preserved. Here, an example of MNA formulation and SV formulation shows the idea before and after conversion by the method described in [10]. The following process has been implemented in MATLAB. For a simple RLC circuit, MNA gives $Ax = B$:

$$A \begin{pmatrix} v_L^{n+1} \\ v_R^{n+1} \\ v_C^{n+1} \\ i_1^{n+1} \\ i_L^{n+1} \end{pmatrix} = B \tag{1}$$

where A is a matrix of conductances, B is a vector of sum of currents through nodes and values of the independent sources at current step n which n is the number of calculated time steps. $v_L^{n+1}, v_R^{n+1}, v_C^{n+1}$ are the voltages across elements at the next time step and i_1^{n+1}, i_L^{n+1} are values of the currents of the supply and inductor at the next time step. In the SV form, the circuit equation is written in the general form:

$$\frac{dx}{dt} = f(t, x(t), u(t)) \tag{2}$$

u is the vector of input sources and state variables stored in vector x. All variables are time dependent. t is time. To transform equation (1) to equation (2), rewrite equation (1) as:

$$\begin{pmatrix} A_d & A_{s1} \\ 0 & A_{s2} \end{pmatrix} \begin{pmatrix} X_1^{n+1} \\ X_2^{n+1} \end{pmatrix} = \begin{pmatrix} B_1 \\ B_2 \end{pmatrix} \tag{3}$$

in which A_s is a sub-matrix containing conductances of only static elements and A_d is a sub-matrix of conductances of other elements – dynamic and static. The minimum number of state variables, r_o, is the number of rows of sub-matrix A_d, A_{s1}, X_1 and B_1. X_1 is the vector of state variables. R is the number of rows and columns of the whole matrix, therefore, $R - r_o$ is the number of internal nodes which are not part of the state variables, and called excess variables, represented by vector X_2. Furthermore, A_d is with the size $r_0 * r_o$ where X_2 and B_2 are vectors with size $r_0 * 1$. The matrix is reordered by converting A_{s2} to $(A_{21} \quad I)$ and I is the unity matrix with size $(R - r_o) * (R - r_o)$:

$$\begin{pmatrix} A_d & A_{12} \\ A_{21} & I \end{pmatrix} \begin{pmatrix} X_1^{n+1} \\ X_2^{n+1} \end{pmatrix} = \begin{pmatrix} B_1 \\ B_2 \end{pmatrix} \tag{4}$$

The transformation is summarized in Algorithm 1. Excess variables, need to be eliminated as well using (5).

Create A and B matrix;

Count number of dynamic elements;

for *counter* $= 1; j \leq no.of dynamic element; counter + +$ **do**

> Move the rows with dynamic elements to the top rows of A and B;
> Move the columns in matrix A with dynamic elements to the left-most columns;

end

while A_{22} *is not the end of the matrix and not a diagonal matrix* **do**

> For the first cell with value '1' in each col, pivot the whole row of the '1' to make the diagonal filled with '1';

end

while A_{22} *is not the end of the matrix and not a identity matrix* **do**

> Divide non-zero value in the diagonal by itself to obtain '1'. For non-zero values outside the diagonal, subtract them by the multiple of other row to make it 'zero';

end

Algorithm 1. MNA to SV conversion

$$A_{sv} = A_{11} - A_{12} \times A_{21}$$
$$B_{sv} = B_1 - A_{12} \times B_2 \tag{5}$$

The equation without excess variables becomes

$$A_{sv} \begin{pmatrix} i_L^{n+1} \\ v_C^{n+1} \end{pmatrix} = B_{sv} \tag{6}$$

The excess variables are evaluated from:

$$X_2^{n+1} = B_2 - A_{21} X_1. \tag{7}$$

Using a simple RC circuit as example, in MNA, after time discretization ($t^{n+1} - t^n = dt$), the left-hand side and the B matrix are:

$$Ax = \begin{pmatrix} \frac{1}{R} & -\frac{1}{R} & 1 \\ -\frac{1}{R} & \frac{1}{R} + \frac{C}{dt} & 0 \\ 1 & 0 & 0 \end{pmatrix} \times \begin{pmatrix} v_1^{n+1} \\ v_c^{n+1} \\ i_{v_1}^{n+1} \end{pmatrix}, B = \begin{pmatrix} 0 \\ \frac{Cv_c^n}{dt} \\ v_{in}^n \end{pmatrix} \tag{8}$$

Transformed it becomes:

$$\left(\frac{1}{R} + \frac{C}{dt} \right) \left(v_c^{n+1} \right) = C \times \frac{v_c^n}{dt} + \frac{v_{in}^n}{R} \tag{9}$$

The equations are still written in a form like (6). In order to solve it using the Runge Kutta method, the equation should be rearranged into normal form as (2):

$$\left(\frac{1}{R} + \frac{C}{dt} \right) \left(v_c^n + dv_c \right) = C \times \frac{v_c^n}{dt} + \frac{v_{in}^n}{R} \tag{10}$$

Rearranging gives:

$$\frac{dv_c}{dt} = \left(\frac{v_{in}^n - v_c^{n+1}}{RC} \right) \tag{11}$$

The form in (11) can be solved by the Runge Kutta or similar method.

3   Solving Circuits with Reduced SV Equations

The proposed method can be applied to circuits with non-linear elements such as MOSFETs. After formulating the circuit matrix by the MNA method, apply algorithm 1 to produce a reduced matrix. Then, it must be rearranged to the set of explicit ordinary differential equations that is ready for the RK4 integration method to evaluate. However, the derivation of the A_{sv} matrix is lengthy, for instance, the entry $A_{sv}(1,1)$ with the sum of conductance for the fulladder circuit shown in Fig.1 is $(G_{dsp1}+G_{dsn4}+G_{dsp2}+G_{dsn5}-(G_{dsp2}*(G_{dsp2}+G_{gsp2})\ldots$ For the sake of simplicity, let $A_{sv}(1,1)$ be written as G_1 , the sum of conductances, $G_2 = A_{sv}(1,2)$ and so on. For B_{sv}, let i_1 be the sum of currents relating to the first state variable, etc. Hence, $A_{sv}X_1 = B_{sv}$ is shown as:

$$\begin{pmatrix} G_1 + \frac{C_1}{dt} & G_2 \\ G_3 & G_4 + \frac{C_2}{dt} \end{pmatrix} \begin{pmatrix} v_1^{n+1} \\ v_2^{n+1} \end{pmatrix} = \begin{pmatrix} \frac{C_1}{dt} v_1^n + i_1 \\ \frac{C_2}{dt} v_2^n + i_2 \end{pmatrix} \tag{12}$$

The sizes of A_{sv} and B_{sv} depend on the number of dynamic elements attached to the network. There must be at least one dynamic element in the circuit when using the approach. For N elements in the circuit, A_{sv} and B_{sv} are $N \times N$ and $N \times 1$. The matrix is then transformed to state variable form $\frac{dv_1}{dt} = f(v_1,t)$, $\frac{dv_2}{dt} = f(v_2,t)$. The first equation is written as

$$\left(G_1 + \frac{C_1}{dt} \right) v_1^{n+1} + G_2 v_2^{n+1} = \frac{C_1}{dt} \times v_1^n + i_1 \tag{13}$$

Rearranging gives

$$G_1 v_1^{n+1} + \left(\frac{C_1}{dt} \right) \left(v_1^n + dv_1 \right) + G_2 v2^{n+1} = \frac{C_1}{dt} v_1^n + i_1 \tag{14}$$

The final form of the ODE for v_1 is

$$\frac{dv_1}{dt} = \frac{i_1 - G_1 v_1^{n+1} - G_2 v_2^{n+1}}{C_1} \tag{15}$$

The second equation can be written in the same way to become

$$\frac{dv_2}{dt} = \frac{i_2 - G_3 v_1^{n+1} - G_4 v_2^{n+1}}{C_2} \tag{16}$$

From equations (15) and (16), it can be concluded that for the circuit equations with M capacitors and hence M state variables, the matrix can be written as $\frac{dv_1}{dt} = f(v_1,t)$, $\frac{dv_2}{dt} = f(v_2,t)\ldots\frac{dv_M}{dt} = f(v_M,t)$. The final form of the set of ODE equations representing the non-linear circuit appears as:

$$\begin{aligned} \frac{dv_1}{dt} &= \frac{i_1 - G_1(v_1^{n+1}) - G_2(v_2^{n+1})\cdots - G_M(v_M^{n+1})}{C_1} \\ \frac{dv_2}{dt} &= \frac{i_2 - G_{M+1}(v_1^{n+1}) - G_{M+2}(v_2^{n+1})\cdots - G_{M+M}(v_M^{n+1})}{C_2} \\ &\vdots \\ \frac{dv_M}{dt} &= \frac{i_M - G_{(M-1)\times M+1}(v_1^{n+1})\cdots - G_{(M-1)\times M+M}(v_M^{n+1})}{C_M} \end{aligned} \tag{17}$$

where n again is the number of time steps. These equations can be solved by the Runge-Kutta method with Newton Raphson iteration.

4 Results

The algorithm is feasible for circuits with dynamic and linear components. The
results of simulation are demonstrated by CMOS inverter, NAND gate and full
adder circuit in Fig. 1. Waveforms generated from the state variable method by C
were compared with the output of NgSPICE which uses traditional algorithm.
The resultant waveforms of fulladder, inverter and NAND Gate are shown in
Figs. 2, 3 and 4 respectively. The differences between the NgSPICE output,
which is in a dotted line and the C implementation of new SV method, which
appears as a solid line, are shown. These waveforms indicate that our result is

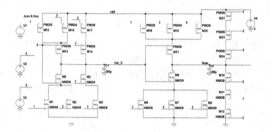

Fig. 1. Fulladder circuit

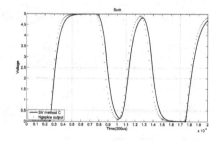

Fig. 2. Comparison between SV approach in C code of output fulladder(solid line) and
Ngspice(dotted line)

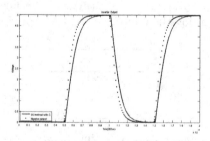

Fig. 3. Comparison between SV approach in C code of output of CMOS inverter

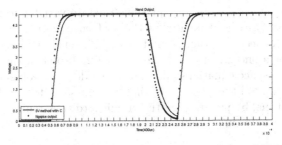

Fig. 4. Comparison between SV approach in C code of output of CMOS NAND Gate

Table 1. Transient runtime comparsion between ngspice and SV method

	Ngspice	SV method in C	Speedup
Inverter(2 transistors and 1 capacitor)	18.20ms	0.18ms	101.11x
NAND GATE(4 transistors and 1 capacitor)	22.40ms	0.25ms	89.60x
Fulladder(24 transistors and 2 capacitors)	100.5ms	5.43ms	18.51x

partially consistence with commercial software but some parts of waveforms lag by 0-6 microseconds. Table 1 lists the comparison of elapsed time of state variable approach in C with Ngspice for each circuit. Surprisingly, the approach can save computation power significantly in very small circuit, such effect,however, is diminished as the circuit becomes larger. Tests are performed on the desktop computer with Intel Xeon W3520 CPU in 2.67GHz and 12GB DRAM. The operating system is Windows 7 Enterprise SP 1.

5   Future Work

In the next stage of this research, the idea of independent time steps and partitioning of the circuit, [11–13], will be introduced. Circuits can be broken down into many subcircuits; each subcircuit acts as a macromodel and can be solved independently. Another approach is to treat each macro-model as a grid and solve it in a similar way to calculating the 2-D heat equation [14]. The explicit Runge Kutta method is generally not stable enough for typical circuit equations. There are more stable numerical integration methods, such as Burlisch-Stoer.

6   Conclusion

There are limitations to massively parallelizing the traditional circuit simulation algorithm and generally, only the device evaluation phase can be easily parallelized. In contrast, matrix solution phase still needs to be done serially. Therefore, we have proposed a new approach that converts MNA equations to SV form and solves the equations by the Runge-Kutta method instead of standard integration methods. An MNA to SV transformer has been developed in

MATLAB. For solving the circuit equations in state variable form, the Runge-Kutta method has been implemented on the SV form equations. The results show the SV approach speeds up the calculation significantly. Although the problem is still solved for a one-dimensional time marching problem, the successful formulation of state space equations allows us to model the problem in a 2-D way, enabling us to explore the hypothesis that we can solve the problem with less dependency on time, by partitioning the circuit into subcircuits and considering them as states to solve independently.

References

1. Gulati, K., Croix, J., Khatri, S., Shastry, R.: Fast circuit simulation on graphics processing units. In: Asia and South Pacific Design Automation Conference, ASP-DAC 2009, pp. 403–408 (January 2009)
2. Poore, R.: Gpu-accelerated time-domain circuit simulation. In: Custom Integrated Circuits Conference, CICC 2009, pp. 629–632. IEEE (September 2009)
3. Bayoumi, A.M., Hanafy, Y.Y.: Massive parallelization of SPICE device model evaluation on GPU-based SIMD architectures. In: Proceedings of the 1st International Forum on Next-Generation Multicore/Manycore Technologies, IFMT 2008, pp. 12:1–12:5. ACM (2008)
4. Perng, R., Weng, T., Li, K.: On performance enhancement of circuit simulation using multithreaded techniques. In: International Conference on Computational Science and Engineering, CSE 2009, vol. 1, pp. 158–165. IEEE (2009)
5. Peng, H., Cheng, C.: Parallel transistor level full-chip circuit simulation. In: Design, Automation & Test in Europe Conference & Exhibition, DATE 2009, pp. 304–307. IEEE (2009)
6. Andjelković, B., Litovski, V., Zerbe, V.: Grid-enabled parallel simulation based on parallel equation formulation. ETRI Journal 32(4) (2010)
7. Nagel, L.W.: SPICE2: A Computer Program to Simulate Semiconductor Circuits. PhD thesis, EECS Department, University of California, Berkeley (1975)
8. Litovski, V., Zwolinski, M.: VLSI circuit simulation and optimization. Springer (1996)
9. Hill, M., Marty, M.: Amdahl's law in the multicore era. Computer 41(7), 33–38 (2008)
10. Kang, Y., Lacy, J.: Conversion of MNA equations to state variable form for nonlinear dynamical circuits. Electronics Letters 28(13), 1240–1241 (1992)
11. Zwolinski, M.: Multi-threaded circuit simulation using openmp. In: LASCAS 2010: IEEE Latin American Symposium on Circuits and Systems (February 2010)
12. Honkala, M., Roos, J., Valtonen, M.: New multilevel newton-raphson method for parallel circuit simulation. In: Proceedings of European Conference on Circuit Theory and Design, vol. 1, pp. 113–116 (2001)
13. Rabbat, N., Sangiovanni-Vincentelli, A., Hsieh, H.: A multilevel newton algorithm with macromodeling and latency for the analysis of large-scale nonlinear circuits in the time domain. IEEE Transactions on Circuits and Systems 26(9), 733–741 (1979)
14. Horak, V., Gruber, P.: Parallel numerical solution of 2-d heat equation. Parallel Numerics 5, 47–56 (2005)

3D CORDIC Algorithm Based Cartesian to Spherical Coordinate Converter

Anita Jain[1] and Kavita Khare[2]

Dept. of Electronics and Communication Engineering, MANIT, Bhopal, India
anitajainone@gmail.com, kavita_khare1@yahoo.co.in

Abstract. The standard Cartesian coordinate set is suitable for most of 3D applications but when dealing with spheres or spherical symmetry, it is easier to use Spherical coordinates. This paper presents a new hardware efficient scaling free 3D CORDIC algorithm based Cartesian to spherical coordinates Converter. Two different architectures i.e. Fully Pipelined and Hybrid Recursive Pipelined are proposed for implementation of above Converter on FPGA. Synthesis is carried out on Xilinx ISE 9.2i, Virtex-5 device. Synthesis results show that the two architectures successfully convert Cartesian coordinates to spherical with maximum operating frequency of 95.786 MHz and 42.29 MHz respectively. The minimum Bit error Position is 12 and region of convergence is entire 3D coordinate space.

1   Introduction

Global positioning system (GPS) consists of three-dimensional Cartesian coordinate system and an associated ellipsoid. It uses World Geodetic System WGS84 as datum in which positions can be described as XYZ Cartesian coordinates or latitude, longitude and ellipsoid height spherical coordinates. To make GPS complementary to geographic information system (GIS), data-focused integration of the two technologies is required. For transfer of data from GPS [1-2] and to conduct spatial analysis directly in the field, Cartesian coordinates are to be converted to spherical counter parts. The Multiple input multiple output (MIMO) systems as in [3] and adaptive beam former in antenna array also require the same conversion.

Overall efficiency of systems that employ conversion definitely depends on the process of conversion. Faster, accurate and area efficient conversion is the demand of all practical applications. CORDIC algorithm has already proven its efficacy in various fields of digital signal processing [4] and 2D coordinate conversions [5]. Here in this paper the conversion through CORDIC has been extended from 2D to 3D.

CORDIC stands for COordinate Rotation in Digital Computer and is a simple hardware efficient algorithm for the implementation of various trigonometric functions. In this paper Cartesian to Spherical Coordinate Converter based on novel 3D CORDIC algorithm is proposed. It covers entire 3D space as its Region of Convergence (RoC). RoC is indicator of maximum angle of rotation which can be realized using finite number of iterations. The proposed design is able to convert any Cartesian coordinate in 3D space to its spherical counterpart.

M.S. Gaur et al. (Eds.): VDAT 2013, CCIS 382, pp. 337–344, 2013.

Two types of architecture i.e. Fully Pipelined and Hybrid Recursive pipelined architecture are proposed for hardware implementation of the Converter. Both architectures are compared for their performance in terms of speed and area. Mathematical verification and error analysis is also carried out for both the designs.

This paper is structured as follows: Section 2 explains the overview of CORDIC algorithm; Section 3 details the steps of proposed scaling free 3D CORDIC algorithm; two different architectures are suggested in Section 4; Section 5 details the FPGA Implementation and results with Section 6 summarizing the conclusions; references are listed in Section 7.

2   CORDIC Algorithm Overview

CORDIC Algorithm is based on Givens rotation of vectors in 2D space using simple shift and add operations. CORDIC Algorithm can operate in two modes namely: rotation and vectoring. In rotation mode, the objective is to rotate a vector through a given angle using series of iteration and to reduce the residual angle to zero after each iteration. Sine and Cosine of given angle can be computed using these iterative rotations.

In vectoring mode, the magnitude and the phase of given vector is computed by rotating a vector iteratively with the aim to align it with x axis. The trajectory of rotation for both the modes can be linear, circular or hyperbolic depending upon the requirement.

2.1   Conventional CORDIC Algorithm

The conventional CORDIC algorithm [6] is derived from general equation of vector rotation. If a vector V with components (Xi, Yi) is iteratively rotated through an angle αi, a new vector V' with components (Xi+1, Yi+1) is formed.

In matrix form, the value of vector after this micro rotation can be represented as:

$$\begin{bmatrix} X_{i+1} \\ Y_{i+1} \end{bmatrix} = K_i \cdot \begin{bmatrix} 1 & -d_i \cdot \tan \alpha_i \\ d_i \cdot \tan \alpha_i & 1 \end{bmatrix} \cdot \begin{bmatrix} X_i \\ Y_i \end{bmatrix}. \tag{1}$$

where $K_i = \cos \alpha_i$ and $\alpha_i = tan^{-1}(2^{-i})$

The sign sequence $d_i \in \{1,-1\}$ is so selected that:

$$\theta = \sum_{i=0}^{w-1} d_i \cdot \alpha_i \tag{2}$$

Where, 'w' is the word-length in bits.

Note that the range of convergence of this algorithm is limited to [-99.99°, 99.99°], which can be extended to entire coordinate space using the properties of sine and cosine functions, using an extra iteration for full-range rotation. The overall scaling-factor of above CORDIC iterations is given by (3).

$$K = \prod_{i=0}^{w-1} K_i = \prod_{i=0}^{w-1} 1/\sqrt{1 + 2^{-2i}} \qquad (3)$$

2.2   Unified CORDIC Algorithm

Walther [7] has extended the scope of conventional CORDIC algorithm to include linear and hyperbolic trajectory along with circular trajectory. Due to this extension, the application and usefulness of CORDIC is broadened since computing of various other functions such as exponential and logarithmic becomes possible. A variable (m) for defining the trajectory was introduced to modify the basic CORDIC rotation matrix and elementary angle 'α_i' as:

$$\begin{bmatrix} X_{i+1} \\ Y_{i+1} \end{bmatrix} = K_i \cdot \begin{bmatrix} 1 & -m \cdot d_i \cdot 2^{-i} \\ d_i \cdot 2^{-i} & 1 \end{bmatrix} \cdot \begin{bmatrix} X_i \\ Y_i \end{bmatrix}$$

where, $K_i = \dfrac{1}{\sqrt{1 + m \cdot 2^{-2i}}}$ and $\alpha_i = \dfrac{1}{\sqrt{m}} tan^{-1}(\sqrt{m} \cdot 2^{-i})$

where $m = \begin{cases} 1 & \text{circular} \\ 0 & \text{linear} \\ -1 & \text{hyperbolic} \end{cases}$

2.3   The Three Dimensional CORDIC Algorithm

The CORDIC algorithm is extended to three dimensional coordinate space by [8-9]. A vector in three dimensional space has Cartesian coordinates (X_i, Y_i, Z_i) and spherical coordinates (R_i, θ_i, Φ_i). The vector can be rotated by an angle α_i around the z axis and by an angle β_i away from the z axis to become a new vector which has coordinates (X_{i+1}, Y_{i+1}, Z_{i+1}) and spherical coordinates (R_i, $\theta_i + \alpha_i$, $\Phi_i + \beta_i$).

$$X_i = R_i \cos \theta_i \sin \Phi_i$$

$$Y_i = R_i \sin \theta_i \sin \Phi_i$$

$$Z_i = R_i \cos \Phi_i \qquad (4)$$

The relationship between the coordinates of original and rotated vector is given by:

$$X_{i+1} = R_i \cos(\theta_i + \alpha_i)\sin(\Phi_i + \beta_i)$$
$$Y_{i+1} = R_i \sin(\theta_i + \alpha_i)\sin(\Phi_i + \beta_i)$$
$$Z_{i+1} = R_i \cos(\Phi_i + \beta_i)$$

To complete the set of iteration equation, the variables U_i, V_i, W_i are introduced which are defined as:

$$U_i = R_i \cos\theta_i \cos\Phi_i$$
$$V_i = R_i \sin\theta_i \cos\Phi_i$$
$$W_i = R_i \sin\Phi_i$$

In matrix form these equations can be represented as follows:

$$\begin{bmatrix} U_{i+1} \\ V_{i+1} \end{bmatrix} = \frac{1}{K_i^2} \cdot \left\{ \begin{bmatrix} 1 & -d_i \cdot 2^{-i} \\ d_i \cdot 2^{-i} & 1 \end{bmatrix} \cdot \begin{bmatrix} U_i \\ V_i \end{bmatrix} - m_i 2^{-i} \begin{bmatrix} 1 & -d_i \cdot 2^{-i} \\ d_i \cdot 2^{-i} & 1 \end{bmatrix} \cdot \begin{bmatrix} X_i \\ Y_i \end{bmatrix} \right\}$$

Similarly

$$\begin{bmatrix} X_{i+1} \\ Y_{i+1} \end{bmatrix} = \frac{1}{K_i^2} \cdot \left\{ \begin{bmatrix} 1 & -d_i \cdot 2^{-i} \\ d_i \cdot 2^{-i} & 1 \end{bmatrix} \cdot \begin{bmatrix} X_i \\ Y_i \end{bmatrix} + m_i 2^{-i} \begin{bmatrix} 1 & -d_i \cdot 2^{-i} \\ d_i \cdot 2^{-i} & 1 \end{bmatrix} \cdot \begin{bmatrix} U_i \\ V_i \end{bmatrix} \right\}$$

Also

$$W_{i+1} = \frac{1}{K_i}(W_i + Z_i m_i \cdot 2^{-i})$$

$$Z_{i+1} = \frac{1}{K_i}(Z_i - W_i m_i \cdot 2^{-i})$$

From the above equation it is clear that four 2D CORDIC rotations are required for a 3D rotation of a vector. Also the scale factor for Z_{i+1} and W_{i+1} is different from that of U_{i+1}, V_{i+1} and Y_{i+1}. They need to be compensated via pre-scaling of inputs or post scaling of outputs with their respective constants K and K^2 whose values are given by:

$$K = \prod_{i=0}^{w-1} K_i$$

$$K^2 = \prod_{i=0}^{w-1} K_i^2$$

3   Proposed Cartesian to Spherical Coordinate Converter

The proposed Cartesian to Spherical Coordinate Converter is based on scaling free 3D CORDIC algorithm. Third order approximation of Taylor series as in [10] is used to derive the CORDIC equation.

The Taylor series expansion of sine and cosine of an angle is:

$$\sin\alpha_i = 2^{-i} - (3!)^{-1} 2^{-3i} + (5!)^{-1} 2^{-5i} + \cdots$$
$$\cos\alpha_i = 1 - (2!)^{-1} 2^{2i} + (4!)^{-1} 2^{-4i} + \cdots$$

But, this approximation imposes a restriction on the allowed values of iterations i as:

$$i = \lfloor(w - 6.906)/5\rfloor$$

For 16 bit word length, the initial value of i required for maintaining the accuracy of the calculations comes out to be 2. It divides the coordinate space into eight equal sectors, each of 45 degrees. The RoC becomes 0 to $\pi/4$ which is extended through quadrant mapping to entire coordinate space.

CORDIC equation for the above approximation reduces to:

$$X_{i+1} = X_i - (X_i \gg 2i + 1) - (Y_i \gg 1) + (Y_i \gg 3i + 3)$$
$$Y_{i+1} = Y_i - (Y_i \gg 2i + 1) + (X_i \gg 1) - (X_i \gg 3i + 3)$$

For Cartesian to spherical conversion, CORDIC is to be operated in vectoring mode. X, Y and Z are given as input and r, θ and Φ are computed as per the conversion equations:

$$R_i = \sqrt{X_i^2 + Y_i^2 + Z_i^2}$$
$$\theta_i = tan^{-1}\{\frac{Y_i}{X_i}\}$$
$$\Phi_i = tan^{-1}\{Z_i/\sqrt{(X_i^2 + Y_i^2)}\}$$

The Pseudo code for the proposed Converter is:

Input: X, Y, Z
Output: r, θ, Φ

Begin
Step 1: Identify and map the sector and quadrant of the input of the vector.
Step 2: Initialize i = 2; v = word length w;
Step 3: Rotate the vector and compute its next iterative value.
Step 4: If MSB of Yi = 1; r_{temp1} = 0; i = i+1;
     Else r_{temp1} = 1;
         i = i+1; go to step 3,
Step 5: Repeat until (i <= word length)
Step 6: Store value of r_{temp1} as θ, and repeat step 1 to 5 with X_{temp1} and Z.
Step 7: Out X_{temp2} as r, r_{temp1} as θ and r_{temp2} as Φ.
Step 8: Restart with new data in pipeline.
End

Scaling factor generated using this algorithm is 1 and hence does not require any pre or post processing circuitry for scaling factor correction which otherwise becomes very complex for 3D space. At present CORDIC based Converter in 3D is not available hence this provides a hardware efficient solution for 3D conversions.

4   Architectures for Proposed Cartesian to Spherical Coordinate Converter

Two types of architecture are proposed for the Converter namely, Fully pipelined architecture (FPA) and hybrid recursive pipelined architecture (HRPA). In FPA two stages of CORDIC pipeline are used where outputs from one stage are fed to the next stage to compute final value, whereas in HRPA, single CORDIC pipeline is used in which one of the output is fed back to the input. Intermediate results are stored in temporary registers till computing in pipeline gets over. Sequence of operation is controlled by 'Enable' signal generated by a counter. The block diagrams for these architectures are as shown in Fig.1 and Fig. 2.

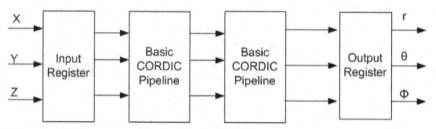

Fig. 1. Fully Pipelined Architecture for Cartesian to Spherical Coordinate Converter

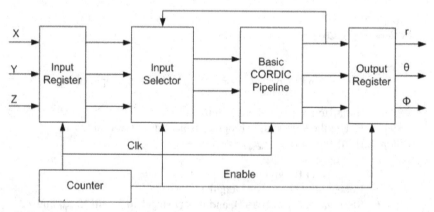

Fig. 2. Hybrid Recursive Pipelined architecture for Cartesian to Spherical Coordinate Converter

Input and output registers used in above design are single bit flip flop which hold the value as per the clock signal. Input selector is a combinational logic circuit which allows a particular set of input to pass through it depending upon the value of 'Enable'. When Enable is 0, it sends X and Y to basic CORDIC pipeline for processing whereas when it is 1, it sends Z and one of the intermediate output of CORDIC pipeline recursively for processing.

Enable signal also acts as a control so that output data from output register is available after every two clock cycle. Basic CORDIC pipeline is responsible for the rotation of the vector in single direction and computes its new value after each iteration using simple shift and add operation as per the CORDIC equation.

5   FPGA Implementation and Results

Functional simulation and Hardware implementation of the proposed Converter for FPA and HRPA is carried out in Xilinx ISE9.2i on Virtex-5 pro device using Verilog. Summary of hardware used is given in Table 1.

Table 1. Hardware Summary for 16 Bits Wordlength Implementation

Parameter	Fully Pipeline Architecture	Recursive Architecture
Flipflops	959	462
LUTs	2939	1482
IOB	101	66
BUFG	1	1
Maximum Freq	95.786 MHz	42.28 MHz

It is evident from the results that hardware utilization of recursive architecture HRPA is less as compared to the fully pipelined FPA. But the Maximum operation frequency of FPA is better than HRPA. The output data rate is one set of data for each clock cycle for FPA whereas it is one set of data for two clock cycle for HRPA.

Error analysis of the results revealed that for 16 bit word length minimum Bit Error Position (BEP) is 12 for both the architectures. This implies that out of 16 bits minimum 12 bits are error free which is sufficient for all practical purposes as per [11]. The BEP for spherical angles θ and Φ are plotted in Fig. 3.

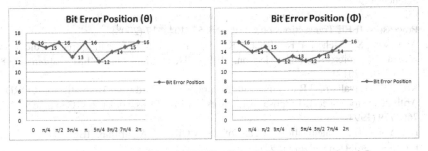

Fig. 3. Bit Error Position (BEP) for Spherical Coordinates θ and Φ

Quantization and finite wordlength are the major source of error in computation as explained in [1].

6   Conclusion

This paper has presented a new Cartesian to spherical coordinate Converter based on scaling free 3D CORDIC. Results have proved its efficacy and accuracy in hardware implementation. There is a tradeoff between hardware requirement and speed of two architectures. FPA can be employed in the applications which demand speed at the expense of area, but where restriction of chip area is applicable HRPA can be used. Both these architectures have a great capability of converting any Cartesian coordinate into spherical because of its RoC being complete 3D coordinate space.

References

1. Li, Y., Mumford, P., Rizos, C.: A real-time GPS/INS integrated system (2008)
2. Li, Y., Mumford, P., Wang, J., Rizos, C.: A low-cost field re-configurable real-time GPS/INS integrated system – design and implementation. In: International Global Navigation Satellite Systems Society IGNSS Symposium (2007)
3. Khan, Z., Arslan, T., Thompson, J.S., Erdogan, A.T.: Analysis and implementation of multiple-input, multiple-output VBLAST receiver from area and power efficiency perspective. IEEE Trans. Very Large Scale Integr. 14(11), 1281–1286 (2006)
4. Meher, P.K., Walls, J., Juang, T.-B., Sridharan, K., Maharatna, K.: 50 years of cordic: Algorithms and architectures and applications. IEEE Transactions on Circuits and Systems I 56, 1893–1907 (2009)
5. Lee, S.-W., Kwonand, K.-S., Park, I.-C.: Pipelined Cartesian-to-Polar Coordinate Conversion Based on SRT Division. IEEE Trans. on Circuits and Systems 54(8) (2007)
6. Volder, J.E.: The CORDIC Trigonometric Computing Technique. IRE Trans. Electronic Computing EC-8, 330–334 (1959)
7. Walther, J.S:: A unified algorithm for elementary functions. In: Spring Joint Computer Conf., pp. 379–385 (1971)
8. Clarke, C., Nudd, G.: Three Dimensional CORDIC with reduced iterations. Technical report, University of Warwick, Coventry, United Kingdom, Department of Computer Science (1994)
9. Elisardo Antelo, J.V., Zapata, E.L.: Low-Latency Pipelined 2D and 3D CORDIC Processors. IEEE Transactions on Computers 57, 404–417 (2008)
10. Aggarwal, S., Meher, P.K., Khare, K.: Area-time efficient scaling-free cordic using generalized micro-rotation selection. IEEE Transactions on VLSI Systems 20(8), 1542–1546 (2012)
11. Kota, K., Cavallaro, J.R.: Numerical Accuracy and Hardware Tradeoffs for CORDIC Arithmetic for Special-Purpose Processors. IEEE Transactions on Computers 42(7), 769–779 (1993)
12. Hu, Y.H.: The Quantization Effects of the CORDIC Algorithm. IEEE Trans. Signal Processing 40(4), 834–844 (1992)

Level-Accurate Peak Activity Estimation in Combinational Circuit Using BILP

Jaynarayan T. Tudu[1], Deepak Malani[2], and Virendra Singh[2]

[1] Computer Science and Automation, Indian Institute of Science, Bangalore
jayttudu@csa.iisc.ernet.in
[2] Electrical Engineering, Indian Institute of Technology, Bombay
malani@ieee.org, viren@computer.org

Abstract. Due to shrinking size of transistor and increasing circuit complexity the instantaneous power became a concern for circuit reliability. Higher IR-drop/Ground bounce induces unpredictable delay and can cause soft error. Higher V_{dd} can cause thermal hot-spot. Appropriate selection of V_{dd} and design of power distribution network(PDN) plays crucial role in alleviating such issues. The design of an efficient PDN entirely depend on the knowledge of power budget and dynamic behaviour of instantaneous activity.

In this work we have proposed an efficient and level-accurate instantaneous peak activity estimation method. The proposed work uses binary integer linear programming technique(BILP). The methodology perform to estimate the peak activity and generate corresponding input vector pair. The experimental results on ISCAS-85 circuit reveals that the level based approach is 10 to 50 time faster than approach based on total-circuit-ILP formulation. The estimated peak activity is 4 to 9 time improved than previous approach.

Keywords: Peak power estimation, Combinational circuits, Integer Linear Programming.

1 Introduction

In todays System-on-chip (SoC) designs, the amount of logic per unit area is very high. Coupled with fast clock rates, the switching power has been on the rise. High power dissipation in certain areas of a chip leads to formation of thermal hot-spots and also impact the reliability of the chip. Besides, high current demand during switching stresses local power grid. This effect is addressed during the design of power delivery network (PDN). Decoupling capacitors are inserted to account for surge demand in current. This solution prevents supply voltage droop from falling below permissible limits, to avoid delay faults.

All these factors mentioned above, need proper estimation of average and peak power demand in a chip. Power grid design can be effective with local observability, especially during peak switching activity. However, the estimation practices are either probabilistic (considering average activity factor) or insufficient (simulation based). This is accounted for by keeping excessive margins

M.S. Gaur et al. (Eds.): VDAT 2013, CCIS 382, pp. 345–352, 2013.

over real power numbers. Probabilistic activity factor ignores local surges and observability, and simulation based estimation is limited due to long-simulation times and input vector combinations. Recently, more exact methods have been proposed to generate worst-case switching scenarios [1] [2] [3].

The method we have proposed here is vector-based approach that considers level-accurate toggling activity in a combination circuit. Our method generates exact pair of input vectors that can result in maximum toggling, at any level of a given circuit.

The rest of the paper is organized as follows. Section 2 gives an overview of previous approaches in power estimation. In Section 3 level-accurate power estimation methodology is elaborated. Section 4 presents a back ground idea on the formulation of BILP problem. We have presented the detail formulation of level based BILP, called Level-BILP problem, in Section 5. In Section 6 the experimental data on ISCAS-85 benchmark circuits and analysis of results is presented. Finally, the paper is concluded with future work in Section 7.

2   Previous Work

Accuracy and computational efficiency are the two motivations for research on power estimation methodology. Two directions has been explored: *Input vector based simulation* and *Vector less probabilistic method*. The simulation based approach generally look for a suitable input vector pair or a set of pairs to trigger the circuit activity to maximum possible value. This kind of approach is motivated by accuracy of the estimation, however such technique suffer from solving an NP-Complete SAT problem to generate input patterns. On the other hand probabilistic approach perform static analysis of circuit based on toggle probability at each node. Such approach are time efficient since static analysis of circuit is a liner time problem. However the accuracy is more pessimistic, which leads to power expensive design[4].

A vector based approach proposed by S Devadas et al.[5], formulated as *weighted max-satisfiability(SAT)* problem, is one of the early attempts. The circuit was represented as *max-satisfiability(max-SAT)* problem and then was solved using exact and approximation SAT solver. The SAT formulation was modified as weighted SAT problem to consider load capacitance. One difficulty with SAT problem is computation time.

The idea of formulating the problem as *Pseudo-Boolean SAT* is explored recently in [6] [3]. H Mangassarian et al.[6] and Sagahyroon et al. [7] have formulated the problem as Pseudo-SAT problem to estimate worst case power and worst case power-up current. The reported results show that the Pseudo-SAT based technique is efficient when the problem is solved using commercial SAT solver like CPLEX[8]. Motivated by the efficiency of CPLEX solver and trade-off between ILP and Pseudo-SAT [9], we have in our previous work [10] explored an alternative idea of formulating the problem as ILP and solving it using CPLEX–a dedicated ILP solver.

Some what different idea, brought from ATPG(Automatic Test Pattern Generation) technique, is proposed by Chuan- Yu Wang et al. [11] [1] in 1996. Two methodologies were proposed in [11] for determining lower and upper bounds on maximum power dissipation. To calculate the lower bound, the authors have proposed an ATPG based technique; while for upper bound they have proposed a *monte-carlo* based simulation technique. An improved version, based on D-Algorithm, of this technique is proposed in [1]. Genetic Algorithm based approach is examined by Hsiao et al[2].

M Pedram and Q Wu et al. have explored probabilistic based ideas [12][13]. Q Wu et al.[13] have proposed a technique based on limiting distribution of extreme order statistics. The challenge in this approach is to show with higher confidence level that the estimated power is indeed the real power. As stated earlier such kind of techniques are time efficient. However difficulty is there in accuracy. More detailed survey of the earlier techniques are carried out by Farid N. Najm[14] and M Pedram[4].

Keeping accuracy and efficiency in forefront in this work we have proposed a *level-accurate* peak activity estimation methodology. Experimental results show the improvement in accuracy and efficiency.

3   Level-Accurate Power Estimation: Methodology

As it is discussed in Section 2, all the power estimation techniques, particularly the peak power estimation techniques, proposed so far perform estimation of the peak power considering the nodes from entire circuit. Such approach leads to pessimistic results because all the circuit nodes does not switch simultaneously. Even though different delay models, zero delay, unit delay, type-1 variable delay, and type-2 variable delay models[2], are taken in to consideration to capture the spurious activity like glitches and hazards this leads to pessimistic value since the toggles are accounted from entire circuit. Our observation is that, since technology is shrinking towards nano meter geometry it is sufficient to estimate the worst case peak activity in a particular level to capture the information on IR-drop, ground bounce, and associated delays.

The proposed *level-accurate* method is demonstrated in following sections.

3.1   Leveling of the Circuit

The different levels of the circuit is determined by assigning the level number at each net. The assignment of level number is performed on per gate basis. For each gate the level number of output net is determined based on the current levels of input nets by following simple formula.

$$L_{out}^i = Max(L_{in1}^i, L_{in2}^i, ...) + 1 \tag{1}$$

where L_{out}^i is the level number of output net of i_{th} gate, L_{in1}^i is the level number of input net-1 of i_{th} gate.

In figure Fig-1 the leveling of each gates along with output net is shown as Level-1, Level-2, and Level-3. For example, for the circuit in Fig-1 the level number of output nets of gate-1.1(XOR gate) and gate-1.2(NAND gate) is 1, in Fig-1 it is shown as Level-1. This is computed using the formula in Eqn-1 by assigning $L_{in1}^{1.1} = 0$ *and* $L_{in2}^{1.1} = 0$ since they are primary input nets. Hence $L_{out}^{1.1} = 1$. The same formula can be applied progressively to determine rest of the levels.

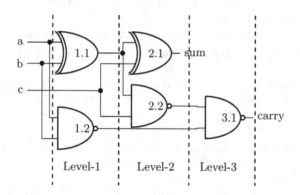

Fig. 1. Group of gates leveled based on the circuit depth

3.2   Power Estimation Methodology

The proposed methodology estimates the maximum instantaneous power by determining the maximum activity among the activity at each levels of the circuit. Mathematically this can be expressed as follows.

$$P_{peak} = Max(A_l) \tag{2}$$

where P_{peak} is the estimated worst peak power and A_l is the maximal activity at l_{th} level of the circuit. Detail is explained in the following section, Section 4.

4   Background on Binary Integer Linear Program

Binary integer linear programing(BILP) is a class of optimization method called linear programing(LP) method. In BILP the variables are constraint to take only 0 or 1 value–a binary digit. The BILP problem is to optimize a given function called *objective function* subject to a given set of constraints. The general form of BILP can be stated as follows:

$$Minimize : f(x), \ Subject \ to : Ax = 0, \ x\epsilon[0,1]$$

In our earlier work[10] we have explored the BILP method to maximize the toggle activity subject to functionality constraints. Summary of the method is presented in Table 1.

Table 1. Summary of BILP as presented in [10]

Function Type	Examples
I/O Constraints	$NOT1 : y = 1 - x_1$
	$NAND2 : y = 1 - x_1 \cdot x_2$
	$NOR2 : y = 1 - (x_1 + x_2) + x_1 \cdot x_2$
	where $y, x_i \varepsilon [0, 1]$
Linearization Constraints	$y = 1 - x_1 \cdot x_2$
	$p = x_1 \cdot x_2$
	$y = 1 - p$
	$s.t. \quad p \le x_1, \quad p \le x_2, \text{ and } \quad x_1 + x_2 - p \le 1$
Toggle Constraints	x_n
	x_{n+1}
	$\overline{x}_n = 1 - x_n$
	$\overline{x}_{n+1} = 1 - x_{n+1}$
	$x_{toggle} = x_n \cdot \overline{x}_{n+1} + \overline{x}_n \cdot x_{n+1}$
Objective Function	$Maximize \sum_{i=1}^{N} x_{toggle}^i$

5   Formulation of Level-BILP

Formulation of BILP for each level is needed to determine the level-max peak activity and the corresponding input vectors in a modified way. For example with respect to Fig-1, to determine the peak activity at Level-1 the toggle variables at out-put net of XOR and NAND gate only has to be included in the objective function. Hence for Level-1 the objective function as given in Table 1 can be rewritten in following way.

$$Maximize \sum_{i=1}^{2} x_{toggle}^{1.i} \tag{3}$$

where $x_{toggle}^{1.1}$ and $x_{toggle}^{1.2}$ are toggle variable corresponding to XOR and NAND gate at Level-1.

Since here the objective is to determine the peak activity at Level-1 the rest of the circuit i.e. Level-2 to Level-3 can be ignored. Therefor the constraint set now will only consider the gates from Level-1.

Similarly when we consider the Level-2 the objective function will optimize the toggle variables corresponding to Level-2. And the constraint set will include the gates from Level-2 back to Level-1. Rest of the gates from Level-3 onwards can be ignored.

Hence from the above demonstration we observed that during the maximization at Level-j(j is the current level at which maximization is being performed) the circuit from Level-[j+1] to Level-L(L is the maximum number of levels) is in don't care state and circuit from Level-1 to Level-j is in active state or care state. Hence the BILP can now be applied only to the part of circuit that is in active state.

Hence the modified objective function can be expressed mathematically as follows.

Formulation of Level-objective Function:

$$Maximize \sum_{j,i} x_{toggle}^{j.i} \tag{4}$$

where j varies from 1 to L where L is the total number of levels and i varies from 1 to n where n is total number of nets in a particular level.

Constraint Set:

All the three constraints, I/O constraints, linearization constraints, and toggle constraints(refer to Section 4), are defined only for that part of the circuit which is currently in active state which mean that gates from Level-1 to Level-j are considered and rest are ignored.

5.1   Computation of Maximum Peak Activity

Now we are all set to compute the maximum peak activity using *level-BILP* formula. The peak power is expressed as Eqn-2. More precisely, the final peak activity is the maximum among the peak activity at each level. Hence by iterative execution of *level-BILP* for every level the level peak activity, A_l in Eqn-2, can be computed. In programing structure this can be written in following way.

for $l = 1$ to L
$$A[l] = Maximize \sum_{l,i} x_{toggle}^{l.i}$$

Now the peak power will be computed using Eqn-2 as $P_{peak} = Max(A[l])$.

6   Evaluation on ISCAS-85 Circuits

To evaluate the accuracy and efficiency of the proposed estimation methodology, we have experimented on ISACS-85 circuits set. We have solved the binary integer linear program(BILP) using CPLEX ILP solver[8]. CPLEX solver is found to be faster for BILP problem[3]. The benchmark circuits are standardised to one-input and two-input gates.

The experimental results are shown in Table 2. Complexity of the circuit is reported in 2nd and 3rd columns,column #PI indicates the number of primary inputs and #Ckt Nets indicates the total number of nets in circuit. The 4th, 5th, and 6th columns reports the activity count. The column #MaxLevelNet indicates the maximum number of nets over the levels, column EstToggle indicates the estimated toggle using proposed method, and columns %Toggle reports the % of estimated toggle activity over #MaxLevel Nets. The last two columns are results from the previous work by the authors [10].

For all the circuits the CPLEX Solver could solve in no more than 546 second which is around 7 time faster than the worst time in [10]. For circuit c499 and c1355 the simulation time is improved. Since in the case of earlier work the ILP problem is formulated for entire circuit which causes around 690 variables and 11K of constraints to be dealt with where as for the level based approach the ILP is formulated for each level and are solved independently in which case only 194 variables and 9K constraints are involved. The estimated toggle activity by proposed method is less than that of the earlier method. For circuits from c432 to c2670 the estimated toggle activity is significantly better.

The c499 and c1355 are both error correction and translation(ECAT) circuits. The % of toggle activity for these circuits are low compared to rest of the circuits because the ECAT circuit consists of xor tree with re-convergent fanout. The % of toggle indicates that i) if it is 100% then the solver has found the solution, ii) if it is less than 100% and solver run time reaches it's time out limit than the solution is approximate, iii)if the solver finishes before time out than the solution reached the maximum achievable toggle activity.

Table 2. Comparison of estimated toggles and simulation time

			Proposed Methodology				[10]	
Ckt	#PIs	#Ckt Nets	#MaxLevel Nets	EstToggle	%Toggle	SimTime in sec.	EstToggle	SimTime in sec.
c01	4	9	4	4	100	0.04	9	0.01
c04	1	4	3	3	100	0.02	4	0.09
c05	3	8	3	3	100	0.03	7	0.05
c11	4	6	4	4	100	0.03	5	0.02
c14	2	4	2	2	100	0.03	3	0.03
c17	5	6	2	2	100	0.04	6	0.02
c432	36	296	27	27	100	9.25	243	8.86
c499	41	626	194	76	39.17	34.45	360	3406.00
c880	60	592	58	58	100	22.34	491	21.55
c1355	41	690	194	76	39.17	44.92	415	3616.48
c1908	33	1291	92	92	100	269.2	832	2371.53
c2670	233	1925	147	144	97.95	545.7	1362	559.65

7   Conclusion and Future Work

In the proposed method peak power estimation in terms of toggle activity count using level based approach is explored. The proposed method generates input vector pair which maximizes the toggle activity for a level. Through experimental results and theoretical analysis we have demonstrated that the level based approach is better than whole circuit approach. The CPLEX solver runs 10 to 50 time faster for this approach than the whole circuit approach.

Extending the work to sequential circuit is a practical necessary and challenge. Consideration of variable delay model along with fanout load could make the estimation realistic. Hence we set forth the above as next step of this work.

References

1. Wang, C.-Y., Roy, K., Chou, T.-L.: Maximum power estimation for sequential circuits using a test generation based technique. In: Proceedings of the IEEE 1996 Custom Integrated Circuits Conference, pp. 229–232 (May 1996)
2. Hsiao, M.S., Rudnick, E.M., Patel, J.H.: Effects of Delay Models on Peak Power Estimation of VLSI Sequential Circuits. In: International Conference on Computer Aided Design, pp. 45–51. IEEE (1997)
3. Sagahyroon, A., Aloul, F.A.: Using SAT based technique in low power state assignment. Journal of Circuits, Systems, and Computers 20(8), 1605–1618 (2011)
4. Pedram, M.: Power minimization in IC Design: Principles and Applications. ACM Transactions on Desing Automation of Electronics System 1, 3–56 (1996)
5. Devadas, S., Keutzer, K., White, J.: Estimation of power dissipation in CMOS combinational circuits. In: Proceedings of the IEEE 1990 Custom Integrated Circuits Conference, pp. 19.7/1 –19.7/6 (May 1990)
6. Mangassarian, H., Veneris, A., Safarpour, S., Najm, F., Abadir, M.: Maximum circuit activity estimation using pseudo-boolean satisfiability. In: Design, Automation Test in Europe Conference Exhibition, DATE 2007, pp. 1–6 (April 2007)
7. Sagahyroon, A., Aloul, F.A.: Using SAT-based techniques in power estimation. Microelectronics Journal 38, 706–715 (2007)
8. Corporation, IBM ILOG CPLEX] optimization studio, in IBM Coporation (2010), http://www-01.ibm.com/software/integration/optimization/cplex-optimization-studio/
9. Li, R., Zhou, D., Du, D.: Satisfiability and integer programming as complementary tools. In: Proceedings of the ASP-DAC 2004. Asia and South Pacific Design Automation Conference, pp. 880–883 (2004)
10. Tudu, J.T., Malani, D., Singh, V.: Ilp based approach for input vector controlled (ivc) toggle maximization in combinational circuits (2012)
11. Wang, C.-Y., Roy, K.: Maximum power estimation for CMOS circuits using deterministic and statistic approaches. In: Proceedings of the Ninth International Conference on VLSI Design, pp. 364–369 (January 1996)
12. Pedram, M.: Advanced power estimation technique. In: Mermet, J., Nebel, W. (eds.) Low Power Design in Deep Submicron Technology. Kluwer Academic Publishers (1997)
13. Wu, Q., Qiu, Q., Pedram, M.: Estimation of peak power dissipation in VLSI circuits using the limiting distributions of extreme order statistics. IEEE Transactions on Computer-Aided Design of Integrated Circuits and Systems 20, 942–956 (2001)
14. Najm, F.: A survey of power estimation techniques in VLSI circuits. IEEE Transactions on Very Large Scale Integration (VLSI) Systems 2, 446–455 (1994)

Design and Optimization of a 2x2 Directional Microstrip Patch Antenna

Cerin Ninan, Chandra Shekhar, and M. Radhakrishna

Indian Institute of Information Technology Allahabad, India
{imi2011004,rs62,mkrishna}@iiita.ac.in

Abstract. In this paper, a 2x2 inset-fed directional microstrip patch antenna is proposed for the industrial, scientific and medical (ISM) frequency band. The proposed antenna is designed at 2.45 GHz for commercially available substrate RT/Duroid 4350 having thickness 0.762 mm and relative dielectric constant 3.48. The EM simulation has been carried out to study the radiation pattern of the proposed antenna using IE3D Software. The simulation results show a gain of 7.3 dBi with a directivity of 9.6 dBi and a 3 dB beam width of $59.8°$. Further the proposed antenna design is compared with other antenna designs.

Keywords: Microstrip patch antenna, Microstrip patch array antenna, Inset-fed.

1 Introduction

An antenna is an electric transducer used to convert electrical power to radio waves or vice-versa. It has its application in wide areas such as radio broadcasting, communication receivers, cell phones and so on [1]. A microstrip patch antenna is used quite often because of its low cost, simplicity of fabrication, light weight etc.

A microstrip antenna consists of a dielectric substrate placed in between radiating patch and a ground plane [2] as shown in Fig. 1. The radiating patch is made of a conducting material like copper or gold which can be of any shape [3]. The dielectric constant normally lies in the range of $2 \leq \epsilon_r \leq 12$ [1]. The radiation from the microstrip antenna is mainly due to fringing field between the patch and the ground plane as shown in Fig.2. A microstrip patch antenna also has some disadvantages such as low gain and bandwidth.The bandwidth, gain and radiation pattern of patch antenna can be improved by using a thick dielectric substrate of low dielectric constant [4,5]. But this type of substrate increases the size of the patch antenna.

In order to compensate these disadvantages, an array of patch antennas is used. This array improves the gain, bandwidth and radiation pattern of the patch antenna [3]. In this paper a 2x2 inset-fed microstrip patch antenna is designed for commercially available substrate RT/Duroid 4350 having relative dielectric constant of $\epsilon_r = 3.48$ and thickness of h= 0.762 mm.

M.S. Gaur et al. (Eds.): VDAT 2013, CCIS 382, pp. 353–360, 2013.

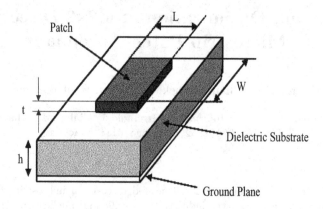

Fig. 1. A microstrip patch antenna [2]

This paper is organized as follows. Section 2 describes the transmission line model in order to analyze the microstrip patch antenna. Section 3 describes the design procedure of a microstrip patch antenna. Simulation results of a 2x2 microstrip patch antenna are given in Section 4. Finally, the paper is concluded in Section 5.

2   Method of Analysis

One of the simplest methods to analyze the microstrip patch antenna is illustrated by transmission line model. In a transmission line model the microstrip patch antenna consists of a transmission line of length L that separates two slots of height h and width W as shown in Fig. 3. Here the microstrip antenna consist of a non-homogeneous line of two dielectrics (substrate and air)

A part of the electric field resides in the air and a major portion lies in the substrate as shown in Fig.2. Due to this the pure transverse-electric-magnetic (TEM) mode of transmission cannot be sustained in the transmission line as the phase velocity of the wave is not the same in the air and in the substrate (dielectric). As a result the dominant mode of propagation in the transmission line is quasi TEM mode. Due to this an effective dielectric constant is attained according to Balanis and given [6] by

$$\epsilon_{reff} = \frac{\epsilon_r + 1}{2} \frac{\epsilon_r - 1}{2} \left[1 + \frac{12h}{W} \right]^{\frac{-1}{2}} \tag{1}$$

where ϵ_{reff} is the effective dielectric constant, ϵ_r is the relative dielectric constant of substrate, h is the height of dielectric substrate and W is the width of the patch.

For the antenna to work in the TM_{10} mode, the length of the patch antenna must be less than $\lambda/2$ (where λ is the wavelength in dielectric medium) [7,8]. But $\lambda = \lambda_0/\sqrt{\epsilon_{reff}}$ (where λ_0 is the wavelength in free space).

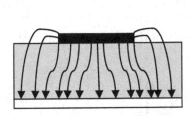

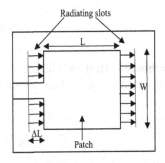

Fig. 2. Electric field distribution in microstrip patch antenna

Fig. 3. Top view of patch antenna

As shown in Fig. 4, the normal and tangential components of the electric field at the edge can be resolved with respect to ground plane. As the length of the patch antenna is $\lambda/2$, the normal components of the electric field will cancel out and the tangential component will add up to give maximum radiation pattern perpendicular to the surface [1] as shown in Fig. 4. Thus the electrical patch will increase and is greater than the physical length. The increase in length is given by Hammerstad [2] as

$$\Delta L = 0.412h \left[\frac{\epsilon_{reff} + 0.3}{\epsilon_{reff} - 0.258} \right] \left[\frac{W/h + 0.264}{W/h + 0.813} \right] \tag{2}$$

Hence the effective length is given by

$$L_{eff} = L + 2\Delta L \tag{3}$$

At given resonant frequency f_0, the effective length is given [9] as

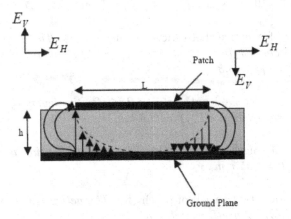

Fig. 4. Side view of patch antenna [1]

$$L_{eff} = \frac{c}{2f_o\sqrt{\epsilon_{reff}}} \tag{4}$$

James and Hall modeled the resonant frequency of the rectangular microstrip patch antenna for TM_{MN} mode [2] as

$$f_o = \frac{c}{2\sqrt{\epsilon_{reff}}}\left[\left(\frac{m}{L}\right)^2 + \left(\frac{n}{W}\right)^2\right]^{1/2} \tag{5}$$

where m and n are modes along the length and width of the patch antenna respectively.

The width of the patch antenna is given by Bahl and Bhartia for effective radiation [10] as

$$W = \frac{c}{2f_o\sqrt{\frac{\epsilon_r+1}{2}}} \tag{6}$$

3   Design Procedure

In this section, the design of a microstrip patch antenna is discussed. The objective is to design an antenna for ISM frequency band (2.45 GHz). The Rogers RT/ Duroid substrate 4350 (Dielectric constant=3.48 and substrate height =0.762 mm) is chosen because of its availability, low cost and low loss. A transmission line model as discussed in previous section is used to calculate the physical dimensions/parameters of microstrip patch antenna. These physical parameters are:

- Calculation of width (W): *The width of the antenna is obtained from (6) by setting $c = 3*10^8$ m/s and f_o=2.45 GHz. Hence W = 27.3 mm*

- Calculation of effective dielectric constant (ϵ_{reff}): *The effective dielectric constant is obtained from (1) by setting ϵ_r =3.48 , h=0.762 mm and W=27.3 mm. Hence ϵ_{reff} = 3.3*

- Calculation of effective length (L_{eff}): *The effective length of the antenna is obtained from (4). Hence L_{eff} =33.6 mm*

- Calculation of length extension (L): *The length extension is obtained from (2). Hence L =0.35 mm*

- Calculation of actual length of patch (L): *The actual length of patch is obtained from (3). Hence L =32.9 mm*

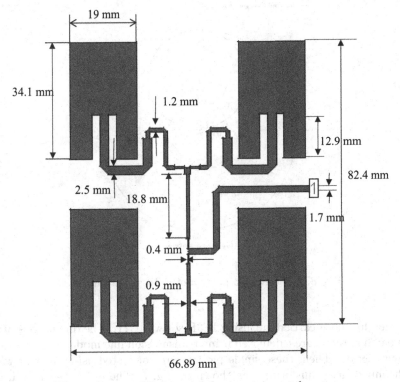

Fig. 5. Proposed 2x2 inset-fed microstrip patch antenna

4 EM Simulation

The proposed 2x2 inset-fed microstrip patch antenna is shown in Fig. 5. The proposed antenna consists of 4 patches and impedance matched feed lines. The EM

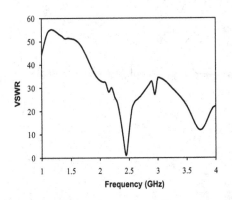

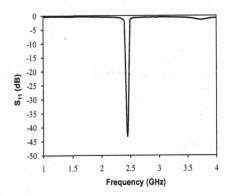

Fig. 6. VSWR of the 2x2 microstrip patch antenna

Fig. 7. S_{11} of the 2x2 microstrip patch antenna

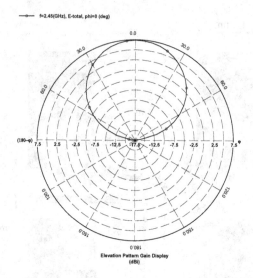

Fig. 8. 2-D elevation pattern of E-Total's at phi=0°

simulation has been carried out using IE3D software [11]. The dimensions of the single patch antenna are calculated using transmission line model as discussed in previous section. Then, these single patches are connected using quarter wavelength impedance transformers as shown in Fig. 5. The optimized length and width of a single patch are 34 mm and 19 mm, respectively. The total size of the microstrip patch array comes out to be 66.89 mm x 87.5 mm.

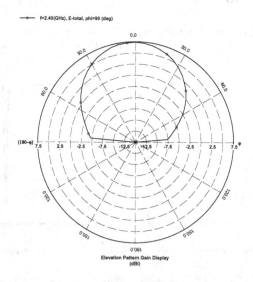

Fig. 9. 2-D elevation pattern of E-Total's directivity at phi=90°

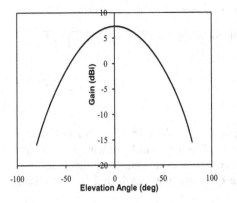

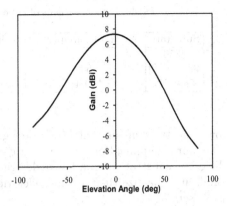

Fig. 10. 2-D elevation pattern of E-Total's gain at phi=0°

Fig. 11. 2-D elevation pattern of E-Total's gain at phi=90°

The microstrip line length and width of 50 Ω, 100 Ω are calculated using lincalc [6]. The microstrip line with a width of 0.4 mm has a length of 2.78 mm and is of 100 Ω whose values were calculated from lincalc. The microstrip line with a width of 2.5 mm has a length of 33 mm. The microstrip line with a width of 1.2 mm has a length of 17.7 mm as shown in Fig. 5. The simulation results provide VSWR = 1.014 and S_{11} = -43.28 dB as shown in Fig. 6 and Fig. 7, respectively. The value of S_{11} is less than -15 dBm and the value of VSWR is less than 2. Hence the attained result will provide a good impedance matching to the 50 Ω load. The 2-D radiation pattern of the antenna is normal to the surface as shown in Fig. 8. The gain attained is 7.3 dBi with a directivity of 9.6 dBi and a 3 dB Beam Width of 59.8° in E-plane. Based on the gain, directivity, and 3 dB beam width attained, it provides a narrow beam with a high gain. Fig. 8 and Fig. 9 show that the 2-D elevation pattern of directivity of total electric field in $phi = 0°$ and 90°, respectively.

Based on Fig. 8 and Fig. 9, the radiation pattern for directivity is normal to the surface with a gain of 9.6 dBi. Fig. 10 and Fig. 11 show that the 2-D elevation pattern of gain of total electric field in $phi = 0°$ and 90^0, respectively. Based on the Fig. 10 and Fig. 11, the radiation pattern for the gain is normal to the surface with a gain of 7.3 dBi.

5   Conclusion

In this paper, a 2x2 directional microstrip patch antenna has been proposed. This antenna is based on a single microstrip patch antenna which is arranged in a 2x2 matrix fashion to facilitate directive radiation pattern. The proposed antenna exhibits the gain of 7.3 dBi and directivity of 9.6 dBi. To provide better insight, the attained simulation results are compared with similar antennas made on RT/Duroid 4003C [12] and on RT/Duroid 5880 [1]. The comparison is tabulated in Table 1. It is clear from Table 1 that a thick substrate with a

Table 1. Comparison of different series of rogers substrates

Substrate	Length of patch (mm)	Width of patch (mm)	Gain (dBi)	S_{11} (dB)
4350	34	19	7.32	-43.2
4003C [12]	34	30	11.5	-16.4
5880 [1]	49.4	41.3	12	-12.2

low dielectric constant exhibits better gain but at the cost of bigger patch area. Therefore, if application needs better gain, efficiency, bandwidth etc then a thick dielectric substrate with a low dielectric constant is chosen. If application needs small antenna size then a thin dielectric constant with high dielectric constant is chosen.

Future works include the fabrication of the designed patch array antenna followed by measurements. We choose RT/Duroid 4350 substrate because of its availability, low loss and low cost. Other substrates will also be evaluated.

References

1. Sandeep, B.S., Kashyap, S.S.: Design and Simulation of Microstrip Patch Array Antenna for Wireless Communication at 2.4 GHz. International Journal of Scientific & Engineering Research 3(2), 1–4 (2012)
2. Rachmansyah, Irianto, A., Mutiara, A.B.: Designing and Manufacturing Microstrip Antenna for Wireless Communication at 2.4 GHz. International Journal of Computer and Electrical Engineering 3(5), 670–675 (2011)
3. Abri, M., Bendimerad, F.T., Boukli-Hacene, N., Bousahla, M.: A Log Periodic Series-Fed Antennas Array Design using a Simple Transmission Line Model. International Journal of Electronics and Communication Engineering 2(3), 161–169 (2009)
4. Kumar, G., Gupta, K.C.: Nonradiating edges and four edges gap-coupled multiple resonator broad-band microstrip antennas. IEEE Trans. Antennas Propag. 34(2), 173–178 (1985)
5. Song, Q., Zhang, X.X.: A study on wideband gap-coupled microstrip antenna arrays. IEEE Trans. Antennas Propag. 43(3), 313–317 (1995)
6. Balanis, C.A.: Antenna Theory: Analysis and Design. John Wiley & Sons (2012)
7. Pozar, D.M.: Input Impedance and Mutual Coupling of Rectangular Microstrip Antennas. IEEE Trans. Antennas and Propagation 30(6), 1191–1196 (1982)
8. Guo, Y.X., Mak, C.L., Luk, K.M., Lee, K.F.: Analysis and design of L probe proximity fed patch antennas. IEEE Trans. Antenna and Propagation 49(2), 145–149 (2001)
9. Zurcher, J.F., Gardiol, F.E.: Broadband Patch Antennas. Artech House (1995)
10. Jackson, D.R., Williams, J.T.: A comparison of CAD models for radiation from rectangular microstrip patches. International Journal of Microwave and Milimeter-Wave Computer Aided Design 1(2), 236–248 (1991)
11. IE3D Simulator, Zeland Software, Inc. (January 1997)
12. Hasan, N., Giri, S.K.: Design of low power RF to DC generator for energy harvesting application. International Journal of Applied Sciences and Engineering Research 1(4), 562–568 (2012)

A New Method for Route Based Synthesis and Placement in Digital Microfluidic Biochips

Pranab Roy[1], Samadrita Bhattacharya[1], Hafizur Rahaman[1]
and Parthasarathi Dasgupta[2]

[1] School of VLSI Technology, Bengal Engineering and Science University, Shibpur, India
[2] Indian Institute of Management, Calcutta, India
{ronmarine14,rahaman_h}@yahoo.co.in, samadrita.bh@gmail.com,
partha@iimcal.ac.in

Abstract. Digital microfluidic Biochips (DMFB) have been developed as a promising platform for Lab-on-chip systems that manipulate individual droplets of chemicals on a 2D planar array of electrodes. Such systems can perform rapid automated biochemical analysis that can be applied to a wide variety of applications including on-chip immunoassays, environmental toxicity monitoring, high-throughput DNA sequencing, point-of-care diagnostics, and biochemical sensing. Design of DMFBs involves system level synthesis -that starts from a given bioassay protocol with a specified biochip architecture and determines the resource allocation, scheduling of individual operations followed by placement of modules and the nets (both in terms of source, targets and mixers) for the said application. In this paper we have proposed a new technique of droplet based route aware synthesis followed by placement to generate a layout that greatly minimizes the utilization of resources in the form of hard blockages termed as modules as well as enhances the routing process in terms of overall completion time for execution of multiple bioassay protocols simultaneously. Using the inherent nature of reconfigurability and scalability of DMFBs the utilization of resources in terms of fixed modules has been greatly reduced and corresponding results tested on three PCRs are found to be encouraging in relation to contemporary works.

1 Introduction

Currently medical diagnostics and biochemical analysis systems rely largely on labor intensive, time consuming and expensive laboratory based bench top methods. A new technology termed as micro-total analysis system (μTAS) has been developed in recent days as an alternative platform for execution of these cumbersome laboratory methods. Such devices known as lab-on-chip systems has major advantages of miniaturization, smaller sample requirements, reduced reagent consumption, decreased analysis time, and higher levels of throughput and automation. Earlier design of LOC devices were based on continuous liquid flow being manipulated through microchannels etched within a substrate. The actuation of flow is implemented through micro-pump and micro-valves and external actuators. The use of permanently etched channels and microvalves largely

M.S. Gaur et al. (Eds.): VDAT 2013, CCIS 382, pp. 361–375, 2013.

reduces the scope of flexibility as well as scalability for multiple bioassay execution within the same device. Hence a new class of device known as digital microfluidic biochip (DMFB) has been emerged in last decade. In DMFBs samples are digitized as nanolitre volumes of discrete fluidic droplets. Such droplets are manipulated using different actuation methods within a 2D planar array of electrodes. The process of manipulation of nanolitre samples are carried out through different mechanisms, viz. electrowetting [1-2], dielectrophoresis [3], thermo capillary transport [4], and surface acoustic wave transport [5]. Compared to continuous flow-based techniques, digital microfluidics offers the advantage of individual sample addressing, reagent isolation, and compatibility with array-based techniques used for biochemical and biomedical application [1, 6]. Electro Wetting on Dielectric (EWOD) is currently used as one of the best actuation methods for droplet manipulation in digital microfluidic systems [7]. The mechanism of electro wetting phenomenon is based on the control of interfacial tension between liquid and an electrode coated with a dielectric layer. An imbalance of interfacial tension is created on application of an electric field to the driving electrode. Due to the difference in contact angle between two sides of the droplet, it is moved towards the energized electrode [8]. Advantages of EWOD devices include ease of fabrication, simple control signal, digital operation, programming flexibility, and minimal fluid consumption.

The basic microfluidic operations performed in DMFBs include droplet generation and storage, droplet transportation, droplet mixing and droplet splitting .The store operation is performed by applying an insulating voltage around the droplet. The mix operation is performed by routing two droplets to the same location, to merge them into one droplet. Since the size of a droplet is kept small, effective mixing can be achieved by fluid diffusion after merging. Finally, the split operation is performed by creating opposite surface tension at the two ends of a fluid droplet and tearing it into two smaller droplets [10].

The microfluidic array contains a set of basic cells that is made up of two parallel glass plates (Figure 1).The bottom plate contains a patterned array of individually controllable electrodes, and the top plate is coated with a continuous ground electrode. The filler medium, such as silicone oil and the sample droplet is sandwiched between the two plates. By assigning time-varying voltage values to turn on/off the electrodes on the digital microfluidic biochip, the interfacial tension of the droplets are modulated- resulting in their transportation around the entire 2-D array and execution of fundamental microfluidic operations for different bioassays. The operations performed by actuating control voltages at the electrodes are also called *reconfigurable* operations because of their flexibility in location and in execution time.

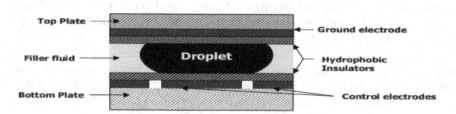

Fig. 1. Schematic for a unit cell used in DMFB

Early research on CAD for digital microfluidics-based biochips has been focused on device-level physical modeling of single components. In modern days a top down system design and test methodology that attempts to apply classical synthesis techniques has been used for the design of digital microfluidics-based biochips. This methodology speeds up the design cycle, reduces human effort, and increases dependability [11].

A behavioral model for a biomedical assay is first manually obtained from the protocol for that assay. Next, architectural-level synthesis is applied to generate a macroscopic structure of the biochip. The macroscopic model provides an assignment of assay functions to biochip resources, as well as a mapping of assay functions to time-steps, based in part on the dependencies between them. Based on the scheduling results, placement algorithms are applied to generate a suitable layout for allocating droplets and modules [12] followed by necessary compaction. Finally droplet-routing algorithms are used to formulate droplet behaviors in a reconfigurable manner for concurrent time multiplexed routing within a 2D planar array of DMFB. The second phase of chip-level design determines the control-signal plan for the underlying electrodes to execute the synthesized result. This phase known as geometry-level synthesis creates a physical representation at the geometrical level. A block level design flow diagram for DMFB design is shown in figure 2. The output is the final layout of the biochip consisting of the configuration of the microfluidic array, locations of reservoirs and dispensing ports, and other geometric details. However it has been found that for all types of microfluidic operation at any given time only one to three electrodes are actually required. Hence it may be possible to dynamically reconfigure any group of cells for performing DMFB operations –in spite of reserving fixed locations for specified operations. In this paper we have proposed a scheduling algorithm to determine a sequence for bioassay operation that can be executed in a time multiplexed manner dynamically at next available locations within the 2D planar array. We further proposed a placement technique for tentative assignment of locations to perform the operations dynamically for a group of predefined nets obtained from the bioassay behavioral model through architecture level synthesis. It has been shown that the method resolves the resource constraint problem for scheduling a bioassay (enhancing execution of microfluidic operations simultaneously) and reduces the overall execution time as well as optimizes the total area to be assigned for the completion of the specified Bioassay protocol.

The organization of the paper is as follows. Section 2 discusses the contemporary contribution on scheduling and placement of biochips. Section 3 describes the details of the reconfigurable transportation based operation and necessary fluidic constraints in DMFBs. Section 4 states the basic scheduling methodology for a given bioassay application. Section 5 defines the proposed method for dynamic scheduling followed by nonreconfigurable resource assignment and final placement within the 2D planar array. Section 6 displays the experimental results for execution of the proposed scheduling and placement techniques employed on PCRs involving different sets of samples and reagents. Section VII presents the conclusive remarks and future scope for further extension of the presented work

2   Related Works

Numerous scheduling techniques are proposed for architectural level synthesis in DMFBs using fixed cell locations termed as hard blocks bound for specified droplet operations. [13] presented modified list scheduling (MLS) and genetic algorithm (GA) based heuristics, as well as an optimal integer linear programming (ILP) model for scheduling microfluidic operations onto a DMFB. Although the GA finds optimal or near-optimal results in much less time than ILP, its iterative nature results in large computation times. MLS generated schedules with lesser time comparable with GA. In [14] the algorithm was modified to include droplet-routing aware physical design decisions. A Tabu search based scheduler proposed in [15] developed an iterative improvement algorithms for DMFB scheduling where virtual devices were considered to be movable (can change their placement) during their operation and significant improvements in scheduling performance were obtained in the process. [16] have proposed a synthesis and placement algorithm which uses a tree-based topological representation and is able to improve on the results from [13]. [18] have proposed an ILP-based architectural-level synthesis and placement approach for DMFBs, which although has the advantage of producing the optimal solution, is only feasible for limited problem sizes. A control path based design is recently integrated to the architectural-level synthesis of DMFBs [19]. In [19], possibilities of errors for each operation is initially measured using an error propagation based estimation technique, and then a check point consisting of a storing operation and a error detection is inserted to the sequencing graph. In [17] a Force-directed List Scheduling *(FDLS)* algorithm for resource constrained assay compilation targeting Digital Microfluidic Biochips (DMFBs) has been proposed. In [17] two methods of FDLS were found to consistently produce schedules of better or comparable quality to MLS while often approaching the quality of GA. Several direct-addressing placement and unified scheduling-placement algorithms [16][20][21][22] using methodologies e.g simulated annealing has been developed. [23] introduced an online synthesis flow for DMFBs, that enable real-time response to errors and control flow. The objective of this flow was to facilitate fast assay synthesis while minimally compromising the quality of results. However it has been found that only in [24] a routing based scheduling method has been proposed where the synthesis problem is transformed into a routing problem. Here the concepts of virtual fixed modules are eliminated and the droplets are allowed to move on the chip on any route during operation execution. The approach was derived from a Greedy Randomized Adaptive Search Procedure (GRASP) and it has been shown that significant improvements can be obtained in the application completion time. In this paper we have used the same concept as of [24] and used a modified droplet route based synthesis methodology to perform the necessary placement and routing for optimization of area and bioassay completion time.

3   Routing in DMFB

The objective of droplet routing is to transmit all the droplets from their respective sources to targets within a 2D grid array while fulfilling all the constraints imposed for the transportation. An efficient routing schedule (virtual route) is often required to be developed to provide an optimal routing in terms of objectives such as latest arrival time and overall cell utilization. Droplet routing problem in *DMFBs* is typically modeled in terms of a 2D-grid (Figure 3). For each droplet, there exists a set of source grid locations, a set of target grid locations, and (optionally) a set of mixers. Each source-target combination is defined as a net. A 2-pin net has a single source and single target. A combination of two Sources, one Mixer and one Target forms a 3-pin net. While execution of routing of multiple nets within a 2D planar array of a DMFB there are possibilities of intersection or overlapping of droplet routes during their concurrent routing in time-multiplexed manner. To avoid such undesirable behaviors following fluidic constraints are introduced.

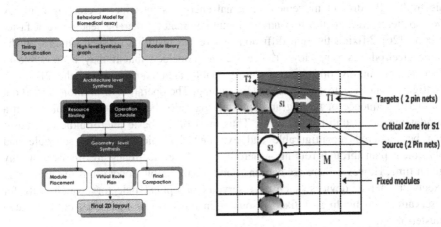

Fig. 2. Top down Design Methodology   **Fig. 3.** Routing with 2-pin nets in a 2D Array For DMFBs

Let d_i at (x^t_i, y^t_i) and d_j at (x^t_j, y^t_j) denote two independent droplets at any given timestamp t. Then, the following constraints, defined as Fluidic *Constraint*s are required to be satisfied for any time t while routing [25]:

Static constraint: $|x^t_i - x^t_j| > 1$ or $|y^t_i - y^t_j| > 1$
Dynamic constraint: $|x^{t+1}_i - x^t_j| > 1$ or, $|y^{t+1}_i - y^t_j| > 1$
or, $|x^{t+1}_j - x^t_i| > 1$ or $|y^{t+1}_j - y^t_i| > 1$

This implies that for any droplet at location (x, y), the locations $(x+1, y)$, $(x-1, y)$, $(x, y+1)$, $(x, y-1)$, $(x+1, y+1)$, $(x+1, y-1)$, $(x-1, y-1)$, and $(x-1, y+1)$ are prohibited for any other droplet to enter at timestamps t and $t+1$ in order to maintain these fluidic constraints. Hence, all the locations adjacent to (x, y) as stated above form a *Critical Zone* (Figure 2) for any droplet at (x, y) at timestamp t. A predetermined time limit called the *Timing Constraint* defines the maximum allowed transportation time for a given set of droplets.

4   Scheduling Methodology in DMFB

The basic microfluidic operations namely merging, mixing, splitting and storage is so far accomplished on predefined fixed module locations comprised of a group of cells within the 2D planar array. In order to avoid conflicts between droplet routes and assay operations, a segregation region is defined around the functional region of each such microfluidic modules. Such locations dedicated for microfluidic operations are considered to be non reconfigurable and fixed. These cells together with a segregation zone consumes considerable area within the DMFB – leaving the overall area for reconfigurable operations e.g routing to be confined within narrow channels. For example mixing is performed by bringing two droplets to the same location and merging them, followed by the transport of the resulted droplet over a series of electrodes. By droplet movement, external energy is introduced, creating complex flow patterns (due to the formation of multilaminates), thereby leading to a faster mixing [26]. Mixing through diffusion, where the resulting droplet remains on the same electrode, is very slow. Hence we can conclude that it may be possible to execute the mixing operation at any available area comprising of the 2D array configuration of electrodes necessary for mixing. The operation of dilution carried out through a sequence of mixing and splitting may also be executed dynamically in a similar manner within the 2D array. Thus most of the basic microfluidic operations can be rendered reconfigurable and executed dynamically as per schedule and placement plan through routing -where one to three electrodes are involved at any given time. However there are certain "non-reconfigurable" operations required to be executed on real devices, such as reservoirs or optical detectors which calls for reservation and binding of fixed resources in the form of individual or segregated cluster of cells.

The conventional architecture level synthesis starts with a sequencing graph representing different assay operations with their mutual dependencies. Each node in the sequencing graph represents an operation and each directed edge represents operation precedence and sequence of execution of each operation. Next, scheduling and binding assigns time-multiplexed steps to these assay operations and bind them to a given number of devices so as to maximize parallelism [27]. In scheduling and binding, each operation will have a set of devices in the form of module library being available for resource binding. Table 1 presents the results of the experiments performed in [26], where several mixing times were obtained for various areas, creating a module library. Figure. 4, shows the type of mixing and the array configuration for modules available to choose. Choice of different modules may result in various reaction area and execution time. Based on the execution time for each module, the start and completion time of each operation are arranged. On the basis of the scheduling result, device placement and droplet routing are conducted to generate a chip layout and establish droplet routing connections between devices in a reconfigurable manner [28][29].

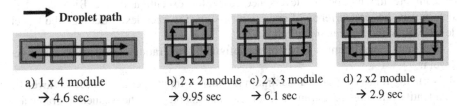

a) 1 x 4 module
→ 4.6 sec

b) 2 x 2 module
→ 9.95 sec

c) 2 x 3 module
→ 6.1 sec

d) 2 x2 module
→ 2.9 sec

Fig. 4. Module library examples for mixing and splitting (details in table 1) with respective droplet path

Table 1. Module library details [26]

Operation	2D Electrode Array	Modules	Time
Mixing/Dilution	2 x 4	4 x 6	2.9 sec
Mixing/Dilution	1 x 4	3 x 6	4.6 sec
Mixing/Dilution	2 x 3	4 x 5	6.1 sec
Mixing/Dilution	2 x 2	4 x 4	9.95 sec
Dispensing	-	-	1 sec
Detection	1 x 1	3 x 3	30 sec

Table 2. Module Library 2

Operation	2D electrode Array	Module	Time
M1 for S1	2 x 4	4 x 6	5
M2 for S2	2 x 4	4 x 6	3
M3 for S3	2 x 4	4 x 6	4
M4 for S4	2 x 4	4 x 6	6
D1 for assay 1	1 x 1	3 x 3	5
D2 for assay 2	1 x 1	3 x 3	4
D3 for assay 3	1 x 1	3 x 3	6
D4 for assay 4	1 x 1	3 x 3	5

5   Proposed Method of Route Based Scheduling and Placement

In this paper we propose a droplet route based method for scheduling together with placement starting with a Sequencing graph.We propose to execute microfluidic operation at a reconfigurable location preassigned during the scheduling phase .Unlike [24] where module operations are precharacterized in terms of routing operation by considering percentage of mixing corresponding to each type of movements – we directly assume the mixing module configuration is determined from the library and is directly assigned in the specified location dynamically (without assignment of any segregation zone). Thereby mixing or splitting operation is executed following the movement patterns referred in the library.

A. Scheduling and placement algorithm

Problem Formulation: Given m number of samples and n number of reagents and buffers with a Bioassay protocol – for providing the details of bioassay operations to be executed within the DMFB. The objective is to develop an efficient schedule for execution of the bioassay followed by placement that optimizes the number of resources N_R , overall assay completion time T and computes the dimensions of the overall 2D array m x n together with location of the fixed resources to ensure overall area necessary for routing and other operations A is minimum. Finally the placement ensures optimized routability with minimum contamination or stalling.

Procedure:
1. Obtain a sequencing graph G_S for a specified Bioassay with each node representing an operation and corresponding edge defines the precedence and dependencies between two operations.

2. compute the number of levels necessary for execution of the Bioassay. This determines the concurrency of operations assigned to each level. Let there be k such levels within the sequencing graph.

3. Determine maximum number of reconfigurable operations to occur at any given level i.

4. Normally it has been found maximum number of Input operations occur at level 1 .

5. identify the non reconfigurable operations denoted in the sequence graph and assign fixed locations for the said operations within the layout.

6. As found specifically in standard testbenches for routing (benchmark suite I) dimension of the 2D array is maintained to be n x n for n number of input operations.

7. It has been found in almost all sequencing graph most of the nonreconfigurable operations occur at level (k-1) while the last level k is assigned to the sink.

8. Tentatively assign fixed locations for these nonreconfigurable operations (with segregation zones) from options available at the module library with execution time prespecified by the Bioassay protocol.

9. Bind the prefixed reservoir locations at the boundary to the input operations.(specifically for level 1)

10. For level i= 2 to k

11.   if i = 2

Reconfigurable mixer modules are assigned for level 2 operation proceeded by level 1 Input operations.

Reconfigurable Mixer locations are assigned at zones that corresponds to the respective I/O operations at level 1 from which the operation is directed in G_S .

12.   For mixer locations at each level we attempt to choose the best options available in the module library in terms of operation execution time.

A compromise in terms of area is made if the layout dimension constraints as mentioned in step 6 permits.

However if area constraint may restrict the assignment we opt for the next optimum choice in terms of execution time.

13.   We assign filler zones of one row or column between neighboring mixer locations to ensure no violation fluidic constraints mentioned in section 3 while concurrent execution of route based reconfigurable mixing operations at the identical level.

14.   If i > 2

Assign reconfigurable module locations at each successive level – such that each Module can be located to share the cells being used in the earlier level for operations with edges directed to the current one.

15.   for any dilution operation that requires mixing followed by splitting – within the reconfigurable mixing zone a cell is assigned for splitting operation after scheduled mixing.

16. next i

17. Compute the maximum time for concurrent operation at each level.

18. Here we use parallel resources at each level – and locations are shared only between different levels for reconfigurable operations.

19. However for non reconfigurable sources being assigned with fixed locations we prefer sequential operation for area constraints.

20. Let maximum number of resources used in any particular level is N_{MAX} and maximum area for any resource is A_M . Let overall fixed area for nonconfigurable resources A_{NR} and overall area for filler zones is considered to be A_F – the total area $(A_M \times N_{MAX} + A_{NR} + A_F) \leq m \times n$.

21. Let maximum execution time for any level is T_{MAX} and execution time for each level i is T_i . Then $\sum_{i=1}^{k} T_i \leq T_{MAX} \times K$.

B. The routing method

1. for i = 1 to k

   If i ≠ 1 and the next operation is reconfigurable Route the output droplets of level (i-1) to the respective start location assigned for Reconfigurable mixing operation. Merge the two droplets at the start location and continue route based mixing by moving the droplets along the respective droplet path as shown in figure 4.

2. The routing is carried out as intermediate steps between mixing and the respective route paths shares the zones comprised of cells being used for respective mixing operation at level(i-1) that has been edges directed to the current operation for which the routing is being performed.

3. If i ≠ 1 and the next operation is non-reconfigurable

4. In such cases a set of nonreconfigurable sources are being used sequentially a t fixed Locations with segregation regions.

5. each output droplet from the previous level dedicated for the specified non reconfigurable operation are routed to the boundary of the segregation zone and stalled at a preferential queue.

6. We follow ASAP assignment technique for scheduling multiple droplets targeted for specific nonreconfigurable operation. This means droplet being routed earliest has been allowed to share resource earlier – while the rest is stalled at predetermined locations to share the resource on next available timestamp – once the earlier operation is complete.

7. However a predetermined fixed time has been assigned between each access to these fixed modules for dispensing of the used droplet as well as to perform wash droplet routing at the operation site to avoid contamination leading to erroneous final output.

8. although placement has ensured optimum routability with no or minimum contamination or stalling – in order to avoid stalling or deadlock we used the biochip routing procedure as mentioned in [30].The procedure is as follows:

9. Sort the nets in descending order of their overall manhattan distance. Preferences are assigned in ascending order with highest preference to the nets with largest distance.

   Start routing of each net starting with timestamp = 0.

   It is also assumed that transition time for a droplet between two adjacent cells to be of one unit.

In the event of collision – which implies a droplet reaching the critical zone of another at the same timestamp – the net with higher preference is allowed to move and the other is stalled till the path is clear to route. Compute the arrival time for each droplet – mark the maximum of all arrival times as the latest arrival time T_{iR} indicating the overall route time occupied between levels (i-1) and i.

10. next i.

11. It has been found that the total route time for bioassay execution is very small as compared with the completion times of other microfluidic operations. In experimental results obtained from [9] it has been found that time required to route the droplet through one cell is 0.01 s.

6   A Real Time Application and Experimental Results

The *in-vitro* measurement for glucose and other metabolites, such as lactate, glutamate and pyruvate, in human physiological fluids is of great importance in clinical diagnosis of metabolic disorders. The behavioural description of an example of a multiplexed *invitro* diagnostics is shown in Figure 6. Four types of human physiological fluid - e.g. plasma, serum, urine and salvir are sampled and dispensed into the microfluidic biochip. Next each type of physiological fluid is assayed for glucose, lactate, pyruvate or glutamate measurement. The result of the biomedical assay is detected by an integrated optical absorbance measurement device.[31]. The tests are denoted as Assay1 for Glucose, Assay2 for Lactate, Assay3 for Pyruvate and Assay4 for Glutamate.

We start with a sequencing graph of one instance of In vitro model involving Three samples (m=3) and Three reagents (n=3) with a module library given in table 2.The sequencing graph is shown in figure 7 a). The number of Input operations are = 2 x m x n = 18 and number of levels k = 4.The number of reconfigurable operations (only mixing) = m x n = 9 that requires three types of mixers M1,M2 and M3. The number of non reconfigurable operations (detection) = m x n = 9 and three types of detectors namely D1, D2 and D3 are used. So we first assigned the non reconfigurable modules into three fixed blocks with segregation region to be used sequentially for each types of assay operation. Hence each detector is scheduled for three assay operations. (Figure 7 b). We schedule to place the non reconfigurable modules to be employed for sequential application and assign a centralized location within the 2D planar array. The dimension of the array is determined to be 18 x 18 for 2 x m x n = 18 samples. Figure 8 a) reorients the graph with fixed modules being aligned at centralized locations. Figure 8 b) assigns zones for the reoriented graph. Figure 8 d) forms the planar triangular graph and the rectangular dualization results are shown in figure 8 e).The corresponding zone placement in 2D array is shown in figure 9 a) .figure 9 b) shows the actual resource assignment in terms of samples and reagents at level 1 and non reconfigurable detectors as D1,D2 and D3 as fixed modules. Finally figure 10 a) shows the actual route performance with the overall scheduling results being shown in figure 10 b).Overall execution time for the bioassay is 21.17 seconds – the route time – 0.21 sec and assay operation time – 21 sec.(we assume route time of 0.01 sec for route through one cell).

The scheduling and placement has been carried out on all five In vitro diagnostics using module library mentioned in Table 2. We assume input operation time of One second. Table 3 displays the detailed results for all five examples. Table 4 shows the comparative results for bioassay execution time obtained using the proposed technique and the ones used in [13].

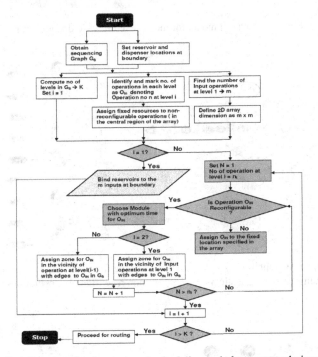

Fig. 5. A flowchart for the proposed scheduling and placement technique

7   Conclusion

In this paper we have proposed route based synthesis and placement technique to employed for execution of Bioassay with a DMFB. We used route based reconfigurability for resources to be reconfigurable resources are assigned with fixed locations. The results show major improvements in terms of areas and execution time for bioassays through application of our algorithms. In table 4 it has been noticed that improvement is more pronounced in comparison to other scheduling methods [13] with increase in problem size. However the algorithm needs to be modified for larger sequencing graphs with higher number of levels as resource sharing for reconfigurable operation may become unmanageable with increase in number of levels beyond a certain value.

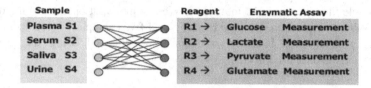

Fig. 6. Behavioral model for multiplexed In vitro diagnostics.[31]

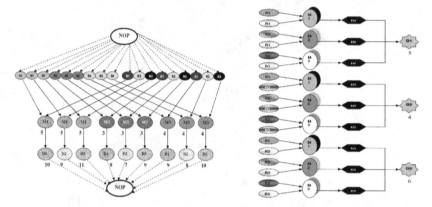

Fig. 7. a) sequence graph for
of In vitro multiplexed diagnostic 3

b) the final graph after sequential assignment
non reconfigurable operations

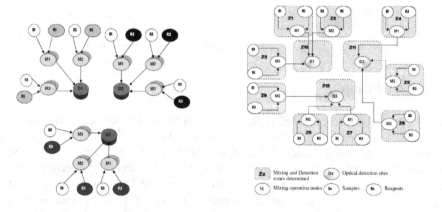

a) reoriented sequencing graph   b) zone assignment

Fig. 8. Zone assignment and rectangular dualization for final placement with resource allocation

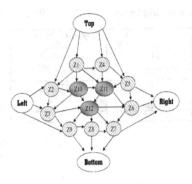

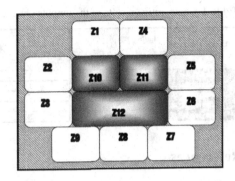

f) The planar triangular graph   g) Rectangular dualization and placement in 2D array

Fig. 8. (*continued*)

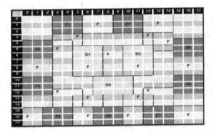

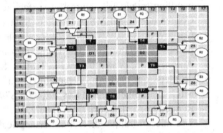

Fig. 9. a) Zone placement with fillers in   b) actual resource assignment with reservoir binding 2D array

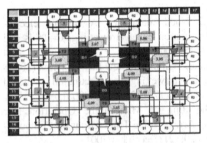

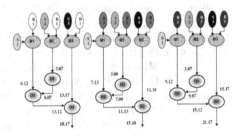

Fig. 10. a) Actual route performance after b) the final scheduling output with resultant sequencing placement graph

Table 3. Detailed results for 5 In vitro diagnostics after scheduling, placement and execution

Experiment	Samples [m]	Reagents[n]	Resources used (detection)	No of Mixing m x n	Overall Execution time (including Route time)	Overall Execution time (excluding Route time)
1	2[S1,S2]	2[R1,R2]	2 [D1, D2]	4	13.08	13
2	2[S1,S2]	3[R1,R2,R3]	3[D1,D2,D3]	6	15.13	15
3	3[S1,S2,S3]	3[R1,R2,R3]	3[D1,D2,D3]	9	21.17	21
4	3[S1,S2,S3]	4[R1,R2,R3,R4]	4[D1,D2,D3,D4]	12	21.24	21
5	4[S1,S2,S3,S4]	4[R1,R2,R3,R4]	4[D1,D2,D3,D4]	16	27.68	27

Table 4. Comparative results of the outputs obtained through droplet based synthesis with [13]

Experiment	ILP [13]	M-LS [13]	GA [13]	Droplet Based Synthesis [our proposed method]
Example 1	15	17	15	13
Example 2	17	19	17	15
Example 3	N/A	26	25	21
Example 4	N/A	27	26	21
Example 5	N/A	35	34	27

References

1. Pollack, M.G., Fair, R.B., Shenderov, A.D.: Electrowetting-based actuation of liquid droplets for microfluidic applications. Appl. Phys. Lett. 77, 1725–1727 (2000)
2. Lee, J., Moon, H., Fowler, J., Kim, C.-J., Schoellhammer, T.: Addressable micro liquid handling by electric control of surface tension. In: Proc. of 2001 IEEE 14th International Conference on MEMS, Interlaken, Switzerland, pp. 499–502 (2001)
3. Gascoyne, R.C., Vykoukal, J.V.: Dielectrophoresis based sample handling in general-purpose programmable diagnostic Instruments. Proc. IEEE 92, 22–42 (2004)
4. Anton, D.A., Valentino, J.P., Trojan, S.M., Wagner, S.: Thermocapillary actuation of droplets on chemically patterned surfaces by programmable microheater arrays. J. Microelectromechanical Sys. 12, 873–879 (2003)
5. Renaudin, A., Tabourier, P., Zhang, V., Druhon, C., Camart, J.C.: Plateforme SAW dédiée à la microfluidique discrète pour applications biologiques. In: 2ème Congrès Français de Microfluidique, Société Hydrotechnique de France, Toulouse, France, pp. 14–16 (2004)
6. Cho, S.K., Moon, H., Kim, C.J.: Creating, transporting, cutting, and merging liquid droplets by electrowettingbased actuation for digital micro fluidic circuits. Journal of Microelectromechanical Systems 12, 70–80 (2003)
7. Arzpeyma, A., Bhaseen, S., Dolatabadi, A., Wood-Adams, P.: A coupled electro-hydrodynamic numerical modeling of droplet actuation by electrowetting. Colloids and Surfaces A: Physicochem. Eng. Aspects 323, 28–35 (2008)
8. Berthier, J.: Microdropes and Digital Microfluidics. William Andrew Inc., Norwich (2008)
9. Pollack, M.G., Fair, R.B., Shenderov, A.D.: Electrowetting-based actuation of liquid droplets for microfluidic applications. Appl. Phys. Lett. 77, 1725–1727 (2000)
10. Ding, J., Chakrabarty, K., Fair, R.B.: Scheduling of Microfluidic Operations for ReconfigurableTwo-Dimensional Electrowetting Arrays. IEEE Transactions on Computer-Aided Design of Integrated Circuits and Systems 20(12) (December 2001)
11. Chakrabarty, K.: Design, Testing, and Applications of Digital Microfluidics-Based Biochips. In: Proceedings of the 18th International Conference on VLSI Design, VLSID 2005 (2005)
12. Su, F., Chakrabarty, K.: Module placement for fault-tolerant microuidics-based biochips. ACM TODAES 11, 682–710 (2006)
13. Su, F., Chakrabarty, K.: High-level synthesis of digital microfluidic biochips. ACM J. Emerging Tech. Comput. Syst. 3(4), 16.1-16.32 (2008)
14. Xu, T., Chakrabarty, K.: Integrated droplet routing and defect tolerance in the synthesis of digital microfluidic biochips. In: Proceedings of Design Automation Conference, pp. 948–953 (2007)

15. Maftei, E., Paul, P., Madsen, J.: Tabu Search-Based Synthesis of Dynamically Reconfigurable Digital Microfluidic Biochips. In: Proceedings of the Compilers, Architecture, and Synthesis for Embedded Systems Conference, pp. 195–203 (2009)

16. Yuh, P.-H., Yang, C.-L., Chang, Y.-W.: Placement of digital microfluidic biochips using the T-tree formulation. In: Proceedings of Design Automation Conference, pp. 931–934 (2006)

17. O' Neal, K., Grissom, D., Brisk, P.: Force-directed list scheduling for digital microfluidic biochips. In: Proc. VLSI-SOC, Santa Cruz, CA (2012)

18. Maftei, E., Paul, P., Madsen, J., Stidsen, T.: Placement-aware architectural synthesis of digital microfluidic biochips using ILP. In: Proceedings of the International Conference on Very Large Scale Integration of System on Chip, pp. 425–430 (2008)

19. Zhao, Y., Xu, T., Chakrabarty, K.: Control-path design and error recovery in digital microfluidic lab-on-chip. ACM JETC 3(11) (2010)

20. Su, F., Chakrabarty, K.: Module placement for fault-tolerant microfluidics-based biochips. ACM Trans. on Design Automation of Electronic Systems 11(3), 682–710 (2006)

21. Su, F., Chakrabarty, K.: Unified high-level synthesis and module placement for defect-tolerant microfluidic biochips. In: Proc. DAC, Anaheim, CA, pp. 825–830 (2005)

22. Xu, T., Chakrabarty, K.: Integrated droplet routing in the synthesis of microfluidic biochips. In: Proc. DAC, San Diego, CA, pp. 948–953 (2007)

23. Grissom, D., Brisk, P.: Fast Online Synthesis of Generally Programmable Digital Microfluidic Biochips. In: Proc. of CODES+ISSS 2012, Tampere, Finland, October 7-12, pp. 413–422 (2012)

24. Maftei, E., Paul, P., Madsen, J.: Routing-Based Synthesis of Digital Microfluidic Biochips. In: Proc. of CASES 2010, Scottsdale, Arizona, USA, October 24-29, pp. 41–50 (2010)

25. Zhao, Y., Chakraborty, K.: Cross Contamination, avoidance of droplet routing in Digital microfluidic biochips. In: Procedure of the Design and Automation Test in Europe (2009)

26. Paik, P., Pamula, V.K., Fair, R.B.: Rapid droplet mixers for digital microfluidic systems. Lab on a Chip 3, 253–259 (2003)

27. Su, F., Chakrabarty, K.: Architectural-level synthesis of digitalmicrofluidics-based biochips. In: Proc. IEEE/ACM ICCAD, pp. 223–228 (November 2004)

28. Su, F., Hwang, W., Chakrabarty, K.: Droplet routing in the synthesis of digital microfluidic biochips. In: Proc. IEEE/ACM DATE, pp. 1–6 (March 2006)

29. Su, F., Chakrabarty, K.: Module placement for fault-tolerant microfluidics-based biochips. ACM TODAES 11(2), 682–710 (2006)

30. Roy, P., Rahaman, H., Dasgupta, P.: A novel droplet routing algorithm for digital microfluidic biochips. In: Proc. GLSVLSI, Providence, RI, pp. 441–446 (2010)

31. Su, F., Chakrabarty, K.: Benchmarks for Digital microfluidic Biochip design and synthesis. Duke University, US (2006)

Defect Diagnosis of Digital Circuits Using Surrogate Faults*

Chidambaram Alagappan and Vishwani D. Agrawal

Auburn University
ECE Dept., 200 Broun Hall, Auburn, AL 36849 USA
cza0011@tigermail.auburn.edu,
vagrawal@eng.auburn.edu
http://www.eng.auburn.edu/~vagrawal

Abstract. Classical single stuck-at faults are analyzed as surrogates for any non-classical fault that may have caused an observed failure. Although multiple stuck-at faults are used as an illustrative example of non-classical faults, proposed algorithms are applicable to any other type of fault. Our effect-cause analysis is less complex than existing methods. The diagnostic procedure adds or removes faults from a set of candidate faults based on the observed circuit outputs, using minimal fault simulation, to obtain a small set of suspected faults.

Keywords: Dictionary-less fault diagnosis; fault simulation; multiple stuck-at faults; stuck-at faults; surrogate faults.

1 Introduction

An ideal fault diagnosis procedure should report true failures with accuracy, i.e., *resolution* (the number of true failures reported among the total number of faults reported) and *diagnosability* (the percentage of correctly identified failures) of the diagnosis result should be high [8]. Previous research on fault diagnosis attempts trade-offs between the resolution, diagnosability and CPU time, but the algorithms become increasingly complex. Two major classes of algorithms are cause-effect and effect-cause types. Cause-effect analysis has a stored simulated response database of modeled faults. The faulty circuit response is compared against this database to find out which fault might have caused the failure [5,7,12,15]. This database, called dictionary, is memory intensive and impractical for large circuits. Effect-cause analysis works on the observed failing signals and searches for the cause by tracing back the error propagation path from the failing primary outputs to identify faults likely to have produced the failure [3,4,9]. Backward implication and forward propagation are used for this purpose [9]. Such procedures use moderate amount of memory.

Although a real defect is rarely a classical single stuck-at fault, diagnostic procedures match observed symptoms to closest single stuck-at faults. This is

---

* Research supported in part by the National Science Foundation Grant CCF-1116213.

M.S. Gaur et al. (Eds.): VDAT 2013, CCIS 382, pp. 376–386, 2013.

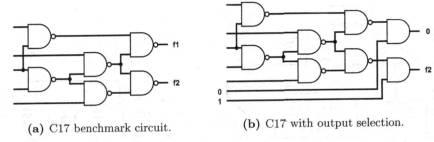

(a) C17 benchmark circuit.   **(b)** C17 with output selection.

Fig. 1. Output selection implementation on C17 benchmark circuit

because the available analysis tools only handle single stuck-at faults. The diagnosed single stuck-at faults then are not real but are "surrogates" meaning that they have some, but not all, characteristics of the actual defect in the circuit. The term "surrogate fault" has been used before in the literature [10,13,16].

2   Preliminaries

A fault simulator reports all single stuck-at faults that can be detected by an input pattern on all primary outputs (POs). To use this information for distinguishing among several faults that could have caused the failure we employ *output selection*. AND gates are added in the simulation netlist at each PO, with the other input of the AND gate being a new primary input (PI). The failing test pattern is duplicated as many times as the number of POs, activating exactly one PI at a time. Thus, new PIs that directly go to the added AND gates are all forced to 0 except for one PI to a transparent AND gate to find the detectable faults at the corresponding PO. Consider C17 benchmark circuit of Figure 1a. A test pattern "abcde" produces good circuit responses 'f1' and 'f2'. Assume this circuit has a failure only at the second output. A typical fault simulator may identify detectable faults without associating them to any PO. With output selection of Figure 1b, the test pattern is duplicated as "abcde10" and "abcde01".

3   Diagnosis Algorithm

The diagnosis algorithm relies on a basic concept that a test pattern fails because a detectable fault is present in the circuit or a test pattern passes because none of the detectable faults is present. For this to be effective, we assume that there is no circular fault masking present in the circuit. Let *'passing_set'* be the set of passing test patterns, *'failing_set'* be the set of failing test patterns, *'sus_flts'* be the suspected fault list, *'set1_can_flts'* be **prime suspect candidate faults** and *'set2_can_flts'* be **surrogate candidate faults**. For simplicity, we will refer to *'set1_can_flts'* as SET1 and *'set2_can_flts'* as SET2.

The algorithm has four phases [6] as shown in the flowchart of Figure 2. Initially, Phase 1 takes the union of all faults detectable by all failing patterns as a list of suspects. Since this set can be large, we need to reduce the list. In Phase 2,

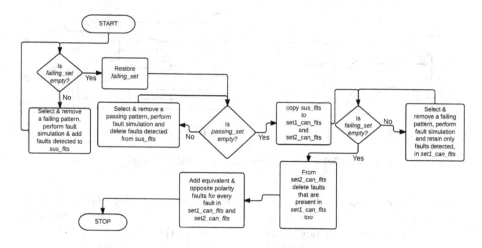

Fig. 2. Flowchart of diagnosis procedure

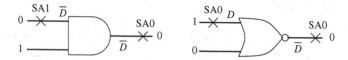

Fig. 3. Opposite polarity fault masking

we take the union of all faults detectable by passing patterns and subtract it from suspect list of Phase 1. Phase 3 takes an intersection of the suspected fault lists of all failing patterns. The resulting faults are called **prime suspects**. These faults are of low priority, but there is a chance that they can be surrogate of an actual fault or one of the actual faults. In Phase 4, equivalent faults of the identified suspected faults are added to the suspect list. To guard against fault masking, we include the opposite polarity faults of the faults that are present in SET1 and SET2, to get the final candidate fault lists. The pseudocode for the entire algorithm is available in a recent thesis [6].

If the actual defect is a single stuck-at fault, the algorithm identifies it as a "prime suspect" in Phase 2. For other defects, it provides a list of surrogate single stuck-at faults "resembling" the actual defect in location or behavior.

Masking. In Figure 3, the top input of an AND gate is stuck-at-1 (SA1) and the output is stuck-at-0 (SA0). To activate the first fault, a '0' must be supplied to the top input and a '1' must be supplied to the bottom input to propagate it. This will produce a $\overline{D}$ on the top input, where $\overline{D} = 1$ if SA1 is present on that input or $\overline{D} = 0$ if the input is fault free. However, $\overline{D}$ will be masked at the output by the SA0 fault. The diagnosis procedure will identify output SA0 as the only suspect. Therefore, SA0s on both inputs are also included as suspects. Similarly, for the NOR gate in Figure 3, when the top input and output have SA0s, the masking occurs. Therefore, Phase 4 enhances the suspect list with all opposite polarity faults for equivalent faults of a suspected single stuck-at fault.

Theorem 1. *If there is only a single stuck-at fault present in a failing circuit under diagnosis (CUD), the diagnosis algorithm will always identify that fault as a prime suspect, irrespective of the detection or diagnostic coverage of the test pattern set.*

Proof. Assume that CUD has a single stuck-at fault that causes $N - k$ out of N test patterns to fail. The remaining k are passing patterns. Because a fault free circuit cannot have any failing test pattern, the presence of failing test patterns indicates the presence of some failure s. In other words, a test pattern can only fail because a fault that it detects is present. Hence all $N - k$ patterns detect the fault s and the remaining k patterns do not detect the fault s. If all $N - k$ patterns detect some fault present in the circuit, it has to be the same fault that all the $N - k$ patterns detect, because there is no more than one fault present in the circuit according to our assumption in the beginning. Moving forward with this revelation, Phase 3 will always come up with one or more prime suspects including the actual fault, as the intersection of the faults detected by all failing patterns. ∎

Many possible cases of single stuck-at faults, multiple stuck-at faults without masking, multiple stuck-at faults with masking, and multiple stuck-at faults with interference have been analyzed in detail [6]. Figure 4 shows the comparison of simulation effort between the proposed diagnosis procedure and the traditional fault dictionary diagnosis method. It is plotted for a multiple (two) stuck-at fault case of C432 ISCAS'85 benchmark circuit. This circuit has a total of 1078 single stuck-at faults in the fault list. The test vector set with 100% diagnostic coverage of detectable faults contains 462 test vectors (with output selection implemented). The dictionary method involves simulation of all faults for all test vectors. Hence, the entire area under the straight black line denotes the simulation effort of the fault dictionary method. The considered failure case produced 31 failing vectors and 431 passing vectors. The proposed fault diagnosis procedure performs fault simulation with the failing test vectors first, which is denoted by the solid red line. This line drops down steeply because, as and when the faults are detected, they are dropped. We process fewer faults as we proceed with the simulation. Next, the fault simulation of passing patterns is performed, which is denoted by the dotted blue line. Note that the faults that were detected and dropped during failing pattern simulation are those to be simulated with passing patterns. In this case too, faults are dropped as and when they are detected by the passing patterns, which explains the drop in the line. Once again the number of faults to be simulated keeps reducing throughout simulation. Beyond a certain point, not many remaining faults are detected by the passing patterns, which makes the curve almost flat. After simulating all passing patterns, the remaining faults become the suspects and surrogates. The area under these lines (solid red and dotted blue) denotes the simulation effort of the proposed procedure that is far lower than the traditional dictionary method.

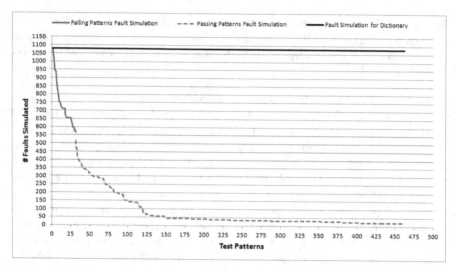

Fig. 4. Simulation effort comparison with dictionary method applied to C432

3.1 Fault Ranking

There is a small probability that the diagnosis procedure comes up with no result, i.e., SET1 and SET2 are both empty after fault simulation. That can happen in a situation like multiple faults with masking and interference such that they together produce faulty output responses that will allow a few of the test patterns detecting them to pass and other test patterns detecting them to fail. For example, consider the case where every fault detectable by failing patters is also detectable by at least one passing pattern. This is a rare phenomenon and only in such cases a ranking procedure is used.

Phase 1 short lists faults in *sus_flts*. For ranking, while carrying out Phase 1 we keep a count of the number of failing patterns that detect each fault. This number is called the weight of the corresponding fault, e.g., if fault F1 is detected by three failing patterns, then the weight of F1 at the end of Phase 1 will be three. Similarly, in Phase 2, which simulates only the faults found detectable in Phase 1, we keep a count of the number of passing patterns for each fault. This number is subtracted from the weight of the fault found in Phase 1. At the end of Phase 2 we get the final weight of every fault. The faults with the highest weight are reported to be prime suspect (SET1) faults and the faults with the second highest weight are reported to be surrogate (SET2) faults.

Note that the final weights can also be negative. This will happen when a fault is detectable by more passing patterns and by fewer failing patterns. Even in this case, the top two highest weights are considered to be suspects. Also, there can be cases where the final weight is zero. This will happen when the fault is detected by the same number of passing and failing patterns.

The fault simulation in ranking is more expensive because it is done without fault dropping. In practice, however, the four phase diagnostic procedure

Table 1. Single fault diagnosis with 1-detect tests

Circuit name	No. of outputs	No. of patterns	DC %	Diagnosis %	CPU* s	Fault ratio SET1	SET2
C17	2	10	95.454	100	0.067	1.100	1.780
C432	7	462	94.038	100	0.189	1.025	6.675
C499	32	2080	98.000	100	0.588	1.029	16.722
C880	26	1664	94.161	100	0.503	1.069	2.248
C1908	25	3625	85.187	100	1.294	1.379	28.290
C2670	140	13300	85.437	100	6.455	1.320	8.207
C3540	22	3520	89.091	100	1.333	1.229	5.200
C5315	123	13899	91.192	100	6.847	1.054	4.204
C6288	32	1056	85.616	100	0.764	1.138	8.255
C7552	108	17064	86.507	100	10.123	1.281	10.765

* PC with Intel Core-2 duo 3.06GHz processor and 4GB memory

returning with zero faults is a rare possibility. Out of numerous tests performed on benchmark circuits, the algorithm came up with no suspect only twice, requiring the fault ranking to provide a diagnosis.

4   Experimental Results

The algorithms were applied to ISCAS'85 benchmark circuits using various test pattern sets. The circuit modeling and the entire algorithm were implemented in Python programming language [2], automatically invoking ATPG and fault simulator of Mentor Graphics FASTSCAN [1] software. VBA macros [11] were used to duplicate the test patterns for output selection. The programs were run on a personal computer (PC) with Intel Core-2 duo 3.06GHz processor and 4GB memory. Results for a circuit are averaged over 100 cases, each with a randomly selected fault. C17 has only 22 faults and its results are averaged over 22 cases.

Results of single fault diagnosis using a 1-detect pattern set are shown in Table 1. The first column states the circuit name, the second column contains the number of primary outputs the circuit has. The third column shows the number of patterns (with output selection implemented) used for diagnosis. So the actual number of patterns in the 1-detect pattern set for any circuit will be the number of patterns shown in the third column divided by the number of primary outputs (shown in column 2) of the table.

Diagnostic Coverage (DC) of the test pattern set based on single stuck-at faults, excluding redundant faults, is stated in column 4. It is defined as [17],

$$DC = \frac{Number\ of\ detected\ fault\ groups}{Total\ number\ of\ faults} = \frac{n}{N} \qquad (1)$$

Column 5 shows the percentage of cases the single fault was diagnosed. For single stuck-at faults, the algorithm always comes up with the actual fault (100% diagnosis), even if the diagnostic coverage of the pattern set is not as high. Simulation time in seconds is stated in column 6. Ratios of number of candidate

Table 2. Single fault diagnosis with 2-detect tests

Circuit name	No. of outputs	No. of patterns	DC %	Diagnosis %	CPU* s	Fault ratio	
						SET1	SET2
C499	32	3872	98.400	100	1.025	1.029	7.970
C1908	25	6425	86.203	100	2.242	1.379	14.798
C7552	108	27756	86.750	100	16.076	1.281	8.023

* PC with Intel Core-2 duo 3.06GHz processor and 4GB memory

faults in SET1 and SET2 are reported in columns 7 and 8, respectively. This is the ratio of the total number of faults reported in each set to the number of faults expected in that set. The expected number of faults includes the actual fault, its equivalent faults and the opposite polarity faults for all equivalent faults, including the actual fault. This ratio denotes the diagnostic resolution of the procedure. The closer the fault ratio is to 1.0, better is the resolution. For single stuck-at faults, the ratio of SET1 faults is almost 1.0 in all cases. Hence, when the faults identified in SET1 are probed (by electron beam or other failure mode analysis procedures), one would locate the actual fault and it will unnecessary to probe the faults in SET2. But in a real situation since we would not know whether the actual fault is a single stuck-at fault or a non-classical fault, the SET2 surrogate faults should not be disregarded.

For circuits C499, C1908 and C7552, the ratio of faults in SET2 is high. This is due to the fact that the diagnostic coverage of the test pattern set is not high enough. To examine the effect of improving diagnostic coverage of the test pattern set on diagnostic resolution, 2-detect test patterns were used to diagnose these three circuits. The results are shown in Table 2. Note that 2-detect patterns provide a marginal, though definite, increase in diagnostic coverage (*DC*). Most increase occurred for C1908, which is only 1.016%. Still, the resolution improved as SET2 ratio dropped to about 50%. So, for patterns with even higher diagnostic coverage, the resolution will be further improved. An utmost efficiency of the diagnosis algorithm can be expected from higher diagnostic capability test pattern set than from just the detection test pattern set.

To verify the relevance of the reported surrogate faults to actual non-classical faults, we examined multiple stuck-at faults by introducing two stuck-at faults simultaneously. One hundred failure cases were generated for each circuit. In each case, two stuck-at faults were chosen in such a way that they are close to each other in the circuit. The reason for considering only two simultaneous faults is that the probability of fault masking is maximum when there are just two faults and this probability keeps reducing as the number of faults present in the circuit increases. This increased chance of fault masking created a pessimistic environment for the algorithm. All diagnosis results are averaged over 100 cases for each circuit. Table 3 summarizes the multiple fault diagnosis experiment with 1-detect test patterns.

Column 4 of Table 3 shows the percentage of cases where both faults were diagnosed. Column 5 shows the percentage of cases where only one of the actual faults present was diagnosed. The sum of these two percentages subtracted from

Table 3. Multiple (two) fault diagnosis with 1-detect tests

Circuit name	No. of Patterns	DC %	% of cases diagnosed			CPU* s	Fault ratio	
			Both faults	One fault	No fault		SET1	SET2
C17	10	95.454	80.950	19.040	0.000	0.067	0.500	2.091
C432	462	94.038	90.566	7.547	1.886	0.135	0.563	3.516
C499	2080	98.000	49.056	20.754	30.188	0.613	0.371	17.589
C880	1664	94.161	86.792	9.433	3.773	0.502	0.900	3.205
C1908	3625	85.187	90.566	0.000	9.433	0.928	0.488	12.764
C2670	13300	85.437	88.679	3.773	7.547	4.720	0.564	7.046
C3540	3520	89.091	86.792	3.773	9.433	1.547	0.488	5.177
C5315	13899	91.192	98.113	1.886	0.000	7.065	0.422	3.886
C6288	1056	85.616	83.018	0.000	16.981	0.888	0.589	5.536
C7552	17064	86.507	96.226	1.886	1.886	7.539	0.358	7.104

* PC with Intel Core-2 duo 3.06GHz processor and 4GB memory

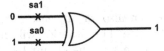

Fig. 5. Fault masking (interference) in XOR gate

100% gives the percentage of cases where both faults were not diagnosed, as shown in column 6. As the results in the table indicate, except for the circuit C499, all other circuits have, at least in 80% cases, a perfect diagnosis of both faults. A point to be noted is that the proposed diagnosis procedure does not assume that fault masking is not present and the reported percentage of diagnosis includes the possible fault masking and interference cases.

The reason for C499 (32-bit single-error-correcting circuit) producing poor multiple fault diagnosis (resulting in irrelevant surrogate faults) even with a test pattern set having very high diagnostic coverage (based on single stuck-at faults) must be examined. We found the presence of circular fault masking in many of the fault cases considered. The circuit has an XOR tree consisting of 104 two-input XOR gates. XOR logic gates are not considered to be elementary logic gates since they are generally constructed from multiple Boolean gates, such that the set of faults depends on its construction. All four test patterns are needed to completely test a 2-input XOR gate, regardless of its construction [14]. Consider the XOR gate shown in Figure 5. The top input has a stuck-at-1 (sa1) fault and the bottom input has a stuck-at-0 (sa0) fault. To propagate a single fault through XOR gate, the other input must be unchanged. But since this is a multiple fault situation, two faults are trying to propagate through the XOR gate at the same time. So a '0' on the top input is required to activate the sa1 fault and a '1' on the bottom input is required to activate the sa0 fault. But since both inputs are changed, the faults mask each other. This phenomenon is called circular masking. Hence the output is '1' which is the same as the good circuit output. Due to this circular masking, the algorithm will not be able to produce the relevant surrogate faults as the actual faults are dropped, since the pattern which should have failed, passes. This is not only for the case where both faults are present on

Table 4. Multiple (two) fault diagnosis with 2-detect tests

Circuit name	No. of patterns	DC (%)	% of cases diagnosed			CPU* s	Fault ratio	
			Both faults	One fault	No fault		SET1	SET2
C499	3872	98.400	49.056	20.754	30.188	0.696	0.371	11.555
C1908	6425	86.203	90.566	0.000	9.433	2.314	0.488	7.232
C7552	27756	86.750	96.226	1.886	1.886	17.291	0.358	5.905

* PC with Intel Core-2 duo 3.06GHz processor and 4GB memory

Table 5. Single fault diagnosis with diagnostic patterns

Circuit name	No. of outputs	No. of patterns	DC %	Diagnosis %	CPU* s	Fault ratio	
						SET1	SET2
C17	2	12	100	100	0.067	1.000	1.780

* PC with Intel Core-2 duo 3.06GHz processor and 4GB memory

the inputs of the XOR gate, but also for any case where fault effects are being propagated through an XOR gate. The situation will improve while considering more than two faults to be present in the circuit because the probability of a complete circular masking decreases with the increase in the number of faults. In circuit C499, the presence of this huge XOR tree increases circular masking and thereby deteriorates the performance of the diagnosis algorithm. But as discussed before, the algorithm does produce reasonable results even in a highly pessimistic environment, where choices (close neighborhood faults selected) are made in such a way that the probability of masking is high. One other ISCAS'85 benchmark circuit, which has (2-input) XOR gates present, is circuit C432. But it has only 18 XOR gates, which do not form a tree and hence the diagnostic percentage is not hurt significantly.

The ratio of faults in SET1 in Table 3 is less than 1 because in most cases, faults reported in SET1 include one of the actual faults, its equivalent faults and the opposite polarity faults. The other actual fault, its equivalent faults and opposite polarity faults are present in SET2. Hence, the resolution of SET1 faults is mostly closer to 0.5 than being 1.0 when we consider two faults.

The same three circuits show a comparatively poorer SET2 resolution. Hence, 2-detect patterns are used to show that the diagnostic resolution improves upon improving the diagnostic coverage of the test pattern set. The results of this experiment are shown in Table 4. Once again it is seen that, for small increase in diagnostic coverage (DC) of the patterns by 1.016% (maximum) for circuit C1908 the resolution is improved by almost 40%. Other two circuits show a similar trend.

The last experiment was to try the diagnosis procedure on a 100% diagnostic test pattern set. The circuit C17 reports 95.454% of diagnostic coverage (DC) with as few as 5 patterns that have 100% detection coverage. The total number of faults in the circuit is 22. There was only one fault pair that was not distinguished. Adding one more pattern that distinguishes the fault pair yielded 100% diagnostic coverage as expected. The diagnostic algorithm was then run using this test pattern set to yield the results shown in Tables 5 and 6.

Table 6. Multiple (two) fault diagnosis with diagnostic patterns

Circuit name	No. of patterns	DC %	% of cases diagnosed			CPU* s	Fault ratio	
			Both faults	One fault	No fault		SET1	SET2
C17	12	100	80.952	19.047	0.000	0.067	0.489	2.102

* PC with Intel Core-2 duo 3.06GHz processor and 4GB memory

Single fault diagnosis with 100% diagnostic coverage vector set produced a perfect diagnostic resolution '1.0' as expected in SET1 and a slightly improved resolution in SET2. Multiple fault diagnosis with this test pattern set improved the resolution in SET1 by a very small amount and decreased the resolution of SET2 by the very same amount. Also, the diagnostic coverage was improved by a very small percentage. Since the 1-detect test pattern set already had a diagnostic coverage of 95.454, there was very little left to improve.

To sum up, the proposed diagnostic procedure, given a failing vector and the cause of failure a single stuck-at fault, will always come up with the actual fault, irrespective of the detection or diagnostic coverage of the test pattern set. If the detection coverage of the test pattern is higher, better will be the resolution of the faults reported. Provided with 100% diagnostic coverage, the maximum resolution can be achieved. If the actual fault is a multiple stuck-at fault without circular fault masking, the diagnostic procedure will come up with surrogate faults that represent the actual faults or the behavior of the actual faults, with higher resolution as the diagnostic coverage of the pattern set increases.

5   Conclusion

We have proposed a lower complexity fault diagnosis algorithm that is based on effect-cause analysis. The algorithm has higher diagnosability and resolution for the surrogate faults identified to represent multiple stuck-at faults without circularly masking, even if provided just with a high detection coverage test pattern set. The same trend is exhibited when the diagnostic coverage of the test pattern set is increased. The algorithm is memory efficient, since it does not require a dictionary and also has reduced diagnostic effort (CPU time), since it works on relatively smaller number of fault suspects and does not require re-running simulations after frequently moving faults to and from the suspected fault list based on heuristics.

In the future, we should examine the performance of the diagnosis algorithm on other non-classical faults by using appropriate fault models and their simulators. Also, redundant faults as one of the interfering fault in fault masking may be examined. Considering that fault simulation tools will always be limited to a few fault models (e.g., single stuck-at or transition faults), we should explore the relationships between non-classical faults (bridging, stuck-open, coupling, path delay, etc.) and the corresponding surrogate classical representatives. For example, some non-classical faults like stuck-open or bridging require an initialization pattern to precede a stuck-at test pattern. Thus, the test result for the non-classical fault agrees with a single stuck-at fault only on a subset of patterns.

Further analysis can establish better correlation between actual faults and their surrogates.

References

1. ATPG and Failure Diagnosis Tools. Mentor Graphics Corp., Wilsonville, OR (2009)
2. Python Tutorial Release 2.6.3. docs@python.org. Python Software Foundation (2009)
3. Abramovici, M., Breuer, M.A.: Fault Diagnosis Based on Effect-Cause Analysis: An Introduction. In: Proc. 17th Design Automation Conf., pp. 69–76 (June 1980)
4. Abramovici, M., Breuer, M.A.: Multiple Fault Diagnosis in Combinational Circuits Based on an Effect-Cause Analysis. IEEE Transactions on Computers C-29(6), 451–460 (1980)
5. Agrawal, V.D., Baik, D.H., Kim, Y.C., Saluja, K.K.: Exclusive Test and Its Applications to Fault Diagnosis. In: Proc. 16th International Conf. VLSI Design, pp. 143–148 (2003)
6. Alagappan, C.: Dictionary-Less Defect Diagnosis as Real or Surrogate Single Stuck-At Faults. Master's thesis, Auburn University, Auburn, Alabama (May 2013)
7. Beckler, M., Blanton, R.D.(S.): On-Chip Diagnosis for Early-Life and Wear-Out Failures. In: Proc. International Test. Conf., pp. 1–10 (November 2012)
8. Bushnell, M.L., Agrawal, V.D.: Essentials of Electronic Testing for Digital, Memory and Mixed-Signal VLSI Circuits. Springer, Boston (2000)
9. Cox, H., Rajski, J.: A Method of Fault Analysis for Test Generation and Fault Diagnosis. IEEE Trans. Computer-Aided Design of Integrated Circuits and Systems 7(7), 813–833 (1988)
10. Grimaila, M.R., Lee, S., Dworak, J., Butler, K.M., Stewart, B., Houchins, B., Mathur, V., Park, J., Wang, L.-C., Mercer, M.R.: REDO - Random Excitation and Deterministic Observation - First Commercial Experiment. In: Proc. 17th IEEE VLSI Test Symp., pp. 268–274 (April 1999)
11. Kofler, M.: Definitive Guide to Excel VBA. Apress, New York (2000)
12. Millman, S.D., McCluskey, E.J., Acken, J.M.: Diagnosing CMOS Bridging Faults With Stuck-At Fault Dictionaries. In: Proc. International Test. Conf., pp. 860–870 (September 1990)
13. Reddy, S.M., Pomeranz, I., Kajihara, S.: On the Effects of Test Compaction on Defect Coverage. In: Proc. 14th IEEE VLSI Test Symp., pp. 430–435 (April 1996)
14. Stroud, C.E.: A Designer's Guide to Built-in Self-Test. Springer, Boston (2002)
15. Venkataraman, S., Drummonds, S.B.: POIROT: A Logic Fault Diagnosis Tool and Its Applications. In: Proc. International Test Conf., pp. 253–262 (2000)
16. Wang, L.C., Williams, T.W., Mercer, M.R.: On Efficiently and Reliably Achieving Low Defective Part Levels. In: Proc. International Test Conf., pp. 616–625 (October 1995)
17. Zhang, Y., Agrawal, V.D.: An Algorithm for Diagnostic Fault Simulation. In: Proc. 11th Latin-American Test Workshop (LATW), pp. 1–5 (March 2010)

Author Index

Agarwal, Alpana   177
Agrawal, Madhusoodan   177
Agrawal, Sachin   138
Agrawal, Vishwani D.   376
Alagappan, Chidambaram   376
Alam, Akhtar W.   44
Anwar, Mohd   169
Azeemuddin, Syed   169

Banerjee, Ansuman   194
Baruah, Ratul Kumar   118
Baskota, Mohit   304
Basu, Prasenjit   194
Bhattacharya, Arani   194
Bhattacharya, Bhargab B.   274, 322
Bhattacharya, Samadrita   361
Bishnoi, Rimpy   304
Boolchandani, Dharmendar   312
Bose, Subash Chandra   10

Chakrabarty, Krishnendu   274
Chattopadhyay, Santanu   74
Cherukat, Saima   242
Choudhury, Priyanka   160

Dana, Abhijit   128
Das, Debesh Kumar   322
Das, Shirshendu   204
Dasgupta, Parthasarathi   361
Dasgupta, Sudeb   146, 214, 267
Deshmukh, Raghavendra   35
Dey, Ayon   294
Dhakshinamoorthy, Esakkimuthu   44

Ganesan, Akash   26
Garg, Lokesh   312
Gaur, Manoj Singh   304
Ghosh, Sandip   257
Ghoshal, Sarmishtha   274
Guha, Anirban   233
Gupta, Anu   108, 185
Gupta, Gaurav   284

Halwe, Prateek D.   204

Jain, Anita   337
Jaiswal, Saurabh   249
Joseph, Jose   153

Kapoor, Hemangee K.   204
Kapoor, Kalpesh   66
Karmakar, Bhaskar J.   194
Kaushik, Brajesh Kumar   146, 214, 267
Khan, Mohammed Zafar Ali   169
Khandare, Amol   35
Khare, Kavita   337
Kole, Dipak Kumar   322
Kondekar, P.N.   138
Korde, Shrirang   35
Krishnamurthy, Rahul   49
Kumar, Jainender   214
Kumar, Manchi Pavan   26
Kumar, Pramod   185
Kumar, S. Santosh   94

Lam, Kai Chi Alex   330
Laxmi, Vijay   304

Mahesh, R.K. Naga   26
Maheshwari, Sachin   100, 108, 185
Majumder, Manoj Kumar   214
Malani, Deepak   345
Mallala, Suresh   294
Manna, Kanchan   74
Mathew, Prince   44
Mondal, Joyati   322
Mudgil, Nandini   284
Mukherjee, Shyamapada   223
Mukhiya, Ravindra   94

Nath, Debanjali   160
Navlakha, Nupur   312
Ninan, Cerin   353

Paily, Roy P.   26, 118
Pal, Ajit   83
Pal, Pankaj Kr.   267
Pandey, Sunil   138
Pandit, Soumya   128
Pant, B.D.   94

Parikh, Chetan D   19
Parikh, Chetan D.   59
Patankar, Sarvesh   284
Patra, Jibesh   223
Patrikar, Rajendra   35, 153
Paul, Somnath   128
Paul, Somshubhra   294
Pawanekar, Sameer   66
Polavarapu, Nagaraju   204
Ponna, Narender   44
Pradhan, Sambhu Nath   160
Pyne, Sumanta   83

Radhakrishna, M.   353
Raghav, Himadri Singh   100, 108
Rahaman, Hafizur   322, 361
Rajahari, Gudlavalleti   10
Rathore, Akhil   59
Raza, Rameez   185
Reniwal, Bhupendra Singh   1
Roy, Pranab   361
Roy, Suchismita   223
Roy, Sudip   274
Roy Chowdhury, Shubhajit   233

Sahula, Vineet   242, 312
Sengupta, Indranil   74
Sharma, Amit   94
Sharma, G.K.   49
Shekhar, Chandra   353
Singh, Brahmadeo Prasad   100
Singh, Jawar   138
Singh, Prashant   249
Singh, Shailesh   74
Singh, Surabhi   146
Singh, Virendra   345
Singhal, Vipul   294
Srivastava, Pooja   249
Srivastava, Rohit   257, 284
Sur-Kolay, Susmita   194

Trivedi, Gaurav   66
Tudu, Jaynarayan T.   345

Varshney, Yashu Anand   10
Verma, Ram Mohan   249
Verma, Vivek   19
Vishvakarma, Santosh Kumar   1

Zwolinski, Mark   330